by J. Allen Jackson

Learn how the secular world has defamed a phenomenon that God intends to use to usher in His own New Age:

CHRIST'S MILLENNIAL REIGN

Supported by evidences from:

- **Reverend Billy Graham**
- **Reverend Chuck Smith**
- **Evangelist Arthur Blessitt**
- **The Roman historian Flavius Josephus** and others
- **Pictorial proofs from Israel & around the world**

All of these renowned evangelists, teachers and historians have unwittingly presented evidences to support this new insight into God's divine plan. A plan that will unfold in the very near future. Don't be alarmed by the subject matter. The real danger lies in ignoring the facts as gathered by this well-informed author. He presents overwhelming evidence to document the UFO phenomenon. But he goes beyond mere eividence into new understanding.

Does the existence of the UFO present an opposing view of the Bible and God's creation of the cosmos? Mr. Jackson responds with a resounding, "No! In fact," he states, "the complete opposite is the case. Their existence fortifies the validity of Christianity like nothing else can," and meticulously points to numerous Scriptures in both the Old and New Testaments as evidence to support his contention.

What many call UFOs (Unidentified Flying Objects) are, in reality, HFOs (Heavenly Flying Objects). These are among the "signs in the heavens" that Christ said would warn us of His soon return.

Until now, the church has held a position that played into the hands of secular New Agers. But Satan's deception is finally and thoroughly exposed in this all-encompassing work. The author believes an enlightened church will result: a New Testament church prepared for Christ's return.

A Reconciliation:
UFOlogy vs. Theology

J. Allen Jackson

Dedicated to Chelsea

My very own angel
and God's precious gift.

Alpha & Omega Publishers
Port Angeles, Washington 98363

ISBN 978-1469988054
Printed in the United States

PORT ANGELES, WASHINGTON

Aliens & In-laws Table of Contents

Part I · Aliens

Chapter 10

Saucer Occupants

Chapter 11

Alien Powers

Chapter 12

Some Mysterious Abductions

Chapter 13

Betty Andreasson's Strange Journey

Chapter 14

What Does Science Say?

Chapter 15

The "Odds"

Chapter 16

Conquering Deep-space Travel

Part II • In-laws

Chapter 17

How Does This Relate to Religion?

Chapter 18

Why Trust The Bible?

Chapter 19

In The Beginning...God

Chapter 20

Wheel Within a Wheel

Chapter 21

HFOs In Other Bible Stories

Chapter 26

Warning: Satan is a Fallen Angel

Chapter 27

Why Are the Aliens Visiting Earth?

Chapter 28

UFOs Are Ready to Invade!

Chapter 29

When You See These Signs

Chapter 30

Christ Returns for His Church

(MORE)

Chapter 31

What Will The World Say?

Chapter 32

The Church Returns

Chapter 33

Space Station Jerusalem

(MORE)

Chapter 34

Your Ticket to Paradise

Foreward

In this modern era it's easy for us Americans to look back smugly at the decades of the forties and fifties as a naive time in our history. After all, we are now the only Superpower in the world. The unchallenged leaders in scientific achievement and economic success. Developers of communications satellite networks that have made possible the hugely popular mobile cell phone and, of course, the ubiquitous personal computer and its accompanying World Wide Web aka the Internet. But let's take a brief walk down memory lane to gain some perspective.

Many of us can remember duck tails and sock hops, cars with fins, nickel candy bars and a thousand other distinctions of that period in our history. We remember those years with a degree of nostalgia. Early television reflected our attitudes with such programs as *I Love Lucy, The Andy Griffith Show* and *Leave It To Beaver.* It was an innocent age.

Hidden among our memories are stories of strange flying machines and little green men in shiny suits with long, slender arms. What an ignorant generation, we've said to ourselves, some actually believed those absurd stories. Nationwide interest in what came to be known as the UFO Phenomenon stimulated Hollywood filmmakers to produce a rash of amateurish films about strange creatures from outer space.

The Blob, The War of The Worlds, The Day the Earth Stood Still, The Thing from Another World and *The Giant Claw* were among the numerous fantasies that got their que from these flying saucer reports. Unsophisticated minds trying to capitalize on an intriguing phenomenon ground out these 'sci-fi' thrillers. But their representation was far from what was actually being reported, and their absurdity defamed sincere UFO witnesses like nothing else could. Still...in the backs of everyone's mind was the unanswered question: *Is there really anything to this whole UFO thing?*

Many decades later, it seems as though every American from every walk of life has either seen some inexplicable object in the sky, or at least has an acquaintance who has. If you don't believe me, ask a few of your friends if they've ever seen anything they would term a "UFO". You may be surprised by just how many have. A 1987 Gallup Poll put the number at 22 million.[F-1] Others more recently estimate that over sixty per cent of the American public now believes that UFOs are real. That would be nearly 150 million Americans.[F-2]

"Well," we say, "If I went around telling everyone about it, they would think I was nuts! Everyone knows the idea of extraterrestrial spacecraft with 'little green men' flying around the Earth is pure science fiction."

Is it? In the following pages I will make a very clear assertion as to the validity of the existence of creatures from another realm and ask only that you do your best to keep an open mind and stay with me as I present the evidence.

Now, there's the matter of a God in this whole scenario. Somehow, in most people's minds, the idea of the existence of aliens from outer space is diametrically opposed to the concept of a Creator, especially as ascribed to by the various Christian denominations.

But Americans are, overwhelmingly, believers in God. Those who are sincerely religious can't understand why everyone doesn't look at the undeniable evidences presented today and see that God truly *must* exist. And not only that He exists, but that He desires to help His creation to live a full and happy life while on Earth. "Why wouldn't everyone want the joy and delectation that God offers to all of mankind?" they ask. "Why do people close their minds to something so wonderful? Don't they seek to know the truth?"

I, too, marvel at our proclivity to make all the wrong choices. We can only do the best we know how with the information we currently possess. This is certainly true in our quest for spiritual knowledge. Unfortunately, the majority of Americans rely on outside opinion when deciding religious matters. They leave it in the hands of their church to figure the whole thing out. Naturally, most of these denominational "experts" believe their interpretations of Bible Scripture are accurate and unquestionable, and pass that along to their laity. However, I'm convinced we need to remain guardedly open minded, especially when it comes to the interpretation of obscure biblical passages like those found in Ezekiel, Daniel, Revelation and elsewhere dealing with visions and future events.

As we draw nearer to the end of this age – and nearly every futurist in the world says we are – we will begin to recognize prophetic passages in the Bible that were not understood by past generations regarding 'End Time' events. New knowledge creates new understanding. "Fiery flying serpents" that can cause great destruction, which are described in the book of *Isaiah, chapter 14 and verse 29*, now have new meaning. Until the advent of guided missiles, past interpretations of this Scripture were usually mystical, rather than literal. Most Bible scholars, until recent times, had interpreted the passage to be merely symbolic phraseology, and with little agreement on just what it symbolized, let alone its significance to modern society.

This honest confusion of interpretation has led many to question the alleged "inerrancy" of Scripture. Probably the majority of Americans see the accuracy of the Bible as questionable – at best. And this, unfortunately, may lead to total disregard of any Christian belief. Religious intolerance among non-believing Americans is widespread today. Unfortunately, the same attitude of intolerance that non-religious or atheistic individuals exhibit toward organized religion is the same one that most religious institutions and clergy display toward the UFO phenomenon.

"How can it be? Surely it's a deception from the devil," they proclaim. "No Godly person would believe that intelligent life from another planet was visiting the Earth. That would conflict with the Bible's view of the Creation of mankind."

I can understand how this viewpoint has persisted. If it weren't for my own experience I, too, would be inclined to think the whole thing simply something from the imaginations of ignorant, undisciplined minds…or considered it a satanic aberration, as do many.

In the following pages I will deal with the reality of the UFO phenomenon as never before. Enough subjective proof exists to convince even the most avid open-minded skeptic (a near oxymoron). But why is the proof only subjective? Why haven't we had more conclusive "scientific" proof? How might the UFO travel from distant planets or galaxies? Just what does the Christian community think of all this? How could the phenomenon possibly have any theological connection? Are there any biblical evidences connecting the UFO to ancient history? More to the point, what about current and future events in God's plan for the New Millennium?

We will examine these provocative questions – and more – in our important journey of discovery. But stay with me. I realize this is a long book, but if you persist, its revelations may change your paradigm of reality forever. And...*please*...don't skip ahead because we need to lay some very important groundwork before we reveal some of the startling evidences presented within these pages.

I wish you Godspeed.

J. Allen Jackson

UPDATE: I want to make an important note about this updated version of Aliens & In-laws. I have purposely confined the data contained herein to its original historical examination of the UFO phenomenon, with a few unavoidable exceptions, i.e., the introduction of new associated phenomena such as Sky Trumpets. Older reports present an infinitely more reliable resource, in my opinion, than to try and include newer sightings without the ability to test the contributor's authenticity, especially with the wide use of deceptive techniques made available through image manipulation programs such as PhotoShop or Illustrator and animators like Maya.

Additionally, and more importantly, to try and include current sightings would be a daunting task. In an age of ubiquitous cell phone cameras and a connected generation of "texters" from across the globe, the amount of data being generated is quite simply unmanageable. The UFO phenomenon has literally exploded in the last five years as never before in our history. Virtually every corner of the globe is reporting UFO activity with certain areas exhibiting above-average heightened activity, such as South and Central America, and especially Mexico. We will explore why that might be within these pages, but to include even a fraction of the available data would take several volumes. So, for the sake of brevity, this is a recent historical examination, not a current indexing. Plus, the points are better made applying this more reliable and manageable method.

Part I
Aliens

In February of 1969 the U.S. Air Force closed its official investigation of the UFO phenomenon. The United States Government claimed that the phenomenon was "non-existent."

On March 9, 1982, The U.S. Supreme Court ordered all files of the United States National Security Agency on the subject of unidentified flying objects (UFOs) to remain top secret, in defiance of the Freedom of Information Act, citing their sensitivity to U.S. security.

My Story

**Phoenix, Arizona
The fall of 1967**

THE TELEVISION WAS ON FULL BLAST AS WAS CUSTOMARY AT MY HOUSE THIS TIME OF NIGHT. TELEVISION WAS MY DAD'S ONE WAY OF ESCAPING THE DEMANDING LIFE ENTAILED IN PROVIDING for such a large family as ours. Having raised a houseful of noisy children, seven in all, full-blast television was almost a necessity in order to drown out all of the inevitable distractions. I was barely eighteen and in my first year at Phoenix Junior College.

Jere, my oldest brother, was in deep conversation with my mom at the half-cleared dinner table. And, of course, I was having my usual battle within trying to pull myself away from the television set. There was homework piling up in the next room because I'd spent all afternoon playing cards with my fraternity brothers John, Rob, Harry and Al, instead of doing my homework.

It was important to belong. And now I'd finally joined a group of guys I could call my friends. Over sixty in all. Although I can't say they were all close friends, at least I was a part of something more exciting than the normal classroom agenda and accompanying tasks of earning a college degree in advertising.

This was "my" club, Gamma Rho: a locally created group organized loosely like a national fraternity. So what, if all we had was a table in the campus snack bar with our "fraternity's" name placed temporarily on the wall above it where we all hung out, rather than at a fraternity house like the big university guys. This was only a junior college, after all. But we were still proud of our organization. And since we all came from the same lower-to-middle-income neighborhoods of Phoenix, we felt comfortable with one another. When we got together at one of the "brother's" homes for an "official" meeting we felt, somehow, smugly important.

I was raised in the very strict home of Pentecostal Christians and I had always played by the rules. But I was growing up now, and I had to make my own decisions. I wanted to belong.

"You've got to come out here right this second!" I was jolted from my daydream as I sat staring at the vacuous (but still wholesome) tube. "Jere! Come on you guys!"

My youngest brother, John, had just burst through the kitchen door directly behind me. He seemed excited and dead serious. Jere was disinterested. John saw I was listening, for a change.

"You've just got to trust me. Come outside, quick!"

Sure, I thought to myself, *I was only going to go do my homework.*

Out we went.

"Come here, hide under the tree...trust me!"

"What's the matter?" I wondered aloud.

"Look at that!" John said in an excited whisper. As I looked up in the direction that he pointed I saw an object in the dusky sky...something I'd never seen before. It reminded me of a donut-shaped space station, at least like the artist's renderings I had seen as a child in the early sixties. A space station, only without the hole in the middle. *Oh, of course, it has to be a satellite,* I thought to myself. *Probably a secret Russian thing.*

"Boy, it sure seems low. What is it?" The strange object that glided slowly and silently through the darkening sky appeared to be lighted. As I recall, it was as if someone had taken an orange or red spotlight and shone it on a metal object. No beam of light was visible, though, only the object itself glowing dimly from within.

Suddenly, something resembling a roman candle shot out directly in front of, and slightly to the right of, the path that the spherical object was taking.

Strange, I thought. *If that were a guidance system on a satellite it would have shot from the rear of the object and thrust it forward*, assuming that it had a front and a rear. There was really no evidence of that, since it was perfectly round. Quickly, another sparkler, only this time in front and to the left. The globe was instantly propelled in its direction. Now, two at once. Again, the object seemed to be drawn toward the sparklers. Back and forth, repeatedly, it worked its way across the sky in a zigzag pattern.

"I've seen this before," John whispered. "I think they can see us. If we get out from under the tree I'll bet it goes out."

We both slid slowly out from under the overhanging branches of the mulberry tree. It was early fall and the tree was still in full foliage. It suddenly dawned on me that the object was as low as an airliner. No satellite flew that close to the Earth. *What the heck was it?*

As we stared up in awe, it suddenly disappeared. It just disappeared! Like a light switch turned off.

"Man was that weird," I said. "What do you think it was?"

John told me he had seen a similar object on two previous occasions. One he was sure was the exact same type of object. He had seen it with his girlfriend as he lay on a lawn chair in her back yard looking up at the sky. It had occurred the previous summer when he was in the 7th grade.

"I told you about it then, but nobody believed me. At least it didn't seem like anybody believed me."

Well, I believed him now because I, too, had seen the strange dimly glowing metal sphere or disc.

As we discussed the incident years later, John said that he had seen some smaller dark, round objects that shot out in front of and slightly below the larger object. They were what caused the shower of sparkling light I had seen. Apparently in my effort to look closely at the larger object I'd missed the small dark discs. But I'd seen some detail on the larger sphere that John had missed.

What I saw appeared to be mechanical irregularities in the surface of the sphere. I say "sphere" because we were almost directly under the object and it was perfectly round with a convex surface. The irregularities were like rivets, or unlit light portals arranged in a somewhat regular pattern. There were other indiscernible shapes that contoured to the surface of the sphere, too, and gave it a definite metallic, mechanical semblance.

There was a lot going on in the world in those days. It was the fall of 1967 and the war was raging in Vietnam. I was busy with school to avoid the draft, and held a part-time job, so I soon dismissed the thought of flying saucers for the more pressing obligations of life.

Fourteen years, a career and several businesses later, I happened upon a book on UFOs in a local bookstore. I had been looking for books on video taping because I was the producer/director for a local informational network called the INN Channel. We broadcast commercials on a cable channel installed within the local resort hotels and thus informed the tourist and business traveler what was available in the form of local entertainment, dining, shopping, civic attractions, etc.

The book caught my eye, so I bought it. I had time for pleasure reading at that time and this UFO business was something that had intrigued me for years for obvious reasons. But I simply had never taken the time to delve into the subject.

I was now on my way to a fascinating journey of discovery that eventually lead to my writing this book.

Credibility

I was to learn, years after the fact, that investigators will usually discredit accounts from multiple witnesses who describe a specific event in identical terms. The probability of remembering an incident exactly as another is almost inconceivable and will usually lead to the suspicion that the witnesses are in collusion, or that one witness copied the other or a common source. A real event is always reported with slightly differing perceptions.[1-1]

The fact that John and I had divergent memories of the event gave it greater credibility. John saw smaller dark spheres precede the "mother" ship. I recalled surface details on the larger glowing sphere, but totally missed the smaller objects, and saw only their sparkling discharges.

*   *   *   *   *

Similar Sightings

Are We Not Alone in the Universe?

As I began to read more and more stories about UFOs I found that there were many others who had seen objects in the night sky very similar to what John and I had seen. In fact, there had been so many that I began to realize they probably numbered in the thousands. What an astounding discovery! We were not alone in our plight. It was somehow strangely comforting to know that the phenomena were worldwide but, at the same time, it was rather frightening. The possibility of mysterious flying machines encircling our globe, under apparent intelligent control and of unknown origin, was a totally disquieting thought. So strange, in fact, that if I had seen the UFO alone, I doubt I would have had the courage to tell anyone about it. I soon found I wasn't the only one who felt that way. Many hundreds of thousands of upstanding citizens all around the world have witnessed similar incidents and voiced similar reservations about reporting them.

When massive sightings occur over a prolonged period of time, it is termed a flap. Several flaps have taken place over the years which have stimulated investigations by several U.S. agencies, the most predominant being the U.S. Air Force. The fact that the Air Force discontinued its official investigation of the phenomenon in 1969, for reasons we shall explore in later chapters, explains why many of the following reported sightings are somewhat dated. In the early years of UFO investigation the policies of secrecy (to be adopted by the Air Force in later years) did not exist. That would explain the preponderance of early

UFO material in my reporting. Just because a report is "dated" – contrary to Air Force opinion – that does not negate its importance.

As another side note in helping you to understand my recount of various incidents, keep in mind that I have attempted to report early sightings first and work forward to more current ones.

Orange Spheres

The earliest modern sighting of "my" UFO, that I am aware of, was recorded in 1870 in London, England. The object, as described by the *London Times*, "…was elliptical in shape with a 'kind of tail.' It crossed the moon from one side to the other in half a minute, and then disappeared."

Astronomer William F. Denning saw a luminous ball emitting sparks traveling "slower than a meteor but faster than a balloon" on October 12th. It was also spotted the same day over Berlin by Lord Brabazon and the same object was seen later that day by a member of the Royal Astronomical Society in Wimbledon, England.[2-1]

In 1952, Bailey Frame of Birch River, West Virginia, saw a large orange ball that was flat on top. He watched as it circled a small valley at Flatwoods. 1952 was a year that produced literally hundreds of UFO stories in newspapers across the nation. Mr. Frame said that after the orange ball had circled for about 15 minutes it sped away at a terrific speed toward Sutton airport.[2-2]

Similar objects have been seen all around the world. On August 31, 1954 in Asnieres-les-Dijon, France, six people happened to be watching the maneuvers of some airplanes from a nearby air base. Suddenly a red disc approached from the east of and above the airplanes. As it traveled overhead it changed from red to orange and then to a silvery shade.[2-3]

That evening in Orly, France, Mme. A. Fouquiau and her family noticed two luminous orange objects streak by overhead in parallel flight. They disappeared quickly to the east, followed soon after by a third, identical object.[2-4] On September 10th that year several witnesses in Limoges, France, observed a reddish-orange disc emitting a bluish trail as it crossed the evening sky.[2-5]

In 1961 there occurred a highly-publicized incident in New Hampshire. The object seen by Betty and Barney Hill was described at one point as a huge, bright-orange ball.[2-6]

On May 24, 1965, a commercial pilot named J.W. Tilse, along with an engineer and two others, was looking out of a hotel room at Eton Range, Australia. An orange glowing object approached the group and settled in a lightly forested area about 300 yards away. They could see that the object was metallic and had a bank of 20 to 30 lights just below a circular platform. They were unable to tell if the object was lit by the row of lights or whether the glow came from within the object itself. The machine soon lifted off revealing what was described as a tripod-like configuration extending below its underbelly and assumed to be the landing gear. At the tip of each leg was a bright-red, pulsating light. The legs soon disappeared, as though retracted, and the object sped away at an incredible rate. Being a commercial pilot, with thousands of hours of flying time to his credit, Tilse said there was no doubt in his mind that the mysterious object did not resemble any known aircraft.[2-7]

In 1966 a book was published called *Incident at Exeter*. Its pages were filled with first-hand accounts of a series of strange sightings that took place during the summer and fall of 1965 in a small New Hampshire town named Exeter. The author of this famous work, John G. Fuller, was a newspaper reporter who wrote at that time for the Saturday Review. In his quest to be ever up with the times he decided to write an article about the popular "UFO craze" currently sweeping the nation. Mr. Fuller randomly chose just one of the numerous sightings being reported around the country at that time and decided to investigate it. He thought it would be interesting to chase down "one of these ghost stories" and prove to himself what he suspicioned: these kooky stories were all either "an illusion, a mistake or, at best, an unsolved mystery."[2-8]

His book is based on interviews with over sixty people who lived in or around the town of Exeter. The mystery that Fuller began to unravel shocked even the skeptics. Here was compelling testimony from practically a whole town attesting to countless visitations by mysterious flying objects...objects that defied the laws of physics.

Mr. Fuller tape-recorded conversations with the earnest local townspeople who told of strange lights and glowing round objects invading their skies. The recorded testimony was sufficient evidence to convince *Look Magazine*, along with several other national publications, to publish the story. The fact that police officers, weather observers, Air Force base and Weather Bureau radar all made separate sightings added even greater credibility to the story. This couldn't be dismissed as mass hysteria, incompetence or mistaken identity because there were simply too many reliable witnesses.[2-9]

During the summer of 1965, Mrs. Ralph Lindsay of South Kensington, New Hampshire, sighted a bright-orange ball outside her kitchen window. She claimed it was almost as large as a harvest moon but that "it was definitely not the moon." As she and her children gazed in astonishment, it moved off toward Hampton.[2-10]

On the evening of October 19th, the Jerline Jalbert family saw an object hovering over their home just outside Fremont, New Hampshire. It was described as a big round metallic object that glowed orange like a light bulb and at times got brighter in color, closer to white. They also reported smaller lights underneath the object that shown red and white as it passed overhead.[2-11]

A Coastguardsman who lived in New Hampshire claimed to have seen a reddish-orange disk one night in 1965 while on watch. It moved slowly up the beach about 15 feet above it and disappeared in the distance.[2-12]

On October 20th, Mrs. Edmund Liscomb claimed she saw a solid orange object hovering in the sky…"like a big, orange ball, nothing but orange."

Over and over again, the residents of Exeter and its surrounding communities claimed to have seen these orange-colored spheres pass overhead. In fact, the author Fuller, himself, while on location for his story, happened to glance up into the evening sky while on his way to an appointment. He and his two companions surprisingly observed a jet in hot pursuit of a dull orange, perfectly round disc. It seemed to glow with a luminous incandescent light. As the object raced in front of the jet, Fuller estimated its size at about one-fifth the size of a full moon. They observed the chase for about 18 or 20 seconds until both objects disappeared into the distant night sky.[2-13]

Smaller Discs

As incredible as it seemed, others had seen the very same aberration that we had. Large orange, metallic-appearing spheres dancing in the night sky. But what about the smaller dark discs that preceded it? If the occurrences were real and were widespread, then it would stand to reason that others would have noticed the mysterious smaller discs leading the way, as John had.

On May 8, 1952, the pilot and crew of a Pan American Airlines DC-4 were settling in with their flight from New York City to Puerto Rico. It was around one o'clock in the morning and they were at an altitude of about 8,000 feet. Relaxed and away from the heavy traffic that required a constant lookout for other aircraft, the co-pilot turned around to look at his number 4 engine. Instantly a glimmer caught his eye. It was dead ahead and closing. He thought it was the taillight of another plane but according to ground control there shouldn't have been any other aircraft in the area. When he realized that they might be in a head-on collision course he nudged the pilot and pointed excitedly toward the light, which by now had become at least ten times the size of a typical landing light. Before either of them could react the large light streaked by the DC-4, narrowly missing the left wing. It was followed immediately by two more smaller balls of fire. When they radioed the tower to tell of their story they caused quite a stir on the ground. Because they were such qualified witnesses, an official from the Air Force met with them the next day to go over their incredible story. As they concluded their story one of them said, "I always thought these people who reported flying saucers were crazy, but now I don't know."[2-14]

On September 27, 1954, near Rixheim, France, two people spotted a large elongated craft shaped like a cigar accompanied by at least ten smaller luminous satellites. A railroad worker on night duty nearby reported a similar formation later that evening.[2-15]

Years later, during the UFO flap in the summer of 1965, dozens of sightings were reported all across the Midwest including Oklahoma, Kansas, Nebraska, Texas and five other states. On July 31st a guard captain at the ordnance depot in Sidney, Nebraska, reported a large saucer followed by four smaller discs in diamond formation. It was witnessed by dozens of others and was tracked on radar by the Weather Bureau at Wichita.[2-16]

An article in the *Christian Science Monitor* related several Texas sightings during the same summer where witnesses described a bright light in the sky, with lesser lights clustered around it. Some reported it as visible for several hours. It wasn't a scientific balloon because there were none in the area according to officials.[2-17]

During the last week of October, 1965, there were several reports from the Los Angeles area, including one of a large, reddish, cigar-shaped object that had been accompanied by several smaller points of light coming out of it and moving along independently.[2-18] This was different than the others because witnesses described an unusual occurrence. The smaller discs apparently went *inside* the larger one.

It made sense. If we were being visited by crews from another world, the need for closer ground-level observation by unmanned probes was the obvious answer. These smaller flying replicas of the larger craft could make pre-landing observations of an area in a hostile environment without risk to the crew. Medium-sized craft, capable of carrying a small crew, would also logically be used for scientific sampling of the planet's surface. That explained why some observers had estimated the size of the objects as anything from 3 or 4 feet up to 300 feet. Different-sized craft for different functions. Of course! (see *figure 2.1*)

And since the smaller craft are so much lighter, they could use a slightly different, or even a combination of power sources conducive to their purpose. That would explain why the shower of sparks on the craft I had witnessed came only from the smaller discs and not the larger one. The power sources needed to lift the objects off the ground and maneuver them at low speed could have produced the trail emitted by the smaller craft.

Our own power sources for transportation also vary in appearance. An automobile, with its relatively short range, is powered by a different form of propulsion than a jet plane or a nuclear-powered submarine.

At Haneda Air Force Base, Japan – now Tokyo International Airport – the midnight crew of the control tower noticed a bright light off to the northeast over Tokyo Bay. As they studied it with binoculars they noticed that the light was emitted from the upper quarter of a large mysterious object. It soon moved out of sight, but within a few seconds reappeared and headed toward the base. One of the radar ground crew called the pilot of a C-54 that happened to be flying in the area and asked him if he could see the unusual light. He wasn't able to spot anything.

With the object still visible, they decided to call a nearby radar site and ask if they had anything registering in their area. Sure enough, a small object appeared on the screen in the direction of the base. For five minutes the radar station tracked the zigzagging motion of the light.

Others were now informed by the tower operators to look at the light. As they observed it they thought it might be a weather balloon. Since they had balloons available to them, they decided to send one up for comparison's sake. As the balloon ascended, they realized that the other object was much larger and lit differently than the balloon. Its estimated size was roughly fifty feet in diameter.

That was enough! An F-94 jet interceptor was immediately dispatched to observe the mysterious light at close range. The plane was scrambled from nearby Johnson AFB shortly after midnight and quickly closed in behind the object. As the radar operator in the rear seat of the F-94 locked in on the target it quickly pulled away and they lost visual contact.

Soon after the jet interceptor left the area the mysterious light returned. As radar was tracking its movement the target broke into three pieces, each spaced about a quarter-mile apart. They watched in amazement as the three lights suddenly disappeared while traversing to the northeast toward Tokyo Bay.[2-19]

In 1952 a formation of UFOs was tracked over the Gulf of Mexico. The radar crew of an Air Force bomber calculated their speed at a fantastic 5,240 mph. Another formation was slightly behind the bomber and paced it for a brief period. Suddenly, a huge craft, estimated later as being over 1,200 feet long, appeared on radar. Within a few seconds the smaller craft raced up toward the larger one and they merged on the radar screen. With the smaller craft having apparently been taken aboard, the huge mother ship accelerated to over 9,000 mph and disappeared off the scopes.[2-20]

Imagine what scientific workshops could be aboard a craft the length of **four football fields**! It could certainly hold a fleet of saucers both in the smaller 3 to 10 foot class and the larger, 20 to 50 foot size. A U.S. space shuttle is only 121 feet long; small enough to fit more than 140 of them into the large mother ship, if you stacked them on 4 levels, or decks, of 4 across and 9 deep (see *figure 2.2*).

Saucer Details

As mentioned in Chapter One, the object that John and I had seen appeared to have details similar to rivets on its underside. It was actually too high up to allow me to see something as small as a rivet. I had speculated that the small protrusions were perhaps light portals, or mechanical appendages or coverings of some sort. Once again, as I delved into reports from around the world, similar observations had been noted by others.

In the rash of sightings mentioned before at Exeter, New Hampshire, one of the witnesses described seeing a round object that changed from a glowing greenish-white to a reddish-orange color. She and her daughter had seen the object fairly close up and described "silver things" hanging down from the underside of the sphere.[2-21]

Another incident at Cherry Creek, New York, was reported to the Fredonia State Police on August 19, 1965. It seems that sixteen- year-old Harold Butcher was in the family barn around 8:30 that evening when the family's three-year-old bull started to make a strange racket as though frightened. When he walked out to investigate, he noticed a "football-shaped" object approximately 50-feet long and 20-feet wide hovering in a nearby forested area. It appeared to have two rows of rivets that dotted the vertical seems of the strange craft. It was silver-chromelike and emitted a beeping noise. A reddish-colored vapor shot down toward the ground from around the two vertical seams. Harold ran into his house to alert his mother, two brothers and a visiting friend. The three youngsters joined him outside just in time to see the object disappear into the clouds in a greenish glow.[2-22]

* * * * *

Figure 2.1 UFOs vary in size from small drone saucers 3 feet in diameter, up to the gigantic mothership class, some estimated at over 1,200 feet (four football fields!) long. Shapes vary within a manufactured mechanical parameter of saucers with and without domes, oblong or acorn shaped, and the much rarer triangle or v-shaped. The smallest objects are unmanned drones. The larger class are typically gigantic cylinders, some transluscent revealing smaller objects (we assume saucers) arranged inside like "peas in a pod." There have also been the rare oval shapes and, even rarer, walnut-shaped (bulging saucer) large mother ships reported, mostly by airline pilots who viewed them in the extreme upper atmosphere.

Figure 2.2 Pilot Kenneth Arnold was responsible for the term "flying saucers" when he described to the press the objects he spotted from his small Cessna aircraft over Mount Ranier, Washington in 1947. Arnold witnessed nine brightly gleaming,"...heel-shaped craft skipping across the atmosphere like saucers across a lake."

Inset: *Kenneth Arnold shows press an artist's rendering of the objects he saw in 1947.*

Endeavor STS-123
A rare night launch

Courtesy NASA

Image Courtesy NASA

Figure 2.3 The large retired American space shuttle was relatively small compared to several gigantic UFOs spotted high above the Earth. It's estimated that more than 140 shuttles would fit comfortably inside the huge "motherships."

Some Very Credible Witnesses

UFO Sightings from Every Nation, Tribe & Tongue

Once I had whetted my appetite for this mystery called the "UFO," my search for an answer to their reality became more intense. It was apparent that some pretty credible people had reported the phenomena. I knew that most people doubted the validity of a story by a 13- and 18-year-old like my brother and me. What about military personnel, scientists, doctors, lawyers, radar experts, politicians? You name the profile or profession and prominent members of those groups had seen the ubiquitous flying saucer or a facsimile. And UFOs were observed in virtually every country in the world. The evidence for their existence was overwhelming. It was nice to know I was among such an elite group of believers. It was even more comforting to know that literally untold millions of others had witnessed similar sightings, some much more incredible than mine, as we shall see. I discovered that others had seen them in Phoenix, Flagstaff, Tucson, Heber, Wilcox and Globe, Arizona. Some were even seen over a military installation near Phoenix called Luke Air Force Base. [3-1] This was getting downright fascinating!

40 Million Americans
Can't All Be Crazy!

Just because there haven't been any major flaps lately doesn't mean that it has never happened. I have to admit that I feel I almost have to make new believers out of my readers. In reality, untold millions of you have seen something you would term a UFO. You must simply remember back to the time when UFOs were big national news. Most of you I doubt remember too much about the 1947, 1952 or 1954 flaps, but many can recall stories during the sixties and seventies. There have been a few publicized incidents since the mid-seventies that some may be aware of, but for the most part we tend to forget yesterday's news with quick detachment.

AUTHOR'S UPDATE: That has certainly changed in recent years with the flood of sightings, especially in South America and Mexico, as we shall explore in later chapters.

For obvious reasons, public interest peaks during these times of high activity and when the public has an interest in a particular area, there are usually public opinion polls made on the subject. Such is the case for the UFO phenomenon. In checking with the Gallup Poll Service, I discovered that their organization had conducted interviews on the subject on many occasions. Beginning in 1947, when those who were polled were asked if they believed that UFOs were "real," 46% said "yes." [3-2]

In a 1973 poll, 55% responded favorably and by 1978, 57% of those polled said they believed that UFOs were a real, not an imagined, phenomenon. [3-3] A more recent poll from the Marist Institute for Public Opinion taken in 1997 put the number of people who believed in intelligent life on other planets at 60%. And a National Enquirer poll in 1996 put the number at 83%. [3-4]

The tendency for the public to believe in UFOs, therefore, is increasing, and I would guesstimate that over 150 million Americans now believe in UFOs. Unfortunately, for reasons which shall be explained in future chapters, the inclination is for most thoughtful citizens to withhold their opinion on the subject, especially if asked by someone they don't know very well. That would open them to ridicule. No one wants to be labeled a "nut" by others.

There are, in fact, over 40 million "nuts" who have openly claimed to have seen something they termed a UFO. According to a recent 2-hour special on UFO sightings from ABC News' Peter Jennings on February 24, 2005, "We have a lot of skeptics – I am very skeptical – but we seriously investigated something a lot of people are serious about," he said. "And when we come to the end, this is wonderfully interesting.

"More than 80 million Americans now believe intelligent beings from somewhere else have come here," he said. "Forty million believe they have seen UFOs, so this is of deep interest to people." [3-5]

No doubt, many of these have seen something that can be explained by natural phenomena. The most common misidentifications are weather balloons, stars, planets, birds and blowing debris. If you think, however, that all forty million of these witnesses are so unobservant that they can't tell the difference between a flying disc and a flying garbage bag, then I challenge you to openly examine some of the reports that follow.

In addition, the Gallup Poll indicates that those with higher degrees of education and larger incomes are, indeed, more likely to believe in the reality of UFOs. Contrary to popular belief, it isn't the stupid people of this country who believe in flying saucers. [3-6]

Astronomers

Few things are as controversial to a scientist as the recognition of the existence of the flying saucer. It is even more so for a scientist who's job it is to peruse the sky. One would naturally think that if the flying saucer did exist, it certainly would have been sighted by every astronomer in the world. The truth of the matter is, those large telescopes perched precariously atop mountains around the world are focused light-years away. And so narrow is their field of view that if UFOs virtually cluttered the atmosphere there would be little chance they'd ever be observed, and even then only for a brief moment.

In spite of this, there have been strange sightings reported by some very distinguished astronomers, not, as you might imagine, while looking through their telescopes but, rather, while away from their equipment, using only the naked eye.

The astronomer credited with the discovery of our farthest planet, Pluto, is also one of the few astronomers to admit he has seen an unidentified flying object. Dr. Clyde Tombaugh was associated with Lowell Observatory in Flagstaff, Arizona, when he discovered Pluto in 1930. Nineteen years later another observation left him with a deeper sense of discovery. While sitting out on the back patio of his home in Los Cruces, New Mexico, discussing the affairs of the day with his wife and mother-in-law, something caught his eye off to the immediate west. Silhouetted against the evening sky was a dark cigar-shaped object with a row of small yellow lighted portholes or "possibly square windows" situated along its horizontal axis. Having had a lifetime of experience viewing objects in the sky, it's hard to discredit such a qualified observer. "The illuminated rectangles I saw did maintain an exact fixed position with respect to each other, which would tend to support the impression of solidity. I doubt that the phenomenon was any terrestrial reflection...I was really petrified with astonishment," stated Dr. Tombaugh. [3-7]

Oddly enough, another astronomer associated with Lowell Observatory reported seeing his own UFO three years later. The highly respected Dr. Seymour Hess, head of the meteorology department of Florida State University, was working at Lowell Observatory at the time he spotted the mysterious object. A small metallic disc appeared moving across the partly cloudy sky. Dr. Hess studied the object for a few minutes, noted the time 12:15 p.m., and then retrieved some four-power binoculars for a closer look. As the object moved from the southeast to the northwest he noticed that it appeared dark against the clouds and bright in the open sky, as though it had caught the sun's reflection on its highly polished surface. Being a scientist, he immediately tried to calculate its dimensions. With the assistance of the Weather Bureau station three miles away he determined that the cloud base was roughly 12,000 feet. Combined with the estimated zenith angle of about 45 degrees, he calculated its size at about 3 to 5 feet. The small object passed under the clouds at roughly 200 mph and against the wind, indicating that it was self-powered. The object passed noiselessly from view by 12:20. [3-8]

On November 1, 1955, Frank Halstead and his wife, Ann, were on their way to California on a Union Pacific passenger train. Frank Halstead was the curator of Darling Observatory at Duluth, Minnesota, for over 15 years and had earned the respect of his distinguished colleagues in the field of astronomy. Approximately one hundred miles west of Las Vegas they noticed a large metallic object moving in the same direction as the train. It appeared to be just above the distant mountain range. Since it was close to the ridges and trees of the mountain it was possible for Mr. Halstead to estimate its size. It was gigantic. At least 800 feet long. That ruled out dirigibles which were only about 200 feet long in that day. The huge cigar-shaped object was soon joined by a second metallic object about 100 feet long. The second was shaped like a disc, flat on the bottom with a low dome on top. For three minutes they watched in amazement as the shapes paced the train, then, without warning, they shot straight up and disappeared from sight within a few seconds. [3-9]

In Canberra, Australia, at Mt. Stromlo Observatory, four witnesses watched a circular, luminous, orange-colored object pass overhead the evening of May 29, 1963. Among the astronomers present was Dr. Bart Bok, world-famous authority on the Milky Way. They all insisted that it was too slow to be a meteor and the object glowed in the dark. There were no planes in the area according to the Department of Civil Aviation. Two days later, the Royal Australian Air Force tried to explain the sighting as two Vampire jets accompanied by a third trainer on a routine flight. It's hard to believe that four highly skilled astronomers could not tell the difference between a glowing orange single sphere and three jets...that two days earlier authorities said weren't even in the area! [3-10]

The big misconception that no professional astronomer has ever seen a UFO can be further dismantled. As early as 1882, E.W. Maunder, eminent member of the Royal Observatory staff at Greenwich reported a large "torpedo-shaped" celestial visitor. This was prior to the building of the first dirigible.

One year later at Zacatecas, Mexico, professor Jose A. Y. Bonilla, the head of the observatory there, photographed some opaque objects moving between his position and the face of the sun. What he saw on the developed plates astounded him and his colleagues. "I had not recovered my surprise when the same phenomenon was repeated! And that with such frequency that, in the space of two hours, I counted up to 283 bodies crossing the solar disc. Little by little, however, clouds hindered the observation until the sun had crossed the meridian, and then only for 40 minutes." That day and the next Bonilla and his associates photographed hundreds of the mysterious dirigible-shaped objects, speculating that they were somewhere in space relatively close to the Earth. This was borne out when other Mexican observatories were unable to locate the shapes from their viewpoint due to an optical law known as parallax which only applies to bodies in close proximity to the Earth. [3-11]

Pilots

Next to professional astronomers, pilots spend more time watching the sky than any other group of people in the world. It would stand to reason then, that there would be many reports of UFOs from these qualified witnesses. Perhaps the most qualified and objective group of pilots would be professional airline pilots. They are put through rigorous training and are rechecked normally two or three time annually to make sure that their flying skills and abilities for making reliable decisions are in accordance with the stringent parameters set by the FAA and the airline industry, itself, since the 1950s. After all, the lives of thousands of passengers and millions of dollars of equipment rests in their hands. Their ability to react to any given crises in a level-headed manner is critical. That's why we don't take lightly the reliability of their testimony. They are not likely to mistake wild geese, weather balloons, comets, the moon, reflections or other identifiable objects for something as mysterious as a UFO.

As one would guess, there have been literally thousands of UFO sightings reported by pilots throughout the world...all of which I would love to record here if I thought it would be any more convincing. Since there simply isn't enough space to report them all, I'll have to settle for selecting a few of the more interesting and better documented cases.

The first UFO case reported in modern times occurred in June of 1947, by a pilot. Kenneth Arnold of Boise, Idaho, was on a business trip when he reported seeing several bright disc-shaped objects near Mount Rainier in the state of Washington. The event captured the imagination of the American press and front page stories appeared across the nation describing the mysterious sighting. Arnold's description of the objects' motion - "Like a saucer skipping across water," was used to coin the term "flying saucer." The descriptive has become so commonplace that it is now listed in Webster's Dictionary and is used around the world to describe just about any unidentifiable object seen in the sky [3-12] (see *Figure 2.2)*.

By the spring of 1950, there were over thirty-five well documented sightings by airline crews across the nation according to Captain Ed Ruppelt, the director of Project Blue Book, the United States Air Force's official investigating agency. In his own words, "It was difficult to believe the old 'hoax, hallucination, and misidentification of known objects' routine," that had become the standard Air Force explanation for these sightings. [3-13]

On the evening of March 31, 1950, the crew of a Chicago and Southern DC-3 were on a flight from Little Rock, Arkansas, to Memphis. The flying conditions were perfect and for co-pilot G.W. Anderson it was a routine flight. Routine, that is, until he happened to glance out of the window. There to his amazement was a dark disc-shaped object with "eight or ten portholes" arranged around its circumference. "Oh no, not one of those things," he exclaimed to the pilot, Jack Adams, who by now was also watching the strange orb. Up until this point they were both avowed skeptics of the UFO phenomenon. Each porthole was glowing with a bluish-white light and a bright-white light flashed from atop the object. "If it had been an airplane we could have seen the passengers and other details very easily because it was so close." It was no airplane they both agreed.

A month later a huge orange-red UFO was spotted by the crew and passengers of a TWA DC-3 flying over northern Indiana.

Over the next couple of years literally hundreds of reports poured into Project Blue Book describing airline pilots' encounters with UFOs. [3-14]

In March of 1952, two TWA personnel, a pilot and co-pilot, were dead-heading home on a C-54 cargo plane from Chicago to Kansas City. The pilot of the C-54 was concerned about oil that had been leaking from engine number 2 and was keeping an eye on its behavior. Suddenly, a silvery disc-shaped object appeared at a position just above the engine. It was about 2:30 p.m. because he had just checked with CAA radio at Kirksville, Missouri. The UFO paced the airplane for five or six minutes before the pilot decided to make a turn toward the object. He seemed to briefly gain on the object but then the UFO made a left turn away from the plane.

As they neared it again, the pilot and co-pilot half-heartedly decided it was a balloon. As a final test they thought they'd make a 360 degree turn around the object. Instead of circling the object, the object stayed in its same position relative to the C-54 and gradually lost altitude. This eliminated the balloon theory.

With his curiosity peaked, the pilot decided to climb several thousand feet at full throttle then turn into the object and glide toward it. As he made this maneuver the UFO sank into the top of the overcast clouds. As the cargo plane flew over the spot where the UFO had disappeared, the crew saw it rise up through the clouds just off the right side of the plane and climb up and out of sight at an incredible rate of speed [3-15] (see *Figure 3.1*).

AUTHOR'S NOTE: *If you are convinced of the reality of UFOs at this time you may choose to skip ahead to Chapter 4. The following cases are more of the same, meant to convince the true skeptic.*

It was a routine flight for the crew of an American Airlines DC-6. They had just left Philadelphia shortly before midnight October 19, 1953, and were headed for Washington, D.C. Suddenly a strange shiny object that reflected the light of the moon appeared in the thin wisps of clouds just ahead. The object was directly in the path of the DC-6. Greatly alarmed, Captain J.L. Kidd ordered his copilot to switch on their landing lights. Just as they directed their beam toward the object to warn it, they were hit with a blinding white light that came directly from the object, as if it were returning their signal. With a startled natural reaction, the pilot jammed the large plane into a steep dive to avoid a collision. Passengers, unprepared for the evasive maneuver, were thrown from their seats and into the aisles of the aircraft.

Fortunately, this near miss caused only a few bumps and bruises but it created quite a stir in the press. The Civil Aeronautics Board (CAB) confirmed the incident but were hesitant, as was their standard position, to discuss the details with anyone outside of the airline industry. [3-16]

At around midnight April 14, 1954, United Airlines flight 193 was over Long Beach, California, when an object appeared directly in the path of the airliner. The pilot, Captain J.M. Schidel, immediately put the plane into a steep climb as his craft narrowly missed the object, which by now had flashed a bright-red light toward them.

A stewardess and a passenger each broke a leg during the ensuing moments of the drastic altitude change. It was described by the official C.A.B. report as a near miss with an "unidentified craft." [3-17]

Pan Am flight 257 was flying west of their normal course to avoid a storm that lay directly in their path from New York City to San Juan, Puerto Rico. As described in newspaper stories in early 1957, the plane was about 150 miles east of Jacksonville, Florida, when Captain Matt Van Winkle was surprised by an intensely bright beam of light coming from an object straight ahead of him. Again, the pilot reacted by forcing his craft into a steep climb, injuring several passengers.

The object had been seen by the crews of seven other airliners in the same general area, all within a few minutes of each other. They all described it as a glowing object with a bright light on its front end, trailing a reddish exhaust or glow. The official explanation of a meteorite or shooting star could not be taken seriously since the object appeared below the horizon. [3-18]

These are just some of the near misses described by the crews themselves. The question is: was there really any need for the drastic action taken by the pilots of these aircraft? If UFOs are intelligently controlled and possess the capability to maneuver at incredible rates of speed and at sudden angles, then it would reason that they are the ones to avoid any collision. I suppose that's easy for me to say, not having ever faced a head-on collision in an airliner!

An interesting side note is that right after several of these near misses in the early '50s the UFOs were suddenly seen with flashing exterior lights. Prior to this time only the glow of the larger craft were visible, apparently not giving adequate warning to approaching pilots and thereby causing overreaction by airline pilots who were surprised to see an object in their path. The flashing lights may have been added by concerned aliens…not concern that the craft might collide, but concern that people were being injured by erratic evasive maneuvers by the airline pilots.

Captain Peter W. Killian was piloting American Airlines flight 713 over Pennsylvania in February of 1959. As verified by N. D. Puncas, a passenger who was also the manager of a Curtiss Write plant, the airliner was approached by a huge glowing round object. The object maintained safe distance between itself and the airliner and soon joined two other identical objects in a position farther away. Again, it approached the airliner, only closer this time. By now the passengers had been alerted and they could see that the object was massive… much larger than the airplane. The pilot prepared to make a hasty retreat just as the UFO pulled away again and then joined the other two at a safer distance. A radio call summoned two other American Airlines' flights in the area and they reported that they, too, could see the objects. After the story broke in the papers, the crews of United Airlines' flights 937 and 921 and the captain of a third, captain A. D. Yates, verified seeing the event exactly as reported by Captain Killian.

All six airliner crews agreed that the UFOs were not any known aircraft and that the sky was clear that night even though the official Air Force explanation said Captain Killian had simply seen stars through broken clouds. [3-19]

Radar Evidence

If crews of commercial airliners have seen these UFOs, what about military flights and radar? Wouldn't they have reported some well-documented cases, too? The answer shouldn't surprise you.

Once again, there have been hundreds of radar reports associated with military sightings of UFOs. Since all military craft are kept in constant radio contact, as well as being tracked by radar whenever possible, any approaching aircraft would also be tracked by the nearest military base. That explains why a large percentage of the military sightings also include radar confirmation. Unfortunately, as we shall later examine, the official Air Force position remains: *"It can't be, therefore, it isn't."*

With rare exception, if there is even a slight chance of explaining away these documented sightings by trained service personnel, then the Air Force's official explanation will do so. The A.F. position on UFOs will be explained in greater detail in *Chapter 5*.

An early sighting in America occurred in Massachusetts on September 21st, 1950. Under contract with the U.S. Signal Corp, several military officers working on a radar project at Massachusetts Institute of Technology reported to Major Tuttle, staff weather officer, 33rd Fighter Wing, Otis Air Force Base, that a strange occurrence had them baffled. While observing two F-86s on radar they noticed a third object make several passes at the jets. The object gave a typical radar echo in all respects with one exception: it had been tracked at well over 12,000 mph! The object had made an unusual turn during its course, also, which they estimated would have produced at least five Gs on the pilot. The fact that the object gave such a good radar echo would indicate that it had irregularities in its surface and that it was comparatively large. For lack of a better explanation, they assumed it was a secret Air Force experimental craft and asked to be advised when it would be in the area again. No answer was forthcoming. [3-20]

Another very well-documented sighting was observed by means of ground visual, air visual, and air radar methods. The object was first tracked by the crew of an Air Force B-52 bomber. While making practice maneuvers near Minot AFB, North Dakota, the radar crew observed an unidentified object approaching at 3,000 mph. It passed off the left wing and took up a position approximately 20 miles out. Several times the object approached the B-52 and each time they experienced electromagnetic interference on their two transmitters as it approached.

In the meantime, the base received a visual report from a maintenance man who saw a bright orangish-red object hovering at about 1,000 feet approximately 10 miles northwest of the base.

The tower immediately called the crew of the B-52 in response to their own sighting and directed them to the area where the maintenance man had reported the object from the ground. As the crew of the B-52 prepared to correct their course toward the object, fourteen ground crewmen from five different locations near Minot AFB saw the same or similar object glowing in the night sky. In astonishment the crew of the B-52 confirmed visual contact with a bright light very near, or on, the ground.

The official AF explanation said that the radar sighting was "a plasma of the ball-lightning class." Also, the 14 separate sightings from the ground were explained as "some first magnitude celestial bodies," in-other-words, planets or stars. It's incredible to think that trained military personnel would risk ridicule and report a star as a hovering, glowing strange orb. Even more ridiculous is the explanation in conjunction with "plasma-balls." And no explanation was even attempted at how trained military personnel could mistakenly identify "planets" as being as bright as the sun and landing or hovering in a nearby field.[3-21] Nice try, but I ain't buying it!

In the well-known 1965 flap in Exeter, New Hampshire, a military radar operator, along with several other witnesses, sighted a UFO through a telescope as it hovered over Pease AFB, then clocked its movement at over 800 mph on radar. On another occasion a bright orange sphere was reported to have landed just adjacent to one of the runways and not far from where several officers and their families lived. The sighting caused such a stir that the base commander ordered the base cut-off from outside phone calls. He dispatched a fire unit to the spot at the end of the runway, but the approaching crewmen were powerless as the UFO sped off into the night.

Portsmouth Navy Base in the same area was constantly reporting UFOs on radar. During this period of 1969 there were innumerable cases of UFOs spotted both visually from the ground, seen while flying and, thirdly, tracked by military radar at both bases. Unfortunately, for their own protection, none of the witnesses' names can be mentioned here. [3-22]

Due to the official United States Air Force position on UFOs some of the best reported radar sightings come from outside of the continental U.S. and were leaked to the media while the modern phenomenon was still relatively new.

During the fall of 1948, off the northwest coast of Kyushu, Japan, a crew of U.S. military personnel were manning an F-61 aircraft on a routine mission that took them out over Fukuoka. Approximately 50 miles northwest of Fukuoka, 2nd Lt. Barton Halter, the radar operator on board, spotted an airborne target. More likely, at least three airborne targets, for he reported it "at a range of five to ten miles…dead ahead and…slightly above us," all within seconds. In his own words:

"…We increased our speed to approximately 220 mph and obtained an advantage of 20 mph. The target showed no evasive action at first, and we thought that it was probably one of the fighter aircraft from our home field. As we closed in, I noticed a slight change in azimuth and a rapid closure between us. Shortly thereafter, a matter of seconds, the target gave the indication of diving beneath us. We dived in an attempt to follow the target and before we could get squared away to follow, it had passed beneath us and was gone. I was notified by my pilot that we were diving at a rate of 3,500 feet a minute at 300 mph. I had intended to ask the pilot to peel off after it split "S," but it was gone too fast.

"The next, or second, interception was from the rear of the target as was the first; however, the target added a burst of speed dead ahead and outdistanced us immediately. On the third interception, my pilot called a visual at 60 degrees port side. By the time I made the pickup it was at 45 degrees port 3,000 feet and 5 degrees below. My pilot made a rapid starboard turn in an attempt to head off the target. By the time we got astern of it, it was off again in a burst of speed and disappeared between nine (9) and ten (10) miles.

"On the fourth interception, the pilot called to me that we had been passed from above from the rear by our target. I picked up the target as it went off my scope from five to ten miles dead ahead and slightly above. On the fifth and sixth interceptions, the target appeared at 9-plus miles doing approximately 200 mph. We had an advantage of 20 mph taking our IAS approximately 200 mph, a safe high-speed cruise for F-61 type aircraft. We closed in to 12,000 feet, then, with a burst of speed the target pulled away to the outer limit of my set which is 10 miles for airborne targets. This took approximately 15 to 20 seconds.

"In my opinion, we were shown a new type aircraft by some agency unknown to us..." [3-23]

A total of six objects were tracked by the F-61 but it was unclear if any of the objects had made more than one pass at the aircraft. The crew was able to discern the shape of the craft because it was a clear moonlit night. They were described as translucent, short (about the size of conventional fighter planes) and stubby without a canopy or any discernible lines. Ground radar reported that there were no other aircraft in the area at the time. [3-24]

The USS Princeton and USS Philippine Sea of the U.S. Navy were involved in a double sighting of several UFOs while on maneuvers off the east coast of Korean. The report to Chief of Naval Operations during this 1951 incident said that SX radar aboard both ships reported identical exceptionally bright targets with some sort of exhaust flames. The report by Lt. H.W. White, a CIC watch officer on the staff of the Commander, Carrier Division 5, said the target approached both vessels and made a sharp 360-degree turn, retreated but then split into two objects. Both objects remained 22 degrees apart and zigzagged out into the open sea at an estimated 1,200 mph. Identical sightings by two radar at the same time eliminated the possibility of malfunctioning equipment. In addition, the targets were observed several times during operations in April and May by the crews of both ships.

On May 31st the following year, two guards on a U.S. military base in Chorwan, Korea, reported seeing a glowing disc make several strange falling-

and-rising motions. The disc would climb to around 4,000 feet then suddenly fall "like a falling star" then stop at about 2,000 feet. It did this several times before an F-94 was scrambled to intercept the saucer. The pilot reported a round glowing object that had the ability to create blinding light at close range. During one pass at 8,000 feet, the object shot up toward the interceptor but maneuvered so quickly that the F-94 was unable to get astern of it. After several such maneuvers, the object simply outdistanced the aircraft and the pilot had to return to his base. The object was observed by the pilot, his radar operator and personnel at the ground radar station but this time they were unable to make radar contact . [3-25]

During August of that same year there was a radar sighting of a similar object at the meteorological station at Villacoubly, France. This was just one of the well-documented radar sightings that accompanied the estimated hundreds of thousands of sightings over France that year. On August 29, 1952, at about 7:30 p.m. several personnel at the station observed a light traveling in an irregular jerking motion across the cloudless evening sky. They watched its strange behavior for twenty minutes before deciding to track it with the station's theodolite. a It appeared on the theodolite "like a luminous bar, white-hot, edged with black and accompanied by bluish trails perpendicular to the bar itself. These trails may have been due to distortion by the lenses of the theodolite." The object was tracked as it traversed from southeast to northwest until it stopped and hovered relatively motionless at about 8:30 p.m. For over four and one-half hours the station had observed the object and recorded its position. Sometime around 8:00 p.m. the object was apparently joined by a second object that appeared as a bright green spot in vivid contrast to the original blue light registered on the theodolite.

To the naked eye of the observers the second object appeared bright red. Suddenly the second light descended, hung motionless for a few seconds, and then sped away toward the east. Two minutes later a similar event took place as the larger object changed its position from east to southeast.

At 10:45 there appeared a red and blue light, which was at first mistaken to be the lights of an approaching airliner. However, the light remained in a fixed position, then it slowly began to move. Through the theodolite it looked like a bright-red, round object that turned from red to yellow to green. It also soon vanished. The objects described were observed by the personnel at the station until midnight at which time observation was discontinued for a good night's sleep. [3-26]

The following telegram issued on November 27, 1953, demonstrates the UFOs presence in Africa, a continent which has had innumerable sightings of its own:

"Headquarters of the South African Air Force announced that on May 23rd, 1953, radar operators picked up an unknown object which passed over the Cape six times at a speed "definitely exceeding 1,250 miles an hour." Each time it passed it was within radar range for sixteen seconds at distances varying from 35,000 to 5,000 feet, and altitudes between 5,000 and 17,000 feet." [3-27]

On August 13 and 14, 1956, a report by the night-watch supervisor in the Radar Air Traffic Control Center at Lakenheath RAF Station, England, had authorities baffled. The officer, along with four other controllers, watched a target on their scopes move from east to west the distance of some 80 to 90 miles over Sculthorpe at a rate of 4,000 mph. Alerted by radar at Sculthorpe GCA Unit, both installations recorded the strange object which apparently possessed the ability for instant acceleration. Several minutes later its speed was calculated at different times as approximately 400 to 600 mph.

A C-47 flying over the base at the same time reported visual contact. The object appeared as a blurred light as it passed under the craft at 5,000 feet.

At first skeptical of the reliability of his own sighting, the officer then decided to contact 7th Air Division Command Post at London, along with his own Commanding Officer at AFCS, Communications Squadron. He repeated all the facts to both parties and updated them as the object was being continually observed. For close to 45 minutes the telephone discussion of the object continued until it was decided to send up two RAF interceptors to investigate.

As the first interceptor, which was scrambled from London, headed toward the area, he was given all the details by the tower at Lakenheath. They guided him toward the object until it was estimated he was approximately one-half mile from it. At that point the pilot reported visual contact and said he was locking his guns onto the target. Before the pilot could respond, the object shot back behind him. Suddenly, it appeared that there were two objects, one behind the other. Through several ensuing maneuvers, designed to shake the UFOs off his tail, the two objects remained in a fixed position precisely behind the interceptor. The pilot decided after several fearful minutes to head back to his base. "Let me know if they decide to follow me," he radioed with great anxiety. The objects followed him only a short distance and stopped. Almost immediately the second interceptor called for directions. He had apparently just left the base in London and wasn't yet sighted by the radar at Lakenheath. After talking to the pilot of the first aircraft about the UFO, he radioed Lakenheath.

"Lakenheath...(identification, aircraft call sign)...can't remember what call sign those aircraft were using. Returning home, my engine is malfunctioning."

The pilot had obviously decided that for him discretion was the wiser part of valor.

The above case was later described by Gordon G. Thayer of the National Oceanic and Atmospheric Administration and member of a scientific panel on UFOs, as "the most puzzling and unusual case in the radar-visual file. The apparently rational, intelligent behavior of the UFO suggests a mechanical device of unknown origin..." [3-28]

Many sightings of the calibre mentioned have been explained by the Air Force spokesmen as caused by lights reflected off the clouds of a weather inversion. This explanation has been used over and over again, even when official weather reports indicate the absence of any inversion. As one radar expert explained, "We are all familiar with the effects of an inversion. When it is strong enough it picks up all kinds of things on the ground: water tanks, buildings, bridges, and so on. But nobody is deceived because it causes huge irregular patches, nothing like the blips which were observed on the 20th and 26th of July – referring to another incident where the AF had claimed the UFO was caused by a weather inversion. During the six years I have spent looking at these scopes no jet plane, however fast, no storm or inversion, in fact nothing at all, has produced radar echoes behaving like that. And yet we have several times had identical atmospheric conditions (as the nights of the UFO sightings)." [3-29]

UFOs have been reported not only by military radar operators but also by other highly trained, qualified observers including NASA spacecraft trackers and FAA air traffic controllers.

Radar Evidence Curtailed

A significant development has taken place with regards to radar procedures since the time of the sightings highlighted above. In recent years, a system has been introduced that incorporates a computer within the radar to filter out uncommon information that would normally be generated on the controller's screens. This is extremely useful in eliminating ground clutter inversions and other confusing data that do not resemble normal aircraft. The computer is fed incoming visual information and it decides whether or not to pass it along to the radar operator. Unfortunately, objects that possess the qualities of a UFO (extremely high velocities, unusual location and dramatic altitude changes) are automatically eliminated by the computer's database of what constitutes a "normal" aircraft. These objects would not even be recorded on the radar screen for observation. That explains the lack of UFO radar evidence in recent years. [3-30]

Astronaut Sightings

If we are being observed worldwide by entities of unknown origin, it is difficult to determine their motives, largely from anecdotal evidence. One element is very significant, however. It would appear that the UFO is very interested in man's progress in exploring his own near space.

UFOs have been present from the very inception of modern man's space program. Early rocket experiments have been shadowed by UFOs, as have many of our manned space flights. From experimental X-15 flights in the early sixties to our manned flights to the moon, there have been frequent reports of UFOs either accompanying the craft or observed in the distance performing strange maneuvers. The following brief synopses of reported incidents is truly incredible, and doesn't even include the Shuttle and Space Station incidents which are notable and numerous:

EXPERIMENTAL V-2   **Various Sightings in 1948**
ROCKET LAUNCHINGS

Launched from White Sands, New Mexico, these rocket flights were often marked by the presence of UFOs. On one occasion a disc approached a rocket traveling at over 1,000 mph, circled it, then shot straight up past it at approximately 5,500 mph. The UFO was observed by various government experts equipped with radar, theodolites, telescopes and by ground personnel with binoculars. From this point onward UFOs accompanied many U.S. rocket experiments. [3-31]

SPUTNIK I & II   November 2, 1957

Dozens of reports from western Texas described an "egg-shaped thing" 200 feet long pass high in the sky just hours after the dog-carrying Russian satellite was launched. 1957 was a year of numerous UFO reports and their presence may have been more than mere coincidence. Dr. Luis Corrales, of Caracas, Venezuela, photographed passage of Sputnik II and, alongside the trail made by the time exposure of the satellite, there appeared a second shorter, zigzagged trail left by an unidentified object which seemed to pace the satellite's trajection. [3-32]

POLARIS MISSILE   January 10, 1961

The official log from the tracking facility at Cape Canaveral, Florida, listed "an unidentified object" that paced the missile for several minutes. The object was so large that ground radar tracked the UFO for fourteen minutes before technicians could get the radar back onto the smaller Polaris missile where it should have been all along. [3-33]

MERCURY CAPSULE   February 20, 1962
John Glenn

The now-famous politician saw three strange objects follow his capsule as it raced in orbit high above the Earth. Each object, traveling at differing speeds, soon shot past him at a fantastic rate. [3-34]

Aliens &
In-laws

MERCURY 3   May 24, 1962
Scott Carpenter

The astronaut observed several objects during his flight that at first appeared like "fireflies." Cmdr. Carpenter claims to have some good shots of an object that looks like a flying saucer. [3-35]

X-15 TEST FLIGHT   May 30, 1962
Pilot Joe Walton

Captain Walton photographed five disc-like objects during early testing of the X-15. [3-36]

X-15   July 17, 1962
Major Robert White

Major White photographed an object the color of "gray-white paper" which paced his X-15 for five or six seconds then darted above and behind the plane and disappeared. [3-37]

MERCURY 4

May 16, 1963
Gordon Cooper

Over one hundred technicians and newsmen saw an object tracked on Perth, Australia radar that Gordon Cooper described as a greenish object with a red tail and traveling east to west (contrary to orbits of man-made satellites). Newsmen were informed that they could not question him about the incident and that any statement about it would come only from NASA. As documented by Maurice Chatelain, former Chief of NASA Communications for the Apollo lunar mission, Cooper picked up voices on special frequency speaking in a strange language. Later examination of the recorded message by expert linguists revealed that the language was unlike any spoken on Earth. [3-38]

MERCURY 8

October 3, 1963
Walter Shirra

Astronaut Shirra was hurtling high above the Indian Ocean when he reported seeing several large mysterious glowing masses. [3-39]

VOSKHOD 1

March 8, 1964

As Russian cosmonauts re-entered the Earth's atmosphere they reported seeing a UFO pace their space capsule. [3-40]

34

GEMINI 1   April 8, 1964

This was an unmanned flight to test whether Gemini could safely carry astronauts into space. Astounded ground technicians watched as four UFOs took up positions around the craft on its first orbit: one below, one behind and two above it. After one complete orbit the objects sped up and away from the satellite. [3-41]

GEMINI 4   June 3, 1964
                          Jim McDivitt

Astronaut McDivitt was startled by a large cylindrical object with "two big arms sticking out" like antennae. At first he thought he would have to alter his course to avoid a collision but the object maintained its distance. He also saw a disc-shaped UFO that paced his craft and he took some 8mm movie film of the objects. Pictures later released by NASA showed an oval with a faint trail and NORAD's explanation of a man-made space device was later discredited by experts. [3-42]

VOSKHOD 2   October 12, 1964
                          Three Russian Cosmonauts

NASA overheard conversations of the cosmonauts when they reported being surrounded by a formation of disc-shaped UFOs. [3-43]

GEMINI 7

December 4, 1965
Commanders Borman & Lovell

The twosome reported being followed by two enormous UFOs apparently powered by "some kind of propulsion system." [3-44]

GEMINI 9

June 3, 1966
Stafford & Cernan

Both astronauts reported seeing several UFOs accompanying their capsule from take-off...also seen by ground stations. [3-45]

GEMINI 10

July 18, 1966
Young & Collins

Both Young and Collins saw two small discs follow their capsule but when they alerted ground control to try to pick them up on radar, the objects quickly disappeared. Later, during the same flight, they observed a huge cylinder-shaped UFO which Young photographed. [3-46]

GEMINI 11
September 12, 1966
Gordon & Conrad

A yellowish-orange UFO was sighted by both astronauts on their flight but as they went for the camera to take its picture the object suddenly disappeared. [3-47]

GEMINI 12
November 11, 1966
Lovell & Aldrin

A strange phenomenon was observed by these astronauts. They saw four spherical objects that appeared to be linked together and assured ground control they were not stars or any normal heavenly phenomenon. [3-48]

APOLLO 8
December 21-27, 1968
Borman, Lovell & Anders

On their second flight as a team, Jim Borman and Frank Lovell reported seeing several disc-shaped UFOs as they circled the moon and gathered information in preparation for the moon landing of 1969. Again, an unknown language was recorded by ground control on space- frequency radio. [3-49]

APOLLO 10

May 18-26, 1969
Stafford, Young & Cernan

The trio saw two UFOs, both when they orbited the moon and on their voyage back to Earth. [3-50]

APOLLO 11

July 16-24, 1969
Armstrong, Collins & Aldrin

Two unidentified spacecraft hovered at the crater's edge as Aldrin and Armstrong made the first moon landing. Prior to that, a large cylinder and two smaller discs watched their approach to the lunar surface from overhead. Aldrin reportedly took several pictures of the objects but NASA has yet to release the photos to the public. The following is an excerpt from the actual recorded voice of Colonel Edwin 'Buzz' Aldrin and NASA Mission Control:

Aldrin: *What was it?...What the hell was it? That's all I want to know.*

Mission Control: *What's there?... (garbled malfunction)...Mission Control Calling Apollo 11...*

Aldrin: *These babies were huge, sir...enormous...Oh God, you wouldn't believe it!...I'm telling you there are other spacecraft out here...lined up on the far side of the crater edge...They're on the moon watching us!...* [3-51]

APOLLO 12

November 14-24, 1969
Conrad, Bean & Gordon

Unretouched NASA image

All three astronauts reported being followed nearly all the way to the moon by two brilliantly lit objects. Ground crews also observed a large UFO with flashing red lights following Apollo 12 as the capsule entered the Earth's atmosphere. [3-52]

APOLLO 16

April 16-27, 1972
Young, Mattingly, Duke

Unretouched NASA image

Lunar module pilot, Charles Duke, was taking a walk while a classic, disc-shaped UFO looked on from an uncomfortable distance. This image was later blamed on lens flare, even though other evidences of such distortion are absent. [3-53]

APOLLO 17

December 7-19, 1972
Cernan, Evans & Schmitt

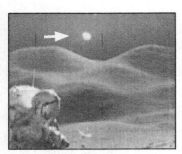

Unretouched NASA image

The threesome reported UFOs on their trip both to, and back from, the moon, as well as observing them near the moon's surface, itself. [3-54]

Some Well-known UFO Proponents

In an effort to disprove the debunkers, I have decided to list some well-known personalities associated with the controversy. The common misconception that only weirdos and eccentrics have claimed UFO sightings is totally false. I could list dozens of respected citizens from every walk of life, including the scientific world, but I think revealing a few of the more public figures will suffice in making the point.

Congressman Gerald R. Ford – who later became President of the United States called for Congressional Hearings into the mysterious UFO phenomenon which had plagued his home state of Michigan. He was the House Republican minority leader at the time and was embarrassed by the "swamp gas" explanation put forth by the Air Force in ridicule of hundreds of credible witnesses. His demands prompted the congressional investigation of 1966. [3-55]

President Jimmy Carter – in one of his Presidential campaign speeches acknowledged that he had seen a UFO and actually filed a UFO report when he was governor of Georgia. He further promised that if elected President, he would "make every piece of information this country has about UFO sightings available to the public and scientists." It was a promise, in a long list of broken promises, that Mr. Carter never kept. [3-56]

Baseball superstar Darrell Evans – Second-base star and member of the 1984 World Series champion Detroit Tigers, Evans claims to have seen a glowing craft with a dome on its top which slowly moved up the hills near his home in Pleasantown, California. He and his wife, LaDonna, were mystified by the sight for over three minutes. As he rose to get a camera the object appeared to move in reaction to his motion. "It was like they knew what I was going to do. They wiggled their ship to say 'goodbye' and began moving slowly away." Evans claims the experience changed his life and credits it with his changing attitude toward baseball. "I was feeling sorry for myself because I wasn't playing," he said. "I put things in perspective after this...this experience helped me regain my positive attitude." [3-57] (see *Figure 3.2*)

President Truman – was in office at the time of the now-famous Washington, D.C. sightings. When UFOs invaded the airspace over the nation's Capitol, in plane view of hundreds of witnesses, Truman demanded an explanation from the Air Force. What he got, at least publicly, was a poor excuse. The AF claimed the strange craft were actually the result of light reflections from a ground inversion, even though official weather records for the date indicated the absence of any inversion. [3-58]

Arthur Godfrey – was a national television celebrity during the 60s who hosted his own show on prime-time network television. In 1965 he revealed to his audience that he'd had a UFO encounter of his own. While flying his private plane with co-pilot Frank Munciello one night over Philadelphia, a strange brightly lighted object approached to the right of his craft. Godfrey maneuvered to avoid a collision but the object stayed positioned just off his left wing. He and Munciello were terrified not knowing the strange craft's intentions but were soon relieved when the object veered away and disappeared. [3-59]

Actor Clint Walker – famous star of the Cheyenne television series and The *Dirty Dozen* movie, among many other credits, claimed he saw a UFO. It was in 1962 when he and a friend were fishing leisurely on a river. Suddenly a disc-shaped object appeared near their boat. The small object caused eddies of dancing water just beneath the craft as if emitting wind from its underside. The object was not more than six feet above the river as it moved slowly and deliberately down the waterway. Not surprisingly, the strange incident prompted the two to retire for the day. [3-60]

Actor Mel Gibson – Hollywood's top-billing male lead, star of the blockbuster film *Signs* and director of *The Passion of The Christ*, has even reported his own UFO sighting in Los Angeles. Gibson described it as the classic disc-shaped UFO which he watched for several minutes before it "descended behind a crosslike object on the ground and disappeared." [3-61]

Prime minister Paul Martin of Canada –– Here's a recent article about the Prime Minister's sighting:

Prime minister's plane has close encounter with UFO in otherworldly incident

March 28, 2004

OTTAWA (CP) - What fate the stars hold for Paul Martin may be unclear. But one thing's certain: Canada's prime minister recently had a high-flying close encounter with a UFO. Martin and his entourage were cruising above Alberta when their Challenger jet came within an otherworldly whisker of a luminous object streaking through the night sky. In a report to Edmonton air traffic controllers, the pilot of Martin's plane noted seeing a "very bright light falling" through the air, with smoke trailing, while the aircraft passed over Suffield, Alta., on Sun., March 21.

People aboard at least two other planes also saw the plummeting object, which was travelling "at a very fast rate of speed" from a high altitude, says the report.

A copy of the one-page form, titled "UFO Procedures," was provided to The Canadian Press by Chris Rutkowski of the Winnipeg-based group Ufology Research of Manitoba.

Rutkowski, a longtime tracker of UFO sightings, obtained the report from the federal Transport Department, which routinely forwards him data on unidentified flying objects.

Martin travelled to a farm near Picture Butte, Alta., to announce an aid package for farmers last Monday.

So was an extraterrestrial envoy trying to convey a message to Canada's new leader?

Unlikely, says Rutkowski. What the prime minister's plane and many others saw that night was almost certainty a chunk of a comet or an asteroid that entered Earth's atmosphere and burned up into fragments.

An amateur astronomer in Calgary captured the blazing streak on videotape. And it appears one or more such fireballs were seen by people across the Prairies and as far east as Quebec.

In any event, it's unclear if Martin or his aides even glimpsed the object that crossed the plane's path.

"I'm not sure of whether the prime minister himself was apprised of what the pilot had seen at the time," Rutkowski said.

Justin Kingsley, a spokesman for the Prime Minister's Office, could not shed light on the question of whether Martin was aware of the celestial sighting. "I don't have any other information than what was provided through the protocol of the pilots," said Kingsley.

Ufology Research* of Manitoba publishes an annual study on UFO sightings in Canada, including many cases involving meteors. [3-62]

> *The group's recently released 2003 survey found that a record 673 reports of unidentified objects were made to various organizations and investigators in Canada.

Dan Akroyd – *In his own words:* "In September of 1986, my wife, Donna, and I were in residence at our home in Chilmark, Massachusetts, on the island of Martha's Vineyard. On this particular occasion there were two houseguests staying with us overnight. At about 2:00 a.m. I arose and stepped outside our bedroom onto the terrace wall to relieve my bladder. The firmament was magnificent, and it was natural for me to look up and observe its beauty and vastness.

"After a minute or so, this contemplation was interrupted by movement at the far right in my field of vision. At an altitude, which I estimated at around 100,000 feet (previous personal observations of the Concord making its turn towards Europe over the island at half that height substantiate my estimate), were two brightly glowing white dots traveling in tandem at high velocity. My immediate shouting awoke Donna who came out to join me. She, in turn, recognized the mysterious glowing objects, and we both vocally around the couple who were asleep in the guest bedroom.

"Drawn by the urgent and excited tenor of our voices, they too emerged and observed these two objects track across the night sky. It took less than a minute for the tiny, perfectly round, luminous bodies to traverse from right to left across the entire celestial array which was visible to us. The speed was evidently quite high.

"We four agreed, through the filters of our pooled experience, that these could not be astral bodies, meteorites, planets, shooting stars, fighter jets, helicopters, airliners, or satellites. To me this was not some stirring revelation, for I have been intrigued since childhood by the possibility of such phenomena's existence. My sighting was a confirmation." [3-63]

President Ronald Reagan – President Reagan had two sightings that he took very seriously. The first occurred on the night that Reagan was invited to a party that actor William Holden was having in Hollywood. He related the he and Nancy had seen the object while driving up the coast in California. They stopped and observed the object for several minutes.

"We followed it for several minutes, Reagan told a reporter. " It was a bright white light. We followed it to Bakersfield and all of a sudden to our utter amazement it went straight up into the heavens."

The second sighting occurred in 1974 just before Reagan ended his second term as governor. The story was told by Air Force Colonel Bill Paynter who, following his retirement from the Air Force, became the pilot of Reagan's Cessna Citation jet plane as governor.

Paynter stated, "it appeared to be several hundred yards away" and it was "…a fairly steady light until it began to accelerate. Then it appeared to elongate. Then the light took off. It went up a 45 degrees angle at a high rate of speed. Everyone on the plane was surprised."

The two incidents appeared to have a great impact on how the president viewed the world after that. Evidences can be seen in several of his speeches. As an example, on September 21, 1987, the President said that, "In our obsession with antagonisms of the moment, we often forget how much unites all the members of humanity. Perhaps we need some outside, universal threat to make us recognize this common bond.

"I occasionally think," continued Reagan, "how quickly our differences worldwide would vanish if we were facing an alien threat from outside this world. And yet, I ask 'is not an alien force already among us?'

"What could be more alien to the universal aspirations of our peoples," he told the Russian president, "than war and the threat of war?"

Again on May 4 in Chicago in the Q&A period following a speech to the National Strategy Forum in Chicago's Palmer House Hotel, where he adopted a more conciliatory tone towards the Soviet Union, Reagan brought up the UFO-alien precedent again. (Reagan's remark was made during his response to the question, "What do you consider to be the most important need in international relations?")

"I've often wondered, what if all of us in the world discovered that we were threatened by…a power from outer space, from another planet?" The president then emphasized his assumption that this would erase all the differences, and that the "citizens of the world" would "come together to fight that particular threat…" [3-64]

Dr. John Jackson – physicist and founder of the Shroud of Turin Research Project, Dr. Jackson was a chief investigator for the film *The Shroud of Turin*. He has also made claims to have seen a UFO in the late '80s while flying over Italy. [3-65]

Here's a short list of some additional noted entertainers, politicians and historical figures who have publicly claimed to have seen a UFO or grouping of UFOs:

Walter Cronkite	Jimi Hendrix	Jamie Farr
Jackie Gleason	Victoria Beckham	*"Corporal Klinger" from MASH*
Muhammed Ali	William Shatner	Rep. Ohio - Dennis Kucinich
Dick Gregory	Billy Ray Cyrus	U.S. Senator Richard Russell
Mick Jagger	David Bowie	Christopher Columbus
John Lennon	Will Smith	*October 11, 1492 - Atlantic Ocean*
Olivia Newton-John	Judy Garland	Alexander The Great
Elvis Presley	Michael Jackson	*329 B.C., Central Asia*

*   *   *   *   *

Illustration Courtesy James Neff

Figure 3.1 UFOs have been regularly spotted by pilots, both private and commercial. These are highly credible witnesses, but the FAA has taken an official position of silence or denial. In fact, they warn commercial airline pilots by invoking the JANAP 146 directive from the federal government which prohibits the declassification of any known report by any military personnel on the subject of Unidentified Flying Objects.

Evans gets boost from UFO sighting

By Mike Kiley
Chicago Tribune

DETROIT — The strength of Darrell Evans' character will be tested now. He has done something that this world doesn't really understand. He has dared to be different, revealing publicly that he saw an unidentified flying object two years ago.

An envelope was waiting for him last week in the Tigers' clubhouse, taped to his locker. The return address was "Flying Saucer Info Center" and attached to it was a sheet with a hand-drawn flying saucer.

"Hi, Darrell," someone said from the spaceship. "Boy, that Ripple looks good." The picture was taken courtesy of "the Darrell Evans Foundation for the Insane." On the outside of the envelope was printed "If you want to see UFOs, drink Ripple."

Evans laughed when he walked in and saw it, and immediately he knew the culprit.

"Bergman," Evans said, meaning first baseman Dave Bergman.

Bergman is lucky that Evans' wife, LaDonna, wasn't on the scene. She might have slugged him.

"I laugh when people are skeptical," Evans said. "I have to live with it. But LaDonna is always so positive about the experience we had. She doesn't let anyone knock down the idea."

Don't let Evans' good humor fool you. He sincerely believes that he saw a machine manned by extraterrestrials.

"The night changed my life," said Evans, the former San Francisco Giants player who signed as a free agent with Detroit last winter.

His night of wonder in June 1982 started out to be another one of frustration. He hadn't played — again — for the Giants. By the time he reached home in the hills of Pleasanton,

Calif., 40 miles away, he was stewing about his recent inactivity.

He and LaDonna went to the porch to discuss his unhappiness. They looked down into a valley and saw a stream of lights for miles on end.

In the distance, one light seemed to be moving slowly toward them. "Must be a helicopter," they thought. As it kept coming, their curiosity was piqued.

"Took 15 minutes for it to travel 10 miles," Evans estimates. "It stopped 150 yards to our right, near our neighbors' house, and hovered. No noise, none at all. By now, LaDonna knew it wasn't a ship made by man. We weren't frightened. We just stared.

"It was triangular in front and flat in back. There weren't a

—Evans, H9

Evans

Continued from H1

series of lights, just a glow. There was a small dome on top. It seemed to be a flat black in color, not a shiny metallic. It was 20 yards across and 15 yards deep. They were there for us to see them and for them to see us."

Evans can't remember if he and his wife spoke during the three minutes they watched the spaceship. The first thing he can recall is LaDonna saying, "Go inside and get the camera."

"Wait a minute," he said, not wanting to leave and miss something. Finally, he rose from his chair to get a camera. The spaceship immediately reacted with motion.

"It was like they knew what I was going to do," Evans said. "They wiggled their ship to say goodbye and began moving slowly away."

He ran breathlessly to the other side of his house, trying to keep the spaceship in sight. Unable to spot it, he returned to LaDonna. Three minutes later, both of them saw it 500 yards to their left and got a final glimpse.

"It took off like a jet," Evans said. "Still no noise. But it was really moving fast when it disappeared behind the hill."

The spaceship has not left their thoughts since then.

"We were talking about it just last night," Evans said. "We kept it to ourselves at first. Then we told a couple of good friends, who told some other people, and they started to give us a hard time about it. Most people take this as a kidding thing. But it will always be serious to us. It will be something special in our relationship."

The incident immediately affected his life, Evans believes.

"I was feeling sorry for myself because I wasn't playing," he said. "I put things in perspective after this, the way I usually approach life, and my baseball situation got better. I've always been a positive person, and this experience helped me regain that attitude."

Evans can identify with Richard Dreyfuss' character in the movie *Close Encounters of the Third Kind*. However, Evans says he would never have the courage to do what Dreyfuss did and leave the earth to travel with the aliens to their planet.

"It takes a certain kind of individual to do that," he said.

"But my wife and I really enjoyed *Close Encounters*, and we talked after seeing it about how beautiful it would be to meet someone from another planet. We have met them, and I hope everybody has the same opportunity someday."

Figure 3.2 *Reprinted from the Arizona Republic, 1985*

Older stories are very often the best referrence source because they were less likely to be distorted by modern precepts and the ease of deception available today.

The Arizona Republic *March 9, 1982*

UFO buffs rebuffed on encountering files

Republic Wire Services

WASHINGTON — The National Security Agency won a Supreme Court victory Monday when the justices rejected an appeal by flying-saucer buffs who demanded access to 135 UFO-related documents held by the NSA.

The court, without comment, decided to avoid a close encounter with a New York City-based group called Citizens Against UFO Secrecy, which sought the materials under the Freedom of Information Act.

The court refused to hear the group's appeal of a lower-court order allowing the NSA to keep the documents secret.

Figure 3.3 *Reprinted from the Arizona Republic, March 9, 1982*

The above policy, upheld by the U.S. Supreme Court, continues to this day with legitimate UFO stories being "Hands-off" material subject to national security and homeland security protections and regulations. There is, to the contrary, a policy of public disinformation which serves to discredit the reality of UFOs. Governments and the military do not like to be thought of as incompetent, as some of these incidents makes perfectly clear. It serves them well to have the general public thinking that UFO witnesses are crazy or delusional.

Flaps & Facts

What's A Flap?

T he term "flap" refers to the occurrence of numerous sightings during a prolonged period of time. The exact number of sightings required to qualify as a flap is strictly subjective, however, certain massive sightings that undeniably qualify as flaps have occurred on many occasions.

The Flap Of 1890

T he first recorded flap in modern U.S. history began in 1890 in the San Francisco Bay area. On November 22, according to several well-documented newspaper stories, several hundred people spotted a large dark object traversing the daylight sky. It was shaped like a huge cigar with "stubby wings." In the ensuing hours thousands of reports flooded in from Santa Rosa, Sacramento, Chico and Red Bluff as they, too, were astonished by the appearance of the strange, silent visitor.

On November 30th, the same or similar object was again seen moving against the prevailing wind. This disproved theories that the object seen earlier had been a balloon.

For several months reports came in from Iowa, Nebraska, Missouri, Wisconsin, Minnesota and Illinois tracking the object's progress across the country. On April 10, it was reported over Chicago and newspaper accounts of the strange craft ended on April 20, 1897. Oddly enough, the same explanations that the Air Force gave a half-century later were used to describe this UFO. Astronomers declared: "...it must have been Venus, the constellation Orion or Jupiter." [4-1]

The 1965 Flap

On August 2nd and 3rd of 1965 a series of sightings by tens of thousands of people, from South Dakota to Texas to the borders of Mexico and beyond, introduced the flap of 1965. Reports flooded into authorities and the nation's headlines heralded the mysterious event. Scores of flying discs were seen flying singly or in groups of up to eight or more and sometimes in diamond-shaped formations. A photograph taken by a fourteen-year-old boy in Tulsa, Oklahoma, showed a disc-shaped object divided into several multicolored sections: blue-green, yellow-orange and creamy white. The picture was shown in newspapers in Oklahoma and Indiana.

A highway patrolman and television cameraman in Sherman, Texas also photographed one of the strange flying discs. Both of these photos could not be disproved, although the "experts" attempted to discredit their authenticity.

The UFOs had swarmed over an area the size of Europe, had been witnessed by virtually tens-of-thousands of people, including policemen, highway patrolmen, military personnel and people from every walk of life. What was the "official" U.S.A.F. response? The cause for all the excitement must have been "... four stars in the constellation Orion; Betelgeuse, Rigel, Aldebaran & Cappella." When further studied, the Air Force explanation was exposed as an obvious lie, or at least gross incompetence. Dr. Robert Risser of the *Oklahoma Science and Art Planetarium* was asked about the possibility of the stars being mistaken for UFOs. The Constellation Orion, it turned out, was "only visible from the other side of the planet" at the time of the UFO sightings.[4-2] Why would the Air Force purposely mislead the entire nation? We shall explore the answers to this perplexing question in the coming chapters of this book.

Other major flaps have occurred in this country in the years 1947, 1950, 1952, 1954, 1957, 1965-66, 1968 and 1973-74. Most of these flaps will be looked at in further detail as we proceed.

When Are Most Sightings Made?

It's interesting to note that the most frequent time that UFOs are spotted is not when you might expect.

Since most of us are traveling around 7 to 8 a.m. going to work, or 5 to 6 p.m. coming home from work, one would speculate that these would be peak times for UFO reports because so many people are in a position to observe aerial phenomena. Strangely enough, just the opposite is true.

Eminent French mathematician, Jacques Vallee, plotted the times of UFO reports in three separate random groups. First he plotted those reports made prior to 1963. Next, those cases from 1963 to 1970 and lastly reports coming only from Spain and Portugal. In each group the time occurrence curve plotted was nearly identical. Peak hours of UFO encounters were:

FIRST ....Around 10:30 p.m.
SECOND.. Around 3:00 a.m.
THIRD .... Just before dawn

These odd hours indicate that the UFOs are, in fact, operating during the most discrete hours. Apparently they have attempted to carry out their purpose – whatever that might be – with the minimum of intrusion into our lives. [4-3]

Flaps Around The World

It's my impression that a lot of Americans believe the UFO craze was something invented by Hollywood to sell sci-fi movies in the 1950s. Nothing could be farther from the truth. What Hollywood did was take documented subject matter and build a sensational story line around it.

Hollywood, or the United States for that matter, was not the place that originated these strange stories. The phenomenon has evidenced itself around the world by cultures vastly different from ours in the farthest reaches of the planet. According to Captain Edward J. Ruppelt, former head of Air Force's Project Blue Book, UFOs have been reported not only in every state in the Union, but by every country in the world. [4-4]

Communist block countries have, in spite of stringent censorship, leaked reports of UFO sightings. Reports of unidentified flying craft were made in 1946 throughout the Scandinavian countries and parts of Soviet Russia. That was *prior* to the infamous Arnold sighting which, as you recall, lead to the now universal term 'flying saucer.' [4-5]

In 1961, an alleged incident took place in the Karelean Associated Soviet Socialist Republic, U.S.S.R., near Lake Onega. It was reported in *UFOs in the U.S.S.R., Vol. II* (1975) by Professor Felix Ziegel of the Soviet Aviation Institute, and Uri Fomin, a soviet state engineer.The official document describes "an aerial object of unknown origin" that descended across Lake Onega on an east-to-west path. A group of 25 hunters watched in horror as the huge oval-shaped object, glowing blue-green, crashed into an inlet bay. A shower of sparks and loud explosion frightened the onlookers speechless. The object, undaunted by its collision with the Earth, proceeded westward with a wobbling motion and disappeared. Subsequent investigations located three trenches apparently dug by the object's impact accompanied by uprooted vegetation. The sight was later investigated by a contingent of soviet civilian and military authorities who located several quantities of a substance (or substances) apparently left behind by the impact. [4-6]

In 1964 a UFO encounter was witnessed by Professor Vyscheslav Zaitsev while flying over Bologoye in a TU-104 aircraft. The UFO, described by the professor as a large gleaming metallic disc with a cabin-like structure on top, had apparently passed under the plane, slowed and paced it for several minutes then raced away.

On July 26, 1965, a large disc estimated at over 300 feet long was spotted in Latvian, S.S.R. The disc, according to astronomers viewing it through telescopes, was accompanied by three smaller round craft. They watched for 15 minutes as the smaller saucers rotated around the larger object then sped away in different directions.

Later that year another Russian astronomer named Lyudmila Tsekhanovick reported a UFO disc with windows or openings. It had been sighted over the Caucasus Mountains near Sukhumi.

In 1966 V.I. Duginov, Director of the Kherson Hydrometeorological School in Russia, along with 45 other witnesses, reported a disc-shaped UFO.

In early 1968 the Soviet Academy announced to AF Intelligence its plans to reveal an official publication with confirmed UFO evidence. But on February 8 they made an abrupt reversal. Instead of revealing new evidence to the Americans, who were themselves in the middle of their own investigation known as the "Condon UFO Commission," the Russians sharply criticized the American UFO commission as "sensational and unscientific." For unknown reasons, top-level Communist Party leaders had decided to put an end to all reports on UFOs and renounce their existence.[4-7]

The European Connection

A remarkable observation was made by Amie Michel in his book, *Flying Saucers and the Straight Line Mystery*. It was noted that the UFO flaps of both 1954 and 1957 had begun first in France and Western Europe. They would then be reported in South America and finally over America and Canada. They seemed to chart a course of action that was similar in both years. I'm not sure if that same pattern held true for later flaps in the U.S., but it did point to some kind of consistent pattern on the part of our visitors. [4-8]

On November 22nd, 1952, eight witnesses in Bocaranga, Africa, observed four silvery discs for over an half-hour. Father Carlos Maria was on his way to Bouar and accompanied by a businessman and six workers. Suddenly a silver disc shot across the path of their truck in the distance and disappeared. As they continued on their journey, once again they came across the strange craft hanging in the sky. This time it was accompanied by three others.

Just before moving, the objects would blaze up "as bright as the sun." They maneuvered in circles in various regions of the near sky then returned to their original spot. The men watched the spectacle for over twenty minutes.[4-9]

A pilot from French Morocco, located in the largely Arab region of northwest Africa, reported a small light that passed under his craft. It was March 25, 1953, and the crew of four was returning from Sale Airdrome to Nouasser Airport near Casablanca. The well-documented evening report described the light's path as it paced the airliner on its approach to the runway. It soon shot off to the left of the plane and performed a series of strange maneuvers in a loose spiral motion, returned to the edge of the runway, and then disappeared. The light was observed for over an hour. [4-10]

In 1965 at Canberra Airport, Australia, Air Traffic Control operators tracked a large glowing object that hung motionless for forty minutes at 5,000 feet altitude. [4-11]

On July 3, 1965, a large "lens-shaped" object was photographed through a theodolite by personnel of the Argentina scientific base, Deception Island, in the Antarctic. The object hovered and accelerated at tremendous speeds and caused strong interference with variometers used to measure the Earth's magnetic field at the scientific base. The incident was reported by Lt. Daniel Perisse, the Commanding Officer at the installation. [4-12]

A large flap occurred in Mexico in the summer of 1965. Virtually every day of the summer, beginning in July, UFO – or in this case OVNI: *objects voladores no identificados* – reports flooded into Government authorities. Some reports described several smaller objects that converged on a larger cigar-shaped mother ship. [4-13]

On October 15, 1954, seven or eight UFO reports came in from Italy. Several Italian peasants saw a cigar-shaped object land near the Po River in Rovigo, Italy. The object left an impression in the soft soil of about twenty feet in diameter. The object allegedly shot straight up and out of sight.

That same day a report came from Calais in the English Channel. A yellow luminous object was seen descending down onto some railroad tracks. According to witnesses it was about twelve feet long and 6 feet high. It soon took off at tremendous speed.

At 2:40, according to newspaper accounts, several Parisians saw four various-colored objects pass overhead high above Paris. [4-14]

During the weeks of September and October of 1954 reports of cigar-shaped UFOs accompanied by smaller discs came in from France, Italy, Switzerland, Austria, Southern Germany, Belgium, England and Spain. [4-15]

The phenomenon was obviously widespread.

UFO's Over Washington, D.C. !

In July of 1952 there occurred one of the most incredible episodes in UFO history. As if to make a statement to the world's power structure, a major series of sightings began near our nation's Capitol, climaxed by the appearance of several UFOs directly over the White House! So astounding was the event that the nation's newspapers dropped their lead story that day on the National Democrat Party Convention and instead ran front page headlines on the well-documented White House sighting.

As related by Edward J. Ruppelt, the head of the U.S. Air Force's Project Blue Book, UFO reports poured into the headquarters during the summer of 1952. By June it was not uncommon to receive 20 or 30 a day. As the Air Force investigators attempted to keep track of the large volume of sightings it appeared the country was in for a shock. On July 1st, two UFOs were tracked on radar in the Boston area of Fort Monmouth, New Jersey, which were heading southwest. Several other reports, apparently of the same two objects earlier that day indicated they were headed in the direction of Washington, D.C. The objects had come down across Long Island and stopped for a short time over the Army's secret laboratories at Fort Monmouth and proceeded toward the nation's capitol. There, one of the objects was seen by a crowd of people as it descended and was blocked from view by the buildings of downtown Washington, D.C. As reported by a professor at George Washington University, the dull-gray saucer was seen by at least 500 people. The incident did little to stir up the press, however, as it was reported on only briefly and the story simply stated that there had been hundreds of phone calls received by the authorities that day from people who claimed to have seen a UFO.

By July 5th the UFO stories had made page two. The crew of an airliner spotted a UFO over the super-secret AEC's Hanford, Washington, installation. On July 12, four hundred people at Montrose Beach in Chicago reported that a "large red light with small white lights on the side" approached the beach, made a sharp 180 degree turn, and then disappeared in the distance. The object was in sight for about 5 minutes and was completely silent.

By now, the number of reports being received by Project Blue Book was highly significant. According to Ruppelt, over 40 percent could not be explained in natural terms and the government was bracing for an invasion by the UFOs.

On July 14 the crew of a Pan Am airliner reported eight UFOs over Newport News, Virginia, around 130 miles south of Washington. And then on July 19 at 11:40 p.m. two radar at Washington's National Airport reported eight unidentified objects southeast of Andrews AFB. Four radar operators watched incredulously as the targets moved along at about 130 mph then burst off the screen at tremendous speeds. One object was clocked at over 7,000 mph. The radar personnel were so amazed that they thought their equipment had malfunctioned and summoned a repairman. The equipment was found to be in perfect working order. Radar at ARTC Headquarters, National Airport Control Tower and Andrews AFB all were tracking the objects as they flew through prohibited airspace over the White House and the Capitol. Immediately, jet fighters were scrambled from Andrews AFB to investigate the intruders but by the time they reached their location they were gone (see *Figure 4.1*).

The same or similar objects were reported that same evening by airline pilots from several different commercial flights.

The headlines the next day read:

INTERCEPTORS CHASE
FLYING SAUCERS
OVER WASHINGTON, D.C.!

Exactly one week later the same radar operators that had reported the first series of UFO sightings had several more unidentified targets on their scopes. Spread in a huge arc formation from Herndon, Virginia, to Andrews AFB, the discs moved in the same flight pattern across the area as those of a week earlier. Two F-94 interceptors were called in from New Castle County AFB a short time later but as they approached the area, the unidentified craft suddenly disappeared off ground radar's screens. The jets inspected the area for a brief time but did not see any evidence of anything unusual and left.

A few minutes later the unidentified targets were back on the radarscopes. Later reports indicated that they had simply moved south to an area near Newport News, Virginia, while the jets were in the area.

Again and again that night as interceptors were vectored into areas where the UFOs were localized, the strange lights would simply disappear and reappear in another location. This uncanny cat-and-mouse game had many military personnel greatly concerned; not knowing the motives or origin of these strange craft. They were greatly relieved when the night finally ended and no incidents of alien contact had occurred.

That next day, Monday, July 27, every newspaper in Washington carried news of the UFO sightings. Typical headlines read:

JETS ALERTED FOR SAUCERS –
INTERCEPTORS CHASE
LIGHTS IN D.C. SKIES

FIERY OBJECTS OUTRUN JETS
OVER CAPITOL - INVESTIGATION VEILED
IN SECRECY FOLLOWING VAIN CHASES

Not surprisingly, the strange event caused a mammoth stir around the country and President Truman sent an aid to investigate. The official Air Force explanation? "The radar targets may have been caused by weather..." even though Project Blue Book's own files listed the phenomena as "unknowns."

The press, equally mislead by the Air Force, ran stories the following week that the Air Force had disavowed the flying saucer explanation in favor of the more acceptable explanation of natural phenomena.

The nation had bought the Air Force's story chiefly because it was a safe, 'logical' one. Everyone knew that only kooks and visionaries saw UFOs! This took a great deal of pressure off the Air Force and the number of reports to Blue Book went from 50 a day to about 10 a day inside a week. They had weathered the storm fairly well and were glad that the reports they feared the most: "UFOs over the nation's Capitol," had finally abated. [4-16]

That monumental event was not to be the last in Washington, D.C. history, however. On May 5, 1954, two huge objects were tracked by Washington National Airport radar. They periodically circled high above the capitol over several days. On June 12 a huge craft was tracked at 79,000 feet above Washington and jets were scrambled to await its descent into firing range. Instead, it simply disappeared. Two nights later it reappeared and coursed through the area between Baltimore and Washington in excess of two hours. Once again, jet interceptors were sent to the area and the coast area went on full military alert. Obviously the Pentagon was expecting contact with the unknown craft at any time and were forced to draw up a contingency plan of action in case the alien craft made an all-out assault.

On August 25, a mysterious object was seen and tracked orbiting the Earth for several days. Officials of the Grumman Aircraft Corporation had reportedly photographed the object and all efforts to discredit the picture had failed.[4-17]

During October of 1954, a French astronomer reported that he had received signals from an unknown object orbiting the Earth. The message was uninterpretable. The objects that the Air Force had been tracking near Washington, D.C., were gigantic and their frequent appearance had the military truly rattled. After all, their purpose was a mystery and they were apparently sending undecipherable (encoded) messages to each other.

By 1955, the appearance of UFOs in the Washington, D.C. area was relatively common. On July 26 a large yellow "grapefruit-like" object was seen moving in an erratic fashion high above the city. As it approached the Washington National Airport it suddenly stopped and hovered over the facility. As it did, the lights at the airport went out. Obviously panicked by the close approach of the object, airport personnel decided to train their searchlights on it. When they did the searchlights also went out. Soon the object moved away and all the lights returned to normal. Although well documented, the event somehow went unmentioned by the newspapers. [4-18] I can only speculate that the press had adopted the Air Force's philosophy: *It can't be, therefore, it isn't!*

Although the next ten years reveals no significant reports in the D.C. area, there may have been numerous unofficial reports. The lack of public support for the validity of the sightings may have prevented many witnesses from coming forward to tell of their own experiences.

Several years later, in January of 1965, after the fear of public ridicule had subsided, several reports again surfaced of UFOs over Washington, D.C. This time a group of twelve Army Communications Specialists reported to the *Washington Star* that they had observed twelve to fifteen egg-shaped objects pass over the Capitol building at about 12,000 to 15,000 feet altitude. They were being chased by two delta-wing jet interceptors and the chase lasted for 3 or 4 minutes. The men had been alerted by friends in the radar section indicating the objects were tracked by military radar.

Preparations had been made for a filmed interview of the witnesses by a television crew when an Army "spokesman" intervened. The men were taken into another room and were told they were not to discuss the event with civilians under any circumstances. Thus, the intended interview was abruptly halted.

When the Defense Department was questioned about the event later they simply replied that the men were mistaken. No such event had taken place and the men "had seen nothing at all." [4-19]

⋆   ⋆   ⋆   ⋆   ⋆

Image Courtesy AP

Figure 4.1 – In the summer of 1952 waves of UFOs flew over Washington D.C. and surrounding areas on several occasions, culminating in a flyover of the White House on July 26, 1952.

Image Courtesy NASA/Hubble Directorate

Figure 4.2 - The "Horsehead" Nebula, taken by the Hubble Space Telescope.

Image Courtesy NASA/Hubble Directorate

Figure 4.3 - The "Ring" Nebula, taken by the Hubble Space Telescope.

Truth or Consequences?

Are UFOs Real?

The reality of UFOs, unfortunately, is still a matter of debate. No UFO has ever landed in a public place and its occupants declared their true purpose or origin. Mystery enshrouds the phenomenon and alien contact is usually isolated and localized (confined to a specific geographic area).

For most of the scientific community, only an open appearance with repeated availability to the scientific 'experts' would constitute proof of their existence. Yet, hundreds of thousands of reliable citizens from around the world have reported the same phenomena. It's ridiculous to suggest that they are all incompetent witnesses or lunatics. As we have shown, some very intelligent and influential members of our society have come forth with tales of mysterious sights in the heavens, even though the admission opens them to public ridicule. How can you explain such sincerity from untold hundreds of thousands of people who have not sought to gain anything from sharing their experiences?

Mass Hallucination?

From the inception of this phenomenon there have been those who have put forth the hypothesis that our society was suffering from mass hallucinations brought on by fictitious reports from the media. They point to the pressures of modern societies which produce mass anxiety and suggest that the unsophisticated public is so desperate to believe the phenomenon that their 'collective consciousnesses' dream up these flying saucers. And all the time the people are really seeing stars or asteroids or airplanes or balloons or who knows what? This position is supported by the group of witnesses who do mistake natural objects as UFOs.

UFO reports have been analyzed by several groups and organizations and their conclusions are all quite similar: approximately three-quarters of the sightings are actually astro bodies, space objects or man-made objects. Roughly twenty to twenty-three percent, however, remain 'unknowns.' [5-1]

One has to question the validity of mass hallucination because if the UFO were only an imagined phenomenon, there would be as many different visual descriptions as there were witnesses who dreamed them up. The truth is, hundreds of thousands of reports and untold millions of sightings around this planet have overwhelmingly described a fairly consistent object possessing very similar flight characteristics. Could this merely be coincidence?

Why are there gaps in our sightings for periods lasting up to eight or ten years? Surely our society lives in the most perilous time in history brought on by the nuclear arms race and the instability in the Middle East and Russia. Would not these pressures cause mass paranoia even more rampant than in the late forties and early fifties? The fact that UFO reports show ebbs and flows in activity dramatically serves to validate flaps in past decades and, frankly, discounts the mass hallucination theory.

USAF Position

And what does our United States Air Force make of all this bothersome noise? As stated before, they have adopted the position of: It can't be, therefore, it isn't. Of course they defend their position by stating that several official investigative committees – made up of panels of scientific experts – support their hypothesis. We will deal with these "unbiased" panels later, but I think it is important to get an overview of the human thought process in making these kinds of determinations.

First, we must explain that the UFO phenomenon doesn't fit into any scientific model and is, therefore, impossible to study in scientific terms. Science dictates that a subject be studied carefully and that rules of consistency be established within the laws of nature...as we understand them. The slippery UFO simply won't cooperate with science. The scientist, being the most practical of types, is naturally not likely to believe something on mere hearsay. If it can't be proven, it simply does not exist!

Bolstered by the scientific community, the Air Force has chosen to simply deny the existence of UFOs. This official position of denial can be explained in one of three ways:

1. The Air Force is not aware of the facts associated with UFO reports (highly unlikely)

2. The Air Force is suppressing the truth for reasons of their own (we will explore this further)

3. There is nothing to the phenomenon (the least likely in light of the avalanche of supportive eye-witness accounts) [5-2]

The Military Vacillates

During the early years of UFO sightings the Air Force seemed, at times, to be leaning toward a position of openly confirming their existence. The onslaught of reports starting with Arnold's sighting in 1947 dictated that the Air Force investigate the phenomenon and determine just what it was that was violating the airspace of America.

A full-scale secret investigation, although never officially admitted, must have ensued shortly thereafter. The Air Force was wrestling with a problem that could neither be proved nor disproved and, frankly, they must have been in quite a quandary over just what to do.

I think that, early on, evidence demonstrates the Air Force was trying to honestly find some answers to this bewildering anomaly. A TOP SECRET report labeled *Estimate of the Situation* was delivered to Air Force Headquarters on August 5, 1948. The result of a six-month study by top American scientists and engineers, the secret report stated flatly that "the UFOs are from another world, observing the Earth for an unknown motive." [5-3] This startling report must have rocked the military power structure. After all, the existence of even one flying saucer would be far more significant than the most decisive battle in the history of mankind.

The astounding conclusion made it past the Directorate of Intelligence before it reached the Chief of Staff, General Hoyt Vandenberg, according to Donald E. Keyhoe in his book *Aliens from Space*. On the general's orders the secret analysis was destroyed...all except one copy which Major Dewey Fournet was able to hold out. The report was seen by Major Keyhoe in 1952. The major was told by Captain Edward J. Ruppelt that the reason the general ordered the report covered up was that he feared a "stampede" by the public. The general had pointed out that the Air Force would have had an impossible task trying to convince the public that the aliens were friendly when, in fact, they weren't sure themselves. [5-4]

And so it was that the Air Force announced in December 1949 that all UFO reports had been disproved and their investigation was ended. Unfortunately for the Air Force, the bothersome UFO was not so easily dismissed. [5-5]

This statement had been, oddly enough, preceded on April 27th by the following statement also issued by the Air Force:

"The mere existence of some yet unidentified flying objects necessitates a constant vigilance on the part of Project 'Saucer' personnel, and on the part of the civilian population...

"Answers have been – and will be – drawn from such factors as guided missile research activity, balloons, astronomical phenomena. But there are still question marks...

"Possibilities that the saucers are foreign aircraft have also been considered. But observations based on nuclear power plant research in this country label as 'highly improbable' the existence on Earth of engines small enough to have powered the saucers...

"Intelligent life on Mars is not impossible but is completely unproven. The possibility of intelligent life on the planet Venus is not considered completely unreasonable by astronomers.

"The saucers are not jokes. Neither are they cause for alarm." [5-6]

The saucers are not jokes, neither are they cause for alarm. This position was to be echoed again in 1952. According to Captain Ruppelt, Air Force Letter 200-5 stated in essence that "UFOs were not a laughing matter, that the Air Force was making a serious study of the problem, and that Project Blue Book was responsible for the study." The letter was officially signed and sealed by the Secretary of the Air Force. [5-7]

In a memo formerly designated "TOP SECRET" but downgraded to "confidential" September 15, 1969, Wilbert B. Smith, Head of the Canadian Broadcast and Measurements Section of the Department of Transport, indicated the interest of the Canadian Government in the U.S. Government's study of UFOs. Dated November 21, 1950, the memo states in part:

> (a) The matter is the most highly classified subject in the U.S. government, rating even higher than the
>
> H-bomb. * (Author's Note: the Hydrogen Bomb was still under development when this memo was issued in 1950)
>
> (b) Flying saucers exist.
>
> (c) Their modus operandi is unknown but concentrated effort is being made by a small group headed by Dr. Vannevar Bush.
>
> (d) The entire matter is considered by the U.S. authorities to be of tremendous significance. [5-8]

In April of 1952 an article in *LIFE Magazine* by Bob Ginna made some very startling revelations. Titled: *"Have We Visitors from Outer Space?"* the author had interviewed the Director of Project Blue Book and had left the impression that "maybe" we were being visited by alien civilizations. It also quoted Dr. Walther Riedel, at the time Director of rocket engine research for North American Aviation

Corporation and an important part of the team that had developed the V-2 missile for Nazi Germany. Dr. Riedel stated that he believed UFOs were from outer space.

In addition, Dr. Maurice Biot, one of the world's leading aerodynamicists was quoted as having been in agreement with Dr. Riedel. [5-9]

When later reflecting on his statement in the *LIFE* article, Captain Ruppelt writes: "...I know that the Air Force had unofficially inspired the article. The 'maybe they're interplanetary' with the 'maybe' bordering on 'there are' was the personal opinion of several very high-ranking officers in the Pentagon – so high that their personal opinion was almost policy." [5-10]

However, soon after this, in the wake of the *Robertson Panel* study on the subject, the Air Force took a solid position of denial...one it has maintained since that time. Even in the face of overwhelming evidence the decision to deliberately debunk UFO reports becomes very obvious to the serious UFO student. As later evidence will show, the Air Force has chosen to cleverly hide facts that even its own advisors have brought to light and has repeatedly released to the public what amounts to absurd statements (in light of the evidence) that there is no such thing as a flying saucer.

Is There A Cover-up?

By Captain Ruppelt's own admission, the Air Force has instituted a policy of 'don't say anything.' In December of 1953, they had issued Joint-Army-Navy-Air Force-Publication (JANAP) 146. The subheading read: Canadian-United States Communications Instructions for Reporting Vital Intelligence Sightings.

> *The Joint Chiefs of Staff made the public disclosure of a UFO report a crime under the Espionage Act, punishable by a one-to-ten-year prison term or a $10,000 fine!*
>
> *JANAP 146 applied to anyone who knew it existed, including commercial airline pilots and all military personnel.* [5-11]

Prior to 1955, even though JANAP was supposedly in force, a clear directive had not been issued by the Air Force. On several occasions Air Force personnel had admitted the validity of UFO reports. But on January 7, 1955, the Air Force issued an *Air Force Services Letter* which put forth the policy which is in effect to this day. The letter said, in essence, that certain Air Force personnel had been talking too much about UFOs and they were ordered to be silent about the subject. [5-12]

Don't expect any cooperation or even open debate on the subject from any Air Force people. They're under strict orders not to discuss it.

Can the Air Force legally withhold information from the public? Absolutely. In Air Force Regulation 11-30, withholding information "in the public interest" is allowed, and in Air Force Regulation 11-7, even Congress may not be privy to certain classified information "even in confidence." [5-13]

According to the Defense Department's Assistant Secretary in 1962, Arthur Sylvester, if the ends justified it, it was not wrong to keep the public in the dark on matters of national security. [5-14]

Have officials withheld information on UFOs?

Airline pilots, whom we have shown to be frequent witnesses to UFO incidents, are under direct supervision from the Federal Aviation Administration through their respective airlines. The FAA is of course a branch of the Federal Government and receives its orders from the executive branch.

In a well-documented story in February of 1959, three huge flying objects were seen by the passengers and crew of American Airline's Flight 713. Captain Peter W. Killian reported to the press that he and all his passengers had seen three huge glowing round objects, much larger than their own craft, approach the airliner. After warning the passengers of the impending danger they prepared for evasive measures if the objects got any closer. Fortunately, the UFOs kept their distance and after some time sped off. The incident, which took place while in air space over parts of Pennsylvania and Ohio, was documented by the crews of no less than six other airliners that were in the area that night.

Needless to say, Captain Killian was anxious to report the incident to the authorities. As he reported himself, his attempts to get action from the FAA were met with indifference. They told him they had no intention of investigating the sighting. "Wasn't the FAA supposed to safeguard airline passengers?" he persisted. Couldn't they..."tell pilots what to do in a tight spot like this?"

The official answer shocked the captain: "FAA's responsibility ends when a UFO report is forwarded to the Air Force. Beyond that, no comment." [5-15]

As reported by famed newsman Frank Edwards in his excellent book *Flying Saucers – Serious Business*, the Air Force had, in the early 50s, been able to effectively stifle reports in the press by giving them misleading information regarding UFOs. This had lead most publications to believe that the phenomenon was simply non-existent.

As an outspoken advocate of UFO realty, having seen one himself, Edwards stated in January 1954, "(there were) only two sources of UFO information at that time: airline pilots and my radio program on Mutual Network," as the Air Force had effectively stopped most other reports.

On February 17, officers of the Military Transport Intelligence met with officials of the Airline Pilots Association in an effort to apply pressure to the commercial pilots. They were "urged" to process UFO reports in the following manner: First, contact the nearest airport immediately and then "make no public statements on such incidents." [5-16]

Frank Edwards continued to be a main spokesman for those who believed in UFOs for many years. Then on June 23, 1966, just days prior to airing a national television show to expose some inconsistencies in the official UFO investigation taking place at Colorado University, Frank Edwards died of a heart attack. [5-17]

In an Air Force public relations booklet *Questions and Answers About the United States Air Force*, the subject of UFOs is addressed in detail:

"The term 'flying saucer' is really a science fiction term that was coined several years ago. No unidentified flying object has given any indication of threat to the national security; there has been no evidence submitted to or discovered by the Air Force that unidentified sightings represented technological developments or principles beyond the range of our present scientific knowledge; and finally, there has been nothing in the way of evidence or other data to indicate that these unidentified sightings are extraterrestrial vehicles under intelligent control." [5-18]

One has to wonder that if the UFO doesn't exist, why has the Air Force been forced into opening new investigations on this non-existent phenomenon on so many occasions?

In a story reported in the *Lake County Republican Herald* the *Geauga Record* and the *Cleveland Press*, an Ohio man named Olden Moore was on his way home from Painesville in northeastern Ohio at about 11:30 the evening of November 6, 1957. Just west of Montville he suddenly saw a bright object in the sky that then split into two separate objects, one going straight up and out of sight, while the other drew nearer and approached his vehicle. As the object got closer it got brighter and quite large and settled into a field about 500 feet from him.

Curious and unafraid, he decided to approach the object which he estimated to be about 50 feet in diameter and 15 feet high with a steeple-like cone on top, making the overall height around 20 to 30 feet. The object was surrounded by a bluish-green haze, like a fog. It also pulsated from a dim glow to a brighter light and then would fade back to its original dim glow. Peering at it in the moonlight he was able to see the highly polished metallic surface of the vehicle as the fog began to dissipate. He walked about halfway to the object and then thought about getting some witnesses, knowing that nobody would believe him. Up until that time he thought anyone who saw a UFO was a kook. He drove 5 miles to his home and got his wife but by the time they got back to the site the object was gone.

An investigation of the area later by Lake County Civilian Defense Director, Kenneth Locke, turned up six footprints that "came from nowhere and went nowhere..." Further investigation located two perfectly round holes about 3 feet deep that had been dug and the earth removed. "They were not like post holes, an observer said: they were perfect."

The story itself was remarkable but what transpired afterward was perhaps equally as mysterious. According to Moore's wife, on November the 14th he came home and reported that he was going away. "When I asked him where, he said he couldn't tell me. I was so mad, I asked him what I was supposed to do if one of the children died, or something." Two days later he returned with the report that he had gone to Washington to talk to some "high officials" and beyond that he would not comment, claiming he was sworn to secrecy. [5-19]

In a study closely allied to Project Blue Book in January 1953, six of the country's top scientists were commissioned to study the UFO phenomenon. One item of particular interest was brought to their attention by Major Dewey

Fournet, formerly assigned as the Pentagon liaison to Projects Grudge and Blue Book. He reported that, at his suggestion, a panel was formed to study the motions of verified UFOs. From this detailed analysis of UFO movements it could be determined whether the objects would have required intelligent guidance. As the study progressed, utilizing hundreds of the Air Force's best reports, the answer became apparent. Without question, the panel concluded, the UFOs were controlled by intelligences with scientific knowledge far surpassing our own technological capabilities.

Captain Ruppelt was very candid when describing this report. "The study was hot because it wasn't official and the reason it wasn't official was because it was so hot. It concluded the UFOs were interplanetary spaceships. The report had circulated around high command levels of intelligence and it had been read with a good deal of interest. But even though some officers at command levels just a notch below General Samford bought it, the space behind the words 'Approved by' was blank – no one would stick his neck out and officially send it to the top." [5-20]

A large outbreak of UFO incidents occurred in 1966 prompting the press and members of Congress to demand the truth. The 'truth' was studied by the Condon Committee and the results issued on January 8, 1968:

"No such thing as an interplanetary spacecraft
and no need for further study."

A familiar tune played in previous years. And as in previous years, the public bought it. This, regardless of objections by many closely associated with the study. Congressman J. Edward Roush: head of the 1968 hearings, Doctor J. Allen Hyneck: noted Harvard scientist and former consultant to Project Blue Book, many top scientific and technical advisors and even the American Institute of Aeronautics and Astronautics, all denounced the conclusions of the Condon Committee. But so it was that the Air Force was able to avert another catastrophe as it denied the existence of the UFO. [5-21]

Obviously, the subject of UFOs has generated a tremendous number of reports and documents. It has been estimated that the CIA, alone, has over 10,000 pages of material relating to UFOs. There has been a concerted effort to obtain some of these top secret documents since the inception of the Freedom of Information Act in 1974, brought on by Watergate.

In spite of the public's right to know, the CIA has managed to keep some "sensitive" UFO-related documents from reaching the hands of civilian UFO investigative groups. [5-22]

Ground Saucer Watch and Citizens Against UFO Secrecy have been denied access to these documents and the courts backed the CIA's right to withhold the information in 1982 on grounds that their disclosure might jeopardize national security [5-23] (see *Figure 3.3*).

Today the public has a certain naive trust in what the Air Force says. Most would think it patriotic to cooperate with the Air Force on matters it deemed national security and that's the way the Air Force likes it, you may rest assured.

Why The Lie?

There may be some very valid reasons for the Air Force's position… valid, at least, from their point of view. The most often speculated reasons are examined here.

Mass Panic

It has been suggested that the Air Force fears a mass panic if the truth were made public. The thought that our skies are being invaded by some alien civilization, and we are powerless to stop them, does breed a real fear that could cause a worldwide panic. [5-24]

As evidence, we can recall a radio broadcast in 1938 by Orsen Wells that caused thousands of people to stampede when alerted that martians had landed. The realistic broadcast called 'The War of The Worlds' was preceded by a brief explanation that it was only a fabricated event. But for those who tuned in after the disclaimer, their reaction was one of terror. Thousands of panic-stricken people rushed into the streets to try to get a glimpse of the invaders and emergency switchboards were overloaded with calls from terrified citizens.

If the Air Force has chosen to remain silent on the issue of the UFO because of this 1938 event, then I think they vastly underestimate our citizen's ability to adjust to the events of a changing world. After all, we have learned to live with the pressures of the impending annihilation of mankind by a nuclear exchange. And the blackout of 1965 failed to cause any mass panic. Quite the opposite, New Yorkers, as an example, tended to show a great deal of compassion and cooperation when faced with hours of total darkness from the power outage.

As proof of our changing attitudes, UFO witnesses have almost universally viewed the mysterious orbs with a strange detachment rather than with panic.

Military Reasons For A Cover-up

It almost goes without saying that any nation in the world who learned the secrets of the UFO would soon assume a position of technological, ergo, military superiority.

The temptation to abuse this newly acquired power would be overwhelming to any leader...but especially to those with less than democratic ideals. Their system of power would dictate immediate destruction and takeover of the "Free World" which, after all, is the main objective of many aggressive societies.

I can understand why such an awesome responsibility to protect the freedoms of our society would cause our leaders to take a position of utmost secrecy.

Steps would need to be taken beforehand to ensure that if ever a UFO were captured, no one would be in a position to expose its existence. One of the dangers of a free press is the common lack of cooperation with certain authorities in guarding the secrecy of national security matters. With its capture a closely-held secret, the military could study the craft and even its occupants with some assurance that its existence would not be leaked to our enemies.

Naturally, a strategy would be devised in the event a crashed or disabled UFO had been captured by our armed forces. By the same token, anyone who might have seen it go down would have to be pressured into remaining silent. How much easier for the armed services to discredit and embarrass all UFO witnesses into remaining silent. That would be a lot more discreet than attempting to quite everyone within hundreds or even thousands of miles of the eventful crash.

Perhaps this is the strategy being implemented now. With all UFO witnesses openly ridiculed and reluctant to come forth, the Air Force would have a much easier task of secreting away any downed UFO. It does sound like a good plan but I think there is contrary evidence to indicate the existence of such a plan. For one, the Air Force vacillated in its early position on the UFO issue, and even though national security may play a part in the Air Force denial, I think the following is a more likely explanation.

The Lack of an Explanation Requires an Official Denial

In the past, every time an Air Force official was the least bit inclined to confirm the reality of UFOs as interplanetary spacecraft, word would soon come from higher-up that the person had erred and the "official" Air Force position was that they did not exist.

Naturally, the press was interested in knowing the inside scoop on the matter. But just what were the unknown details that the Air Force could provide?

Can you imagine a general standing in front of the press corps and saying: "Ladies and gentlemen, today I am going to release to you the Air Force's proof that UFOs do exist. Here are some very interesting photos and videos of apparently intelligently controlled objects in the skies, and I have gathered together some distinguished guests who claim they have seen these giant metallic, luminous 'saucers' flying in our air space. Of course, we don't know where they come from or what their intentions are...we're not sure if they are friendly or hostile...and we have no idea of their method of flight which seems to totally contradict our understanding of the laws of physics. In fact, we don't even have one piece of evidence from a UFO nor have we ever been contacted by the humanoid occupants of these craft." [5-25]

Obviously, the Air Force would be made to appear ridiculous. Worse yet, their ineptitude in dealing with the phenomenon might encourage overreaction and paranoia throughout the entire Free World.

Political Suicide

How confident would you be in a Government who couldn't explain a foreign object invading the very air space that it has sworn to defend? The admission of ignorance would undoubtedly serve only to usurp the power of the military and would prove to be political suicide to the ruling political party.

As much as world political leaders want to know the truth, I am sure they are wise enough to want it told to them in private. Public awareness of our defenseless position would jeopardize the very hierarchy of power. It's natural that political leaders would cooperate with the military in keeping the truth from ever being known by the masses.

And what of long-range planning in an uncertain future? How would the nation's economy fare with unchecked fears about long-term investments? The stock market would plummet overnight. Who would invest in futures and options or even in real estate or autos under these uncertain conditions? I think that such economic panic would be almost certain. Therefore, it would behoove the leaders of the world to keep such news secret until undeniable contact is established by the 'aliens' themselves. [5-26]

Reasons to Tell the Truth

There are some very good reasons for the Government to reveal the truth to the public, not the least among them: the public's right to know as guaranteed by the U.S. Constitution. However, in this particular instance, the stakes are just too high and the potential harm just too damaging. The public's right to know is outweighed by the urgency of protecting our democratic society.

There are those, however, who would seek to prepare the public for the inevitable. There is also some merit to this point of view. If the Government fears a massive panic if ever our alien friends decide to reveal themselves, the best way to confront the problem is by allowing small, relatively unalarming bits of conclusive evidence to be leaked to the press over a long period of time. As previously stated, we have learned to cope with the anxiety of impending nuclear holocaust, but it has been a slow and painful process.

Perhaps the most pertinent justification for the truth would be to prevent an accidental war. If the Superpowers mistook a wave of slow-flying UFOs for an incoming enemy missile attack, pandemonium would break out. The risks of a defensive counterattack could be very real; the results Earth-shattering, to say the least. [5-27]

There is, however, the possibility that such news would bind humanity together. It might stimulate worldwide cooperation in an attempt to combat a common "enemy." Just such a scenario will be examined in the second half of this book.

*　*　*　*　*

![The Eskimo Nebula — Image Courtesy NASA/Hubble Directorate]

Figure 5.1 — The Eskimo Nebula Credits: NASA, Andrew Fruchter and the ERO Team [Sylvia Baggett (STScI), Richard Hook (ST-ECF), Zoltan Levay (STScI)]

Military Investigations & Cover-ups

A Brief History

This chapter could conceivably fill volumes. Since space doesn't allow a thorough review of the subject matter, I'll try to be brief, yet convincing.

The Air Force, evidence indicates, has been forced into reopening its official investigation time and again dating from 1947 to as recently as 1965. The pesky UFO simply won't leave well enough alone. Each time the Air Force has closed the books on the matter and declared that UFOs don't exist, up would pop another major flap.

The earliest investigation was called *Project Sign*, set up in December of 1947. Then came *Project Grudge,* and finally *Project Blue Book.*

What I find incredulous is that at no time was there evidence that the Air Force had set up a full-scale project to either prove or disprove, once and for all, the existence of UFOs. There is evidence, however, that several such projects were suggested over the years but none came to fruition. Likely the Air Force feared that any such study would subject them to open questioning about their newly acquired evidence.

Several early efforts had been planned to prove the existence of UFOs when the Air Force position was still unsettled. One such plan was to create a system of cameras on air bases at strategic points around the country. The cameras were equipped with a diffraction grid placed over their lenses. The sensitive equipment was attuned to capture the color spectrum of any passing object. UFOs were known to emit strange light that changed at random. The plan was to measure any unusual light patterns and thus detect any foreign object. Color spectrum of known objects could then be analyzed and compared with photographs of the suspect object. The Air Force set up about a hundred of these cameras at air bases around the country for testing.

About the same time Ruppelt suggested setting up astronomical cameras nationwide in conjunction with ground radar stations. The system would be tied-in with a network of scientists who would take measurements of every possible, available type whenever a UFO was spotted. The plan was scrapped, however, for no apparent reason, the Air Force explaining it had decided to rely on the diffraction grid system instead.

A problem arose almost immediately during testing of the diffraction grid camera system. The grids were decomposing after a few weeks and were unable to separate the light spectrum as designed. While the Air Force on the one hand chose to continue with the grid system after a full year of testing, it apparently ignored the significant problem of decomposing camera grids. They were effectively able to squelch Ruppelt's plan and abandon their grid camera system, both in one smooth transaction. After the Robertson Panel's conclusion (which we will investigate further) the Air Force announced it would abandon all future attempts to collect data on the "non-existent" phenomenon. [6-1]

Project Sign

A few months after Kenneth Arnold made national news with his story of flying saucers, the Air Force began its first official investigation of the phenomenon.

Project Sign, as it was called, was formed in September 1947. It was referred to by the public, however, as 'Project Saucer.' On September 23, 1947, Lt. General Nathan F. Twining, the Chief of the Air Technical Intelligence Center known as ATIC, sent a letter to the Commanding General of what was then the Army Air Force. This incredible letter marked 'SECRET' and 'CONFIDENTIAL' for 15 years was finally made public through the Congressional 'Freedom of Information' Committees of UFO reports from the flap of 1947, General Twinning sent the following classified letter:

1. As requested by AC/AS-2, there is presented below the considered opinion of this Command concerning the so-called "Flying Discs."...This opinion was arrived at in conference between personnel of the Air Institute of Technology, Intelligence T-2, Office, Chief of Engineering Division; and the Aircraft, Power Plant and Propeller Laboratories of Engineering Division T-3.

2. It is the opinion that:

a. The phenomenon reported is something real and not visionary or fictitious.

b. There are objects probably approximating the shape of a disc, of such appreciable size as to appear to be as large as man-made aircraft.

c. There is a possibility that some of the incidents may be caused by natural phenomena, such as meteors.

d. The reported operating characteristics such as extreme rates of climb, maneuvera- bility particularly in roll), and action which must be considered evasive when sighted or contacted by friendly aircraft and radar, lend belief to the possibility that some of the objects are controlled either manually, automatically or remotely.

e. The apparent common description of the objects is as follows:

(1) Metallic or light reflecting surface

(2) Absence of trail, except a few instances when the object apparently was operating under high performance conditions.

(3) Circular or elliptical in shape, flat on bottom and domed on top.

(4) Several reports of well kept formation flights varying from three to nine objects.

(5) Normally no associated sound, except in three instances a substantial rumbling roar was heard.

(6) Level flight speeds normally above 300 knots are estimated...

3. It is recommended that: a. Headquarters, Army Air Force issue a directive assigning a priority, security classification and Code Name for a detailed study of this matter...

4. Awaiting a specific directive AMC will continue the investigation within its current sources..."

N.F. Twining,
Lieutenant General, U.S.A.
Commanding Officer. 6-2

The existence of the secret document was denied by the Air Force many times and when Captain Ruppelt wrote about the directive in 1956 his claim was immediately labeled false. "The Air Force is not hiding any UFO information. And I do not qualify this in any way," stated Assistant AF Secretary Richard E. Horner during a nationwide telecast in 1958. [6-3]

Captain Ruppelt quotes a Senior Intelligence Officer with Project Sign as saying:

'The powers-that-be are anti-flying saucer and to stay in favor it behooved one to follow suit.' [6-4]

On December 27th, 1949, two years after being set up, Project Sign was disbanded. The Air Force claimed that all UFO reports had been disproved and their investigation had ended.

Project Grudge

In reality, as the Air Force was later forced to admit, its investigation of UFOs had never really ended. It had just been renamed and shifted to a top secret operation.

When top scientists and intelligence officers working from Wright-Patterson AFB on Project Sign concluded that the UFOs were in fact a real phenomenon, they suggested to General Hoyt Vandenberg, Chief of Staff, that he prepare the public for the startling news.

But fearing a "stampede" the general had refused the advice and decided instead to cover up the evidence. He ordered the report destroyed according to Captain Ruppelt, but one report escaped the censors and was secreted away by major Dewey Fournet, as I indicated in an earlier chapter. [6-5]

Soon after General Vandenberg's decision to deny all UFO reports, the Air Force closed Project Sign and on February 11, 1949, Project "Grudge" was formed (aptly named considering the new attitude adopted by the Air Force). According to Ruppelt, the name change was very significant with, no doubt, a lot of intended hidden meaning. [6-6]

The new policy under Grudge was to disprove or deny all UFO reports. The Air Force found it a lot easier to deny the phenomenon than to explain it. Grudge continued until December 27, 1949, when it was officially closed out. The final report quoted contracted astronomer J. Allen Hynek (at the time working at nearby Ohio State University) and concluded that the UFO was either a hallucination, misidentification or a hoax. What it didn't point out was that by its own admission, 23 percent of all the UFO reports studied by Hynek were labeled "unknowns," meaning the Air Force could not identify them. This was an obvious contradiction to their own conclusion. [6-7]

Project Blue Book

Less than two years later the Air Force was forced to reopen its investigation. On October 27, 1951, prompted by another major UFO wave and public pressure, the new Project Grudge was officially established. It was to continue for eighteen years and eventually adopt the name of Project Blue Book. [6-8]

The man selected to head the new Project Grudge was Captain Edward J. Ruppelt who had been recalled to active duty in January 1951 and assigned to ATIC as an intelligence officer. [6-9]

This low priority organization headed by a captain was simply a project within a group. Its status indicated the Air Force's obvious attempt to downplay the subject. But prompted by an ever increasing flow of UFO reports it had soon outgrown its status.

By March 1952 it had become a separate organization and was renamed Project Blue Book. Using logic that perhaps only the military can understand the project was named after those small books used in college exams. [6-10] It was to continue under this name until 1969 when the Air Force concluded its official investigation of the subject.

It was during the Blue Book days that the Air Force received its largest number of UFO reports. The average number of reports had doubled within three months prior to Blue Book's formation. During Ruppelt's reign at Blue Book he decided to subscribe to a newspaper clipping service to monitor the reports around the country. After all, not everyone reported their sightings to the Air Force. In March, 1952, the service was sending reports in letter-sized envelopes. By May they had resorted to old shoe boxes to hold the large number of clippings. And then in June the largest flap ever to hit this country had the nation teaming with UFO sightings from coast-to-coast. The newspaper clippings began arriving at Blue Book in large cardboard cartons and reported sightings poured into headquarters at the astounding rate of fifty a day. In all, over 1,500 UFO reports were received during 1952 by Blue Book. [6-11]

The Air Force had a huge problem on its hands and with their policy being what it was, it was vital to debunk the subject as soon as possible before the whole lid blew off. On Tuesday, July 29th, Major General John Samford directed the longest press conference ever held by the Air Force since WW II. The press was very anxious for some answers to a phenomenon the Air Force had denied existed. Some of those present were true believers that UFOs were visitors from outer space and they wanted to force General Samford into admitting that the Air Force had been hiding the truth.

They chose a particularly disturbing report that occurred with accompanying radar evidence. The sightings over Washington, D.C. (described in detail in an earlier chapter of this book) had the press stirred up. On one occasion both ground radar at Washington National Airport and radar on board an F-94C sent to investigate had tracked the same fiery object for a considerable length of time. The brightly glowing orange object and the jet played a cat-and-mouse game for several minutes with the object shooting away at terrific speeds each time the interceptor approached. This highly documented report was one of the best "unknowns" in Air Force files.

But General Samford skillfully fielded the barrage of questions without ever admitting to the existence of UFOs. He and his assistants in fact had insinuated that the radar sightings "may" have been caused by temperature inversions and that the pilot's visual sighting was probably ground lights reflected off a layer of haze. He offered this poorly conceived explanation in spite of the fact that there was no inversion on the night in question sufficient enough to produce the effects that the General had suggested.

However, the Air Force got the results they were looking for. The next day the headlines read:

AIR FORCE DEBUNKS SAUCERS AS JUST NATURAL PHENOMENA

Within weeks UFO reports at Blue Book dropped from fifty a day to ten a day. The Air Force had effectively discredited the phenomena and much to their relief the pressure was off. [6-12]

It never ceases to amaze me to find out just how the Air Force treated the UFO situation. Here was potentially the greatest event in all of human history: the discovery of extraterrestrial life, and the Air Force assigns a captain to take charge of the investigation. One would certainly think the subject deserved the attention of at least a colonel if not a general. Captains, after all, can't order investigations or assistance from ranking members of his club. And there were many instances that called for such authority. This fact, alone, proves in my mind that they were deliberately down playing the phenomenon.

In his book *The Report on Unidentified Flying Objects*, Captain Ruppelt apologetically described a couple of situations where his rank stifled his ability to carry out his assigned task. In one instance while in Washington, D.C., investigating perhaps the most crucial UFO report in history, "flying saucers over the Capitol," he explains that he had planned a full day of work starting at Washington National Airport. Next, he would go to Andrews AFB, airline offices, the Weather Bureau and "a half-dozen other places" in his quest for first-hand knowledge of the situation. But when he called the transportation section of the Pentagon to get a staff car he was told (as if he wouldn't already have known it) that only senior colonels or generals were allowed the use of a staff car. He goes on to explain that on his measly salary and his $9 per day per diem he just couldn't afford to hire a cab to help him investigate the most critical UFO case in history! Unbelievable! [6-13]

On another occasion during November or December of 1952 the U.S. was planning to explode its first H-Bomb during Project Ivy. As Ruppelt explained, "Our proposed trip to the Pacific to watch for UFOs during the H-Bomb test was cancelled at the last minute because we couldn't get space on an airplane." [6-14]

We're supposed to believe that the U.S. Air Force didn't have any planes available for the leader of Project Blue Book? Something just doesn't seem quite right here!

Ruppelt reports that prior to taking command of Blue Book he was assigned a desk near those who were supposedly in charge of the UFO investigation. He puzzled over an incident in the office when a UFO report came in from the crew and passengers of an airliner. Rather than take the report seriously he reports that the officers in command reacted with "a great big, deep belly laugh...This puzzled me because I'd read that the Air Force was seriously investigating all UFO reports." [6-15]

Dr. J. Allen Hynek

One of the greatest debunkers and the most often quoted scientific expert during the Blue Book days was an astronomer named J. Allen Hynek. Doctor Hynek was an authority on astronomy and was at one time in charge of the U.S. Optical Satellite Tracking Program. [6-16] He went on to become Head of the Department of Astronomy at Northwestern University but while at Blue Book he was an assistant and associate professor at Ohio State University. [6-17]

Hynek was hired by the Air Force as a consultant in 1949 and remained with Blue Book through 1969.

Hynek was just what the Air Force needed. A young, up-and-coming scientist who was not likely to rock the boat and someone who was known for his skepticism of the UFO subject. Hynek was an ideal "team player" who could be quoted by the Air Force as an "expert" from outside the military. He frankly admits he was more concerned about his own career at the time than in proclaiming his doubts about the Air Force investigation. [6-18]

It was Hynek who put forth the now famous "swamp gas" explanation for a sighting in the swamp area near Dexter, Michigan, on March 20, 1966.

Preceded by a major flap in 1965, the 1966 sighting was of tremendous importance because of the number of people who reported the phenomenon.

Very credible witnesses, including dozens of police officers, saw strange light formations on several occasions even prior to the March 20th event. On March 14, at 3:15 a.m., two Deputy Sheriffs saw several lights above Dexter, Michigan. Several other agencies reported the lights moving in single-file and in an erratic fashion.

"This is the strangest thing that Deputy Foster and myself have ever witnessed ...These objects could move at fantastic speeds, and make very sharp turns, dive and climb, and hover, with great maneuverability," said Deputy B. Bushroe.

Even though the sighting was substantiated by radar at Selfridge AFB, the incident was met with little interest by the press. [6-19] That indifference was to end in a few days.

In his excellent book entitled *The UFO Controversy in America*, David Michael Jacobs reports:

"On March 20, 1966, eighty-seven women students and a civil defense director at Hillsdale College saw a football-shaped, glowing object hovering over a swampy area a few hundred yards from the women's dormitory. The witnesses claimed the object flew directly at the dormitory but then stopped suddenly and retreated back to the swamp. The object 'dodged an airport beacon light,' appeared to dim when automobiles approached the area, and then 'brightened when the cars left.' The witnesses watched the object for four hours. The next day five people - including two police officers - in Dexter saw a large, glowing object rise from a swampy area on a farm, hover for a few minutes at about 1,000 feet, and then leave the area. *Over one hundred witnesses saw objects on these two nights in two Michigan cities sixty-three miles apart.* The story of these somewhat routine sightings caught fire.

"Within a few days virtually every newspaper in the country and all national news shows carried the report. Reporters put intense pressure on the Air Force to investigate the incidents and arrive at a solution immediately." [6-20]

I can recall, as a teenager, the swamp gas story because it made national headlines. What I didn't recall was why it caused such a stir. Apparently Dr. Hynek, in a hurry under orders from the Air Force to explain the sighting immediately, had put forth a totally absurd explanation for the hovering lights seen in Michigan. Not able to explain the reports of flying discs he concentrated on the ground lights stories. He suggested the lights may have been caused by marsh gas from decaying vegetation in the swamp. The chemical reaction created by the decaying matter may have produced a gas that could spontaneously ignite under certain conditions and is often referred to as foxfire or will-o'-the-wisp. Hynek later accused the press of misquoting him but the damage was done. Headlines around the country read:

AIR FORCE INSULTS PUBLIC
WITH SWAMP GAS THEORY!

All across the nation the press had recognized the absurdity of the Air Force explanation and *The Indianapolis News* even called for a Congressional inquiry. House Minority Leader, Gerald Ford, resentful of the ridicule his home state of

Michigan was getting, also demanded a Congressional investigation. Political cartoons around the country defamed Hynek and the Air Force. The public had just about had enough! [6-21]

It was this kind of pressure that finally forced the Air Force into forming a panel of "unbiased" experts to investigate the UFO phenomenon. Called the Condon Committee, the formation of the panel took the heat off the Air Force and allowed them to manipulate the committee's results behind the scenes without arousing suspicion. We shall study this committee and its conclusions in the next chapter.

Not long after the swamp gas incident Dr. Hynek mustered enough courage to change his long-standing position on UFOs and actually announced his suppressed suspicion that something unexplainable was indeed going on. Although I am somewhat skeptical of his prolonged delay in making his true opinions known, it is an understandable position. Who would have believed an associate professor at Ohio State when there were Nobel Prize winners (Doctors Robertson and Alvarez) who had openly denied the existence of UFOs. As he explained later, he feared being labeled a nut while with Blue Book. It would not have benefited anyone, he claims, for him to come out and deny the Air Force position. The result of an open defiance would have been his immediate dismissal and would have prevented him from gathering facts for future UFO investigators. In other words, he felt like he was the man on the inside for those who believed in UFOs. [6-22]

Hynek was able to share his knowledge in later years when he published his books *The UFO Experience, A Scientific Inquiry* and *The Hynek UFO Report.*

Blue Book 1952 to 1969

Captain Ruppelt left Blue Book in August of 1953 as his staff dwindled to two. He was replaced by Airman First Class Max Futch. In March 1954 Captain Charles Hardin was appointed head of Blue Book. His two-man staff was too small to investigate reports so they simply filed them away. Investigating reports then became the task of 4602d Air Intelligence Service Squadron (AISS) a division of the Air Defense Command.

Hardin, Hynek and members of the 4602d devised a "UFOB Guide" to assist personnel in identifying and reporting UFOs. In August UFO reports labeled "unknowns" by AISS included 60 percent of all reports. This was totally unacceptable to ATIC so they told the Commander of AISS to try to solve as many of the reports as possible using common sense.

Common sense, they reasoned, obviously ruled out the possibility that witnesses could have seen anything that was extraterrestrial. [6-23]

As reported by Hynek, Blue Book reports were classified according to descriptions. If a report said the UFO looked like a balloon – the Air Force labeled it a balloon. All "possibles" and "probables" were dropped. An an example, "probable star" became "star." [6-24]

Under this new procedure unknowns fell to 5.9 percent by 1955 and 0.4 percent by 1956. [6-25] The Air Force would maintain in years to come that the reason unknowns were so high in the early years of Blue Book was because they had an inadequate system for reporting and classifying UFOs.

In April of 1956 Captain George T. Gregory became head of Blue Book. Gregory was an ardent UFO debunker and under his guidance all reports from youths age ten to seventeen were labeled "figments of their imaginations" and therefore unreliable. [6-26]

In July of 1957 the Air Defense Command disbanded the 4602d and reassigned UFO investigation duties to the 106th Air Intelligence Service Squadron.

1006th continued in its duties until July, 1959 when the assignment went to the 1127th Field Activities Group stationed at Fort Belvoir, Virginia. [6-27]

In October 1958 Major Robert Friend took over as head of Blue Book. Major Friend was different from the other Blue Book directors in that he had a solid scientific background (having studied physics in graduate school). Under his guidance Blue Book files were organized as never before. He planned to microfilm the old Blue Book files because he felt too many good reports had been lost or pilfered. Unfortunately, the Air Force decided the project would be too costly. [6-28] Some years later the Condon Committee would use the files of NICAP (a civilian organization) for their investigation, finding the Air Force files incomplete and in total disarray.

In 1963 then Lt. Colonel Friend was replaced as Blue Book head by Major Hector Quintanilla who continued until 1966. In June of that year the Air Force moved to take UFO responsibility out of the intelligence community and place it under the jurisdiction of the scientific arm of the Air Force where it belonged.

General James Ferguson, deputy Chief of Staff for research and development, took responsibility for the UFO program and the Air Force changed the rules for handling UFO reports. This allowed Blue Book to send UFO cases directly to the Condon Committee. [6-29]

Colonel Raymond S. Sleeper took over as head of Blue Book later that year. Colonel Sleeper was the Commander of the Air Force's Foreign Technology Division and remained with Blue Book until its termination. [6-30]

In 1969, after the conclusion of the Condon Committee, which suggested that there was nothing to the "UFO craze" and therefore nothing for the Air Force to study, the Air Force closed Project Blue Book and its investigation of UFOs permanently.

* * * * *

Non-military "Impartial" Investigations

The Robertson Panel

The Air Force had been lucky with the press in 1952 when General Samford was able to sell them his bill of goods. But the tenuous situation called for more substantiated "proof" to support their contention. The concept of a "non-military unbiased" second opinion was the answer. A panel of scientific experts would be formed to research the phenomenon. If they could prove to the public that even the "experts" felt that UFOs were fictitious, then the heat would be off. The Air Force could simply refer to these scientific findings whenever their own opinion was questioned. The panel would be helpful in supporting the Air Force policy of debunking all UFO reports, but it was vital that no one suspicioned any Air Force influence in the panel's final outcome.

The Robertson Panel was formed in 1952 under CIA sponsorship which further removed any Air Force connection. The panel's formation has been called the pivotal point in UFO investigation. Based on the outcome of this study the Air Force changed its official opinion from that of open, or at least unsure, to a position of total denial.

The panel was headed by Dr. H.P. Robertson, a Nobel Prize winner who was Director of the Weapons System Evaluation Group in the Office of the Secretary of Defense and was a CIA classified employee. He was an expert in mathematics, cosmology and relativity. Dr. Luis Alvarez another Nobel Prize recipient for physics in 1968, and a key figure in the development of the atomic bomb during WW II, was also on the panel. Thornton Page, deputy director of the Johns Hopkins' Operations Research Office – the third panelist – was a physicist at the Naval Ordnance Laboratory during World War II and was later employed by NASA in the Manned Spaceflight Program in Houston. The final panelist was Lloyd Berkner a director of the Brookhaven National Laboratories who had been with the Carnegie Institution's Department of Terrestrial Magnetism as a physicist. He was in charge of the radar section of the Navy Bureau of Aeronautics and had served in the Department of Defense's Research and Development Board during WW II. He was later to become a special assistant to the Secretary of State. [7-1]

The panel convened on January 14, 1953, spent a total of 12 hours studying the subject over the next five days, examined eight cases in detail, fifteen in general (all from Blue Book's files) and then saw two purported UFO movies, before deciding the most controversial subject in history.

After their "thorough" review of the data the panel concluded that they had found no evidence that UFOs represented any kind of threat to national security. In fact, the "continued reporting of such phenomena threatened to clog the channels of communication in the military." The real threat, it concluded, was the UFO *report*, not the UFO.

Furthermore, the panel made four recommendations in secret to the Air Force. These recommendations weren't made public until the Air Force was forced to reveal them in 1967:

First, it suggested that the Air Force totally abandon Dr. Hynek's plan to upgrade Skywatch but thought that the diffraction grid camera plan and the radarscope plan could both be used to record natural phenomena and thus allay public anxiety.

Second, they suggested that civilian UFO investigative organizations, specifically NICAP and APRO, were in danger of being used as subversive tools by our enemies.

Third, they sought to demystify the UFO phenomenon by educating the public and by down playing the subject within the military.

Last, they proposed a detailed program for training the public and debunking witness sightings in an effort to eliminate reports. They suggested hiring psychologists familiar with mass psychology in an effort to explain how a gullible and uninformed public could conjure up such visions. [7-2]

The panel's conclusions sent a loud message to the Air Force's Project Blue Book which cut back its staff and stopped investigating UFO sightings. It became more of a UFO report collection center than anything else and the two men at BB that had openly questioned the UFOs' existence, Edward Ruppelt and Major Dewey Fournet, were soon to leave. By 1953 the Project was headed by Airman First Class Max Futch, who's rank indicated the importance placed on the project. [7-3]

In December of 1953, less than one year after the Robertson Panel convened, the Joint Chiefs of Staffs of all the branches of the U.S. military reached a decision to further protect the secretive nature of UFO investigation. Under the auspices of the joint Army-Navy-Air Force publication, they issued JANAP 146 making it a federal crime under the Espionage Act to reveal any information on UFO investigations, punishable by a one-to-ten-year prison term or a $10,000 fine. This applied to all military and included the commercial airline pilots who were under the authority of a federal organization: the FAA. [7-4]

The Battelle Memorial Institute's Report

In 1953 the Air Force had concluded its statistical study of UFOs which had been started by Ruppelt in 1951. The Battelle Memorial statistical study set out to prove a theory put forth by Dr. Menzel of Harvard, an avowed UFO skeptic, who hypothesized that all UFO sightings could be explained by their connection with temperature inversions. He thought that ground lights were reflected and passed through layers of warm and cold air masses. As these air masses moved in opposite directions of each other the light would be diffracted and appear to move.

The statistical study was also referred to as the *"Special Report Number 14."* It's been labeled by its critics as incomplete and inconclusive, charges that are substantiated by the fact that the Air Force did not even release it until it needed further evidence in 1955, some four years after its inception. [7-5]

NICAP & APRO

Public concern about the UFO phenomenon naturally produced several public sector organizations. Spawned in large part by the Air Force's denial of UFOs, the two main groups to emerge in the mid-fifties were the National Investigations Committee on Aerial Phenomena (NICAP) and the Aerial Phenomena Research Organization (APRO). NICAP emerged as the leading spokesman for the pro-UFO view and had a running battle with the Air Force for many years even up to the time that the Air Force "got out of the UFO business" in 1969.

NICAP was headed by retired Major Donald Keyhoe who was a noted author on the subject. Keyhoe used his contacts within the military to give credibility to his own investigative organization. Keyhoe maintained that the Air Force was engaged in a long-standing cover-up of the true evidence on UFOs. He used his sources to cull information from within the military ranks and became a best-selling author on the subject.

In 1954 Keyhoe released his book *Flying Saucers from Outer Space* in which he substantiated his claims of an Air Force cover-up. The book was an instant success and it helped to increase public awareness of the phenomenon. When a new flap occurred after release of this book, the Air Force blamed Keyhoe with instigating the latest series of reports.

And in 1955, when Keyhoe released his third book, *The Flying Saucer Conspiracy*, the Air Force countered by releasing *Special Report Number 14* claiming that, once again, scientists had proven the flying saucer phenomenon to be totally unfounded. The study had been the Air Force's ace in the hole, having been concluded in 1953, and authorities disingenuously waited for the most opportune time to publish it. [7-6]

The ploy went unnoticed for the most part by the press and the report effectively attracted favorable attention for the Air Force position.

Keyhoe wanted to maintain NICAP's integrity so he wisely refused to publish any contactee stories (several wild stories had been circulating at that time). He avoided the lunatic fringe that was naturally drawn to the controversy. His efforts paid off because the group was able to attract some very credible members.

Among the board of governors for NICAP were retired Rear Admiral Delmer S. Fahrney (former head of the Navy's guided missile program), Vice-Admiral R.H. Hillenkoetter (the first director of the CIA), retired Rear Admiral H.B. Knowles, J.B. Hartranft (president of the Aircraft Owners and Pilots Association), Army Reserve Colonel Robert B. Emerson, and retired Marine Corps Lieutenant General P.A. delValle, all of whom naturally had to be retired or they would have been tried by the military on grounds of treason (see *JANAP 146, p.61*).

By 1958 NICAP had over 5,000 members and published a newsletter to its membership periodically in which the latest Air Force explanations were refuted and stories of well-documented sightings were published.

The only other organization in the country with a substantial membership was APRO. APRO was founded in 1952 by Jim and Coral Lorenzen. It was an active group with a large membership but it lacked the desire or funding to take on the Air Force or Congress like NICAP did. They were also more prone to report contactee stories and were viewed by the public as somewhat less credible than NICAP.

In 1957 the Air Force was, once again, caught in a major UFO wave. Over one thousand sightings came in that year in spite of efforts to debunk the phenomenon. [7-7]

During the peak of the 1957 wave an incredible event occurred in and around Levelland, Texas. It began on November 2 when several witnesses claimed to have seen a glowing yellow and white "torpedo-shaped" object. Two witnesses reported that the object flew over their car and as it did, the engine and lights turned off. They quickly exited the auto to investigate and as they did the object passed low overhead again. Considerable heat forced the two to dive for the ground. Once the object left the area they were able to restart their car as if nothing had happened.

An hour later at midnight, and four miles away, another witness reported seeing a "glowing, egg-shaped" object resting in the middle of the road. Once again, the witness' auto engine automatically shut off and its lights failed. Estimated at 200 feet long, the huge object slowly rose and then suddenly disappeared. And again, as before, the witness was able to restart his car.

The same (or similar) object was seen intermittently during the night and next day by many startled witnesses, all with accompanying effects on their autos.

In all, twelve people had seen the mysterious object up close, and three others claimed to have seen an unusual flash of light during the three day period. Witnesses included Patrolman A. J. Fowler, Sheriff Clem and Deputy McCulloch, Patrolmen Hargrove and Gavin and Constable Lloyd Ballen, all investigating the strange phenomena on tips from concerned citizens. They state that the sky was slightly overcast with some light rain but no lightning or thunder.

The sighting attracted national attention because of the quality of its witnesses and this forced the Air Force to respond.

According to Hynek, the "official investigation" consisted of a "one-man team" from the 1006th who took two auto trips to visit three witnesses and, thus, concluded his "thorough" investigation.

The official Air Force conclusion? Only three people "could be located" who had seen the "big light...visible for only a few seconds, not sustained visibility as had been implied." The climatic conditions at the time of the sighting lead to the natural deduction that the sightings were caused by "weather phenomenon of electrical nature, generally classified as 'Ball lightning' or 'St. Elmo's Fire,' caused by stormy conditions in the area..." And as for the auto ignition and light failures: "wet electrical circuits!" [7-8]

The Air Force blamed the latest wave on the public's tendency to overreact to the Soviet's satellite program and the launching of Sputnik I and II. However, constant pressure from civilian groups and the press began to raise the issue of a Congressional Hearing. NICAP, with Keyhoe as spokesman, was in the forefront of public pressure that, along with the combination of good sighting reports and bad Air Force explanations, soon created an overwhelming demand for a Congressional Hearing.

1966 Congressional Hearing

The Air Force had been able to effectively head off Congressional Hearings for several years by presenting their side of the story to various Congressional Committees. On several occasions the Air Force was allowed to explain their program at Project Blue Book and state exactly their position on the issue. These one-sided discussions lead to the dismissal of any further investigation on the part of Congress, the Congressional Review Committees having been satisfied with their explanations.

The 1957 flap at Levelland, Texas, had been sufficiently squelched by the Air Force's release of *Special Report Number 14* and constant reminders that the Air Force had conducted other investigations…all dismissing the existence of UFOs…helped to stave off public pressure. So it went for several years. Each time a flap produced pressure for a hearing, a Congressional Review Committee would put the fire out, relying on information produced by the Air Force itself.

There hadn't been an official Congressional inquiry into the phenomenon since 1963 and for the next few years interest in the subject declined. [7-9] Then in 1965 a new wave of sightings again revived public interest in the subject. By August, Blue Book had received 262 reports for that month, alone, and, once again, was saddled with the task of explaining the mysterious occurrences. [7-10]

With the pressure on from the public, several Congressmen joined in demanding a full Congressional hearing. Gerald R. Ford, who was the House Republican minority leader at the time, was particularly influential and was under pressure from his Michigan constituency. The Dexter-Hillsdale incident was an embarrassment to Ford and he wanted an answer. "Swamp gas" wasn't good enough.

On April 5, 1966, Congress held its first open hearing on the Air Force's handling of the UFO controversy. But, as in Congressional Review Committees, The Congress invited only witnesses from the Air Force to testify. Those questioned were the Secretary of the Air Force, Harold D. Brown; the current director of Project Blue Book, Hector Quintanilla; and J. Allen Hynek, at the time still allied with the Air Force investigation.

The one important outcome of the hearing was that it forced Secretary Brown to promise that he would recommend a private study of the subject by a panel of civilian scientists who were to be totally unbiased. Thus, was born the Air Force's final authority on UFOs: The Condon Committee. [7-11]

The Condon Committee

The UFO wave continued, even as Congress tried to decide what to do with the issue. And the issue was red-hot, for the public no longer trusted the Air Force's explanations.

To put an end to the problem the Air Force agreed to appoint a panel of civilian scientists to study the phenomenon. In May of 1966 the Air Force announced that the University of Colorado in Boulder had agreed to host the project.

Dr. Edward U. Condon, former head of the National Bureau of Standards – also in Boulder – was appointed the project director. Dr. Condon was a scientist with a good reputation and credentials, having co-authored the country's first textbook on quantum mechanics and had written extensively in the field of atomic spectra.

Also on the panel was Robert Low, Assistant Dean of the Graduate School at C.U. and two psychologists Franklin Roach and Stuart Cook.

The investigation was welcomed by both factions of the UFO controversy. Donald Keyhoe of NICAP called it "the most significant development in the history of the UFO investigation." [7-12]

However, this amiable relationship quickly soured as the Condon Committee found itself ensnared in controversy almost as soon as it began. In early 1967, in a speech to the Corning Section of the American Chemical Society, Condon openly claimed that there was nothing to the UFO phenomenon and that the Air Force should "get out of the UFO business."

The speech almost prompted Keyhoe to withdraw NICAP support of the project, but a hasty letter from Condon, claiming he was misquoted, averted such a disaster. [7-13]

NICAP's participation was vitally important to Condon because he needed their support to lend an air of credibility to the study.

There were many groups in the country who distrusted anything that was even remotely affiliated with the Air Force, and Keyhoe had been the major spokesman for this faction. His participation ensured ,in many people's minds, that the study would be impartial.

In addition, Condon soon found that NICAP's reports were superior to those provided by Blue Book. BB's files were disorganized and many reports had been lost or misfiled. When Condon made requests for reports from BB, their response was irritatingly slow. [7-14]

As the allegedly impartial Condon study proceeded, Keyhoe was frustrated by the attitude of its members and the methods of study imposed. Condon disregarded some of the very best evidence claiming that he could only study current sightings. Anything from the earlier flaps were dismissed because witnesses would have trouble remembering the details.

Suspicion was growing within the UFO "insider community" that the Condon Committee was not as impartial as it had claimed to be. Then the bottom dropped out.

In July of 1967, staff member Roy Craig uncovered a memorandum written in 1966 – well before the study had even begun – from Low to members of the University's administration. Low, in airing his view of the project's intent, expressed his opinion that "...the trick would be to describe the project so that, to the public, it would appear a totally objective study but, to the scientific community, would present the image of a group of nonbelievers trying their best to be objective but having an almost zero expectation of finding a saucer."

Furthermore, he suggested that by emphasizing "...the psychology and sociology of persons and groups who report seeing UFOs...rather than examination of the old question of the physical reality of the saucer, I think the scientific community would quickly get the message." [7-15]

His plan called for a preconceived conclusion by skeptics who would discredit the witnesses of UFOs and, thus, keep the focus off the actual phenomenon itself.

When Condon was confronted with the memorandum he exploded. In his flurry of accusations he fired the two people associated with the committee that he thought were responsible for making the memorandum public.

Condon's reaction brought great internal strife within the committee and convinced Keyhoe to withdraw NICAP's support. Of the original twelve people on the Condon staff, only two remained, including Low, in the wake of the scandal. [7-16]

As if Condon hadn't already enough trouble, the continued wave of UFO sightings around the country, and the unfavorable press generated by the disclosure of the Low memorandum, prompted a new Congressional Investigation.

1968 Congressional Hearing

As the country was reeling under the onslaught of a new UFO wave that lasted, for the first time in history, three full years, pressure was being applied for another Congressional Hearing.

The Air Force had received over 3,000 reports from 1965 to 1967 and a book had been released documenting a massive sighting at Exeter, New Hampshire, as previously described. [7-17]

To recap, author John G. Fuller, an avowed UFO skeptic, decided to check out one of the many flying saucer stories circulating around the country at the time. He randomly chose a sighting reported in Exeter by two local policemen. In his book, *Incident at Exeter*, Fuller documented an ongoing series of UFO sightings by over sixty witnesses from the small New Hampshire town. The book captured the imaginations of the nation and thrust Fuller into a position of prominence as an expert on the reality of UFOs.

Public pressure mounted for an explanation on the phenomenon and finally produced the Congressional Hearing of July 29, 1968.

The hearing under the jurisdiction of the House Science and Astronautics Committee was more encompassing than the one in 1966. The participants included Dr. Hynek; Dr. James McDonald, senior atmospheric physicist at the University of Arizona's Department of Atmospheric Sciences and a noted authority on the UFO phenomenon; Carl Sagan, a well known astronomer; sociologist Robert L. Hall; engineer James A. Harder and astronautics engineer Robert M. Baker.

The symposium served to allay public alarm and several members suggested further study of the subject, leaving the issue open on whether the phenomenon was real or not. However, the Science and Astronautics Committee expressly prohibited criticizing the Condon Committee, saying that any criticism of the Air Force or Air Force project was the responsibility of the House Armed Services Committee. [7-18]

Thus, the Congressional Hearing of 1968 ended with all eyes on the final outcome of the Condon Committee.

Condon's Conclusion

Condon had somehow survived the Low memorandum scandal and the withdrawal of NICAP support and had pressed on, wounded but intact. Press coverage of the committee had become virtually non-existent since February of '68, the media choosing to withhold judgement until its final outcome was announced. Condon wisely kept a low profile refusing any public appearances. [7-19]

The final report compiled by the Condon Committee consisted of nearly 1,500 pages. On January 8, 1968, the voluminous report was released to the media with directions for release the next day. The report's first two sections, however, were purported to be an overview of the report by Dr. Condon himself. In it he concluded "that nothing has come from the study of UFOs in the past 21 years that has added to scientific knowledge. Careful consideration of the record, as it is available to us, leads us to conclude that further extensive study of UFOs probably cannot be justified in the expectation that science will be advanced thereby." He claimed, further, that the committee had found "no direct evidence whatever of a convincing nature...for the claim that any UFOs represent spacecraft visiting Earth from another civilization."

He recommended that teachers stop giving credit to students for studying the phenomenon and warned that the abundance of false information available to students could cause them to be "educationally harmed." [7-20]

The National Academy of Sciences panel of scientists, (prohibited from consulting with members of Congress who were informed on the subject, or members of the Condon Committee itself) gave the report its official stamp of approval. They agreed with Condon that most UFO reports could be credited to misidentification or hoaxes and concluded that there was no official secrecy and that the UFO investigation by our government should be ended. [7-21]

The panel's conclusions naturally outraged the civilian UFO groups for obvious reasons.

NICAP was furious to find that even though they had culled over their ten thousand reports to present only one thousand of the best to Condon, the committee had used precious little of the evidence. The study that took well over two years to complete and over five hundred thousand dollars of taxpayers' money to fund, reported that only 59 cases were actually studied in any great detail! Many of those were "obvious hoaxes" from Blue Book files that should have been summarily eliminated to begin with.

A remaining forty sightings were evaluated without a full-scale investigation ever having taken place. [7-22]

Of the evidence presented to Condon, over 98 percent was totally disregarded, including many of NICAP's very best reports. Not one case from the Michigan sightings of 1966 – which had prompted the study to begin with – had been examined! [7-23]

But the ploy had worked for the Air Force. The press, eager to get the story out, published headlines the next morning claiming the Condon Report proved that UFOs did not exist. They had obviously read Condon's conclusions, as instructed by the Air Force, and never took the time to read the full report. If they had, they would have discovered buried within its voluminous text, thirty mysterious reports that could not be explained, some of which strongly suggested the cases involved genuine UFOs... in direct contradiction to the Condon Committee's own conclusions. [7-24]

Percentage Of "Unknowns"

For the most part, the public believed the Air Force when they said that only a small percentage of reports filed with Blue Book were still unknown. Logic, the Air Force argued, dictated that if more were known about the "unknowns" they too would be explained as natural phenomena.

As Dr. Hynek explained in 1975, "they boasted that they had only two or three percent unknown and based on that they would argue in a very interesting circular-reasoning way: We have solved everything but two or three percent (hence it follows that if we really tried harder, if we had a little more data in these cases, we would have solved the other two or three percent, after all its only three percent!). Then they would complete the circle of reasoning: If that is the case, no point in trying. But it wasn't two or three percent. It was twenty percent." [7-25]

According to Edward Ruppelt, head of Project Blue Book in the early fifties, Project Grudge (which was closed out in 1949) had 23 percent of its reports classified as "unknowns." [7-26]

In addition, data compiled by Ruppelt showed that of the Air Force reports studied by Blue Book from 1947 to 1953 some 26.94 percent fell into the "unknown" category.[7-27] He further stated that "...our investigation and analysis were thorough and when we finally stamped a report 'unknown' it was unknown. We weren't infallible but we didn't often let a clue slip by." [7-28]

In 1967 noted French scientist and mathematician and former faculty member of Northwestern and Stanford Universities, Jacques Vallee, cataloged all of the cases in the Air Force files with the aid of a computer. He concluded that fully 23 percent of the reports qualified as "unknowns." [7-29]

As mentioned previously, the Air Force had incorporated a method of eliminating "possible" and "probable" from all existing reports. As an example, "similar to a balloon" became "balloon." This new method for reclassifying reports, in addition to the newly adopted policy of debunking all reports even remotely questionable, gave the Air Force the small percentage of "unknowns" that it needed to satisfactorily "document" the lack of evidence supporting the phenomenon. [7-30]

Blue Book Ends with Condon

And so, with the official sanction of the Condon Committee, the Air Force was finally able to fulfill its longtime desire to get out of the UFO business. With the welcomed cooperation of the mysterious flying saucer (reports had dropped dramatically by 1969) the Air Force was able to quietly close the book on the bothersome phenomenon. [7-31]

In December of 1969, the Air Force ended its official investigation of UFOs for the final time, informing the public that if anyone saw a strange occurrence in the sky, *"Don't call us!"* It can't be, therefore, it isn't!

The 1973-74 Flap

Satisfied with the Condon conclusion and convinced that there was nothing to the story, the press almost totally ignored the subject for many years. By the early seventies the UFO controversy was all but forgotten. But that was to end.

1973 was billed as "the year of the miniflap." With official Air Force involvement ended and Blue Book closed, statistics on the flap are unavailable for the most part. However, private UFO groups have calculated that the "miniflap" of 1973 was as significant as the flaps of '52, '57 and '65 - '67. One researcher reported over 500 sightings in Pennsylvania, alone. Literally thousands of people saw strange lights and craft all across America. By 1974 the numbers of reports began to subside.

Ohio governor, John Gilligan, and wife, reported seeing several "amber-colored" objects near Ann Arbor, Michigan.

People from all walks of life were reporting all the known types of incidents as in earlier flaps, including electromagnetic interference, landing traces, and reports of occupants. This time, however, there was no official government agency to report to. Past pressures served to discredit the new wave of witnesses. The Air Force refused to reopen its investigation, citing the Condon Committee and other past reports as proof that flying saucers did not exist. [7-32]

So the flap of '73-'74 died a quiet death. Since that time there have been scattered reports of UFO incidents including some very interesting occupant cases. But for the most part, it has been calm and the press has remained silent on the issue.

AUTHOR'S UPDATE: since I first penned this book there have been several major flaps, some lasting for years such as those in south america and mexico (see *Figures 9.9 to 9.11).*

According to the pattern set since 1947, another major flap is overdue. Since 1947, a major wave has occurred in the U.S. every six to ten years. This time, however, don't look for widespread notoriety or press coverage of the ordeal. All the powers that be are anti-UFO and publicity will generally be of the negative type. You can count on it.

Who's In Charge Now?

When the Air Force closed its investigation in 1969, it appeared that the U.S. government was through with the UFO. There are those, however, that claim the investigation has not really ended, it has just gone underground.

Almost from its inception, Project Blue Book had viewed the problem as one more of public relations than anything else. Records indicate the Air Force explanations have always avoided the real issue: Why have so many solid citizens reported such consistent evidence?

The best solution, as experience has borne out, has been to simply remain silent on the issue. Early investigations by the Air Force simply compounded the problem. Even the less active function as an information collection center put the Air Force in an uncomfortable position trying to explain (disprove) the phenomenon. The flap of '73 - '74 proved that the public could be placated by simple silence. And ,thus, "silence" remains the policy – as far as is known – of military and governmental powers to this day.

But silence does not always reflect the activity associated with secret projects. In his book, *Aliens from Space*, Major Donald Keyhoe asserts that the Air Force has always had a silent partner in its cover-up: the CIA. The CIA has authority over all the military services and can apply strong pressure when necessary to the FAA, The Coast Guard, the FCC and most other governmental agencies – this is a fact that is not well known in the public sector. The veil of secrecy surrounding the CIA places it in a position to monitor and control policy regarding the UFO phenomenon without detection.

Keyhoe claims that it was the Secretary of the Navy who forced the flying saucer investigation onto the CIA in early 1952. It seems that Secretary Dan Kimball, while en route to Hawaii, spotted two silvery discs which sped by his executive aircraft. Following close behind the Secretary's plane was another Navy plane carrying Admiral Arthur Radford. Kimball's pilot radioed the second plane to see if they, too, had seen the strange discs. Kimball reported, "In almost no time the UFOs were now circling their plane – they'd covered the fifty miles in less than two minutes. In a few seconds the pilot told us they'd left the plane and raced up out of sight."

Kimball was obviously deeply affected by the incident and reported it to the proper authority: the Air Force. However, the Air Force's reaction was not what Kimball had expected. They refused to discuss the incident, or offer any explanation.

It was a mistake to ignore Kimball. Not one to be pushed around, Kimball was ready to blow the lid off and he ordered all Navy and Marine reports "to be kept separate from the Air Force project."

The Air Force was worried that Kimball might take his experience public and feared that such publicity would directly undermine their efforts to debunk the UFO.

The current major UFO wave had the Air Force's hands full. All they needed was to have a highly credible military witness like Kimball to go public with his story.

In the meantime, Kimball was busy studying and compiling UFO reports, and had in his possession a color film – taken by Warrant Officer, Delbert C. Newhouse – of a whole formation of flying saucers near Tremonton, Utah.

This startling new evidence rechanneled Kimball's efforts and he ordered Navy experts to examine the film. After 600 hours of scientific evaluation the Navy experts concluded the film was indeed authentic. Their findings disproved any explanation that the objects filmed were either aircraft, birds, or balloons. Conclusion? "Unknown objects under intelligent control."

Behind the scenes the CIA was keeping an eye on the controversy. They had been keenly aware of the phenomenon and were solidly behind the Air Force cover-up since 1948, according to Admiral Hillenkoetter, the CIA director at the time.

Hillenkoetter was so convinced of the reality of UFOs that he later became a member of the board of directors of NICAP.

The CIA was greatly concerned about Kimball and weighed their alternatives. He had to be stopped. They suggested that the Air Force stall Kimball until after the elections of 1952, knowing that a new administration would likely replace the Secretary. Their gamble paid off when Eisenhower defeated Truman and promptly replaced Secretary Kimball with a Republican of his choice.

Meanwhile, the CIA had forced its hand with the Air Force. They had suggested that the Air Force gather a group of CIA-selected scientists to help disprove the phenomenon.

What they didn't know was that at the time there was a certain element within the Air Force investigation who firmly believed the cover-up should end. Among those in this camp were Pentagon liaison Dewey Fornet, Captain Edward Ruppelt and Albert M. Chop, HQ press official in charge of Blue Book press releases. They apparently thought that open discussion was the best policy for the Air Force to follow but were unaware of the CIA's position on the matter. The CIA revealed its true position during the ensuing conference. The discussion was directed by three CIA representatives – agents Philip G. Strong and Ralph L. Clark, and CIA scientist Dr. Marshall Chedwell.

For five days, starting January 12, 1953, the CIA-directed panel discussed the phenomenon. It was apparent that the CIA was committed to discrediting the bothersome issue and all discussions were aimed at negative evidence. The agents excluded credible witnesses – including airline pilots, top military personnel and scientists – and threw out a plan by Ruppelt for the implementation of a special UFO tracking system.

They stood firm on their position and ordered, "...a national debunking campaign, planting articles in magazines and arranging broadcasts to make UFO reports sound like poppycock," according to Chop.

NICAP's Donald Keyhoe quoted Blue Book's director as saying, "We're ordered to hide sightings when possible, but if a strong report does get out we have to publish a fast explanation – make up something to kill the report in a hurry, and also to ridicule the witness, especially if we can't figure a plausible answer. We even have to discredit our own pilots. It's a raw deal but we can't buck the CIA. The whole thing makes me sick – I'm thinking of putting in for inactive."

Within a short time, Albert Chop quit the Air Force, Major Fornet was put on inactive duty and Captain Ruppelt was replaced at Blue Book.

The CIA, it would appear, is (and has been) in charge of the UFO investigation since the outset, and has dictated the U.S. military policy regarding the phenomenon. [7-33]

* * * * *

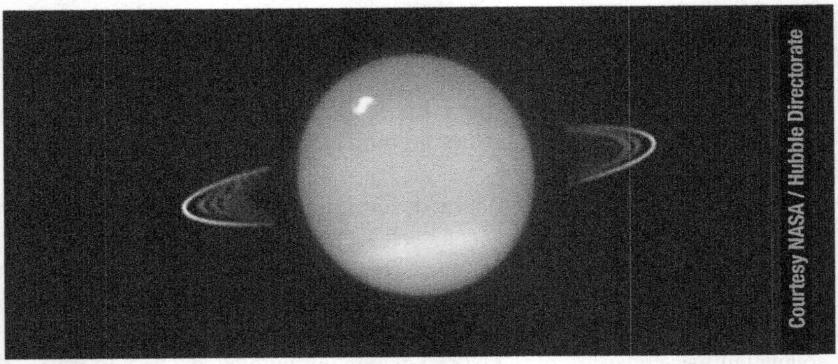

Figure 7.1 Uranus 2005 – Credit: NASA, ESA, and M. Showalter (SETI Institute)

UFO Photos

Do UFO Photos Exist?

One of the first questions that comes to mind when dealing with the UFO phenomenon is the question of photographic evidence.

It's true that several photographs have surfaced that have been authenticated by experts, but the real problem has been convincing a wary public that they are real. It's very difficult to distinguish the real from the forgeries with the naked eye, so we must rely on the testimony of the experts.

Why so few authentic photos exist is another mystery worthy of thought. If truly hundreds of thousands of these strange craft have been sighted, why haven't more people taken pictures of them?

The answer unfolds in several logical explanations. First, not many people carry cameras in their cars, or around their necks, and many of these sightings occur on deserted stretches of highway, or in isolated areas. Second, the phenomenon usually only lasts a few fleeting minutes, or seconds, and witnesses are so entranced by the sight that they simply don't think about taking a picture. Thirdly, most sightings occur from great distances and usually at night. On several occasions an attempt at taking a picture of the moving target has resulted in only a blur of light, hardly what one could consider conclusive evidence. But any captured image is proof that at least something was there when the picture was taken. In combination with credible eyewitness reports, photographs can add a great deal of validity to the phenomenon.

AUTHOR'S UPDATE: With our modern obsession, where nearly everyone carries a mobile phone equipped with a built-in camera, and the widespread distribution of PhotoShop to manipulate photography, most current sightings are a mixed bag. Sightings are now much more commonplace, but so is skepticism that these images are forged. Several incidents, however, are unchallengeable. During the mid-nineties, mostly in South America, a major wave of UFO activity erupted which continues to this day. Numerous photographs and video footage have surfaced of this massive, ongoing flap. In fact, in one high-profile incident, several million residents of Mexico City witnessed silvery discs and formations of lights dancing in the sky for extended periods (days and sometimes weeks). This is well documented and can be proven with even a cursory 'Google' of the incidents (see *Figure 9.11*). You are very likely to have seen the amazing footage of one giant disc-shaped craft wobbling between two apartment buildings in the heart of Mexico City...as it has been widely distributed on cable TV and online. It's hard to discredit an entire nation's eyewitness accounts, even though many have tried.

Several other high-profile incidents and flaps have also emerged since my first draft of *Aliens & In-laws*, including regular monthly visitations in Baturite, Brazil, in 1993 and 1994, with very similar exhibitions as is described later in this book in *chapter 22* titled *"Miracles, Apparitions & Dancing Suns."* The hovering objects had been observed by up to ten thousand people each time they appeared, which was at precisely 2:00 p.m. on the first Saturday of the month. The local peasants, being primarily Catholics, were claiming accompanying visions of Jesus and Mary. They believed the spinning discs, which turned varying shades of red, blue and green, were signs from God.

Forgeries Exposed

The UFO phenomenon, unlike anything else in history, has produced a variety of kooks and deliberate forgeries. Seeking notoriety, or fortune, this small nucleus of deceptive individuals has done a great deal to discredit sincere UFO research. Usually this group of fanatics is associated with contactee stories including wild claims of communicating with "space brothers," being told the secrets of the universe, or being given rides to mars and back on-board the alien craft.

Among this group of imposters are those who have deliberately faked photographs of UFOs. Some have been lured by the temptation of benefiting monetarily. Others have forged their pictures as a joke and the joke simply got out of hand.

A favorite technique has been to throw a hubcap into the air and take a snapshot as it sails by. Another is the easily executed double exposure. However, these techniques of deception are readily exposed in the laboratory.

Close examination of the evidence will always expose these imposters for what they are, but too often an eager press has published their accounts as factual. Had they done their homework reporters would have dismissed most of them. But once published, retraction does little good because the damage has been done.

In the minds of many, anyone linked with the UFO phenomenon becomes guilty by association with liars and nuts.

There Are Some Authentic Photos & Films

The existence of several authentic UFO photos has been substantiated by both military and civilian experts. Upon thorough examination by top technicians the photos have been declared genuine. These are the cases we shall concern ourselves with here.

The Trent Photos

One of the earliest and best UFO photographs was taken in McMinnville, Oregon in 1950. Actually two photos were taken in sequence by Mr. and Mrs. Paul Trent on their small farm 10 miles southwest of McMinnville.

It was May 11th in the late afternoon when the Trents first spotted the bright metallic object approaching them from a nearby field. As the object got nearer they realized this was no ordinary sight. Mr. Trent immediately ran back into his house and grabbed the family camera.

The object was wobbling as it flew toward the Trents and they noticed it had a rounded dome-like structure on top but was flat on the bottom. They estimated its size at over 20 feet in diameter. Mr. Trent was able to get two good shots of the object before it disappeared in the west. The whole sequence lasted only a few minutes.

One of the most convincing elements of this account is that the Trents never tried to benefit in any way from the existence of these photos. In fact, they waited some time before even telling anyone about their encounter for fear of ridicule.

As word finally got out of the existence of these purported UFO photos, the Trents were contacted by the local newspaper in McMinnville. When the negatives were analyzed by the newspaper staff they were declared authentic and were immediately published (see *Figure 8.1*).

Soon, several papers carried the story in their pages and a *LIFE* Magazine correspondent picked up the story. Wishing to substantiate the Trent's claim, *LIFE* requested the original negatives for inspection. Upon close examination their staff, too, declared the photos authentic without question of forgery and quickly published the pictures.

Some years later, during the official investigation by the Condon Committee, staff photo analyst William K. Hartman declared of the McMinnville photo. "This is one of the few UFO reports in which all factors investigated, geometric, psychological and physical, appear to be consistent with assertion that an extraordinary flying object, silvery, metallic, and evidently artificial, flew within sight of the two witnesses." [8-1]

Subsequently, scientist Dr. Bruce Maccabee studied the photo further under photogrammetric analyses and concluded that the object in question could not have been a small object close to the camera, as some had maintained, but was at a considerable distance and, henceforth, approximately as large as the Trents had asserted.

When a request was forwarded to the offices of Blue Book regarding the Trent photos, Dr. Hynek reports that the following letter was received from the Office of Information of the Air Force:

"Dear Mr. Case:

Your letter to the Department of Science has been referred to this office as a matter pertaining to the Air Force.

The Air Force has no information on photographs of an unidentified object taken by Mr. & Mrs. Trent of McMinnville, Oregon.

In this regard, it should be noted that all photographs submitted in conjunction with UFO reports have been a misinterpretation of natural or conventional objects. The object in these photographs have a positive identification.

John F. Spaulding
Lt. Col. USAF" [8-2]

The only thing in the letter approaching the truth is that the object in the photos indeed had a "positive identification." It was an unidentified flying object. (see *Figure 8.1*)

The Lucci Photos

On August 8, 1965, amateur photographer James Lucci of Brighton Township, Pennsylvania, was making time exposures of the moon as part of his hobby. He was with his brother and a friend, Michael Grove, in the driveway of their home when a UFO suddenly appeared over a hill behind the house.

Round and glowing brightly, Lucci was able to take two quick shots of the object before it climbed up and out of sight.

When the photos were later examined they discovered something more. Not visible to the naked eye, the camera had picked up a luminous halo and strange misty trail left by the object.

Again, as with the Trents, Lucci was reluctant to share his ordeal with anyone other than close friends and family members. He was finally coaxed into taking the photos to the *Beaver County Times* where they were tested by staff photographers. Conclusion: The photos were genuine.

Before publishing the photos, the editorial staff interviewed the boy and found him to be very sincere. In addition, the boy's upstanding character was attested to by the Brighton Township Chief of Police, his high school principal and several other prominent citizens who knew young Lucci personally. [8-3]

The Heflin Photos

Five days earlier, four vivid UFO photographs were taken near Santa Ana, California. Mr. Rex Heflin, a Los Angeles County Accident Investigator for the Highway Commission, was driving along Myford Road just outside Santa Ana when a strange small flying object appeared. It was approaching his vehicle on the opposite side of the road and appeared to be a small (approximately three feet in diameter) metallic disc.

Being a traffic accident investigator, Heflin was equipped with a small Polaroid camera. Thinking quickly, he was able to take several photos of the strange craft from inside his truck. In the meantime he attempted to radio his office but his radio malfunctioned. He jumped out of the truck and snapped off a forth shot of the disc as it disappeared down the road. When he got back in the truck, the radio suddenly worked perfectly.

UPI photographic specialists examined the photos some weeks later and concluded that they were taken just as Heflin had claimed. They had no explanation, however, for what it was that he had photographed.

The photos were also thoroughly examined by John Gray, an engineer at North American involved with the Apollo space program; engineer Ed Evers, an unidentified photogrammetrist with another major space industry in Los Angeles (choosing to remain somewhat anonymous); and several others associated with NICAP. Their conclusion was that the photos were indeed authentic.

After the photos attained notoriety nationwide, Heflin was approached by a man purporting to be from NORAD. Unfortunately, he convinced Heflin to give him the original photos for "official study."

When Heflin later tried to get the photos back, the Air Force and NORAD denied ever having them. (see *Figures 8.2 & 8.3*)

This absence of the original photos, however, did not prevent the Air Force from totally denying their authenticity. They labeled them hoaxes deliberately disputing what others had claimed and offered as proof the fact that 3 Polaroids could not possibly have been taken as quickly as Heflin had claimed.

This argument was quickly knocked down by NICAP investigators who went to the spot and reenacted, with ease, Heflin's reported experience.

The Air Force avoided one of the most glaring proofs within the photo itself. On close examination, a patch of dust appears rising up directly underneath the disc. Nowhere else is the earth disturbed (see *Figure 8.2*) except directly beneath the object. This phenomenon has been associated with UFOs on numerous occasions. Apparently the flying discs can at times cause a force field or exhaust just beneath them and thus created circular patterns of disturbances directly below them. The Air Force, obviously aware of the phenomenon, failed to even mention it in their official denial. [8-4]

Other authentic photos exist but for lack of space I hope those listed represent a convincing sample.

Tremonton Movie

On July 2, 1952, Navy Warrant Officer Delbert Newhouse and his family were driving to his new assignment in another state when they spotted 14 strange objects high overhead near Tremonton, Utah.

Since Newhouse had been a Naval Aviation photographer, he was carrying his 16mm Bell & Howell movie camera on his journey. Equipped with a three inch telephoto lens he aimed the camera at the strange formation of luminous round objects and reeled-off forty feet of film. He followed the path of the objects as they flew at high speeds and then concentrated on one object that had broken away from the others. As he followed the one object until it disappeared, he didn't notice what had transpired with the main body of objects and when he looked for the others they also had disappeared.

The existence of the film was of great interest to Dan Kimball the Secretary of the Navy who had, himself, observed a UFO as discussed in an earlier chapter. As mentioned, Kimball was miffed at the Air Force's reception to his report and thus ordered the Navy lab technicians to evaluate the Newhouse film for themselves rather than turn it over to the Air Force.

After 600 hours of extensive study by the very best photo analysts available to the Navy, the following conclusions were made of the film:

> **Aircraft:** "With the lens used, aircraft would have been identified clearly five miles away. The objects' speed at that distance would have been 653.3 miles an hour...At that time, there was no group flying capable of such speeds, and certainly not capable of such maneuvers at those speeds."

Balloons: "With the telephoto lens used, balloons could have been identified up to five miles. The speeds of the objects if they were only 2 1/2 miles away would be 326.75 miles an hour, in excess of windblown balloons."

Birds: "No bird is sufficiently reflective to cause the film to react as strongly as it has done." Detailed evidence of the objects' speeds also excluded the possibility of birds.

Conclusion: "Unknown objects under intelligent control." [8-5]

When the Air Force made their own investigation they were stumped in their efforts to debunk the film.

The Robertson Panel was allowed to study the film, too, because Ruppelt thought it was among the best evidence that BB possessed. After all, the staffs of two of the country's best photo labs (the Navy lab at Anacostia, Maryland and the Air Force lab at Wright Field, Ohio) had concluded the objects were true UFOs. Yet the Robertson Panel totally ignored the experts and concluded after simply viewing the film twice that the objects were actually seagulls. Absurd in light of the fact that the Navy had estimated their speeds at over 650 mph. [8-6]

When the press got wind of the film, Ruppelt moved to have it declassified and shown at a press conference later in 1952. However, according to Ruppelt, the press conference was called off at the last minute because Air Force officials knew their "seagull" hypothesis was weak. [8-7]

Several years later during the Condon Investigation, Dr. Robert M. Baker was asked to testify regarding his analysis of the Tremonton film. Dr. Baker was an eminently qualified witness as senior scientist with the Computer Sciences Corporation in southern California. As such, he had access to the latest technology for photo analyses. He was also a former astronomy and engineering professor at UCLA. He concluded that the Newhouse film and another film, the Mariana film (which we will investigate next) were almost assuredly made by an object or objects that possessed qualities unlike anything on Earth. He also suggested further study of the possible existence of extraterrestrial life. [8-8]

Condon, however, chose to ignore the testimony in favor of the shaky explanation put forth by the Air Force.

Great Falls, Montana Film

Another movie film taken by a credible witness was made in 1950. On August 5, Nicholas Mariana and his secretary were inspecting a baseball field at Great Falls, Montana. Mariana was the manager of a local team and was checking out the conditions of the field prior to a game when he happened to spot two strange lights in the sky. Recognizing that they were not ordinary planes, but huge round lighted objects, Mariana ran to his car and got out his 16mm movie camera.

He was able to photograph the two objects as they moved across the sky, at one point passing behind a water tower, and moving against the wind.

The water towers would later provide the reference point for investigators to calculate distance, altitude, size, azimuth and time duration and thus approximate speed of the objects. The Air Force concluded they were flying too fast to be birds and too slow to be meteors. [8-9]

The Mariana film like the Newhouse film was studied by military experts and intelligence officers from all over the world. Both the Robertson and Condon Committees were shown the film.

The explanation that the military put forth was that the objects photographed were reflections of two F-94 jet fighters known to have been in the area that day. What they failed to acknowledge was the fact that the two fighters were seen by the witnesses a minute or two after the lights disappeared but in another part of the sky. By Blue Book's own calculations the F-94s that landed at Great Falls AFB could not have been in the part of the sky that the film was shot. They also ruled out reflections because the lights Mariana filmed were glowing with a steady light.

At first, Blue Book labeled the objects "unknowns" and kept the film classified. After several years, however, the Air Force declassified it and claimed the film showed the reflections of aircraft. [8-10]

The Swiss Encounters

Another film that has gone through extensive testing was taken near a small farming community of Canton Zurich in Switzerland. In fact, there exists a whole series of films, tapes and photos taken by Eduard "Billy" Meier beginning in January of 1975.

Since very few books on UFO sightings have been published in recent years and precious little information is available (the Air Force does not investigate the phenomenon any longer) the publication of *UFO - Contact from the Pleiades* is certainly an important event.

I don't wish to establish the reality of UFOs by quoting undocumented testimony but the photos and films of Meier are of incredible significance.

Meier, as of 1979, had shot seven 8mm films and literally hundreds of photographs revealing five different "models" of flying saucers. He claims that an ongoing contact has produced the incredible evidence.

The films and photos reproduced in the book are of tremendous quality and clarity. Meier's story was investigated by several American specialists including Colonel Wendelle C. Stevens, former ATIC officer in intelligence for the Air Force. Colonel Stevens, as an expert in the field of aircraft technology, participated in the peace negotiations with Japan prior to the end of WW II. He also helped to structure the Bolivian Air Force, among many other major achievements in his illustrious career. For over 30 years Stevens has studied the UFO phenomenon and is considered a leading expert on the subject.

Along with Col. Stevens, Lee Elders, Director of Intercep, a prominent counter-measure security firm based in Phoenix, joined the investigation as a security expert.

These two spearheaded a team of security, computer, laser and photographic specialists from around the country. In addition, Jim Lorenzen of APRO was consulted in the ensuing investigation.

The research was extremely thorough and utilized the very latest technology including:

COMPUTER FUNCTIONS

Histogram - defines light intensity values, Z scale

Edge Identification - clearly shows all lines (edges) in pictures

Edge Enhancement - improves visual quality of edges in pictures

Spatial Filtering - separates different light values (frequency)

Contour Identification - topographic (3-D) map of object

Focus Index - identifies edges as function of distance

Contrast Enhancement - improves visual quality of hazy picture

Image Enhancement - improves edges and finer detail of object

Geometry Function - calculates size, distance, aspect ratio of objects

LABORATORY EQUIPMENT

Vidicon Tube - converts picture to electronic image

Digitizer - converts vidicon image to 300,000 computer cells called pixels

Image Process Computer - defines, analyzes, measures elements of photo

Electron Microscope - powerful close-up microscope

Microdensitometer - measures density of film grain

Interferometer - measures waveform/frequency of film crystals (as lenses)

Infraredometer - measures infrared light not visible to naked eye

After months of exhaustive study the research team had concluded that the photos were not faked in any way. The only answer is that they are, indeed, genuine photographs and 8mm film frames of UFOs. [8-11]

(see *Figure 8.4*, also see *Author's Update* at the end of *Chapter 26*)

* * * * *

The Trent's Photo

Used by permission of Wikimedia Commons / GNU Free Documentation license

Figure 8.1 One of the 1950 Trents' photos, also known as the McMinnville photos, after the city in Oregon where they were taken, is evidence of one of the earliest, most documented sightings of a classic UFO. Note its wobbly (tilted) flight path while in slow movement in close proximity to the earth's surface.

Figure 8.2 – The first of three photographs taken by a Los Angeles County highway employee named Heflin on the morning of August 3, 1965, near Santa Ana, California. Note the disturbance on the shoulder of road just beneath the object, apparently caused by its flight mechanism.

Figure 8.3 – Another Heflin photo. As the object approached his car the car radio malfunctioned, but returned to normal after the small UFO passed from view.

The Meier Photos

Figure 8.4 – Close-up of an alien craft taken by the one armed eye-witness Eduard "Billy" Meier of Switzerland in 1975. This was long before the common use of Photoshop and digital imaging. These were all printed on old-fashioned photo paper using continuous tone lab printing techniques which makes it very difficult to manipulate.

Description & Properties of Various Craft

Size Of Craft

U FOs have been reported in varying sizes from small unmanned discs no larger than two or three feet, all the way up to massive structures known as "mother ships" and estimated on radar to be 1,200 feet long. That's the length of four football fields! Although there have been literally scores of different estimated sizes as reported from around the world, I would tend to classify them in the following general categories:

1. Under 20 feet (drones)   3. 50 to 200 feet
2. 20 to 50 feet (most common)   4. 200 feet & over (motherships)

Possibly the most common size encountered are the ones in the medium range, particularly around 20 to 30 feet in diameter. The second most common would be the small drone saucers and then the larger sizes around 100 feet. The rarest would be the extremely large ships which are usually spotted far above the Earth's surface only by pilots and by both air and ground radar (see *Figure 9.2)*.

A fairly common description by both radar and ground sightings have described smaller saucers which have merged or gone inside of other larger craft. This has been seen as a mysterious occurrence, however, further thought reveals a logical explanation.

The frequency of sightings of various sized UFOs fits a definite pattern of use. In fact, the pattern shows an obvious and logical implementation of technology. Evidence indicates the following scenario: Medium sized saucers, usually containing two to six passengers, jettison from their gigantic mother ships while still high above the Earth. As they advance into our atmosphere they often use smaller probes to precede them. This action is similar to the technique NASA employed when America sent unmanned probes to the lunar surface prior to landing men on the moon.

Since these small probes can't be seen in daylight from too great a distance, it would stand to reason that more sightings would be made of the larger manned craft.

However, the presence of the smaller craft in our atmosphere would ensure that they would be spotted on many occasions especially when in close proximity to witnesses. At night these smaller discs can be seen more readily because they apparently use the same or similar type of power system as their larger counterparts. This power mode apparently produces differing intensities and colors of light. The presence of small extremely bright lights making quick, drastic maneuvers in our atmosphere has been reported on numerous occasions.

The largest sized UFOs are rarely seen in close proximity to Earth but have been seen in a few instances as large columns of cloud. The cloud cover is obviously for camouflage because the sight of a huge metallic craft hovering over a town would no doubt send panic throughout the area. Strange moving clouds are much less threatening to an unsuspecting populace.

UFO Shapes

There are basically six or eight general shapes of craft that appear with regularity.

DISC - As we examined the volumes of reports the most plentiful UFO is the flying "saucer" or disc. The disc has been described in numerous sizes from two feet up to 300 feet or larger. The smaller ones have been solid or have slightly differing shapes on the top and bottom i.e. rounded tops and flat bottoms. The mid-sized craft are often seen with transparent domes on their tops or portholes on their sides. And the larger ones either have no noticeable openings or a series of portholes at mid-point or slightly above their circumference. The saucers have been described with totally smooth mirror-like surfaces or variations of surface structures including rivets and mechanical protrusions, railings and lights.

CIGAR - Perhaps the second most-often described shape is the cigar or egg-shaped craft. These elongated discs have been noted with similar surface characteristics as the circular saucers and are usually estimated larger than 100 feet long.

SPHERE - Another very commonly described configuration, the sphere is the shape most often described by those who observe UFOs at a distance, especially at night. The nighttime sighting of these objects always include their luminosity. It may very well be that the discs or cigar-shaped objects give off so much light while in certain phases of flight that their shape is indiscernible and can only be described as a sphere. It may also be that discs viewed from their rounded undersides take on the appearance of a sphere to the untrained eye. The last alternative is that the sphere-shaped machine is yet another class of UFO. Most likely, all three account for the large number of spherical sightings.

TOP - Also among the fairly common shapes is the acorn or inverted top-shaped UFO. These are generally of the middle-sized category with rarely a larger size being described (50 feet or over). Usually the object is seen spinning rapidly. These objects have also been described as light bulb or mushroom-shaped.

COLUMN - Column-shaped craft are of the larger "mother ship" class. Very often they are seen merging with smaller objects on radar and apparently can hold many such craft. These craft have also been described as cigar or carrot-shaped. A strange phenomenon associated with this UFO is that the column is usually enveloped in a cloud when viewed in close proximity to Earth.

Although rare, they have been seen throughout the world and most notably invaded the airspace of Europe, from Italy to England, in 1954. Dozens of newspaper reports came from France, alone, and described the huge mother ships "like a cigar standing on end" with 5 or 6 smaller discs entering and leaving from one end of the column.

About 250 miles southwest of Paris in the region of Vendee, hundreds of witnesses from a half-dozen small villages observed one of these strange column-shaped clouds.

67-year-old Mme. Pizou of St-Prouant was standing in a cabbage field working her small farm on September 14, 1954, when she happened to look up.

> "My attention was first attracted about 5 o'clock by the arrival of a strange carrot-shaped cloud that seemed to have detached itself from the ceiling of clouds that were moving fast, carried by the wind. It came near us, point downward, and then straightened up. It looked to me as if another, smaller cloud then formed above the carrot, making a kind of hat for it.
>
> "Then white smoke came out like a thread from the base of the vertical carrot and began to draw designs all around it. Then the trail went away toward the valley, where trees hid whatever happened next; I was told that a disk came out of the trail, but I cannot say that I saw it, because from where I stood the treetops reached almost to the base of the vertical cloud. In my opinion it was not a real cloud, for it stayed motionless and kept its shape while other clouds were gliding away very fast above it, toward the horizon.
>
> "Finally, when I had been watching for about half an hour, it moved down into a horizontal position again, and went away rapidly in the direction toward which it was slanted." 9-1

Again and again, the giant column was seen throughout the region. At night the cloud-like appearance of the object changed to a faint glow. According to witnesses, the object appeared pale white while at rest, but once it started to move the light intensity would increase and cause the object to take on a violet or blue caste.

JELLYFISH - This extremely rare shape has been seen most frequently in Europe. Described as a yellowish globe with luminous vertical filaments hanging from its underside, it is not clear if the filaments are structural or simply light projections from the object. The filaments vary in color including green and violet. [9-2]

In America an object that might be described as the jellyfish UFO was seen by a Kansas Highway Patrolman and the editor of the *Arkansas City Daily Traveler*. On a tip from the Hutchinson Naval Air Station the two drove to Emporia in search of a UFO that was reported earlier that evening in the same area. As they drove out to a hillside overlooking the city they were joined by an Arkansas City Police cruiser and both vehicles waited to spot the object.

Shortly before midnight they noticed a "tear- drop shaped blob of light" approach from the north. The large craft appeared to have "prongs, or streams of bright light spraying downward toward the Earth" from beneath it. The trio watched in astonishment several minutes as the object moved across the city skyline.

The next day hundreds of reports poured into the police headquarters and newspaper offices describing the object. Editor Coyne reported: "I have tended to discount stories about flying objects, but, brother, I am now a believer." [9-3]

DELTA WING - Another extremely rare shape for a UFO is the delta wing. Their existence has been substantiated, however, by some very competent witnesses including professors, scientists and two Air Force colonels who recognized the objects as nothing in existence in the U.S. arsenal. The craft have no tails or "pilot's canopies," as one witness said, just a clean upper surface with a ridge running from the leading point across the object to the tail. [9-4]

AUTHOR'S UPDATE: The delta wing, or v-shaped formation, has become much more prevalent in current times. It is now considered commonplace in the UFO community, but I can't conjecture why.

SMALL SPHERES - Some as small as a ping pong ball have been observed by several pilots. Allied forces during WWII often reported being accompanied by these small "friendly" observers during combat missions. In 1986, a Brazilian film crew took live footage of one of these smaller objects and the film was shown on network television across America. [9-5]

OTHERS - Other descriptions have included small vertical cylinders and an elongated egg with one edge pointed and the other rounded, as well as a variety of others. These are so rare, however, that I tend to discount their accuracy, charging them instead to misidentification, distorted viewpoints or unreliable witnesses. [9-6]

AUTHOR'S UPDATE: In an age of internet saturation, PhotoShop trickery and You-Tube, it is very difficult for the uninformed public to decipher between truth and fakery. There are many more doctored representations than genuine photos or films of UFOs. And the type of craft being portrayed by malicious individuals are only limited by their imaginations. That's why the only way to really understand this phenomenon is through an historical work, such as this manuscript. It takes study to gain a true perspective for weeding out the frauds among us.

Surfaces And Lights

Without exception, UFOs have been described as having a metallic surface when viewed in the daylight either as stationary objects or while in slow flight. Of course, the cloud-covered columns are not fully visible when close to the Earth and it is assumed that they, too, would appear metallic if the cloud were removed.

Often described as flat gray, like aluminum, the craft take on a brilliant glow when in fast flight. The texture of the surface is either dull or metallic silver, sometimes to the point of a mirror-like finish. Depending on the "model" of UFO, the color of this glow may change during certain phases of flight. The most common color is orange or red-orange and is usually exhibited while the object is in slower flight. But the color may change from a red to a yellow or amber to green or greenish blue. Sometimes the color changes in succession, from red to yellow to green. These same objects are often seen glowing much brighter during rapid transit, most notably a bright white, like a star.

Some objects remain one particular color without any perceivable color change. The phenomena called "green fireballs" describes the most notable example of this. It is my opinion that green fireballs represent the smaller drone class of saucer while those that change color are of the larger, manned class. The larger craft have a different mode of propulsion, perhaps even utilizing more than one flight technology. This would explain the reason for the color change. Obviously, I am speculating, but whatever their mode of flight, it apparently induces dramatic color changes which are probably relevant to their varying speeds.

The colors, particularly the oranges and reds, are very gentle on the eye, however, the bright yellows and whites can become blinding even to the point of rivaling the sun in intensity.

RIM LIGHTS - Another specific area of light emission originates in the rim of the disc. Sometimes identified as portholes or openings at the edge of the saucer's rim, this area on many UFO's emit varied colored lights and vapor. In all likelihood the emission is associated with the UFO's atmospheric propulsion system.

SPARK EMISSIONS - Sparks, too, accompany many of the movements of these craft, especially while in slower flight. It may be that the flight system used for the smaller drone saucers incorporate more basic thrust propulsion as a part of their terrestrial flight mode because this phenomenon is generally associated with the smaller objects.

LIGHT BEAMS - Another fairly common occurrence is the emission of light beams. The exact purpose of these beams is unclear, however, it's unrealistic to assume that their only purpose is to eliminate objects like a powerful weapon. These beams may very well be information gathering devices or even control mechanisms. There is some evidence that they are used for all three: information gathering, as stunning weapons and as guidance systems.

In August of 1965, a woman and her young daughter were lying on cots in their backyard in New Jersey gazing up at the summer constellation. Suddenly a bright light much larger than a star raced across the sky and stopped directly over them. According to Ms. Bennett, a very bright light shot down on them at that instant which illuminated approximately one-quarter of an acre directly around them. Terribly frightened, the two were frozen in terror for a brief moment, but after the light went out they regained their composure and raced into their house to tell Mr. Bennett about the amazing event.

Once they started to explain what had happened they discovered that they had not seen the event in exactly the same way. The daughter did not notice the bright light but she did observe that two smaller objects dropped out of the larger one and flew off in different directions. [9-7] Again, it's reason for suspicion if two individuals describe an event in exactly the same way. This event was apparently authentic.

Sound

Generally, there are no reported sounds associated with the UFO because most sightings are made from a distance. However, in a great number of the cases when witnesses have gotten close to the objects, audible sounds have been reported. Usually, the sound resembles a hum or buzzing like an electric generator might make. Sometimes higher, shriller sounds have been observed and, on occasion, even an explosive boom as the object jumped into motion.

One interesting sighting was made by a New Mexico City Patrolman in 1966. Patrolman Lonnie Zamora had been chasing a speeding car when something else grabbed his attention. He noticed a blue flame near an area where he knew there was a dynamite shack. Concerned that there had been an explosion his attention turned from the speedster to the potentially dangerous flame. As he pulled his car off the main highway and down a dirt road he approached what he thought at first was an overturned vehicle. Beside the distant object he saw two figures in light-colored "overalls" who acted alarmed by his presence. The two figures were too far away for him to make out any details. Since Zamora was on an adjacent hill, he maneuvered his car down another dirt road which would bring him closer to the wash where he first saw the two figures. He parked his car and got out and scouted the area but soon discovered the two had left. Suddenly two loud bangs interrupted the silence of the desert wash, followed closely by a loud roar. Startled and shaken, Zamora watched as a large egg-shaped object lifted up off the desert floor exiting a bright-blue flame from its underside. Once the object had attained an altitude of about twenty feet, it leveled off and the roar was replaced by a high-pitched humming sound. Quickly, the thirty foot object took off toward the east at a high rate of speed and disappeared. Later examination of the area revealed four rectangular impressions in the hard-packed desert soil where the object apparently had rested. The surrounding vegetation was charred and smoldering. [9-8]

Movement

Consistently common characteristics of movement exist within the UFO phenomenon. The mode of propulsion, as discussed previously, may utilize at least two methods of movement. One for traveling within the gravitational field of our planet and another for use in interplanetary travel.

SPEED - It has become apparent that UFOs can travel at tremendous rates of speed. U.S. radar teams have tracked these objects in excess of 25,000 mph over great distances and in exacting formation. Many observers have estimated their speeds in excess of 1,000 mph, which appears to be the speeds used to traverse the planet at relatively high altitudes. More common than rapid transit is the slower more deliberate speeds around 150 to 300 mph, speeds they use when approaching the Earth's surface. Military and civilian pilots have reported slower speeds with intermittent bursts over 1,000 mph. These same objects have been observed standing absolutely still for long periods of time. In addition, they have been observed stopping instantly with no apparent slow down, just instant deceleration. And, of course, the opposite: instant acceleration.

ZIG-ZAG FLIGHT - One characteristic distinct to the UFO is the zigzag pattern of flight. It is very common for observers to describe this zig-zagging, starting-stopping pattern. But it is usually associated with the slower flight speeds estimated at around 300 to 600 mph. This is one of the unusual characteristics that my brother John and I observed when we saw our UFO in 1967. Faster speeds are usually flown in straight or curving patterns, especially when speeds are in excess of 1,000 mph.

SHARP 90 DEGREE TURNS - In addition to the zigzag, UFOs possess the ability to make abrupt right angle turns or even to reverse their course instantly. These characteristics are particularly disturbing to modern scientists because they violate the accepted – and I emphasize "accepted" – laws of physics.

POSITION OF FLIGHT - The most often observed position taken by the saucer, egg, top, jellyfish and delta wing-shaped objects is the horizontal position. However, many have been seen flying in a tilted or even perpendicular position. I know of no instances where these craft have rolled 180 degrees to fly in the upside-down position but I would certainly not dismiss the possibility.

THE WOBBLE - One strange but very common phenomenon associated with flight is the fluttering or wobbling effect especially while descending. This effect is always seen while the object is either descending, moving slowly or hovering, but never at high speeds. Many witnesses have described the descent of these objects with colorful analogies such as: "Like a falling leaf" or "like a rowboat in choppy water" (see *Figure 9.3*).

FLIGHT PATTERNS - Groups of UFOs have been observed flying in formation more often than in random flight. The diamond position for four or more craft is very common, as is the two abreast position. However, I know of no recorded instances where saucers flew one over the top of the other in a stacked position. Evidence would indicate that the UFO produces a field of force directly below it which prevents flight formations in the vertical position.

In addition to flying in formation in the horizontal position, these objects have been seen flying in variously tilted, fixed positions.

On Friday, October 3, 1958, on a run from Monmon, Indiana, to Indianapolis, a group of four discs made several passes at a freight train as the startled crew watched intently. Conductor Ed Robinson and flagman Paul Sosby were riding in the caboose. The rest of the crew including Harry Eckman, engineer; Cecil Bridge, fireman; Morris Ott, head breakman, were all in the cab of the diesel engine at the head of the procession.

"We got a good look at them," said conductor Robinson, "as they sailed over the train and over the caboose. They were four big disc-shaped things maybe forty feet in diameter. They glowed like white fluorescent things, sort of fuzzy looking around the rims. After they had gone half a mile or so behind the train they seemed to stop for a few seconds and then Sosby and me went out on the rear platform to watch them. They seemed to be bunched up, right over the tracks, by this time about a mile or so away."

"Then they swung off the tracks, one right behind the other, and started moving to the east. The faster they went the brighter they got. The boys in the engine were able to see them again by this time and they yelled at us over the radio."

The men noticed that as the "V" formation sped up, their glow got brighter and as they slowed they went from a bright white color to a "muddy yellow-orange."

Suddenly the procession reappeared but this time they were in a strange formation. Robinson continued, "The two which were over the tracks were flying on edge...by that I mean the rims were vertical. The ones on either side of these two were flying at angles of about forty-five degrees, with the upper rims tilted in toward the discs over the tracks. They sort of resembled a huge letter 'M' in white lights."

The objects continued to pace the train darting back and forth until they got to Kirklin, about 38 miles northwest of Indianapolis and "...they just zipped off to the northeast and we never saw them any more." [9-9]

SPINNING - It's not clear whether all of the egg or disc-shaped objects spin but a great number of accounts exist detailing the phenomenon. Usually an outer rim of larger discs will spin. With smaller discs, the whole object appears to spin. This spinning motion is not always a continuous movement because many accounts tell of the rings beginning to spin after the object has ascended to a certain height. Often as the object approaches the Earth the outer rim will begin to spin, indicating that the rim can be engaged at will as part of a flight or stabilizing system.

Some Speculation on Movement

Some very interesting theories have been put forth regarding the power and associated flight characteristics of the UFO.

The zig-zag motion, it has been speculated, allows the UFO to travel slowly without reducing its force of propulsion. The simple shifting of the "eccentric spot" may produce a pendulum effect. As the pendulum swing reaches its maximum extension, the shift in the object's center weight would produce movement in the opposite direction without reducing the actual force of the object's momentum. [9-10]

This same shifting of weight, or mass, may produce the force needed for descent, also without loosing momentum. This may explain the erratic swings of descent resembling a falling leaf.

Another frequently reported effect, that of spinning, may be associated with the stabilization of the object once it has maximized the pendulum maneuver for its desired result. Witnesses have often described the wobbling descent followed closely by the object's spinning, at which point the wobbling stabilizes. It has been suggested that this spinning produces a gyroscopic effect which stops the random oscillation of descent. [9-11]

For a more thorough explanation of this effect, I would suggest reading *The Truth About Flying Saucers* by Aime Michel, especially for his section on the Plantier theory of UFO flight.

Another theory put forth that appears to make some sense is that the craft may use some form of servo system. A servo system is one that is composed of three basic parts:

1. A means of accepting an instruction

2. A means of carrying out the instruction

3. A monitor to determine when the instruction has been carried out

The thermostat on some heat-pumps work in this manner. First, you set the desired temperature. The thermostat will then automatically trigger either the heater or the cooler depending on the existing temperature. When the desired temperature range is achieved, both systems remain off until a sufficient heating or cooling occurs, at which point the thermostat gives the appropriate signal to resume operation.

Out of necessity, however, there is a range of temperature variance when neither the cooler or heater are in operation. This is called the "dead zone." If it weren't for this dead zone, each appliance would automatically trigger the other in an endless chain reaction.

Servo systems are used on our planet to guide devices where human judgement and reactions are too slow. Presumably the same type of system is used by our alien friends for descent. The wobbling movement of a UFO may be caused by the craft wandering from one limit of the dead zone to the other as it strives to achieve a desired altitude. Once achieved, apparently the outer rim's spinning mechanism is engaged by the saucer's occupants and its gyroscopic effect eliminates the seemingly erratic wobbling motion of descent. [9-12]

Other Details

WINDOWS - Most often the manned craft have some method for its occupants to observe the terrain. Windows, or portholes have been seen an many craft, usually lined up on the object's circumference.

DOMES - As an alternative to the portholes, some of the smaller one or two-man craft have sported a clear dome on their tops.

LANDING GEAR - There have been many reports describing landing gear attached to UFOs. Usually in a tripod arrangement and sometimes with 4 extensions, these landing arms are tipped with a dish-like or squarish object for support and often have a small light on their ends.

The landing protrusions have been observed being retracted by the craft. Once retracted, they become an integral part of the craft's surface and disappear from sight.

Many photos of depressions left by the landing gear give evidence of their existence. In addition to the marks left in soil or grassy areas, there have been accompanying circular patterns left in the foliage apparently created by the circular movement or exhaust of the craft.

VAPOR TRAIL - Several incidents report a type of condensation trail left by the objects during daylight observation. Since they are not common I would suggest that the phenomena only occur during certain phases of flight and/or under specific weather conditions.

LADDERS, RAMPS & RAILINGS - There exist several descriptions of UFOs with ladders, ramps and railings. In one case, the Reverend Gill incident, witnesses observed several humanoid creatures on a deck-like platform which circumscribed the saucer-shaped UFO. The incident occurred in June of 1959 and involved several humanoid aliens apparently making repairs on a crippled UFO. The incident took place in plain sight of at least thirty eight witnesses including an Anglican missionary named Rev. William Booth Gill who gave the most detailed account of the incident. The craft hovered above Reverend Gill's compound for two days while the aliens made their repairs. They were apparently unconcerned about the stir they were causing and on several occasions even waved to the villagers some two hundred feet below. [9-13]

In the famous case of Betty and Barney Hill, (full details in chapter 12) the witnesses described an "...object coming down from the bottom of it." Mr. Hill recalled, "I could see through the binoculars...I thought of a ladder, but I didn't really know what it was." [9-14]

There have been several other reports of ramps or walkways that protruded from the craft and when retracted, either became a part of the smooth surface or disappeared into an opening in the craft.

DOORS - Several configurations of openings into the craft have been reported. Some have seen sliding doors that opened to produce a smooth entrance into the craft. Next, a ramp would protrude for the witnesses to walk up and into the craft. Some have reported a combination door/walkway that flips open to produce an entrance way. Entrances both on the outer skin of the object and somewhere near the center of the craft have been reported. Access from the top is rare and is usually seen only on the small one or two man-sized craft.

WINGS - Some of the larger saucer or egg-shaped craft have been described with wing-like attachments on two sides. Not usually noticed at first, these retractable protrusions are visible when the craft is either hovering or after it has landed.

I would speculate that these wing-like devices are used on some models of the larger craft to stabilize or minimize the wobbling effect associated with their descent. A two hundred foot wide craft that is attempting to land in a small clearing in a forest, for example, might do considerable damage to nearby trees if it swung in a pendulum-like manner as it neared its destination.

Drone Saucers

As described earlier, there is evidence of small drone saucers accompanying the mid-sized craft. Obviously, these small reproductions don't possess all the capability of their larger brothers. No windows or landing gear and often their appearance is that of a bright light at night or a flat metallic disc during the day.

Effects Of Close Encounters

Although the following phenomena are not necessarily common to all classes of UFOs their existence has been reported with regularity.

ELECTROMAGNETIC EFFECTS - Very common to the UFO is accompanying effects on electromagnetic devices. Pilots have reported that their instruments have malfunctioned while in close proximity to UFOs and have returned to normal function once the craft has left the area.

Motorists are the most common source of this report. Automobile engines die and lights and electrical systems all fail while close to a hovering or landed craft. Again, they return to normal function once the alien craft has left. Although rare, engines have been known to mysteriously restart by themselves after the UFO has gone. Radio and television sets have also been affected by low flying UFOs.

RADIOACTIVITY - Routine UFO investigative techniques include the measurement of radioactive traces in the area of a landing incident. It was discovered early on that there could be some danger in getting too close to an active UFO because some of them have left excessively high radioactivity in their paths. The radioactive contamination usually dissipates within hours leaving a landing area safe to explore. Crop Circles only leave elecro-magnetic traces.

HEAT - Heat is another phenomenon associated with some UFOs. Although not too common, there have been reports by those who have gotten too close to an active UFO who have suffered from heat-exposure and a sunburn-like condition. Apparently some UFOs give off dangerous amounts of heat and/or ultraviolet radiation.

NAUSEA - Several witnesses have described a nauseous feeling accompanying a close encounter with these strange craft.

REPULSION DEVICE - The alien craft possess the advanced technology to repulse and incapacitate aggressors. Several witnesses have reported being repelled by beams of light or energy when they have ventured too close to a UFO.

ANIMAL REACTIONS - One piece of evidence that helps to verify that UFOs are indeed a real, not an imagined, phenomenon is the recognition of their presence by animals. On numerous occasions family pets and livestock have been driven to react violently or to cower from fear of the strange objects.

Some Rare Properties/Associated Phenomena

ANGEL'S HAIR - One of the most mysterious phenomena associated with the UFO is something aptly called angel's hair. On several occasions saucers have been observed discharging a substance in the form of long gelatinous strands. These stringy discards usually dissipate before reaching the ground, but in at least one case they were collected by several witnesses. Almost immediately the strange strands began to disappear as if they had evaporated. More on this in the chapter called "Miracle at Fatima" (see *Figure 9.1*).

OTHER DISCHARGES - In addition to angel's hair, other unlikely substances have been known to fall mysteriously from a clear sky. Items like ice, bean pods and fish, and even pieces of raw meat, have reportedly fallen from the sky. Such accounts are usually scoffed at, but credible witnesses have sworn that they've been hit by the unlikely falling debris and their testimony has been believable.

Although no explanation has been accepted, the UFO may be connected to these strange incidents. If the creatures aboard these craft have stocked up on earthly food for the duration of their assignment, it is highly likely that they may oversupply themselves with the local food source from time to time. If this were the case and their stay had ended, or if they were called back home prematurely, they might need to discard their supply of food. It's possible they would simply jettison it overboard at sea and go on their way. Upper atmospheric winds may carry it over land masses and dump it on unsuspecting humans.

Earthly food might not be suitable for hyperspace transport or perhaps there is concern that the food would spoil on the long journey home. Whatever the case, this hypothetical scenario would explain the mysterious phenomena.

CATTLE MUTILATIONS - Although there is not too much evidence, there have been several reports of strange hovering lights associated with the widely known mystery of cattle mutilations. Missing eyes, tongues and other organs have been mysteriously removed with surgical precision from range cattle all across the southwest. Perhaps various parts of the cows have been used for medical purposes by the aliens. There really is no other plausible explanation for the mysterious phenomenon. [9-15]

ATTACHED UFOs - Another very strange and very rare occurrence is that of connected saucers. Several witnesses have reported two or more saucers connected somehow by a greenish light or arc of light.

One notable account was reported by the crew of Gemini XII. Jim Lovel and Edwin Aldrin reported seeing four UFOs linked in a row that were "definitely not stars." [9-16]

One speculation is that this light or electrical connection serves the same purpose as our own conventional in-flight refueling procedures. The author of this theory further supports his contention by citing one such occurrence in France. The eye-witness account describes two UFOs connected for a time that landed and the two "pilots" exchanged craft. He speculates that alien craft left on active duty in our atmosphere would need a recharge from time to time. The ship which came to refuel the craft would also carry a fresh relief pilot. [9-17]

I think it more likely that these electrical connections are some sort of safety device used to keep the saucers from banging into one another while in close formation and especially while landing in a relatively tight area. We must remember that these craft normally wobble or swing like a pendulum while descending and some safety measure would be necessary to prevent them from crashing into one another.

This would explain one report of several craft linked to one another that entered into a large mother ship. The mechanical separation device would be used in just such cases where several craft must enter into exacting formation while in descent [9-18] (see *Figure 9.4*).

AUTHOR'S UPDATE: Three (and now four) more phenomena associated with UFO sightings must now be included since I first penned this text. The first is the now very familiar crop circles.

CROP CIRCLES - Crop circles are appearing across this planet with such regularity that claims of forgery must be dismissed. The precision and shape of *authentic* crop circles cannot be replicated by human means, although many pranksters have tried. The phenomenon first gained notoriety in 1983 when an engineer, named Colin Andrews, recorded six patterned circles in a field in England. Subsequently, literally tens of thousands of patterns have appeared in the UK and elsewhere around the globe. Mr. Andrews's research has led to little explanation for the phenomenon, other than to reveal that 80 percent are fabricated, while 20 percent remain inexplicable. Authentic crop circles reveal bent, not broken, stocks on plants in a circular pattern made with perfect precision. The effected plants start their flattened appearance in exact center points and generate outward, often in weaved patterns. The flattened plants continue to mysteriously grow in their altered growth direction, rather than die, as do damaged plants in fabricated patterns. Magnetic abnormalities have also been detected near patterns' centers, such as enhanced cell phone reception. Those who have claimed they've mischievously created crop circles cannot reproduce the anomaly in exacting detail, when challenged by credentialed researchers. In addition, there have appeared many odd shapes, most of which have been fabricated by hoaxers, along with the circular designs. The mystery is further deepened by the fact that authentic circles appear overnight, no matter how intricate the pattern created, and are often accompanied by UFO sightings [9-19] (see *Figure 9.5*).

FLEETS OF UFOs - Another phenomenon has surfaced in recent years that is even more astounding than crop circles. That's the amazing appearance of UFOs in giant fleets, some estimated at 300 to 400. The preponderance of sightings began in the early 1990s in several South American nations, and especially in Mexico. [9-20] But even sightings over the M25 highway near London at Middlesex, England, have been videotaped by passing motorists. [9-21] This is a very significant development in the purpose of our alien visitors. In this age of "Jackass – The Movie," it takes more than a single UFO to get our attention. As much as I hate it, this is exactly what our nation has come to expect. An extreme UFO sightings makeover! Wake up people! ...*sorry for the outburst* (see *Figures 9.10 & 9.11*).

FLYING CROSSES - lastly, is the flying cross. Actually, a flying formation in the shape of a cross. This one is of particular interest to me because that was the shape of my second UFO sighting. It occurred on January 13, 2005 on my way home from my niece's home in Washington state. I live in a rural area and was quite surprised by the sight. It was early evening and I recognized the object as something out of the ordinary. I say "object" because it moved as one. There was no sound and no flashing red and green lights on its wing tips, as is required by the FAA for single engine aircraft. That was the approximate airspace it was occupying. There were several dimly glowing circular objects inside of, or attached to, the shell. They looked like low-wattage florescent lights inside the "mother ship", for lack of a better description. I can't be sure if the wingspan was three objects across or five, but arranged in a definite cross shape. There was also a small flashing red light in the center, at the intersection of the two rows of cross-shaped lights. It moved slowly in the direction of Seattle and disappeared into the night. I've read of other flying cross UFOs and was skeptical, as is my nature, because of their rarity, but I am now a confirmed believer (see *Figures 9.7 & 9.8*).

AUTHOR'S UPDATE: Starting around March of 2011, and dramatically heightened the second week of January 2012, a new phenomenon has gripped our planet.

SKY TRUMPETS - Sounds from Space are being heard around the planet. The eerie sounds have unsettled residents from Hawaii to New York, Alberta to Toronto, across Australia, the UK, Spain, The Ukraine, Russia, Czech Republic, Belgium, Denmark, Costa Rica, Mexico and numerous other nations...all over the same period of January 16th to around the 23rd. The phenomenon has taken over You Tube as the key interest among Web surfers, and for good reason. The sounds that seem to eminate from the open skies sometimes even cause the earth to vibrate, according to some, because of their intensity. The first incident of notariety occurred on August 23rd, 2011 at a Tampa Bays Rays vs. Detroit Tigers baseball game. It persisted throughout most of the game and the mystified announcers took notice and said that it sounded "haunting" and "supernatural." It couldn't have been a simple malfunction of the P.A. system because the sounds were heard outside the domed stadium, as reported from many places in the area that evening. No plausible explanation has been forthcoming to resolve the phenomenon, although there are the usual "experts" offering absurd causes like nearby trains (even though many are in rural areas nowhere near any trains), pre-earthquake noises (that would be the first time in history), or as one quack scientist said on television, "It's not really a noise, it's a magnetic waive or image..." who's sound is being picked up by "...an environmental antenna that just happens to be there." Just normal electromagnetic sound "...from the aurora above our heads or the radiation belt...a nice natural noise." [9-22] I'm not sure what "normality" he exists in, but you can't hear and record anything unless it's in the form of a sound wave. When is the last time you held a magnet up to your ear to hear its vibration? Absurd. You know what they say about experts. We'll explore this newest phenomenon in our section called *"The Trumpets of God"* in the second half of this book (see *Chapter 32, pages 426 and 432*).

* * * * *

Figure 9.1 – This amateur illustration by an actual eyewitness records the rare phenomenon called "angel's hair." The small gelatinous filaments fell from the entourage that flew over Orloron and Gaillac, France in 1954, and dissipated into thin air after only a few minutes. Notice the huge "mothership" shaped like a giant column. The flying pillar, cloaked in smoke or mist, flew behind and well above the formation. The giant "cloud", according to several eyewitness accounts, actually held some (perhaps all) of the smaller craft that precede it in this illustration.

Figure 9.2 A – Composite of UFO shapes based on published UFO photographs was prepared by Dr. R.N. Shepard, a research psychologist at Stanford University, as an identification aid and included in a paper submitted to the House Committee on Science and Astronautics in July 1968. Below is an illustration by JasonArt.com with a more updated record of shapes. Most of these images are from the 1950s and their shapes are consistent with what is still being seen. Logic would tell you that if this were a man-made phenomenon many more shapes & sizes would be reported.

UFO SIGHTINGS

Figure 9.2 B Photoshop artists have produced flying humanoids, cows and other obviously fake imagery as seen on YouTube, but they are fairly easy to spot as frauds. Unfortunately, many are lured into false beliefs of wierd unorthodox shapes. One or two sightings of frightening, or aggressive creatures are overshadowed by the many tens of thousands of sightings with classic Human-looking creatures or a smaller class of large-headed, grayish creatures with large nearly black eyes that can tilt up in the corners, with a very small mouth, nose and chin.

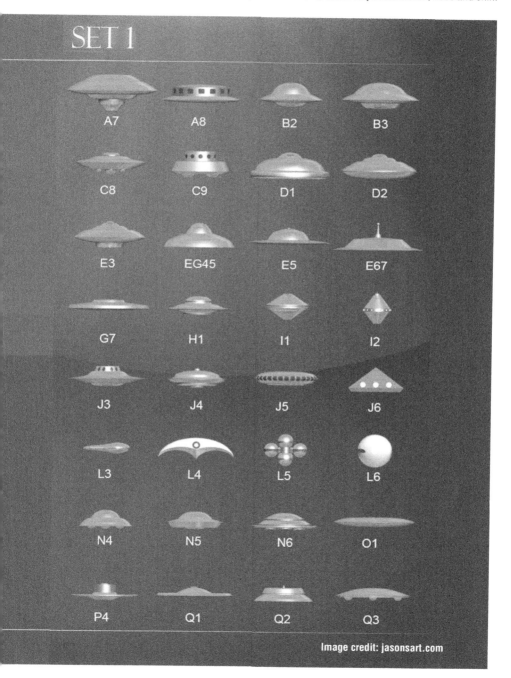

SET 1

A7　A8　B2　B3

C8　C9　D1　D2

E3　EG45　E5　E67

G7　H1　I1　I2

J3　J4　J5　J6

L3　L4　L5　L6

N4　N5　N6　O1

P4　Q1　Q2　Q3

Image credit: jasonsart.com

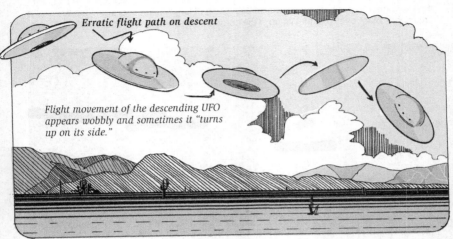

Erratic flight path on descent

Flight movement of the descending UFO appears wobbly and sometimes it "turns up on its side."

Figure 9.3 – A major characteristic of the UFO is its descent to near the Earth's surface. Usually the UFO will slow or stop first, then descend "like a falling leaf" or a "boat in choppy water." This descent causes the craft to tip and wobble erratically.

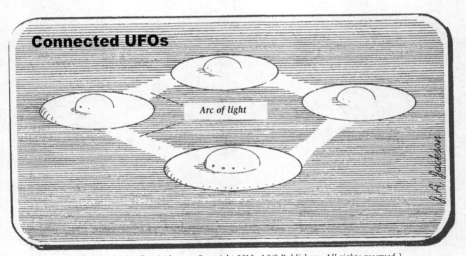

Connected UFOs

Arc of light

Figure 9.4 – An arc of light appears to enjoin formations of UFOs that must land in close proximity to one another. Perhaps this strange beam of light keeps the craft from banging into one another during the erratic activity of descent (called the "falling-leaf" effect).

Note: in the above right-hand column of images I've overlayed each pattern with geometric lines to reveal some of the "sacred geometry" of the five plantonic solids of which they are made. They often contain several of those shapes including the Tetrahedron, Hexahedron, Octahedron, Dodecahedron, and Icosahedron.

Figure 9.5 – The crop circle phenomenon has become very prevalent in recent years, advanced by its New Age proponents and discredited by many amateurish attempts at duplicating legitimate anomalies. To the professional investigator, legitimate crop circles show unmistakable properties, including altered growth patterns of effected crops and magnetic abnormalities near their centers. The prophet Joel forewarned that in the last days there would be "signs in the heavens and on the earth," to alert us to Christ's soon return (Joel 2: 30). The designs (above) all have overlapping tetrahedrons with encasing radii. (Top right) Design called the "Seed of Life." The double tetrahedron should be familiar. It's the symbol Israel uses on their flag. It's also called "The Star of David". The star has six points plus the center point making seven, or the number of completion. Also, 13 is a very special number, as there are 13 spheres in the star tetrahedron (far right). Consider: the United States originally had 13 colonies. Interesting.

Figure 9.6 — This is a quick sketch of an object, or objects, I saw on the evening of January 13, 2005 near a place called Kountry Korner in Kingston, Washington. I actually sketched this three days after the fact, and can't be certain how many lights there were, but they were arranged in a perfect 'cross' with a flashing smaller red light in the center where the two rows of lights intersected. The lights glowed dimly like a very low-watt fluorescent bulb and were perfectly round, remaining stationary in relation to one another as it moved toward the general direction of Seattle from Hansville. It was visible for several minutes, and continued its flight path until out of sight over the tree line.

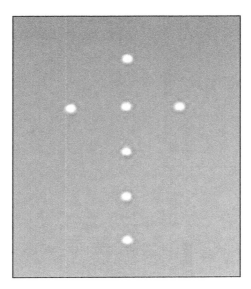

Figure 9.7 – This is a frame from a flying cross video taken over Florida on August 25, 2005, while hurricane Katrina slammed into the Gulf Coast of the U.S. and is very similar to the one I saw in 2005. As I recall, its lights were larger and more plentiful, but maybe not. Truthfully, I can't be sure, but I do remember a flashing red light in its center, which this formation does not have.

Figure 9.8 – Interestingly, this seven-studded turquoise crucifix is called a 'Latin Cross'; the most common and recognizable symbol of Christianity in Spanish-speaking Mexico, Central and South America, where the majority of sightings are taking place today.

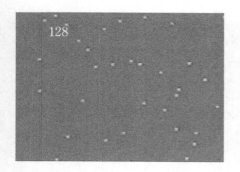

Fleets/Armadas of UFOs are now commonplace

Figure 9.9 – Groups of flying spheres were seen by dozens of neighbors in San Luis Potosi, on the morning of June 24, 2005. Several reports from residents told of a strange formation of luminous globes coursing over the area for two days. One of these sightings was videotaped by Rosario Oviedo at daylight just outside her home. The number of objects frightened her at first. A portion of a video lasting nearly 3 minutes is seen to the left.

Figure 9.10 – The same day at 10:30 AM at least 14 objects were seen at a political event at casa Veracruz in Xalapa, Mexico. This stunning sighting was witnessed by Xalapa's governor, Fidel Herrera Beltran, members of his staff, many officers of the Xalapa police department, newspaper and television reporters, and many others gathered at Casa Veracruz for an official ceremony for the delivery of new police patrol cars to the police department. The local press featured the incident, left, on its front page.

NOTE Below: These are some still clips from videos which can be found on the popular video sharing sites such as YouTube (but beware of fabricated fakes, as always).

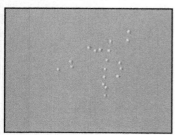

Guadalajara – June 10, 2004

Figure 9.11 – Although this is not the first time fleets of UFOs have been seen, it is a relatively new occurrence – starting in the early 1990s and continuing through to current times – for so many to be reported. The area where fleets are spotted regularly is South America and especially Mexico.Why is anybody's guess, but I would conjecture that it is because these nations are primarily Catholic and they seem to be prone to watching for signs in everyday life. But I think there is a more sinister reason they are patroling the skies of our southern neighbors. Drug lords have taken over much of the border and I expect the lawlessness to intensify over the next few years. the second half of this book will deal with these issues of purpose and motivation of HFOs.

Tula Hidalgo – March 18, 1998

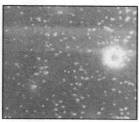

Space Shuttle - NASA 2011

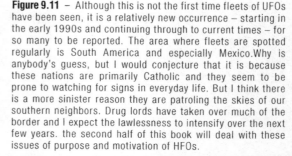

Taylors Hill, Australia Nov.18-2013

Saucer Occupants

would hope by now that I've been able to convince you of the validity of the UFO phenomenon and the associated cover-up perpetrated by various world powers. It's real folks! No jokes or illusions. The proof is voluminous. One need only search for the truth and it will be revealed. If you're still not convinced, then I challenge you to investigate for yourselves. Begin by asking several of your friends if they have ever seen a UFO. Chances are good that several have. Then compare what they've seen to what I've reported in this book. I can guarantee you it will fit into the flying saucer "jigsaw puzzle" neatly.

The next piece of the puzzle is fairly obvious. The question must be asked: "If there really are alien craft entering into the Earth's atmosphere, then by what or whom are they being controlled?"

Some put forth an early theory that the saucers themselves were creatures from another dimension. This theory is closely paralleled by what the prophet Ezekiel described in the Old Testament of the Bible, as we shall discuss in the second half of this book. Somehow, this theory speculates, the saucer-shaped creatures were momentarily caught in Earth's time/space warp and were materialized and visible to humans until they were able to return to their own dimension.

This theory, of course, was pretty far out, but no more so than the speculation that the objects were manned by aliens from another planet or, perhaps, another solar system in some distant galaxy.

The living entity explanation, however, has been abandoned due to the existence of yet another phenomenon: visual contact of saucer occupants.

The report of two-legged creatures in connection with visual sightings of saucers is very common. Exactly when the first sighting was made is debatable, however, sightings have become more and more commonplace.

The abundance of UFO sightings in the early fifties created such a jolt on the public that just dealing with the saucer's existence was enough. Trying to go beyond that was simply too much to be expected. Occupant stories were either ignored or laughed-off as the figments of overactive imaginations. But as the public became more mindful of the controversy, the provocative nature of the idea of some intelligent form controlling the UFO became more palatable. Slowly the public began to accept such a possibility. Discussions centered on such possibilities by the mid-fifties on several of the nation's talk shows and, of course, Hollywood got in on the act.

The natural tendency, for the sake of a good story, was to portray these aliens as gruesome diabolical monsters bent on capturing or destroying the human race.

Nothing could be farther from the truth. All documented alien contact has revealed a friendly, if not somewhat indifferent, attitude exhibited by the inhabitants of UFOs.

Their actual physical appearance, as well, has been highly distorted by our film makers. (One notable exception is Stephen Spielberg's *Close Encounters,* although he did take liberties with the length of creature's neck). Actual eye-witness accounts have consistently described only two types of alien astronauts.

Human-like Occupants

It would take volumes to substantiate all of the stories associated with the physical descriptions of these entities, however, the following overview will help to abbreviate the task.

For the most part, these aliens are very much like any normal human form with the exception that they are all exquisite examples of the human physique. There are no stories of aliens with ugly scars, missing teeth or limbs or any other malady that might be present in a comparable cross-section of the human species. No acne or bald heads or wild haircuts and tatttoos like some of our youth.

Simply magnificent human-like specimens. Very idealized in a human context. Their hair has been described as brown or blonde in most cases and blue eyes seem to be prevalent. Some have sported beards but most are clean shaven.

These human forms have been seen inside the craft through transparent domes or windows as the craft hovered nearby. They've also been observed on numerous occasions going in or coming out of landed craft.

Smaller Occupants

By far, the most often observed alien form is the small human-shaped creature. Their existence has been espoused by thousands, if not hundreds of thousands, worldwide. These are the life-forms that have given rise to the "little green men" descriptive that has become so legendary.

Very few people, in my opinion, realize that the "little green men from another planet" narrative is based on real fact. Almost.

At least one-third of the colorful description is accurate. They are little. Usually described as around three and one-half to four and one-half feet tall. However, the color of their skin is usually described as pale gray or a putty-like color. Not a bright green as would be expected by the descriptive phrase. I would guess that some journalist, in an attempt to discredit the UFO phenomenon, coined the phrase in mockery.

Additionally, these creatures are not really very much like men. They are similar in that they have the basic human shape with two legs with feet, two arms with hands, and a head attached to a torso. However, their head is much larger in proportion to their bodies than a normal human as is their chest cavity. The head has a very large cranium and the face is dominated by extremely large slanted eyes. "Like a cat's eyes," some have said. The mouth, by contrast, is not very large at all. Usually just a slit in the face. The nose, too, is almost unnoticeable appearing like a bump with two small openings for nostrils. And the ears are either not seen or are described as two small holes in the sides of the head.

Some of these small creatures have longer than normal arms and hands with long skinny fingers. Others are normal length with three or four digit hands, often described as appearing like claws or pincers.

The texture of the skin is very soft and flat or putty-like in appearance (see *Figure 12.1 p.154*).

These creatures often waddle, much like a duck, when they walk and have sometimes been reported to simply float effortlessly as they move about.

Two Types Together

Although rare, there have been a few instances where both types of aliens have been seen together in the same craft. It would appear that this Universal Federation of Brotherhood is made up of all space creatures, ourselves included, if and when we attain their status. I certainly think some of us will, as I shall explain in the second half of this book.

Apparel

The aliens of both types dress very much the same. They are almost always seen wearing a shiny tight-fitting body suit. On several occasions the one-piece uniform or space apparel has had glowing properties, a glowing or slightly luminous light apparently being emitted from the garment itself.

These body suits or "diving suits," as they have often been described, come in many colors. Black, dark blue, brown, light blue, silver and white are the most common colors.

Very often the uniform is topped off with a helmet or transparent bubble. Some cases of hoses attached to the helmets have been reported and have included the use of a back-pack of some kind, possibly for use in flight (like a jet pack), or perhaps, a device to maintain the proper atmosphere for the alien's intake.

Uniforms or dress often appear to denote rank. In the Betty and Barney Hill incident the witnesses recalled, under hypnosis, that the being in charge wore a black shiny uniform, a long black scarf that fell over the left shoulder and a black cap with a visor. The other aliens aboard his craft behaved like his subordinates and wore dark blue uniforms made of denim-like material that reminded Barney of a Navy pea jacket [10-1]

In addition to the helmet, other headgear has included a tam O' shanter type of hat.

Uniforms usually don't include too many accessories as is normal with man's military apparel. However, descriptions of different colored belts and shoes are fairly common. Insignias and medals of rank are extremely rare but a few such accounts have surfaced.

Very often the shoes appear to be the same color as the uniform and blend into their overall appearance. Often the shoes don't include a heel. Usually the hands are covered with gloves made from similarly colored material as the suit.

Alien Contact

To my knowledge, the first recorded incident of physical contact with an alien occurred in France in 1954. On September 10, near the town of Mourieras, France, a 50-year-old farmer named M. Antoine Masaud was on his way home from the fields at dusk (about 8:30 p.m.).

He was carrying a pitchfork over his shoulder as he walked along the deserted dirt road to his house about a mile away. After stopping to roll a cigarette, he was suddenly confronted by a strange looking man.

> "This 'person' was average height and was wearing a sort of helmet without any ear flaps, something like the ones motorcyclists wear," said Masaud. At first he was frightened by the odd appearing stranger.

> "My first reaction was to grab my pitchfork," he said. "I was frozen with fear. The 'other one' also remained motionless. Then very cautiously, he came toward me, making a sort of gesture with his arm above his head. I thought it meant he wanted to reassure me, perhaps speak to me, or express his friendship. His other arm was extended toward me, but I did not have the impression of a threat, rather the contrary.

> "I didn't know what to do. After a moment of confusion when I wondered who and what this was, I thought that he must be a crazy man in disguise. As he continued to advance slowly toward me, making peculiar gestures and low bows, I decided that he had no intention of attacking me.

> "He was right in front of me. Then, still holding my pitchfork in my right hand, I rather hesitantly held out my left hand to him. He seized it eagerly and shook it very hard – then he suddenly pulled me right up to him, drawing my head against his helmet.

"I really saw stars. All this had happened in complete silence. Recovering from my astonishment, I ventured to say 'good evening.' He made no reply, passed in front of me, and went a few yards away, into the dense shadow of the woods. It seemed to me that he then got down on his knees. A few seconds later I heard a low hum, like a bee buzzing, and I saw rising among the branches, toward the sky, almost vertically, a kind of dark object, which seemed to me to have the shape of a cigar swollen out on one side, about fifteen or twenty feet long. It passed under the high-tension wires and disappeared into the sky toward the west, in the direction of Limoges.

"It was only then that I recovered my wits – I rushed toward the place where he had disappeared, but of course it was too late then." [10-2]

As UFO sightings became more prevalent, so too, did alien contact. The existence of these human-like creatures is now accepted as a very integral part of the UFO phenomenon.

*   *   *   *   *

Image Courtesy NASA / Hubble Directorate

The M81 Galaxy "just" 12 Million Light Years from Earth! Galaxies appearing much like our own Milky Way are abundant throughout the known universe.

Alien Powers

Technological Capabilities

The existence of aliens from another world is, in itself, an incredible thing to accept. The ability of another race of non-human and human-like forms to travel to our planet from light years away requires technology far beyond normal human knowledge. But we are being visited by craft that defy present-day scientific knowledge. If these aliens have the ability to develop such advanced vehicles for travel, then they also would almost certainly possess other capabilities far beyond our present comprehension.

Some of their capabilities far surpass our own physical and mental abilities, as well. The following brief descriptives, however, are most likely associated with the laws of physics and their use via mechanical means.

Electric Presence – Many witnesses have described an eerie tingling sensation when in close proximity to space vehicles, even when no aliens are seen. This usually precedes the next physical occurrence in close contacts.

Freezing Animate Objects – Witnesses who have approached objects too closely or have held threatening poses have either been frozen in their tracks or have experienced extreme electric-like jolts. Described variously as red-hot or icey-cold, these jolts are administered normally by a beam of light and result in instant repulsion.

Controlling and Moving Objects – Numerous stories have surfaced of people loosing control of their automobiles as if drawn up by some force coming from a hovering UFO. Autos have been automatically steered and turned, even with their motors turned off, according to hundreds of such accounts.

Normally, witnesses experience this just after spotting a UFO and don't remember much afterward other than seeing the UFO leaving the area.

The evidence of possible abductions in such cases is very convincing. But that's another discussion.

Psychological/Physiological Properties

Communication by Telepathy - When confronted by space creatures, the first reaction of almost every witness has been extreme fear. Fear is a natural reaction to such a bizarre event, but is totally unfounded. As witnesses have gotten close enough to speak to these superhuman forms they are instantly overcome by feelings of friendliness and well-being. This "feeling" is usually communicated by a "voice" that is known rather than audibly heard. "Don't be afraid...we won't hurt you." Somehow the thought is implanted into the frightened witnesses who later compare the experience to mental telepathy. The first point of contact, however, is always eye contact. Apparently the need for eye contact to be established, *prior* to communication, is crucial. Once that has been accomplished, the alien can then transfer thoughts without the need of speaking.

They Can Speak, too – The aliens are so far advanced in their mental capabilities that it seems they've developed the ability to read human thoughts and to communicate without the burden of speaking. But they are capable of speaking audibly, too. When they speak to humans it is always in their (the witnesses') native tongue. They've been known to speak French, Spanish, Portuguese, English and many other languages as reported by witnesses from around the world. However, when they communicate with each other audibly they speak in low, guttural sounds, or with a strange clicking noises.

They Have a Written Language – Several credible witnesses have observed books in the possession of these creatures. Often described as hieroglyphic like, strange symbols fill their pages. In one case the pages of the book glowed faintly and its pages appeared to be so thin they were almost transparent. No human has been allowed to keep any of these texts...apparently the aliens want to remain a mystery to the general public. Spacecraft have also been observed with strange markings on their sides indicating a written language.

Mind Control – Close contact with aliens has consistently produced descriptions of being controlled mentally when eye contact has been established. Once the impression has been implanted into the minds of the witnesses that the aliens are friendly (and even loving), the normal reaction of fear is replaced with one of trust. The aliens are then able to introduce thoughts and control body movements, if necessary.

Levitation – One of the abilities of the aliens is to move witnesses about without the witness consciously cooperating with the movement. Witness accounts have described being "floated" into the alien craft via artificial means. The process has been perceived as being one of mind control, however, evidence would indicate they may use some sort of force field or mechanical device rather than mental levitation. The same witnesses also describe themselves as walking about under their own power once allowed to do so.

Self-Levitation – The aliens themselves are able to either walk normally (the small aliens actually walk rather awkwardly with a kind of waddle) or to float or glide along on a supposed cushion of air. Both methods of movement have been cited for the same creatures at different moments.

Pass Through Objects – Rarely these creatures have been seen passing through hard objects like doors and walls. It is assumed that they all possess this ability. Even though it would reason that any object that can pass through a solid wall would be etherial, such is not the case. The same creatures that were able to do this have also made contact with the witnesses in a normal physical manner, indicating that they can interact with natural elements or defy natural laws as if made of a different molecular structure. More on this in the section called "Parallel Universes."

Can't Be Killed – On several occasions witnesses have shot the smaller creatures with shotguns, rifles and handguns, all with the same result. In each case the creature has been knocked back by the blast but has leaped up immediately and run away as if never having been fired upon. The shots simply seem to bounce off, making a sound as though they were ricochetting-off metal. One case, the Kelly-Hopkinsville incident, described the small creatures as glowing brighter when struck by bullets. [11-1]Another case in Brazil in 1954 cites a situation where a man attempted to stab an alien with his knife. This, too, resulted in the knife glancing off the creature as though striking metal.[11-2]

Glowing Properties – This phenomenon has been covered earlier but to recap, the aliens do at times seem to glow with a faint light. It's not clear if the glow comes from their clothing or if it emanates from the creatures themselves.

* * * * *

A billowing tower of gas and dust rises from the stellar nursery known as the Eagle Nebula. This small piece of the Eagle Nebula is 57 trillion miles long (91.7 trillion km)

Credit: NASA, ESA, and The Hubble Heritage Team (STScI/AURA)

Some Mysterious Abductions

The UFO phenomenon naturally brings out the crackpots and those unscrupulous individuals who would try to benefit from the whole affair. Many have made wild claims about creatures from Mars, or elsewhere, who have visited with or even abducted them. Usually outlandish claims are made of imparted knowledge and warnings of the future and man's corruption of the environment. Most of these contact stories have proven to be lies. There do remain, however, a few credible cases of possible abductions by aliens.

I have carefully weeded out the ones that are obvious deceptions. Especially those in which witnesses have refused to take lie-detector tests or subject themselves to any other investigative technique by qualified professionals. I've also avoided the cases where the "victim" has tried to benefit from his experience, such as the highly publicized Adamski case, or the more recent claims by authors Bud Hopkins and Whitley Strieber.

The three that I have chosen to write about are truly mysterious and apparently real. In each case the witnesses have never attempted to benefit monetarily (although Travis Walton did write a book about his case in an attempt to prove to a skeptical world that he was telling the truth), and have subjected themselves to expert scrutiny.

Hypnosis As A Reliable Tool

Hypnosis has been used in several abduction cases to bring out facts that had been suppressed by the subconscious minds of witnesses. Although greatly misunderstood, it has proven to be a reliable tool in many cases for both therapeutic reasons and as a means of gathering new information.

We should clarify, for those who are unaware of the procedure, just what hypnosis encompasses. The use of hypnosis by a qualified practitioner can be a great aid in revealing certain information that has been withheld by the subconscious of many individuals undergoing psychotherapy treatment.

Not everyone is susceptible to hypnosis because, contrary to popular belief, hypnosis can only be achieved with the subject's full cooperation. A lot of modern stigmas have been attached to hypnosis, much the same way the UFO phenomenon has been discredited. The true danger of hypnosis lies in the qualifications, or lack thereof, of those who administer it.

The following excerpt is from *Interrupted Journey* by John G. Fuller and attributed to Dr. Benjamin Simon who will play a significant part in the Betty and Barney Hill abduction case which we will examine shortly.

"There are generally described three stages of hypnosis: light, medium, and heavy. In the light stage, catalepsy of the eyelids (inability to open the eyes at will) can be produced on suggestion, and a certain degree of general suggestibility is present. Post-hypnotic suggestions may be given, and a great deal of treatment can be accomplished..

"In the medium stage, paralysis of volitional control of the larger muscles of the body may be produced - major catalepsy. In this stage, analgesia, insensitivity to pain, may be successfully suggested...

"In the third stage, or somnambulistic stage, almost any phenomenon can be produced, and the patient will be amnesiac unless he is definitely told to recall the trance state. (This will play an important part in the Hill's treatment.) Positive or negative hallucinations may be induced, and post-hypnotic suggestions given in this somnambulistic stage will be very effective. Activity of the automatic nervous system and slowing of the pulse can be produced...

"Ninety five percent of hypnotizable persons can attain the first stage, but only about 20 percent can be brought to the third or somnambulistic stage...Any intelligent adult and most children above the age of seven can be hypnotized; in fact, children are more easily hypnotized than adults. Very psychotic individuals and the mentally retarded are very resistant to hypnosis...

"...In a variety of conditions, hysterical, psychosomatic and others, hypnosis may help to shorten the time of therapy by facilitating the approach to unconscious conflicts, as has been described. Hypnosis has dangers and yet is not dangerous. The essential dangers lie in its use by those not bound by a professional code of ethics, and who are not adequately trained." [12-1]

Through exacting exercises of relaxation and concentration a subject can be induced into a "state of hypnosis" where he can recall candidly certain repressed events in his past.

Most psychiatrists agree that the brain has a stored memory of every event that has ever occurred to an individual. It's also generally agreed that we use only 3 to 5 percent of our brain's capacity in our normal lifetimes. Much of the brain's powers remain dormant or hidden.

Hypnosis can retrieve much of the stored information that has been repressed by the subconscious in its attempt to prevent an individual from "overloading" their mind. Psychiatrists have claimed that the release of these hidden thoughts can help to alleviate anxiety in repressed individuals.

Although information obtained through regressive hypnosis is not accepted in a court of law as legal evidence, the use of hypnosis by the legal community is extensive. [12-2]

Many cases have been solved through the use of hypnosis. In 1976, in Chowchilla, California, twenty six school children had been kidnapped by several gunmen who ordered them off their school bus and into an awaiting van. Through hypnosis the bus driver was able to remember enough of the license number to allow police to find the getaway van which eventually led to the capture of the children's abductors. [12-3]

In 1980, the murder of a cellist at the Metropolitan Opera House had police mystified. A witness had seen the cellist with a young man prior to the brutal murder but could not recall what he looked like. Under hypnosis she was able to remember enough to allow police to make an accurate composite sketch of the suspect. The sketch led to the eventual arrest of the suspect. [12-4]

Many victims who have been subjected to the particularly traumatic experience of rape have been unable to identify their assailant. Through the use of hypnosis, enough details have been recalled to lead to the rapist's arrest.

Clearly, the courts recognize hypnosis as a useful tool and many police departments routinely use it as a means of obtaining valuable information for the apprehension and conviction of criminals when normal techniques fail. [12-5]

*   *   *

Betty & Barney Hill's Experience

The Sighting

The earliest substantiated abduction case goes back to 1961. Although not revealed until 1963 under hypnotic investigation, the case has become quite well known in UFO lore. In fact, a movie was made of the bizarre hypnotic sessions that revealed the strange sequence of events.

Bothered by a nagging sense of anxiety and a bleeding ulcer, Barney Hill, a black postal worker from Portsmouth, New Hampshire, decided to take the advice of a doctor friend and seek help from a reputable psychiatrist.

Dr. Benjamin Simon first interviewed Barney along with Barney's wife, Betty, on December 14, 1963. During the course of the ensuing treatment it became apparent to the doctor that a great deal of their anxiety was associated with a certain event and resultant time lapse that had occurred several years prior.

As their story unfolded the doctor found that Betty and Barney Hill had decided to take a leisurely drive one afternoon in September of 1961. They thought a sightseeing trip to Canada would be a relaxing way to spend the weekend. During the drive home through the White Mountains of New Hampshire they had spotted a strange light in the starry night sky that seemed to be following their car.

At first Barney tried to explain it away as a satellite (sound familiar?) that had gone astray, but as they continued to watch the object from their moving car, they noticed it was moving in an erratic fashion. Barney re-evaluated the sight and promptly labeled it a "military plane, maybe a search plane. Maybe it's a plane that's lost."

As they continued watching, the object came closer and they were able to tell that it was a large, oblong lighted object. Betty was beginning to get annoyed at Barney because of his insistent attempts to explain the strange craft in conventional terms. She insisted that Barney pull over and take a closer look at it through the binoculars they had brought along.

As Barney stopped the car for a quick look, he admitted hoping to himself that someone would come along on the deserted stretch of highway and share in their discovery. Someone else to help explain this unexplainable object. "Perhaps it was a helicopter or a military plane," he thought. He got back in the car and drove on in silence. He was, after all, an avowed skeptic of UFOs. And, yet, he somehow felt as if the object was following them. "Impossible. But what about the family dog," who was whimpering and cowering at Betty's feet. "How do you explain that?" he thought to himself. Barney was beginning to get frightened.

By now the object was only a few hundred feet above the dense forest of the White Mountains. Betty was spellbound. She couldn't take her eyes off the object as it cast off multi-colored patterns of blinking light. Alternating shades of red, then amber, then green and blue. The object seemed as though it was spinning too, but as it got closer to the tree tops the spinning stopped and the blinking lights changed to a steady, white glow.

As she gazed at the object through her binoculars she was aghast at what she saw next. It appeared as if the object had two rows of windows which had only appeared as a streak of light from farther away. Slowly two wing-like structures began to slide from the sides of the object. Each was tipped with a red light.

She'd had enough... "Barney you've got to stop! You've never seen anything like this in your life!" Barney, trying to hide his growing fear, pulled the car to a stop almost in the middle of the road and jumped out (see *figure 12.1*).

For reasons unknown to him, even though extremely frightened, he started toward the object which was now hovering several hundred feet away. It's size was enormous, he estimated it was larger than a commercial airliner and shaped like a huge glowing pancake.

Barney walked to a field directly across the road from his idling car and trained the binoculars on the object.

By now Betty was screaming from inside the parked car "Barney you damn fool, come back here!" But Barney was engrossed by the sight of the object, for just inside the windows of the craft he could see men-like beings staring back at him intently. Extremely terrified he watched as one figure dressed in a shiny black outfit gave a command and the others stepped back to a wall directly behind them. It looked to Barney as if this were some sort of control panel and the crew had been instructed to carry on with their task of operating the huge object.

From underneath the object he could see something being extended down toward the ground. "I thought of a ladder," he said. More likely it was another type of special gear being lowered in preparation for what was about to happen

Contact.

By now totally terrified, Barney felt an overwhelming urge to stare into the large cat-like eyes of the figure in black. With all the strength he could muster, Barney ripped the binoculars from his eyes and ran for his automobile. He arrived just as Betty was about to come looking for him in the darkness.

Somehow he sensed that these creatures wanted to capture them and in a state of panic he sped down the road screaming to Betty "We have to get out of here before the 'thing' gets us!"

Barney was sure that the object was following them but Betty could see nothing in the darkened sky. She later realized neither could she see any stars directly above them.

Suddenly a strange beeping sound could be heard. The sound came from the rear of the car and it seemed to vibrate the whole car as it beeped at irregular intervals. With each beeping sound they felt an odd tingling sensation and accompanying drowsiness.

Some time later they again heard these strange beeping sounds, but found they were thirty-five miles south of Indian Head where they had pulled over to look at the UFO.

When they arrived home they realized that it was after 5:00 in the morning. They should have been home by two-thirty according to the calculations they made prior to their departure. They had lost over two and one-half hours somewhere!

The loss of time and an urgent sense that something had happened created a bothersome anxiety in the couple. They would periodically gaze up at the morning sky half expecting to see the strange craft again. But why?

As they unloaded the car Barney felt some pain in his lower abdomen. For some unknown reason he was anxious to examine his pubic area, the area where he felt the odd aching sensation. The urge to look over his entire body puzzled him. He felt that something strange had happened that night but his initial reaction was to dismiss the entire episode. He simply wanted to put the thing out of his mind and get on with life as usual.

But this was impossible. Somewhere down inside of him he felt sure that something had happened during the time lapse of that mysterious night. He needed to know what.

Betty, too, began to show signs of anxiety. She began to have repetitive nightmares associated with the event. Something else had happened that night and it was emotionally disturbing.

Sometime later Barney discovered that an odd ring of warts had formed, arranged in a neat circle, around his testicles. Just what had caused them was a complete mystery to him, although he suspicioned that it may have been linked somehow to the September 19 experience.

Barney attempted to forget the whole affair but Betty had a more persistent nature and wanted to get to the heart of the problem. She was reluctant to discuss the incident with most people, but confided in her sister who claimed to have seen a UFO herself. After some coaxing, Betty reported the incident to officials at Pease Air Force Base nearby. The AF officials patiently listened to the Hill's story and even called them the next day for a few more details as if they were interested in sincerely investigating the event. But that was the last they heard from them.

Seeking Help

Still not satisfied with the explanations that Barney expounded, Betty learned of a Major Donald Keyhoe and his organization called NICAP. She decided to write him and tell of their experience. The letter resulted in a visit by Walter Webb, a scientific advisor to NICAP, on October 21, 1961.

The ensuing 8 hour interview convinced Webb that the Hills were a sincere, intelligent, honest couple who fully believed they had encountered a UFO. Further, he was convinced they weren't seeking any publicity and were not attempting to benefit from a fabricated story. They were simply looking for answers to the mystifying, anxiety-inducing event.

Webb's conclusion lead to further investigation of the couple by two more eminent members of NICAP, Robert Hohman and C.D. Jackson. They, too, were struck by the Hills' sincerity and were particularly interested in what had happened during those missing two and one-half hours.

Each time they would get to the part where Barney looked through the binoculars at the craft and into the eyes of the "leader," Barney would have a complete memory lapse. It had lasted until both he and Betty "came to" on the road back to Portsmouth.

Further discussions about the missing period of time lead to the suggestion that they try hypnosis to help them remember exactly what had transpired. Keyhoe reasoned that the Hills had undergone some sort of traumatic experience that produced a type of "shell-shock." Hypnotherapy had been used successfully in relieving the anxiety of battlefield neuroses and amnesia during wartime and he thought the Hills might benefit from the same type of therapy.

The Hills agreed to the idea and felt it might help them to clear up the mystery, once-and-for- all, and hopefully release their pent-up anxiety over the whole affair. However, for reasons of their own, they waited until March of 1962, to actually take the advice of NICAP members and visit a psychiatrist. Like many of us, they waited as long as they could, hoping that somehow it would work itself out.

During the yearlong postponement they took several trips retracing their path, attempting to remember more details, all without much new light being shed on the mystery.

At the referral of a close friend they visited the office of Dr. Quirke, a psychiatrist in nearby Georgetown, Massachusetts. The doctor suggested that they postpone any further treatment unless their problems persisted.

Barney Hill, with an IQ of nearly 140, was an intelligent, sensitive human being who was deeply involved in human rights issues. He was, at that time, Chairman of the Portsmouth NAACP and also a member of the state Advisory Board of the United Civil Rights Commission, on the Board of Directors of the Rockingham County Poverty Program and won a special award for his work that was presented to him by Sargent Shriver.

Barney suffered mixed feelings about his racial status and his relationship to his father. Although never expressed openly, he tended to agree with his family doctor that there might be some deep-seeded problems because of his interracial marriage to Betty. Those, along with several other minor personal problems lead to high blood pressure and a bleeding ulcer. He had pushed aside in his own mind any possibility that the UFO experience may have had any effect on him and instead sought psychiatric help for his other deep-rooted psychological problems.

Betty was also an outstanding community member. As a child welfare worker for the state of New Hampshire, she was deeply committed to the social issues of the day. It was this mutual deep commitment to fellow humans that had attracted Betty and Barney to each other. They knew that their interracial marriage would present its share of problems, but their common interests helped them to remain a close and loving couple. After her normal work day Betty would spend time at her other job as assistant secretary and community coordinator for the NAACP, and as United Nations envoy for their family church: the Unitarian-Universalist church in Portsmouth.

Barney wrestled with his medical problems until 1963, when his family physician, doctor Stephens, suggested that he visit a well-known Boston psychiatrist and neurologist, Dr. Benjamin Simon.

Dr. Simon was eminently qualified. He graduated from Stanford with a Masters Degree and received his M.D. from Washington University School of Medicine in St. Louis.

According to an excerpt from John G. Fuller's *Interrupted Journey*, Dr. Simon became interested in hypnosis while an undergraduate at Johns Hopkins University... "when he served as a subject in some experiments conducted by the Psychology Department there. During psychiatric and neurological training, he developed proficiency in techniques and procedures. While on a Rockefeller Foundation Fellowship in Europe in 1937 and 1938, he further extended the knowledge which was to prove so useful a few years later.

"In World War II, he found it a very useful adjunct in the treatment of military psychiatric disorders, first as Consultant Psychiatrist to the General Dispensary in New York, and later on a very extensive scale as Chief of Neuropsychiatry and Executive Officer at Mason General Hospital, the Army's chief psychiatric center in World War II.

"The responsibility of bringing treatment to three thousand patients a month made necessary the use of all the varied types of treatment, especially those which could be used in briefer therapy and with groups. Hypnosis, and its companion therapeutic procedure, narcosynthesis (the so-called "truth serum"), fulfilled these requirements expeditiously and became well established as therapeutic agents.

"When John Huston produced his outstanding motion picture documentary on psychiatric treatment, '*Let There Be Light*,' at the Mason General Hospital, Colonel Simon served as advisor, and personally did the scenes involving hypnosis and narcosynthesis. For his work as Chief of Neuropsychiatry and Executive officer, he was awarded the Legion of Merit and the Army Commendation Medal. Mason General Hospital and its personnel received the Meritorious Service Unit Award. After leaving military service in 1946, Dr. Simon maintained his interest in these special procedures, though their place in civilian psychiatric practice was much more restricted." [12-6]

On December 14, 1963, Barney's first session with Doctor Simon began. During the course of this first consultation, it became apparent to Dr. Simon that Betty, too, had need of therapy in relieving a certain amount of anxiety that she had, at least on the surface, repressed successfully.

Although somewhat intrigued by the Hill's story of a UFO encounter, the doctor's main concern was to aid the couple with their psychological problems. His conclusion was that the Hill's could benefit from hypnotherapy by penetrating their amnesiatic period. Hypnosis had proven particularly effective in dealing with amnesia patients and he felt it was a central factor in obtaining relief.

One of the more interesting aspects of the case was Betty's recurring dreams of being captured by small humanoid creatures and taken aboard the UFO for a physical examination. She was quite bothered by the dream and began to wonder if the vision represented reality. After all, they did have a blank to fill-in on the night of September 19, 1961. Finding out what had happened was the reason they were with the doctor.

What was to be revealed during these incredible sessions was to change the course of UFO history.

Therapy lasted for six months during which time Betty and Barney subjected themselves to deep hypnosis on many occasions. Dr. Simon recorded each visit on tape so that they could listen to their past sessions as treatment progressed. Remember that deep hypnosis generally is purposely accomplished with the patient's lack of recall. Dr. Simon thought it would be best to protect them from any excessive stress that recalling the traumatic event might induce.

Dr. Simon found both to be extremely good subjects and deep hypnosis was fairly easily accomplished. From the outset, the purpose was to reclaim the lost two and one-half hour period.

As therapy continued the couple was able to recall enough details to form a fairly clear picture of what happened that mysterious night.

Parts of the story were remembered slightly differently, as is normal, but the following description of events emerged from the sessions.

The Hill's conscious memories blanked out about the time they heard the beeping sounds coming from the rear of their car. The mesmerizing sounds had put the couple into a trance-like state. For some unknown reason Barney then took a dirt road turn-off and made another quick sharp left down a thickly forested dark road.

A short distance down this road they could see approximately six humanoid figures trying to flag them down. About this time the car engine died and the headlights went out. The family dog, Dulce, cowered under the front seat as Barney, in a state of total panic, tried desperately to restart the car without success.

Betty, too, was overcome with fear and wanted to escape into the forest and hide from these strangers in the road, three of which had started toward the car.

Friendly Vibes

By the time she reached for the car door handle, the strangers had arrived and opened it for her. Somehow she heard a voice in her head that said "Don't be afraid...we won't hurt you."

Barney had made eye contact with the one he called the leader and was told, telepathically, the same reassuring phrase. The alien instructed him to close his eyes and not to be afraid.

Both were overcome with feelings of friendship and their fear quickly left them. Betty, however, having a stronger will, fought to regain consciousness. She didn't want to be put to sleep. As the creatures surrounded her, she felt herself unable to resist them. Somehow she struggled to regain her senses long enough to turn around and see Barney, eyes closed, with one alien on each arm, being escorted toward the spacecraft. He stood much taller than his captors who Betty estimated to be about four and one-half feet tall.

"Barney, wake up!" she yelled out, but Barney was in a deep sleep, his eyes tightly closed.

Later Barney recalled that the aliens dragged him along in his unconscious state and had scuffed the tops of his shoes as his limp feet banged into the undergrowth and rocks. He felt in his mind, however, like he was floating.

Betty, on the other hand, walked under her own power but was escorted by three aliens.

As they neared the edge of the spacecraft she tried to resist again. "Don't be afraid. You don't have any reason to be afraid. We're not going to harm you, but we want to do some tests. When the tests are over with, we'll take you and Barney back and put you in your car. You'll be on your way in no time." The voice seemed somehow reassuring.

Sitting in a clearing in the forest in a kind of depression was the huge craft they had seen earlier. From one side there extended a ramp. Betty and Barney were escorted up the ramp, took a couple of steps on a sort of platform that ringed the disc, and stepped into a doorway in the side of the craft. Betty had the impression that the platform surrounding the craft was capable of rotating, "maybe like a huge gyroscope."

Once inside, she saw that the craft had a hallway around its circumference. Betty was taken to a room just off the hallway as Barney was escorted past the doorway and into another room farther down the hall.

"What are you doing with Barney? Bring him in here where I am," Betty insisted. She was promptly informed that there wasn't enough equipment in one room to examine two at once and it would take too long for them to be examined individually.

In the lightened room of the spacecraft Betty was able to get a clear view of her captors. Scarcely human, the gruesome creatures had oversized heads with an enormous cranium. Much shorter than humans, they did have the same arrangement of appendages, but their chest cavity appeared somewhat larger than normal. Their eyes were the dominant feature of their faces, very large and expressive. Barney described at one point how he felt they had smiled with their eyes because they never moved their mouths. The mouth was small with no lips. It looked more like a simple slit in the face. Their noses, too, were understated, basically a small convex area with two slits for nostrils. They didn't have ears as we know them either, just small holes in the sides of their heads. The head was totally devoid of any hair, as were their bodies, and the skin looked grayish, almost metallic.

In spite of their fearful appearance, Betty felt as though they were very friendly and meant her no harm. Another creature now entered the room and the others left. He wanted to examine her and run a few simple tests, he informed her. As he spoke, Betty noticed that he had a strange accent, unlike any she had ever heard. When the aliens conversed among themselves it was totally foreign to her.

Physical Examination

She was asked to sit on a stool as a second alien came into the room. They began to examine the skin of her hand with what looked to Betty like a large microscope. Then, with a tool that looked something like a letter opener, one of the "men" scraped across her arm. The other one carefully placed the specimen on a piece of glass or plastic, covered it with another piece, much like a slide, and wrapped the whole affair in a piece of cloth.

Next, they placed Betty's head in a headrest type of bracket that extended from the stool and examined her eyes, throat, teeth and ears using a small light. Then with a cotton swab type of instrument the examiner took a sample from her left ear and placed it on another piece of glass and put it in a drawer that retracted from the smooth surface of the wall.

The room was very clean and sterile, lit by a kind of bluish-colored light that engulfed the entire room. The walls were smooth and the same light-metallic color as the floor and ceiling. In one corner was the equipment they used in their examination.

The "doctor" then took a small sample of Betty's hair from the back of her neck. Next, they took off her shoes and examined her feet and hands, cutting off a small sample of her fingernail.

Betty was then requested to take off her dress and lie down on a small table in the middle of the room. With a strange device "like an EEG machine only without a tracing machine," they began to gently touch her head and temples and parts of her face. The strange machine looked like a cluster of needles with wires attached to them. It didn't cause any pain as they touched it to the various parts of her body. Down her neck and spine under her arms, around her hips, legs and feet they pressed the odd looking machine. At several points her limbs jerked involuntarily as the machine touched them. She thought maybe they were recording the process somehow, although no screen or other recording device was seen.

Then one of the men approached with a large needle about six or eight inches long. "What are you going to do with that?" she asked. "Don't worry it won't hurt. It's a simple pregnancy test and we're going to put it in your navel for a minute."

As the examiner thrust the long needle into her abdomen through her navel Betty began to feel great discomfort and eventually pain. Apparently whatever sedative the aliens had used, its effects were beginning to wear off. "It's hurting, it's hurting, take it out, take it out!" Quite alarmed, the leader rushed over and rubbed his hand across Betty's eyes. The pain immediately left. Somehow he had controlled her pain without injecting any foreign substance into her body. Apparently their abilities to control the thoughts of humans includes the control of pain. "Oh thank you, thank you for stopping," Betty sighed. "If we had known that it would cause you such pain we wouldn't have done the test," the kindly alien replied. Betty could feel the concern in his voice and once again began to trust the sensitive creature.

Physical Evidence – Almost

They decided to end the test at that point and Betty was allowed to dress. "Where's Barney?" she implored. "He'll be along soon. It's taking a little longer with him."

The alien who had been in charge of examining Betty left the room and she began to speak with the leader figure. "No one will ever believe me. This is totally unbelievable." The leader laughed, apparently beginning to warm up to Betty's simple sincerity. "What I need is some kind of proof," she said. "What kind of proof do you need? What would you like?" "Well," Betty said, "if you could give me something I could take back with me, then people would believe me."

"Look around and see if there's something you would like."

"How about a book?" Betty had spotted a large dictionary-sized book sitting on a nearby table.

"Yes, you may have it," said the leader. As Betty looked through the book, she saw that it contained strange symbols unlike anything she had ever seen before. The words were arranged in vertical columns.

Under deep hypnosis Betty began to describe what she saw in the strange book: "...it had sharp lines, and they were, some were very thin and some were medium and some were very heavy. It had some dots. It had straight lines and curved lines. And the leader laughed and asked me if I thought I could read it. And I told him no. I laughed too. I said no, but I wasn't taking it to read. But this was going to be my proof that this happened. That this – this was my proof. And so he said I could have the book if I wanted it. And I picked it up and I was delighted. I mean this was more than I had ever hoped for."

About that time several other aliens rushed into the room in an excited state and communicated with each other in their indiscernible tongue. It had something to do with Barney, she thought.

The examiner came over to Betty and started checking her mouth again, tugging at her teeth for some reason. "What are you doing?" she asked. The little man said that he was baffled. Barney's teeth came out but her's didn't. She then explained to them that Barney was wearing dentures. And she explained why some people needed them when they got older, and they conversed for awhile about what happened to people who got older.

He asked her several more questions that she was not able to answer with much detail. Questions about life on Earth and the concept of time.

"I am a very limited person, when trying to talk to you. But there are other people in this country who are not like me. They would be most happy to talk with him, and they could answer all his questions. Maybe if he came back, all his questions would have answers. But if I did, I wouldn't know where to meet him. And he laughed, and said, 'Don't worry, if we decided to come back, we will be able to find you all right. We always find those we want to.' "

Through the door she could see the others bringing Barney down the hallway, his eyes still tightly shut. As Betty and the leader fell in line in front of Barney and his escorts, several of the aliens began to converse with each other. The leader instructed Betty to wait for a minute while he determined the problem. After a brief discussion with the others the leader came back over to Betty and said he had to take the book back.

Angrily Betty responded, "You promised that I could have the book."

"I know it, but the others object."

"But this is my proof."

"That's the whole point," the leader said. "They don't want you to know what happened. They want you to forget all about it."

The aliens then escorted Betty out of the craft and to her car.

Barney's recollection was more limited than Betty's, and for good reason. Apparently the aliens could sense his tendency to panic and for his own protection had instructed him to keep his eyes closed. That explained his lack of any visual substantiation to support Betty's story.

Although he kept his eyes tightly closed, he could feel the aliens performing tests on him. They had instructed him to lie on a short table. It was obviously too small for Barney's large frame because his feet hung over the edge. The next thing he felt was a cold sensation in his groin area. He also felt like something was touching various parts of his body. Something pressed down his spine and stopped at the small of his back. Before he knew it they put his shoes back on having concluded the examination.

The alien leader, himself, had said they had run more tests on Barney, but Barney's testimony remained short. Perhaps it was because he didn't want to deal with the reality of the incident. He was, according to Dr. Simon, excessively sensitive. It was difficult to convince Barney that the event might have actually happened. He insisted it "was more likely just a dream. UFOs can't be real. They probably just saw the full moon that night." His persistent use of conventional explanations masked his deep fear that something bizarre may have taken place.

Safely Back Home

Barney was the first to be taken to the car and was left in the driver's seat. Their pet dog was still hiding under the front seat. Barney was soon joined by his wife who stood outside the car gazing up at the sky.

"Come on out and watch them leave," she said. Suddenly a large orange ball appeared on the horizon. Look there's the moon, Barney thought to himself. "Well, now do you believe in flying saucers?" Betty chided. "Oh, Betty, don't be ridiculous," Barney responded. The next thing they knew, they saw the highway 93 road marker and felt as if they had suddenly come to consciousness from a kind of hazy sleep.[12-7]

Two years later, reports from New Hampshire flooded into Air Force headquarters. Hundreds of witnesses reported seeing dancing lights and strange disc-like craft racing about and then suddenly disappearing. The book, *Incident at Exeter,* thrust the phenomenon, once again, into national prominence. The New England area, it appeared, was being invaded by strange craft from another world and the Air Force's only response was: "No comment."

* * * * *

Figure 12.1 Betty and Barney Hill encounter their hosts in the woods of New Hampshire in 1961, the earliest modern-day documented case of "alien abduction".

Figure 12.2 Position of the "whirling apparatus" that Betty Andreasson described.

Two Types of Aliens Encountered[*]

Figure 12.3 – *A through E*

HUMAN-LIKE ALIENS

A. *As illustrated for contactee Arthur Shuttlewood in 1978.*

B. *As illustrated by Dr. Wanda M. Lockwood*

SMALL ALIENS

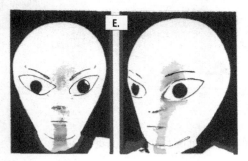

C. Above. *Drawing made after hypnosis of William Herrmann (1979) of one of his abductors. The incident occurred in 1978 near Charleston, South Carolina. Note similarity of head shape, eyes, mouth, and the differences in the shoulders to alien types on left.*

D. Top Left. *Rendering of Steven Kilburn's abductors from his hypnotic ally retrieved recollections.*

E. Bottom Left. *Reconstruction of the aliens who took Betty Andreasson on a glorious ride.*

Figure 12.3 – *F through J*   155

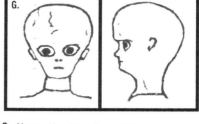

F. *Sketches of one of Travis Walton's "marshmallow skinned" abductors. Incident occurred near Heber, Arizona on November 5, 1975.*

G. Above. *Sketches of one of Sergeant Charles Moody's abductors. His incident occurred near Alamogordo, New Mexico, on August 13, 1975. Note the strong facial similarities, and the resemblances of both figures to the kilburn, Herrmann and Andreasson abductors.*

H. Far Left. *Artist's reconstruction of one of Steven Kilburn's abductors.*

I. Left. *Drawing by Betty Andreasson of one of her abductors. The incident occurred in January 1968, in South Ashburnham, Mass. Note the similarity of head shapes, neck and shoulders, and the differences in torso and limbs.*

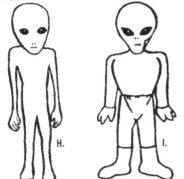

*NOTE: Several of the alien encounters illustrated here are not mentioned in this book and are shown simply as a point of interest. The truthfulness of their claims has not been authenticated by the author of Aliens & In-laws.

J. *Travis Walton was abducted near Heber, Arizona in 1978. After the small spacecraft he had been taken in had apparently landed inside a large mother ship, he frightened-off the small alien creatures seen in the rendering above. He also encountered several human-like aliens (both men and women) who wore crystal-clear helmets. Apparently both type of aliens were working as a team.*

156

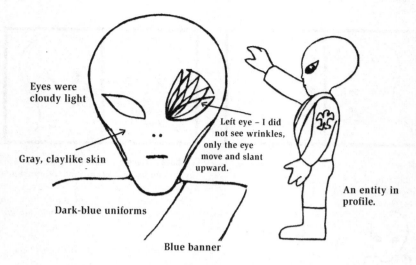

Eyes were
cloudy light

Gray, claylike skin

Dark-blue uniforms

Left eye – I did
not see wrinkles,
only the eye
move and slant
upward.

An entity in
profile.

Blue banner

Figure 12.4 – Above. The leader Quazgaa as he appeared to
Betty Andreasson in the kitchen of her home.

Figure 12.5 – Betty Andreasson's rendition of how the entities
appeared through the closed kitchen door: they "moved in a jerky
motion, leaving a vapory image behind."

Saucer's Drive Mechanism

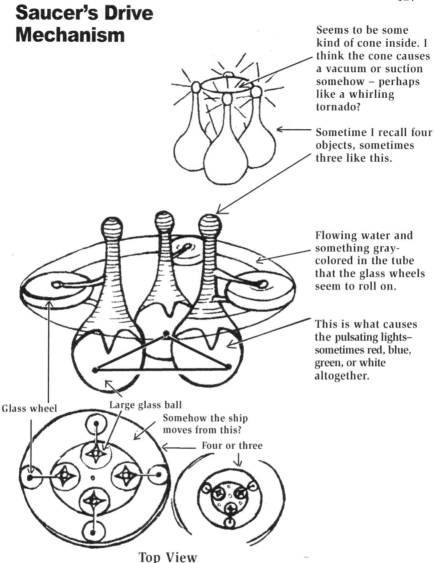

Seems to be some kind of cone inside. I think the cone causes a vacuum or suction somehow – perhaps like a whirling tornado?

Sometime I recall four objects, sometimes three like this.

Flowing water and something gray-colored in the tube that the glass wheels seem to roll on.

This is what causes the pulsating lights– sometimes red, blue, green, or white altogether.

Glass wheel

Large glass ball

Somehow the ship moves from this?

Four or three

Top View

Figure 12.6 – Betty Andreasson sketched what she thought to be the flight mechanism of an alien craft that changed from "red to blue, green or white altogether." The view from directly beneath the craft reveals what would accurately be described as a "wheel within a wheel."

Hyperspace
flight preparation

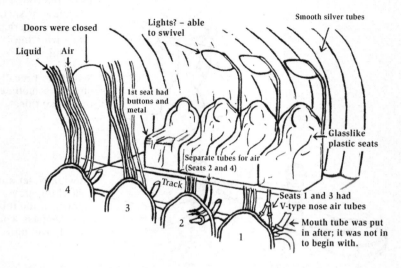

Figure 12.7 – Betty Andreasson sketched the room where her abductors prepared her for flight. Note similarities to other witnesses' drawing below.

Figure 12.8 – Although not covered in this book, the incident described by Sara Shaw and Jan Whitley bore very many similarites to Betty Andreasson's journey.

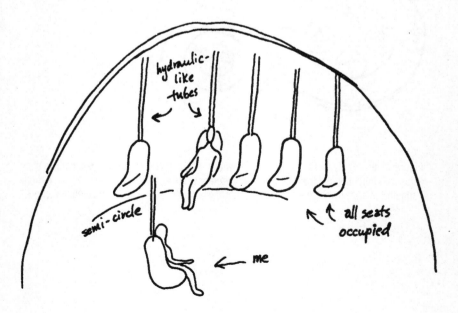

Betty Andreasson's Strange "Journey"

13

Oddly enough, the single most significant UFO abduction case in history occurred the same year that I saw my UFO.

The year was 1967, and Betty Andreasson was just getting settled in her new home in South Ashburnham, a small town in northern Massachusetts, when bad news came. Her husband James had been in a severe auto accident and had barely escaped death. James would be in traction and would require hospitalization for several weeks. They decided to ask Betty's aging parents to stay with her and help with the duties of caring for seven children.

Waino and Eva Aho, Betty's Finish parents, gladly responded to the family crisis and had settled in with their daughter and grandchildren. They had always been a close family perhaps because of Betty's deep religious conviction. As a member of the Pentecostal Church, Betty stressed faith in a Supreme Being and attempted to instill the same moral Christian values in her children. Betty's faith was to play a significant part in what was about to happen.

Dinner was just over and Betty was cleaning up afterwards standing at the kitchen sink. The children were settled in, watching an evening children's show on TV with their adoring grandparents. Three-year-old Cindy, the youngest, was happily curled up on Grandma's lap.

Suddenly the power went off. Startled, the children huddled together in the living room. Outside the kitchen window Betty could see a bright pulsating glow coming from the winter mist in her backyard. "What is that?"she thought to herself. "Shhhh! Be quiet!" Betty ordered to the children. Perhaps whatever it was would go away if they were very quiet. Her father, Waino, moved to the kitchen to see what was causing the eerie flashing light that began reflecting through the kitchen window. In a state of disbelief Waino watched as several little men bounded toward the house "...just like grasshoppers. They were just like Halloween freaks. I thought they had put on a funny kind of headdress imitating a moon man."

It was a snowy, foggy winter night and heavy mist engulfed the back yard. Suddenly the strange little creatures spotted Waino gazing at them through the window. "When they saw me looking at them they stopped... the one in front looked at me and I felt kind of queer. That's all I knew.."

Waino's memory went blank at this point. As with the Hill's, eye contact was established just prior to his memory lapse.

Betty, too, remembered only parts of what was to occur next. She remembered a small blue book in her possession that she studied for the next several days, telling her oldest daughter, Becky, then eleven, that she was instructed to read the book but not show it to anyone. "Promise me you won't tell anyone about it," she told her young daughter. Then one day the small book with its thin luminous pages disappeared from its hiding place in Betty's closet.

Betty would periodically remember small bits and pieces of something else. Something else had happened but she just couldn't remember what.

These recurrent flash-backs over the next several years prompted Betty to respond to an article published in the local paper in August of 1975. It was an article by Dr. J. Allen Hynek of the Center for UFO Studies in Chicago. The story solicited many new reports by UFO witnesses for scientific study.

Hynek sent a copy of Betty's letter to a group called the Mutual UFO Network, or MUFON, who was compiling a computerized listing of all close encounters of the third kind (any account which included alien occupants at fairly close range: 500 feet or less).

It was Jules Vaillancourt who first contacted Betty Andreasson about her encounter. He was the MUFON field investigator for Massachusetts and was therefore asked to check out her story for the organization.

Almost immediately Vaillancourt recognized the significance of her story and was convinced of the various witnesses' sincerity, including Betty's father Waino and daughter Becky.

Learning of the great success achieved through hypnosis in the Hill's case, MUFON representatives decided to seek the assistance of a qualified hypnotherapist for Betty and her daughter Becky. There were many unanswered questions including a period of time that was unaccounted for, much like the Hills had experienced.

One of MUFON's field investigators, Merlyn Sheehan, had undergone hypnosis to relieve the nauseating side effects of her chemotherapy treatment. A deep trusting relationship in the ability of the respected doctor ensued. It was through this doctor/patient relationship that Harold J. Edelstein became involved with his first UFO case.

Doctor Edelstein, a well-recognized expert in the practice of hypnosis, was the director of the New England Institute of Hypnosis at the time. He was also used extensively by the law enforcement community and served on the faculties of three colleges. Additionally, his reputation as a likeable, effective professional lead to many referrals from area hospitals in the treatment of their medical patients.

The Session Begins

During initial testing, Dr. Edelstein concluded that both Betty and Becky had truly undergone some kind of traumatic experience.

Application of a lie-detector test indicated that the witnesses were telling the truth and so the sessions began.

Both Betty and Becky proved to be good subjects and through the use of "key words" and "slight pressure" (common techniques in hypnotherapy) Dr. Edelstein was able to induce deep hypnotic states with great ease during the ensuing regressive hypnotic sessions.

Accompanied by a team of MUFON investigators, Dr. Edelstein would systematically interview Betty and Becky over the next several months. Here's the incredible story that surfaced from the numerous sessions.

Betty Andreasson's Story

Waino and Betty stood in the kitchen watching in astonishment as four or five small creatures approached in single file. The pulsating glow outlined the silhouetted forms as they leaped closer.

Betty looked at her father, he seemed to be frozen in his place. As she glanced back in the living room she saw that her family, too, seemed inanimate. What was happening?

Without warning, one of the creatures entered through the kitchen door. Three others followed close behind. "How did they do that?" Betty thought to herself. It appeared as if the small creatures has passed right through the door! They just floated through, one after the other (see *Figure 12.5*).

Betty's religious teaching came to the forefront during this moment of crisis. What should she do? Her faith in a protective God kept her from totally panicking like so many of us would have.

"I'm thinking they must be angels, because Jesus was able to walk through doors and walls and walk on water. Must be angels...And scriptures keep coming into my mind where it says, Entertain the stranger, for it may be angels unaware."

As she gazed at them she was immediately overcome with feelings of trust and friendliness. She no longer feared the frightening little creatures with oversized heads. They had the appearance of a mongoloid with their unusually large craniums. The eyes, too, were extraordinarily large, dominating the other facial features. The mouth was just a small slit and the nose and ears were represented only by small depressions or holes. Devoid of any hair, the soft-skinned aliens appeared to be light gray. Their hands had three digits and were covered with gloves.

A small banner was strung over one shoulder that extended to the waist, and on the left sleeve was an emblem of an eagle. The emblem contrasted with the shiny dark blue, full-length uniform. On their feet they wore high-top boots without any heels.

The leader of the group appeared slightly larger than the others. His name was "Quazgaa," he said. Although the words were not formed by his mouth or audibly spoken, Betty could hear the words in her head.

Wanting to extend a friendly gesture to the aliens, Betty inquired, "Do you want something to eat?" They seemed to nod their heads in approval.

Betty moved to the refrigerator and took out some meat and busied herself with the task of cooking the token meal.

"We cannot eat food unless it is tried by fire," she heard in her head. "OK, I can burn it for you," she thought. When the meat began to scorch, the resultant smoke seemed to take the creatures by surprise. As they stepped back from the stove, Betty got another mental impression.

"But that's not our kind of food. Our food is tried by fire, knowledge tried by fire. Do you have any food like that?"

"Yes, I think I have some like that...It's in there." *I'll go and get the Bible*, she thought to herself. As Betty entered the living room she once again saw that the whole family was motionless, as if frozen in time.

Betty got the small book off the table and handed it to the leader. In return, Quazgaa gave her a small, thin blue book.

What happened next defied all logic. The investigative team knew Betty had nothing to gain by lying about the event. She was only seeking relief from personal anxiety and the persistent nightmares. After all, she had passed a lie detector test administered by a certified stress analyst. *Yet, surely she must be mistaken*, they thought to themselves. This was to be only part of a mysterious venture that was to leave all those present, changed forever.

Quazgaa held the small Bible in one hand and waved his other hand over it. As he lifted his hand, there appeared several copies of the book, each a little thicker than the original.

This was reminiscent of the event in Bible history where Jesus reproduced enough loaves and fishes (from the original seven loaves and a few small fish) to feed a crowd of well over four thousand people. In fact there were seven baskets left over after all the people had feasted.

Quazgaa handed each of the aliens a copy which they quickly read by flipping through its pages in rapid succession. Betty noticed that the pages were a luminous white. So were the pages of the thin blue book which she began to study.

At this point, eleven-year-old Becky regained consciousness, as it was later revealed by hypnotizing her. "It's...it looks like a clay man...talking to my mom. Some kind of man-creature. And behind him, right behind him toward the right, there's one, a little one – and there's two after him that are just exactly like triplets."

Becky's first reaction was fear because of the "scary" little men, even though she sensed that they were very kind and friendly. Noticing that Becky was conscious, Quazgaa looked into her eyes and Becky lost all consciousness instantly.

The next series of events are reminiscent of the Betty and Barney Hill examination with one exception. They asked Betty Andreasson if she was willing to come with them.

"Will you help us?"

"If you are of God. If you are here to help and are of God. I would follow, but do not deceive me."

The entities asked again, "Will you follow us?"

"Oh, Lord show me what I'm supposed to do," Betty prayed.

"We will not harm you. Will you follow us?"

The alien's persistence finally won out. "All right," Betty said quietly.

She was directed to stand behind Quazgaa. As she did they were all suddenly moved through the door and floated to an awaiting spacecraft.

The huge object was partially obscured by a heavy fog that engulfed the entire back yard of Betty's house. It was sitting on a slight slope and what must have been landing gear supported its weight. The rear landing gear were retracted somewhat to compensate for the slope and kept the shiny "gold-silver" craft level (see *Figure 12.2*).

As they approached the huge glowing disc, Betty was again overcome with fear.

"...you can trust me. Look over the ship." Quazgaa in an apparent effort to win her confidence then began to show her the ship's power source.

Instantly the bottom of the ship became transparent, as if a shield were lifted, and Betty could see several strange objects on its underside.

Later Betty was able to draw what she saw. Three or four bowling pin-like objects arranged in a circle were the main thing she recalled. They were capable of rotating at high speeds and create what she described was a tornado-like vacuum or suction. The bottoms of these objects appeared as glass balls and these, apparently, were the objects that created pulsating light. "Sometimes red, blue, green or white altogether." (see *Fgure 12.6*)

Quazgaa raised his hand and a door appeared on the side of the craft. They were soon all whisked inside.

The next series of events, which included a thorough examination, were described in great detail by Betty, but for lack of space, I will summarize.

Prior to testing, she was exposed to a powerful light with intermingling streaks of bright lightning-like areas. She was told that it was a cleansing device and would not cause any discomfort.

As with the Hills, Betty was subjected to a rigorous physical examination. The aliens were able to control her extremities and move her about the craft into several different rooms for the various tests.

As with Betty Hill, she also was subjected to the painful needle-in-the-navel examination. This particular test seemed to cause the aliens some concern perhaps because of a hysterectomy, Betty surmised, which she had undergone a few years earlier.

The aliens also pushed a large needle up Betty's nose into her head. As she began to feel pain, the aliens would simply touch her forehead and the pain would subside. Remembering the ordeal caused Betty a great deal of stress and they decided to end the sessions for a few days.

The Mystery Deepens

With each successive event, the mystery deepened. During the routine Saturday afternoon hypnosis sessions, attended by up to eleven specialists connected with the MUFON investigation, the witnesses were continually astounded by the unfolding story.

Betty was allowed to recall the events exposed through her hypnotic sessions and they all openly discussed their meaning. It was obvious to all that Betty was merely a cooperative and sincere subject. She was as mystified by the account as any and her main concern was to find out exactly what had happened to her on that fateful night in 1967.

Under regressive hypnosis a subject will pick up at exactly the same point where they left off during the preceding session. On June 18, 1977, once again Betty was induced into her trance-like state by Doctor Edelstein as the others watched intently.

Betty began where she had left off the week prior. "He's taking that thing out now (the long needle that had been inserted into her left nostril). Oh! It feels funny. (sigh) They took it out, and it looks like, there is some kind of a ball on the end of it – something on the end of it. A little thing, whatever it was, on the end of the needle. It's kind of hard to see what it is (sigh)."

It was unclear whether or not the small ball with tiny prickly protrusions had been there when the needle was inserted. Some have speculated that perhaps the aliens were retrieving some kind of device that they had inserted into Betty's head during an earlier abduction. This, of course, is pure speculation, for it may have been present when the needle was first inserted and Betty just hadn't noticed it. It may also have been the residue of blood or tissue from the test the aliens had just administered.

As Betty relived the event under hypnosis, they began pushing another needle deep inside her abdominal cavity through her naval. She screamed out in agonizing pain, startling everyone present at the session. It was almost too much for the witnesses to bear. They were totally engrossed in the event and felt deep empathy for this poor, simple woman, recognizing the terror and pain she was experiencing.

"I don't want any more tests! Get that thing out of me!" Betty emphatically ordered.

Quazgaa reached out and gently touched her forehead again, and just as before, the pain subsided. After a few more simple tests she was allowed to put on her own clothes.

Next, the aliens took her down a long corridor to another room. Inside were eight strange chair-like devices arranged in two rows of four with each row facing one another (see *Figures 12.7 & 12.8*).

Betty was instructed to sit in one of the chairs and a hard, clear plastic covering was pulled down over her. A sensation of cold air rushed into the enclosed chamber of the seat.

"It feels very cold...It feels like...feels like moisture is even being drawn from me...And it's cold. The moisture is coming right out of me."

The aliens had complete control of Betty and she was unable to move. Whatever it was they used to hold her in place caused an uncomfortable prickling, tingling sensation. Betty repeatedly complained of the uncomfortable heavy feeling in her arms, hands, legs and feet whenever this force was applied

After what seemed like a long time, the covering was lifted and Betty was levitated in the "weightless" chamber into another chair that was located in the opposite row of seats.

Again, a covering was lowered and locked in place over Betty's body. She was instructed to close her eyes and keep them shut tightly. Next, tubes were inserted through the plastic or glass covering and fitted into her nostrils. Another larger one was inserted into her mouth and then the seat's chamber was filled with liquid. Soothing vibrations began to pulse rhythmically through the liquid which immediately relaxed Betty and put her into a state of peaceful bliss.

It was while immersed in this soothing liquid, breathing through her nostrils and being fed pleasant, sweet-tasting syrup through the mouthpiece, that Betty had apparently been taken on a long journey to a distant destination.

The chair-like chamber had apparently protected her from the forces of rapid flight to another galaxy. Perhaps she had even experienced suspended animation while in transition.

After some time she heard a voice telepathically that awakened her from her blissful sleep in the tank-like apparatus. The chamber was so pleasant that she was hesitant to wake up.

As the liquid slowly began to drain from the chamber Betty again felt the heaviness in her arms and legs. When she opened her eyes she was surprised to see the aliens standing in front of her with black hoods over their heads.

Apparently this provided a shield from the atmosphere they were about to encounter.

Betty was then levitated out of the chair, her extremities held firmly in place by some unseen force, and floated to a doorway in the craft while still dripping wet with the liquid that had immersed her during flight. The door swooshed open and they all floated in single file down a long dark corridor, the aliens still wearing their black hoods.

The tunnel was dark like a coal tunnel and they passed other tunnels that intersected the main corridor. The inside surface was lit only by the glowing uniforms of the aliens. Straight ahead appeared a mirror-like obstruction in the tunnel, but Betty and the aliens all passed through it like it wasn't there. Suddenly, they burst into a new, totally red atmosphere.

The shimmering red environment had some large buildings with window-like openings in them. As Betty glanced down she realized that a black track had been carrying them through the darkened tunnel from the ship. The narrow strip of black that passed between the buildings was somehow mysteriously suspended in mid-air.

As they glided along the track they came upon a mass of small red monkey-like creatures with large protruding eyes. The ugly creatures darted back and forth among the red buildings. Their sight frightened Betty but soon they passed by them and through the red atmosphere into a green atmosphere.

It's interesting to note here that Dr. Edelstein later referred to these strange frightening creatures as lemurs. The lemur is a nocturnal mammal related to the monkey family with large eyes, a pointed muzzle, and soft woolly fur. These nighttime creatures are found mainly in Madagascar. As I looked the word up in the dictionary I happened to see the word "lemures." According to Roman mythology, lemures (lem' yoo-reez) refers to the night-walking spirits of the dead. Are the similarities between the creatures Betty saw in this hell-like atmosphere and the mythological definition pure coincidence? One has to wonder.

The aliens removed their hoods once they entered the green atmosphere. The escalator-like track on which they were riding (or perhaps gliding above) took them by a beautiful large green lake or ocean. The beauty of the place overwhelmed Betty. It reminded her of some legendary underground kingdom with its vast array of beautiful strange plants and its misty horizon. Off in the distance she could see what looked like a gigantic city shrouded in mist. What a magnificent sight!

As they continued along the track for what may have been hundreds of miles (Betty was unclear of the distances traveled), they passed by several indescribable buildings and other odd structures. The track at this point began to criss-cross several others both above and below their course. At one point they stopped for something to pass on an intersecting track and then proceeded. The track took them high above several large mysterious pyramid-shaped objects and past other objects that Betty was unable to describe with the human vocabulary. On past a rainbow of radiant crystal-like structures with a magnificently bright light beyond. Like a huge inviting glow in the distance, Betty was stricken with the light's beauty and drawn to it like a moth to a flame.

Without warning, the track stopped and the two aliens got off. Betty was frozen to the track as it proceeded toward a giant object that stood in front of the radiating light.

As she neared the object she could see that it was a huge bird towering over the entire city. "It looks like an eagle to me. And it's living! It has a white head and there is light in back of it – real white light...It's beautiful, bright light."

Her attention was drawn again to the large bird. "It was too big to be real, and yet it looked as if it were alive."

Like a towering beast from a Japanese sci-fi film, the huge bird glistened and sparkled with a magnificent light.

As Betty got closer to the huge bird the heat became unbearable. Golden specs began to fly out from it. As the eagle got brighter, the heat became more unbearable until Betty closed her eyes and cried out in agony.

Again the investigative team from MUFON sat anxiously on the edge of their chairs, totally amazed by what she was re-living.

"Oh, Lord Jesus, I'm hot. Help me."

"Oh-h-h-h-h (heavy breathing) Oh-h-h-h-h. I'm so hot! Oh,oh,oh,oh,oh-h-h-h-h! Take me out of it! Take me out of it! Take me out of it! Oh, Oh, Oh! (quick breaths) Ah,ah,ah...I can't feel my hands! Oh, wow, wow, wow! Oh, my hands and my legs. My feet. Oh, oh. Oh, it feels like my hands are just vibrating so much and my feet are just vibrating like – oh, oh."

The pain and torment expressed by Betty was almost too much for the interviewers to take. They felt an overpowering sympathy for her as she relived her ordeal. Hypnotic trances can induce total recall right down to actually experiencing an unpleasant sensation. And Betty was experiencing a terrifying ordeal. "This was no act," all twelve experts agreed as they sat in horror watching the poor woman.

Finally the pain began to subside and every one in the room felt a tremendous relief.

Betty recalled opening her eyes and noticing that the bird was gone. All that remained was a small fire. The fire soon dwindled down to glowing coals.

As the fire subsided the agonizing heat was replaced with cold. Betty began to shiver.

As she stared at the glowing coal the feeling began to return to her feet and hands. The glowing coals were now turning gray and started to take on the shape of a large gray worm.

"Now, looks like a worm, a big fat worm. It just looks like a big fat worm...just lying there."

Suddenly a loud booming voice filled the empty air. It sounded like many voices blended into one and it was overpowering.

"BETTY," the omnipotent voice echoed out "YOU HAVE HEARD. DO YOU UNDERSTAND?" (pause) The voice bellowed out again, "BETTY... DO YOU UNDERSTAND?"

"No...I don't understand...what this is all about...why I'm even here..."

"I HAVE CHOSEN YOU."

"For what have you chosen me?"

"I HAVE CHOSEN YOU TO SHOW THE WORLD." The voice sounded like many, yet, somehow it seemed like one personality.

"Are you God? Are you the Lord God?"

"I SHALL SHOW YOU AS YOUR TIME GOES BY."

A Religious Connection?

The team of interviewers were astonished at what was transpiring. "...a religious connotation caused great consternation among us. It seemed somehow completely out of place," wrote Raymond Fowler in his book *The Andreasson Affair.* And yet they knew that under deep hypnosis a subject will never purposely lie. What was being described was definitely believed by Betty.

"And we believed her, too. Her simple honest approach was totally convincing," related Fowler.

"Are you my Jesus?" Betty continued.

"I would recognize my Lord Jesus."

"Oh, it says - 'I love you. God is love, and I love you...' " that simple transmission appeared to overcome Betty's reservations. Their conversation continued:

"Why was I brought here?"

"BECAUSE I HAVE CHOSEN YOU."

"Why won't you tell me why and what for?"

"THE TIME IS NOT YET. IT SHALL COME. THAT WHICH YOU HAVE FAITH IN, THAT WHICH YOU TRUST."

Betty again began to proclaim her religious affirmations out loud: "It is true," she said ecstatically, "I have faith in God, and I have faith in Jesus Christ. Praise God! Praise God! Praise God! There is nothing that can harm me. There is nothing that can make me fear. I have faith in Jesus Christ!"

"WE KNOW CHILD...WE KNOW THAT YOU DO. THAT IS WHY YOU HAVE BEEN CHOSEN. I AM SENDING YOU BACK NOW. FEAR NOT...BE OF COMFORT. YOUR OWN FEAR MAKES YOU FEEL THESE THINGS. I WOULD NEVER HARM YOU. IT IS YOUR FEAR THAT YOU DRAW TO YOUR BODY, THAT CAUSES YOU TO FEEL THESE THINGS. I CAN RELEASE YOU, BUT YOU MUST RELEASE YOURSELF OF THAT FEAR THROUGH MY SON."

Betty's reaction to the voice and her accompanying joy was something that the team of investigators would never forget. Her face beamed with delight and she cried streams of tears with a joy that was indescribable.

"Oh, praise God... praise God...praise God! (crying) Thank you Lord! – (crying, sobbing) I know, I know I am not worthy. Thank you for your Son. – (Uncontrollable sobbing) Thank you for your Son."

The experience was totally foreign and out of place to the research team. "The very concepts of UFOs and extraterrestrial life had no place within the confines of fundamentalist Christianity," wrote Raymond Fowler. And what about the strange incident with the large bird. They knew of the legend of the Phoenix Bird, which was what Betty had unwittingly described. But what did that have to do with fundamentalist Christianity?

Later investigation revealed some startling facts. It was learned that the Phoenix Bird played a key role in early Christian art and literature. The death and subsequent resurrection of the bird were used as symbols of Christ's resurrection and immortality.

After the bizarre encounter with the large bird Betty was taken back to the spacecraft via the same route she had arrived.

This time she was placed in a chair that had buttons or controls on the arms and metal bands inlaid in the seat and arms. As Betty was levitated into a sitting position in the chair, one of the aliens came forward and pressed a button on the chair. Betty was suddenly convulsed from two electric shocks that surged through her body. The shock had apparently caused her eyes to close because one of the aliens came and opened her right eye, most likely to check her conscious state.

Again, she was levitated into the immersion chair and prepared as before for the journey home.

After the apparent Journey ended, Betty was awakened by a tapping on the glass cover.

"They're tapping on that glass thing for some reason. And they are saying, 'Betty, are you comfortable?' Yes, I like it in here. They said they are going to let me stay a few more moments ...oh feels good."

After the liquid had drained out of the chair, Betty was placed in yet another chair where warm soothing air blew over her entire body.

As they left the room where the two rows of seats were positioned, one of the aliens carried two white glowing spheres, one in each hand. Next, they took her into another room and told her to wait for Quazgaa because he wanted to speak with her.

Quazgaa entered the room wearing a shiny luminous silver suit, different from the dark blue uniform he wore when he first appeared in Betty's kitchen. It was the same type the aliens had worn when they had taken her to see the huge bird.

At this point the leader, Quazgaa, looked into her eyes and imparted some secret knowledge. Somehow Betty knew that this knowledge had to do with scientific formulas and some sort of a master plan for the human race. She knew the general context of the information, however, she was unable to recall any of the specifics of Quazgaa's message. Much of the information must still be lying dormant in Betty Andreasson's mind, for even hypnosis could not extract the secret information.

A Message To Mankind

Quazgaa gave Betty some advice, "He says my race won't believe me until much time has passed – our time...They love the human race. They have come to help the human race. And, *'unless man will accept, he will not be saved, he will not live... All things have been planned. LOVE IS THE GREATEST OF ALL . They do not want to hurt anybody – but because of great love,'* they said. *'...because of great love, they cannot let man continue in the footsteps that he is going...It is better to lose some than to lose all...'* They have technology that man could use *'...It is through the spirit, but man will not search out that portion.'* "

An excerpt from The Andreasson Affair vividly records Betty's retelling of her conversation with Quazgaa:

"*'Man must understand many of the natural things on earth...If man will just study nature itself, he will find many of the answers that he seeks...Within fire are many answers, within ashes – within the highest of the high and the lowest of the low are many answers...Man will find them through the spirit. Man in not made of just flesh and blood. It would be easy to hand them to us, but that would show that we are not worthy to receive those...The knowledge is sought out through the spirit, and those that are worthy are given...Those that are pure of heart, that seek with earnestness will be given... Energy is 'round about man that he does not know of. It is the simplest form of energy. It is within the atmosphere – this atmosphere...It has all been provided for him... Many riddles will be given...Those that are wise will understand...Those that seek will find...They must remain hidden in this way because of the corruption - the corruption that is upon the earth...If they are revealed outright, man would use it.'* (sigh) He keeps telling me of different things, of what is going to take place, *'Man is going to fear because of it...Many are going to be astonished...Yet many are not going to be afraid because they have overcome fear...'* He says that he has had others here *'...Many others have locked within their minds, secrets...'* He is locking within my mind certain secrets (sigh)...They will be revealed when the time is right...Again, he's putting both hands up on my shoulders. And he's saying, *'Go, child, now, and rest.'* "*

After Quazgaa's long discourse had ended, Betty was taken by the two smaller aliens to the exit door of the spaceship. Out they floated, through the back yard of Betty's home which was still enshrouded in fog. Back toward the house in single file they went, through the porch door and into the kitchen. There, Waino stood in frozen silence, just as he'd been left.

The two aliens each carried a small white glowing globe. One was about 4 or 5 inches in diameter and the other about twice as large. The aliens apparently used these devices to control the movement of the unwitting subjects. As one alien neared Waino he held out the white ball and he began to move. Slowly, still in a trancelike state, Waino walked into the living room where the others were. One by one the children stood and marched to their rooms in single file. Next the aliens directed their attention to Betty's parents. They walked slowly to their rooms and went to bed as if instructed by some unseen force.

Another alien suddenly appeared in front of Betty. He said his name was 'Joohop.'

"What is this all about, Joohop?"

"You will see as time goes by."

Betty could hear a voice in her mind *'Betty you will have to forget this – you and your family – for the time being. There are many other things that we have told you. They will come out at the appointed time.'*

The next morning Betty awoke with a feeling of extreme happiness. The family was carrying on as if nothing had happened. Betty knew better. She had a small blue book with luminous pages to prove it. Over the next few days she would take the book out of its hiding place and study its strange pages for hours – not really knowing what she was reading. On the tenth day it disappeared. That was basically all Betty could remember until the hypnotic sessions helped her to remember the details of her ordeal.

The temptation to extract the 'secret' information was too great for the MUFON investigators. With Betty's permission Dr. Edelstein continued the sessions in hopes of learning just what was locked in Betty's mind.

Betty's main concern was the effect it might have on her religious beliefs. She was reluctant to publish the details of her encounter for fear of what the religious community would think of her. The tale was just too bizarre for anyone to believe, even though the experience actually affirmed the most significant doctrines of fundamentalist Christianity.

The Session Continues

It was several weeks later when the sessions continued on July 16, 1977. What was about to happen caught everyone by surprise, even the highly trained investigators. As Dr. Edelstein probed Betty's mind for answers, the question was asked: "Did these aliens give you any predictions for the future?"

"Yes," Betty replied.

"Can you reveal these now?"

Betty's face suddenly contorted as she struggled with some unseen force in her mind.

All those present knew that a subject under deep regressive hypnosis is incapable of deliberately lying. Whatever is said, is said with complete candor. Betty, of all people, had proven her sincerity and honesty in dealing with the mystery. Yet, somehow, what was occurring went beyond all reasonableness.

"They – have things – in control...I don't like them controlling my words!"

Betty was apparently experiencing the alien mind control as she lay on the doctor's table!

One of the investigators quickly asked, "What does it feel like, Betty?"

She described the same heavy, tingling feeling she had experienced while being physically controlled by the aliens during her abduction. Her arms and legs were totally immobilized as she struggled against their control. Suddenly she spoke out in a strange tone of voice:

> *"Oh-tookurah bohututah mawhulah duh duwa ma her duh okaht turaht* (sighs) *nuwrlahah-tutrah aw-hoehoe marikoto tutrah etrah meekohtutrah etro indra ukreeahlah* (sigh)."

The strange message had even surprised Betty. "I don't know what it is. They're just saying it to me. I don't know what they are saying."

As Betty was questioned while under hypnotic trance there were several more outbursts of this strange tongue, followed by Betty's conscious struggle to decipher the mysterious message. It was as if the aliens were trying to give the investigators a message directly. She continued:

> *" 'Man seeks to destroy himself. Greed, greed, greed, greed. And because of greed, it draws all foul things. Everything has been provided for man. Simple things. He could be advanced so far, but greed gets in his way. Freely it will be given to those that have loved.' "*

While the investigators stopped to take out the recorded cassette tape and put in a fresh one, Betty was taken out of her hypnotic state. After the brief interruption the hypnotic session continued.

There was one area of inquiry that had been on several of the investigators' minds, as the sessions revealed an apparent direct link to alien entities. During the mysterious blackouts of New York, and several other regions of our nation, in 1965, several witnesses had reported seeing strange glowing spheres in the sky. There was never any real explanation for the power outages by the power companies. The power came back on as mysteriously as it had gone off, without any subsequent mechanical failure. Since the power generating equipment had simply returned to normal, many serious UFO investigators have speculated that the phenomenon may have been caused by the UFOs, but for unknown reasons. If they had direct contact with an alien, as Betty was claiming, then this was a possible opportunity to find out if her abductors had anything to do with the blackouts.

Betty continued:
"They have powers. They can control the wind, and water and even lightning."

Investigator: "Did they tell you what the purpose of the blackout was?"

Betty: *"It was to reveal to man his true nature."*
"What is man's true nature?" the investigator asked.

Betty: *"Man seeks to destroy himself. Greed, greed, greed..."*

Again Betty began to speak in the strange indiscernible language. It was as though someone else were speaking through her:

Betty: *Even-now-you-cannot-see. Even-now-we-speak.*

Investigator: We are trying to see. Do you have a message for us?

Betty: *You-try-to-seek-in-wrong directions.* (The words were hesitant and strained as if Betty was resisting the entity taking control of her voice.) *Simplicity-'round about you.-Air-you breathe-water you drink- (sigh) -fire-that-warms-earth-that-heals. -Simplicity-ashes-things-that-are-necessary-taken-for-granted.-Powers-within them-overlooked.-Why-think-you-are-able-to live? Simplicity.*

Investigator: Betty, are you telling us this? Are you interpreting this for us?

Betty: No, I'm not telling you those things.

Investigator: How do your arms and legs feel right now?

Betty: Terrible...That feeling in my hands – to hold my hands down.

Investigator: Do you feel that the beings are using you?

Betty: Yes, they are. (softly) And I don't know how they're doing it.

Investigator: What do they want us, as seekers of the truth, to understand right now?

Betty: *The truth-freedom-love-to understand man's hatred-to deal with it righteously.*

Investigator: Are they trying to protect man from himself? Is that true?

Betty: *No, and yes. No, because-because other worlds are involved in man's world. Man-is very-arrogant-and greedy-and he thinks-that all worlds- revolve around-him.*

Investigator: But not all men think this way.

Betty: *Only-because-Love is present.*

Investigator: Will the blue book help us to understand the message?

Betty: *You-would-be-in-just-as-much-darkness-about the-blue-book.-First-seek-out-the-simple forms-of your-selves.-Man is-arrogant-because-his-image makes-up-everything-that-is-condensed-and-pride-dwells-there-because-of-the-image-that-man-has-been-given.* (sigh)

Investigator: Do the beings want us to understand? Does Quazgaa want us to understand?

Betty: *Quazgaa-is-just-an-official officer-under-the-clan-like-many-others.*

Investigator: But my question is, do they want us to understand and gain knowledge?

Betty: Yes.

Investigator: Betty, where are they from?

Betty: They said, *'you will know the truth, and you will know once you find the truth.'*

Investigator: Betty, what is the truth?

Betty: I've told you the truth before. *'Jesus Christ is the truth. He is the answer for mankind. He's the only answer.'*

AUTHOR'S NOTE: At this point the investigators thought that Betty was answering from her religious convictions and not allowing the alien to answer through her. I wouldn't be so sure of that... it seems to me that the investigators weren't really listening to her message...they simply chose to overlook any religious overtones and missed the incredible implication that Christianity might be more than a man-made religion. Obviously reacting from their own personal "scientific" convictions, the questioning continued:

Investigator: I have a question for the beings. I would like to know if they are willing to help us to find knowledge. Can we find out if they are willing to help us?

Betty: *You-would-not-have-gotten-this far-nor-gained-this-much-information-had-we-not-desired-to-help-you.*

Investigator: Then I would like to have some indication of their help for us to proceed any further. What must we do for the next step? How do we proceed further?

Betty: *Search.*

Investigator: In what direction?

Betty: *That-which has been given to you-seek-search. We-shall-help-reveal. Certain-pieces-of-the-puzzle-will-be-fitted. -Try-to-understand-yourselves. -Seek-spiritually.-Seek.-Doors-have-been-left-open-to-you. -The-Great Door-shall guide.*

Investigator: What is the great door?

Betty: It is the entrance into the other world. The world where light is.

Investigator: Is that available to us as well as to you, Betty?

Betty: No, not yet.

Investigator: Is it available to you?

Betty: Yes.

Investigator: Do you understand what is on the other side of the great door?

Betty: Yes, I understand and believe in it.

Investigator: Can you help us to understand?

Betty: If you will accept it.

Investigator: Will they permit you to guide us?

Betty: No, they want to guide.

Again the pressure on Betty's limbs causes her great discomfort. After a few more irrelevant questions and answers, the interview continues:

Betty: The future and the past are the same as today to them.

Investigator: Does time exist?

Betty: Time to them is not like our time, but they know about our time.

Investigator: They recognize time as our dimension, but they have something else, through time?

Betty: Yes, they can reverse time.

Investigator: They can reverse our time?

Betty: Uh-huh.

Investigator: Are the beings able to come here again?

Betty: They travel freely. They travel freely throughout our whole earth.

Investigator: Can they travel inside the earth?

Betty: Yes, their density is much different, although they have metals that they cannot penetrate. They have to have those metals.

Investigator: Are those metals in the earth?

Betty: (softly) Some of them.

Investigator: Is that one reason they're here?

Betty: Mmmm, no. But some of the metals in the earth are enough to carry man to where they are. Then, when they get to their certain station, they are able to subtract ores from that planet for the use of going on farther.

Investigator: Have they been visiting the earth for very long?

Betty: Since the beginning of time.

Investigator: Our time?

Betty: Yes.

Investigator: Can they travel freely throughout the stars?

Betty: Certain ones.

Investigator: Are these stars nearby to the sun and the earth?

Betty: Yes, and they are beyond.

Investigator: What do you mean by 'beyond?'

Betty: Beyond ours there are others, but they are in a different plane. They're in a heavier space.

Investigator: What do you mean by a 'heavier space?'

Betty: They're in a heavier space than we are.

Investigator: Why are they restricted to some stars and not others?

Betty: Why are we restricted to earth and able to go only to certain stars, and not others?

Investigator: Is that the answer or is that another question?

Betty: That is the answer and the question.

Investigator: Betty, do they have enemies as we have enemies?

Betty: There is one planet that is an enemy, and also many men are enemies, only because they do not understand.

Investigator: Men of this earth, you mean?

Betty: Yes.

Investigator: Betty, are there many of these clans or races visiting the earth right now from many planets?

Betty: Yes.

Investigator: How many?

Betty: Seventy.

Investigator: Seventy different planets or races?

Betty: Races.

Investigator: Do these races work together?

Betty: Yes, except for the offensive one.

Investigator: They come from different planets, then? They don't come from the same planet? Is that correct?

Betty: Some. Some come from realms where you cannot see their hiding place. Some come from the very Earth.

Investigator: This very earth?

Betty: Yes, there is a place on this very earth that you do not know of.

Investigator: Can they see the future?

Betty: Definitely.

Investigator: Can they tell whether we are going to come up with an answer?

Betty: The answer is here already.

Investigator: When will we recognize it, in our time?

Betty: When you give your heart over.

Investigator: When the heart is given over to what?

Betty: To love and truth.

Investigator: Does that mean that some people have already seen this many, many years gone by, and some will never see it?

Betty: Yes, and it is sad, because it was there for all mankind.

Investigator: Betty, what is your personal function in revealing this?

Betty: They said that they have chosen me to reveal it because of the initiation, because of going through what I had gone through, because it was planned.

Investigator: Why were you chosen?

Betty: Because I did not object.

Investigator: Betty, have other people like yourself been involved in being taken on board their craft and examined?

Betty: Yes, but they quiet them. They tell them to be still. It's hidden within them. As time goes by, mysteries are going to be unlocked from man. These people are very afraid.

Investigator: Did they tell you how many such cases there have been of people being taken aboard?

Betty: Many, many, many, many, many. Many, many cases. Many, but few have gone to the fullness.

Investigator: Have some of these people been taken back to the planets of the beings? Have some earth people been taken back?

Betty: Yes, and they're going to return, and people are going to be afraid because of it.

Investigator: Were you taken to their home planet?

Betty: (Long pause and weak voice) I was taken to the high place, higher than their home planet.

Investigator: You mean a more important planet?

Betty: It is not a planet, it is a place.

At this point the investigators decided to end the hypnotic trance because of Betty's visible fatigue. They decided after a few more sessions, with little else revealed, that it was time to move on to other things. Betty had been helped, they felt, by the sessions and she soon decided to seek employment in another state.

Thus ended one of the strangest sagas in the annals of UFOlogy. The subsequent sessions revealed very little else and to this day Betty is apparently living a "normal" life somewhere in America and has since remarried, living under another name. [13-1]

* * * * *

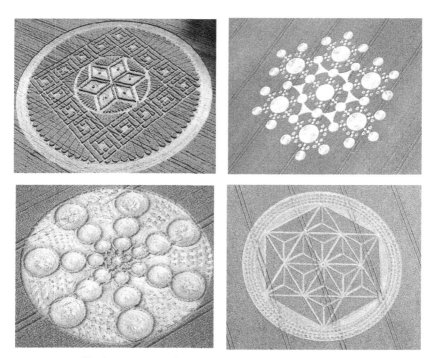

Figure13.1-4 – The beauty and precision of authentic mysterious crop circles is astonishing.

Some Provocative Conclusions

This story, on the surface, seems too strange to be real, but could it be true? One is reminded of what it says in the Scriptures: The opposite of faith is fear. Was it Betty's faith which allowed her to experience what very few people have ever experienced: direct contact from God, Almighty. Sounds bizarre, I know, I know. So do many Bible stories of contact with God and His angels. But we accept them, as strange as they are to us.

Does Betty's experience conflict with Scripture in any way? That's the acid test to me. The following verse from the Bible should answer that question:

> Hereby know ye the Spirit of God: Every spirit that confesseth
> that Jesus Christ is come in the flesh is of God: And every spirit
> that confesseth not that Jesus Christ is come in the flesh is not
> of God.
>
> **II JOHN 4:2**

Moses, Ezekiel, Daniel and the apostle John, among others, all claimed to have been taken off the planet by angels of the Lord and stood in the presence of God. Their experiences were no less sensational than were Betty Andreasson's. In fact, as I shall point out in the second half of this book, their experiences closely parallel Betty's close encounter with "aliens" from another world. Are, what we call aliens, actually God's angelic force, both honorable and fallen?

*   *   *   *   *

14

What Does Science Say?

What Is The Scientific Position?

The scientific community's position on the existence of UFOs is probably best exemplified in the opinion of noted scientist and lecturer, Dr. Carl Sagan. Dr. Sagan has said that there is absolutely no proof that we are being visited by alien beings but he believes that in eons past the Earth was probably visited by some advanced civilization. The odds for the existence of such civilizations are overwhelming. He further believes that probably sometime in the future, likely thousands of years from now, man may get another random isolated visit or two by some passing space vehicle.[14-1]

In other words, he believes that UFOs (interplanetary space travelers) have been here in the past, will visit us in the future, but there's no chance that they are visiting us today.

What is the premise for this obviously absurd position?

Reasonable Men

To understand the mind of a scientist we must first understand the discipline of modern science.

Science-fiction writer and biochemist Isaac Asimov states:

"Science deals only with phenomena that can be reproduced; observations that, under certain fixed conditions, can be made by anybody of normal intelligence; observations upon which reasonable men can agree." [14-2]

The UFO is controversial for precisely these reasons. We have no substantial, reproducible proof that they exist other than several films and photographs, and the word of many reasonable men. Unfortunately, science, in an act of self-preservation, must label UFO witnesses "unreasonable men" even though they come from very respectable backgrounds...even from within their own ranks.

Asimov goes on to say:

> *"Unsophisticated human beings with limited experience are impatient with puzzles and seek solutions, often pouncing on something they have vaguely heard of if it satisfies an apparently fundamental human need for drama and excitement.*
>
> *"Thus, mysterious lights or sounds, experienced by people living in a society in which angels and demons are commonplace beliefs, will invariably be interpreted as representing angels and demons - or spirits of the dead, or whatever.*
>
> *"In the nineteenth century, they were described as airships on occasion. In the days after World War II, when talk of rocketry reached the general public, they became spaceships.*
>
> *"Thus began the modern craze of 'flying saucers' (from an early description in 1947) or, more soberly, 'unidentified flying objects', usually abbreviated as UFOs.*
>
> *"That there are such things as unidentified flying objects is beyond dispute. Someone who sees the planet Venus, with its image distorted near the horizon or by mist, and mistakes it for something much closer, has seen a UFO...*
>
> *"There is, however, no reason so far to suppose that any UFO report can represent an extraterrestrial spaceship. An extraterrestrial spaceship is not inconceivable, to be sure, and one may show up tomorrow and will then have to be accepted. But at present there is no acceptable evidence for one."* [14-3]

It has been speculated that the two disciplines that would be most adversely affected by the open landing of a UFO would be science and engineering, because these two professions are the most closely related to the mastery of nature.[14-4]

Another area that would obviously feel the effects of such a visitation would be the religious community. It's interesting to note that the Bible states that it was Satan's ego, his desire to be like God, that caused his fall and the eventual fall of mankind: his separation from God. The discipline of science produces many men who are diametrically opposed to religion for this very reason. The "brains" of science like to think that they have all the answers (or will, at least, eventually discover them) and anything that challenges their authority is met with great hostility. I'm not too fond of being called "unsophisticated" simply because I have enough courage to admit to seeing an unknown (i.e. unknown in scientific circles) phenomenon. I know what I saw.

According to Asimov:

"Those UFO reports that seem to be most honest and reliable report only mysterious lights. As the reports grow more dramatic, they also grow more unreliable, and all accounts of actual 'encounters of the second or third kind' would seem utterly worthless.

"Any extraterrestrials reported are always described as essentially human in form, which is so unlikely a possibility that we can dismiss it out of hand. Descriptions of the ship itself and of the scientific devices of the aliens usually betray a great knowledge of science fiction movies of the more primitive kind and no knowledge whatever of real science.

(Author's note: infamous last words?)

"In short, then, once we allow the practicality of easy interstellar travel, we are forced to speculate that Earth is being visited or has been visited, is being helped or at least left alone by a Federation of benevolent civilizations.

"Well, perhaps, but none of it sounds compelling. It seems safer to assume that interstellar travel is not easy or practical.

"The final conclusion I can come to at the end of the reasoning in this chapter, then, is that extraterrestrial civilizations do exist, probably in great numbers, but that we

have not been visited by them, very likely because interstellar distances are too great to be penetrated." [14-5]

Copernicus was crucified for even suggesting that the Earth was not the center of the universe. If we were able to go back in time and talk to those "scientific experts" just two hundred years ago, I'm sure that we would have an impossible time convincing them that one day man would be able to send images and sounds through the air for thousands of miles in the form of television, or that electronic digits would rule our society.

Was J. Allen Hynek A Reasonable Man?

J. Allen Hynek aptly put it when he said Twentieth-century scientists tend to forget "that there will be a 21st Century science, and indeed, a 30th Century science, from which vantage points our knowledge of the universe may appear quite different...we suffer, perhaps from temporal provincialism, a form of arrogance that has always irritated posterity." [14-6]

These same vain scientists wonder, "if creatures from another world are visiting us, why haven't they contacted us?"...usually having all the answers, Asimov this time asks "...why haven't we heard from them? Why hasn't any civilization come calling?" [14-7]

Captain Edward J. Ruppelt, former head of Project Blue Book, asks the pertinent question: "What constitutes proof? Does a UFO have to land at the River Entrance of the Pentagon near the Joint Chiefs of Staff Offices? Or is it proof when a ground radar station detects a UFO, sends a jet to intercept it, the jet pilot sees it, and locks on with his radar, only to have the UFO streak away at a phenomenal speed? Is it proof when a jet pilot fires at a UFO and sticks to his story even under the threat of court-martial? Does this constitute proof?" [14-8]

Unfortunately, the answer for the scientific community is best summed up by the following statement by Dr. Walter Dornberger, wartime head of the German V-2 rocket development. "No one," he said, "is going to convince me of visitors from space, until they bring in one of those little guys and sit him on my desk." [14-9]

What Is A Skeptic?

The position of the skeptic is very aptly described by General L. M. Chassin, former General Air Defense Coordinator, Allied Air Forces, Central Europe (NATO), when he wrote,

"...Obsessed with the notion of his own omniscience, it enrages him to be confronted by phenomena that do not agree with his conviction. Finding in his limited armory no explanation that satisfies him, he chooses to doubt anyone rather than himself, and rejects the most obvious facts in order to avoid putting his faith to the test. The mistaken pride and anthropocentrism that supposedly went out with Copernicus and Galileo make him a peril to science, as history abundantly proves.

"...In spite of the indifference – not to say hostility – which almost all the official groups in the world have so far displayed toward the pioneers of research in this field, the public has shown more judgment. The man in the street has an instinct for such things; he had accepted airplanes while a Sorbonne professor was still arguing the utter impossibility of heavier-than-air flight.

"That strange things have been seen is now beyond question, and the 'psychological' explanations seem to have misfired. The number of thoughtful, intelligent, educated people in full possession of their faculties who have 'seen something' and described it grows every day. Doubting Thomases among astronomers, engineers, and officials who used to laugh at 'saucers' have seen and repented. To reject out of hand testimony such as theirs becomes more and more presumptuous.

"Moreover, what is testimony? If a policeman testifies in court that 'I saw a man armed with a revolver run across the road after another man, and both of them disappear into the woods,' it does not occur to the jurors to dispute this testimony. And if three other policemen confirm the statement, and if their combined evidence convicts a murderer, we can be certain that the murderer's head will roll. But let these four policemen submit a report that 'We saw a cigar-shaped object approach rapidly from the north, stop motionless over town for several seconds, change color, and disappear in the east at lightning speed' – let them say this, and many a solid citizen will suddenly question their sanity or sobriety. There will be talk of 'hallucination,' of 'a weather balloon,' of 'helicopters,' of 'electrical phenomena.' Would these same citizens dream of acquitting the murderer if his lawyer argued that what the four policemen really saw was a couple of dogs playing in the road?" 14-10

* * * * *

Figure 14.1 – Saucer emitting "Angel's Hair" discharge which dissipates within minutes. Taken with infrared camera.

The "Odds"

What The Experts Say:

W hat are the mathematical odds for the existence of other civilizations elsewhere in the universe? One of the most valid cases made for the existence of interplanetary visitors comes, oddly enough, from the very community that refuses to acknowledge them.

Several well-known scientists, among them Nobel prize winners Dr. Melvin Calvin & Dr. C. F. Powell; Dr. Clyde Tombaugh and others all agree that there are as many as one million planets in our galaxy with beings similar to those on earth.[15-1]

In a secret meeting held at Green Bank in November of 1961, several eminent scientists gathered to discuss and estimate the number of planets capable of sustaining life as we know it on Earth. In attendance were some very prominent opponents of the UFO controversy, including: Dr. Carl Sagan, Dr. Otto Struve, Dr. Melvin Calvin, Dr. John C. Lilly, Dr. Frank Drake and several others.

Their conclusion known as the Green Bank Formula was as follows:

"There are between 40 and 50 million worlds which are either trying to signal us or are listening for messages from Earth." [15-2]

According to Dr. Harlow Shapley, former head of Harvard Observatory:

> *"There are at least one hundred million inhabited planets. On many of them the inhabitants will be far superior to us."* [15-3]

T.A. Heppenheimer's Odds

In an exercise of scientific/mathematical probabilities, author T. A. Heppenheimer has calculated the probability for the existence of earthlike planets using stars formed between 4.5 and 11 billion years ago. [15-4] (our sun is thought to be 4.5 billion years old)

Stellar spectral type	Mean stellar mass (Sun = 1.0)	Fraction of stars with this spectral type	Habitable range of distances from star (Earth from Sun = 1.0)	Probability of finding a planet in that range
F6	1.18	0.00474	1.536 – 1.591	0.0621
F7	1.14	0.00484	1.382 – 1.445	0.0791
F8	1.10	0.00499	1.240 – 1.309	0.0965
F9	1.06	0.00512	1.115 – 1.181	0.1027
G0	1.02	0.00520	1.009 – 1.061	0.0894
G1	0.985	0.00531	0.921 – 0.961	0.0753
G2	0.955	0.00534	0.850 – 0.880	0.0612
G3	0.930	0.00586	0.793 – 0.815	0.0481
G4	0.900	0.00628	0.728 – 0.742	0.0334
G5	0.870	0.00751	0.666 – 0.673	0.0182
G6	0.850	0.00810	0.627 – 0.630	0.0083
G7	0.825	0.00892	——	0.0

Probabilities for Existence of Earth like Planets*

* Data in the first three columns are taken from *Habitable Planets for Man* by Stephen H. Dole, (New York, Blaisdell, 1964), pp. 102 and 104. The fourth column was computed from equations given by Michael Hart; see references to papers in the Bibliography. The last column again uses data by Dole, pp. 91 and 92.

According to Heppenheimer, "A bit of explanation is in order. Astronomers classify stars by the appearance of their spectra, thus furnishing a convenient way to refer to groups of similar stars. The fourth column gives the range of planetary distances over which Earth might have formed so as to avoid thermal runaways while progressing to the Cambrian revolution. The last column assumes that planet distances are distributed as in our own solar system. For example, a typical star in spectral class F9 has a mass 6 percent greater than the Sun; some one-half percent of all stars are of this type. One would find an earthlike planet only between distances from that star of 1.115 and 1.181 times Earth's distance from the Sun, but there is a bit better than a 10 percent chance that a given star of that type would actually have a planet there.

"Of the 130 billion stars that are the right age, a great many of them suffered the planetary hang-up and failed to form worlds such as Earth. In view of the carnage wrought by Jupiter within our solar system, it is risky to imagine that planets exist where a star has a binary companion larger than Jupiter. Following the estimates ... discussed...this would rule out 90 percent of these stars. We thus have 13 billion candidates.

"From the table, we find that only about one-third of 1 percent of these would have the right combination of stellar mass together with a planet in the proper range of distances. We thus are down to 46 million planets. Earlier we noted that to avoid the end of life, a planet must be between 86 percent and 130 percent the mass of Earth. If planets throughout the Galaxy have the same distribution of masses as in our own solar system, then there is only a chance of 1.9 percent that a given planet has the right mass. This brings us finally down to 880,000 worlds like ours in this Galaxy.

"So we finally come down to an estimate of 880,000 planets suitable for life. Nevertheless, this now is the real McCoy, the genuine nitty-gritty. We expect that each of them will be virtually a dead ringer for Earth, of similar size and appearance, with a similar star for its sun, and at the right distance and age to have experienced the Cambrian revolution upward of half a billion years ago. Moreover, it is likely that every one of them is (or soon will be) the abode of an intelligent species. These are just the worlds we would seek in space. Yet by these calculations, there is only one such planet for every 227,000 stars." [15-5]

Isaac Asimov

You remember Isaac Asimov's statement regarding the total absurdity of the belief in UFOs by "unsophisticated minds." He said, "Any extraterrestrials reported are...so unlikely...that we can dismiss it out of hand. It seems safer to assume that interstellar travel is not easy or practical...very likely because interstellar distances are too great to be penetrated." [15-6]

I sure hope none of the distinguished scientists who disagree with him ever read his slanderous statements. The sad commentary on such narrow-minded thinking is that Asimov, himself, calculates there are many millions of planets within our single Galaxy that have civilizations "more advanced than we are."

In his book, Extraterrestrial Civilizations, Asimov makes the following cerebral calculations:

1. The number of stars in our Galaxy= 300,000,000,000

2. The number of planetary systems in our Galaxy = 280,000,000,000

3. The number of planetary systems in our Galaxy that circle Sunlike stars = 75,000,000,000

4. The number of Sunlike stars in our Galaxy with a useful ecosphere = 52,000,000,000

5. The number of second-generation, Population I, Sunlike stars in our Galaxy with a useful ecosphere = 5,200,000,000

6. The number of second-generation, Population I stars in our Galaxy with a useful

ecosphere and a planet circling it within that
ecosphere = 2,600,000,000

7. The number of second-generation, Population I,
Sunlike stars in our Galaxy with a
useful ecosphere and an Earthlike planet
circling it within that ecosphere =
1,300,000,000

8. The number of habitable planets in our
Galaxy = 650,000,000

9. The number of life-bearing planets
in our Galaxy = 600,000,000

10. The number of planets in our Galaxy
bearing multicellular life = 433,000,000

11. The number of planets in our Galaxy
bearing a rich land life = 416,000,000

12. The number of planets in our Galaxy on
which a technological civilization has
developed = 390,000,000

Furthermore, "of the 390 million civilizations in our Galaxy, only
260 are as primitive as we are... All the rest," (389,999,740) "...are
more advanced than we are." [15-7]

Carl Sagan's Odds

Asimov admits this is a very conservative figure and quotes the
late Carl Sagan, one of the leading investigators of the possibility
of extraterrestrial intelligence, who said that

*"...there may be as many as one billion
habitable planets in our Galaxy."*

As you can see, even the scientists can't agree on the number of inhabited planets in our own Galaxy, but they do agree that the possibilities are abundant.

These are conservative figures and consider only our own Galaxy: the Milky Way. What about the other seemingly infinite numbers of Galaxies within the vast wasteland of space?

Are not the chances of a highly technologically advanced civilization developing a means of interplanetary – and, yes, even intergalactic – space travel also infinite?

*   *   *   *   *

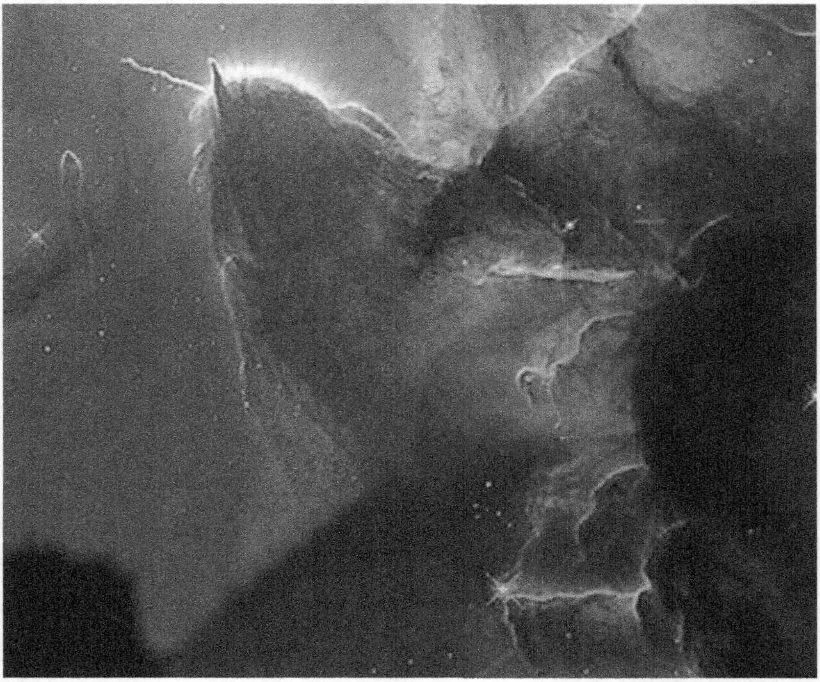

Figure 15.1 – A deep-space cosmic nursery - taken by the Hubble Space Telescope.

16

Conquering
Deep-space Travel

The Speed of Light

cience points to the impossibility of traveling the vast distances of space as the main deterrent to interplanetary space travel.

And it's no wonder. With our primitive technology today we are only able to travel at several times the speed of sound (741 miles per hour) within our atmosphere.

The nearest star to Earth, other than our sun, is estimated to be eleven light years away. Light travels at 186,000 miles per second ! Therefore, if you could travel at the speed of light, it would still take eleven years to get there. The possibility of achieving speeds even approaching the speed of light, with today's technology, is about as remote as the probability of scientific acceptance of the existence of UFOs.

We can travel just under 2,200 miles per hour in our fastest jet aircraft – the SR-71. What about six hundred sixty-nine million, six hundred thousand miles per hour? That's what it would take to travel at the speed of light. It's easy to see why scientists think that the distances required for interplanetary travel are totally impossible to negotiate.

There's another slight problem – at least within the constraints of Einstein's theory of relativity – that we might encounter if we were physically able to transport humans at this phenomenal speed. We would be everywhere at the same time, or nowhere at anytime. Poof!

It may be more than a mere coincidence that this is precisely what happens to a great many of the UFOs seen flying in our skies. They simply disappear into an unknown realm, be it movement or dimension.

As I have suggested before, their mode of flight may include two or more systems. One, or more, for use in various maneuvers within a planet's gravitational field, and the other for use in interplanetary space travel.

The strange metallic devices that transport these aliens, however, have never been seen to disappear while on the ground. They always ascend into the air several thousand feet, usually traveling at this point horizontally at around 150 to 300 mph, often-times moving in a zigzag motion and structurally emitting various colors of light in exacting sequence (the sequence suggests a connection between the light emission and the energy source of the craft). Then, without warning, they simply disappear. Poof!

Parallel Universes

Several theories of how UFOs might achieve their maneuverability have been put forth, but they usually apply known technological principles in their solutions.

It remind me of a 13th Century scientist trying to explain the likely principles utilized in creating the image in a television set. He might describe it as a box with very nicely painted pictures being flipped in rapid sequence by the power source, most likely a mouse on a wheel hidden inside the box...but, of course, having no explanation for the ability to change from one moving picture to another or its ability to emit numerous synchronized sounds. Pretty absurd in light of our modern understanding of the principles of electricity and sound waves.

There is one explanation for space travel that has captured my imagination, however, and it may include the existence of a parallel dimension.

Scientists would all agree that a pretty good case has been made for the theory of atoms, molecules, etc. as being the building blocks of all creation. Everything, they say, consists of small moving particles rotating around each other in either a neutral, positively or negatively charged form. They label these small units neutrons: neutrally charged particles; and protons: positively charged particles. They make up the nucleus of an atom. Around this center rotates one or more electrons: negatively charged particles; their number being equal to the number of protons in the nucleus.

The whole unit makes up an atom. Combined with similar units, these atoms make up the various molecules of each element in our universe.

Science has assigned an atomic weight and number to each of the know elements. Hydrogen is the lightest with an atomic weight of 1.0080. Lawrencium is the heaviest man-made element with an estimated atomic weight of 256. Uranium is the heaviest natural element.

Combinations of these elements make up what is known as compounds and create every form known to man. Water consists of 2 parts (atoms) hydrogen and one part oxygen and is denoted chemically by the symbol H_2O.

For most, all of this is old hat, but the reason I've included this refresher course in chemistry and physics is to show you the significance of what we know compared to what we don't. For instance, the space between the mass of the nucleus of an atom and the mass of the electron(s) that circle around it is roughly equivalent to the spaces between our Earth, the accompanying planets, and our Sun.

It's roughly 93 million miles form the Earth to the Sun. There is certainly plenty of room for something else to fit into the vast space between us and our neighbors, wouldn't you agree? [16-1]

By like reasoning, there is plenty of room for other invisible objects to rotate within the spaces that separate our own atomic structures. This is the case made for the possibility of parallel universes, or even antimatter, as science has hypothesized.

The spacecraft that we see on occasion may actually exist in harmless unison in a hidden dimension of the universe. They may possess the ability to interact with Earth's physics and to disappear at will into the vast spaces between our world's atomic structure.

Einstein's Theory of Relativity

Einstein's theory of relativity is, quite literally, the law of all creation [16-2] Simply put, Einstein theorized that the universe is made up of indestructible matter/energy. You can change matter into energy or energy into matter but there will never be a loss of either…only change. The rest-energy of a particle determines its mass. In other words, the more energy (movement) a particle has the less mass it has. A rock is made up of various compounds of atoms that are not very energetic, which coexists in a relatively snug fit, thus it weighs a great deal more (has more mass) than air, which is made up of more energetic elements that are separated by greater spaces, thus producing less mass. The energy of which we speak manifests itself to humans in the form of light. These energy-carrying light particles are emitted from various atoms in a constant procession and strike the retina of the eye much like sound waves cause movement on the ear drum.[16-3]In fact, sight and hearing are both perceived frequencies of matter. Higher frequency is light and lower frequency is sound but the phenomena are caused by the same source: energy/movement of particles.

The Big Bang!

Light travels faster than anything in the universe. According to Einstein's theory of relativity, the energy of light can be transformed into mass – or rest energy – without any loss of the energy. It simply changes form. However, the process of creating matter (mass) requires a great deal of energy, indeed. Inversely, the process of creating energy, or changing mass into energy, releases a tremendous amount of energy. That can be demonstrated by the devastating force of an atomic bomb in which we split the atoms of the uranium isotope 235 and transform its mass into energy in a rapid and radical chain reaction. Actually, the destructive force which we associate with the process is, in reality, the side effects of creating energy (movement).

As this energy moves outward from its center, the atoms of the objects in its path are actively disturbed and produce heat. The process of producing this super intense heat changes these object (or matter) into energy, thus they burn up, or more graphically, instantly vaporize.

Even the most highly efficient nuclear reaction taps, at the most, no more than one percent of the rest-energy that is available in its fuel. Incredible!

Inversely, it would take the same tremendous amount of energy to change light particles into matter, or to "create" matter, rather than transform matter into energy, as does the A-Bomb. This is how science formulated its "Big Bang" descriptive for the creation of the universe. They speculate that one day eons ago there was an incomprehensibly energetic Galactic Explosion and the energy of the universe suddenly formed all matter as we know it. [16-4] It would be more accurately labeled: "The Infinitely Powerful Big Bang Theory!" The amount of energy released in less than one percent of just 29 pounds of uranium fuel leveled Hiroshima. The demonstration of this terrifying force produced an allied victory in WW-II. It's impossible to imagine the amount of energy it would take to create our entire universe.

Isn't it interesting to realize that the more science tries to disprove a Creator through scientific reasoning, the better it makes the case for His existence?

> GENESIS 1:3 *And God said let there be light:*
> *and there was light...*

* * BANG!!! * *

According to the Bible, God is light and truth...the creative energy of the universe!

> FIRST JOHN 1:5 *This is the message which we have*
> *heard of him, and declare unto you, that God is*
> *light, and in him is no darkness at all.*

> DANIEL 2:22 *And the light dwelleth with him.*

> JAMES 1:17 *Every good gift and every perfect gift is*
> *from above, and cometh down from the Father*
> *of lights, with whom is no variableness, neither*
> *shadow of turning.*

Black Holes

Einsteinian theorists have discovered mysterious phenomena in deep space that appear as massive areas totally devoid of any light. These "black holes", as they've been labeled, are, in theory, a star with such great mass, and therefore gravity, that any light or mass in their area is sucked in by gravitational pull at speeds that eventually exceed the speed of light.

As these particles of light or mass – space debris and gases – are sucked into the black hole something very strange happens. Because of the tremendous speeds they attain as they approach the center of the black hole they disappear or, perhaps, simply cease to exist. Poof!

Several theories have surfaced during the past several decades to explain what happens to this light, or mass, as it exceeds the speed of light.

Some scientists speculate that nothing can exist on "the other side" of the speed of light. Matter-energy that goes beyond the light barrier simply ceases to exist. Others speculate that time would reverse itself beyond the speed of light.

Some have described these mysterious holes as the "windows" to a parallel universe made up of particles of antimatter. Still others describe a resonating universe on the "other side" consisting of units called "tachyons" rather than the units of energy-mass we call atoms.

If there were beings who existed in the Tachyon dimension of rapidly rotating matter, what would happen if they were able to slow down their atomic, or subatomic, structures? Would they not simply appear in our world as if from nowhere? There is a great deal of merit to this theory in explaining the properties of angels, as we shall investigate in the coming chapters.

Whatever the case, these strange dark holes have given science something to think about.

Time in the Universe

Another very interesting aspect of Einstein's theory of relativity has to do with the existence of time. He postulated that a clock would either lose or gain time if put into high-altitude, high-speed flight for two reason: (1) Altitude would increase its mass and, (2) Movement with or counter to the Earth's rotation would either increase or decrease the mass of the clock and, thus, alter its time.

In 1971, two American scientists pioneered an experiment to see if Einstein was correct. They put two extremely accurate atomic clocks aboard two jets and sent them around the world in opposite directions flying a straight course above the equator.

* * BANG!!! * *

Figure 16.1 – Just a few of the incredible images of deep space taken by the Hubble space-based telescope. Larger images are galaxies being "born". These images are dramatically enhanced when presented in full color, full screen and if you haven't already seen them, I'd suggest a Google search of Hubble images. *All images courtesy NASA*

They discovered that the eastbound clock lost time and the westbound clock gained, just as Einstein had speculated. The measurements of change were in nanoseconds and thus very slight, but the speeds at which the jets traveled in relation to the speed of light were also very minimal.

Einstein further postulated that if an object (or person) were able to travel at a rate of one thousand to one. In other words, if an Earthling were to leave this planet and travel in a large circle in space at speeds approaching 186,000 miles per second and journeyed for the length of one year, when he/she returned to Earth they would discover that one thousand years of Earth time would have elapsed. Let's not forget that Einstein, of course, was dealing in theory.

And what does the Bible have to say about time and its relation to the Creator?

> II PETER 3:8 *But, beloved be not ignorant of this one thing, that one day is with the LORD as a thousand years, and a thousand years as one day.*

> PSALMS 90:4 *For a thousand years in thy sight are but as yesterday when it is past, and as a watch in the night.*

Since God is light *(First John 1:5)* it would stand to reason that His time reference is positioned with the speed of light. Are the above biblical passages mere poetic verse, or is there a deeper truth being revealed? Perhaps, as levelheaded, logical human beings, we had better pay closer attention to what's been explained within the mysterious pages of God's inspired Holy Word.

*   *   *   *   *

Part II

In-laws

...and fearful sights and
great signs shall there
be from heaven.

**Jesus in
Luke 21:11**

Anyone who ponders these
things will find that God cares for
mankind, and in all possible ways
foreshows to His people the means
of salvation, and that it is through
folly and evils of their own choosing
that they come to destruction.

**Flavius Josephus
37-93 A.D.**

Surely the LORD GOD will do
nothing but first he revealeth
his secret unto his servants...

Amos 3:7

How Does This Relate to Religion?

Is Theology Relevant?

So, how does all this UFO stuff relate to religion? If you believe that UFOs are real and agree that the evidence of their existence is overwhelming, then how does this phenomenon relate to our precepts of Christian theology?

The fundamentalist Christian – one who believes the Bible is the inspired, infallible word of God – also believes that God created all things in the universe. If all things include UFOs, as it must, then what do these strange alien forms have to do with Christianity? Do we dare investigate answers to this perplexing question, or do we, as have so many in the past, simply dismiss the phenomena as something from Satan? Is it just a grand scheme of deception to dissuade modern minds from the Truth as presented in the Bible, or something much more mysterious?

Betty Andreasson's UFO experience is the only one I am aware of with any connection suggested between the "alien" creatures and the God of Christianity.

Why was Betty Andreasson given such a comprehensive experience? Was she different than other contactees? The one key difference was her willingness to cooperate. Could it be that her religious faith in a protective God alive within her kept her from experiencing the debilitating fear that others have experienced? Her total cooperation was based on her faith in a living, protective God. This would suggest that the lack of a deep Christian faith is what has prevented others from having a fuller experience with their "captors."

Most Religious Institutions Scoff at the Idea of UFOs

To most, the idea of visitors from other planets seems, somehow, diametrically opposed to a God of creation. If a UFO were to land on the lawn of the White House and its occupants proclaim their reality, the fear is that it would irreparably alter, if not totally undermine, the church's precepts of deity. Naturally, the church is not eager to self-destruct.

Man, apart from theology, has always considered his world the center of the universe. There has been no room in the scheme of things to include creatures from distant star systems, let alone angels from the spirit realm; a dimension he cannot even see.

The Christian church has been indoctrinated into a similar "pheology" (philosophy+theology). Although open to the concept of angels as messengers of God, most denominations believe that these were symbolic spiritual experiences for an age that has long passed. "Any levelheaded, thinking man couldn't possibly believe stories of angel visitations in this modern era," voice the majority of America's learned theologians and religious institutions.

With that kind of humanistic logic, it would be doubly impossible to expect them to embrace any phenomenon as controversial as the UFO.

I, for one, don't hope to change these deeply embedded notions within any institution. However, for those who are not afraid to re-evaluate their long-standing preconceptions, there is hope for some startling revelations within the pages of this book.

Embraced by the Occult

Among the factors that serve to discredit the UFO phenomenon is the willingness of certain groups to embrace it and attach their own metaphysical agendas which have no basis in fact.

There are several publications that proclaim the validity of the UFO while in the same breath they ask for donations for miracle healing ointments, or speak of Martian visitations to help keep mankind from destroying itself. It is information very close to the truth, as foretold in Scripture, and therefore often swallowed as the whole truth.

The New Age Movement's proponents speak of a coming time of spiritual enlightenment brought on by man's inner understanding of cosmic forces, and are quick to point to the UFO phenomenon as proof of a higher Cosmic Consciousness.

In my opinion, these groups all purposely employ techniques of deception that include the subtle use of half-truths to establish their own credibility. They have embraced partial truths and then introduced totally false precepts within the same context. Obviously this ploy is used by self-serving persons and organizations. It is nothing new.

I think that all this rhetorical attachment has probably helped to discredit the phenomenon as much as the press' willingness to publish bizarre contactee or abduction stories by obvious nuts and liars.

Please remember that I have attempted to weed out the phoney abduction cases by including only those that are well-documented, experienced by witnesses that have not sought to benefit financially from their encounter and who's stories have been supported through the administering of unbiased lie detector tests...emphasis on 'unbiased.'

As we now explore the possibility of some connection between the UFO phenomenon and the events described in the Bible it is important to understand the biblical premise of accuracy. Can we trust the Bible, or is it totally irrelevant to our "modern" society? The next chapter will deal with that pertinent question.

*   *   *   *   *

Figure 17.1 – Dead Sea Caves, Qumran, Israel.

Figure17.2 – Cave 4 interior - This most famous of the Dead Sea Scroll caves is also the most significant in terms of finds. More than 15,000 fragments from over 200 books were found in this cave, nearly all by Bedouin thieves. 122 biblical scrolls (or fragments) were found in this cave. From all 11 Qumran caves, every Old Testament book is represented except Esther. Naturally, no New Testament books or fragments have been found at the site.

Figure 17.3 – Cave 6 exterior. Note the small inlet of the Dead Sea in the background.

Why Trust
The Bible?

Is The Bible
Historically Accurate?

There are several questions that come to mind when dealing with the Bible. Where did it come from? Is it historically accurate? Why doesn't everyone agree with what it says? Is it really the inspired word of God, Almighty, or just a collection of stuffy old Hebrew parables and confusing rhetoric written in the ancient past and interpreted into tiresome Elizabethan English? Is it simply a book of philosophy, a collection of individuals' thoughts, like so many others?

For most Americans, the Bible is of little importance in the way they conduct their daily lives. And the Church has done a poor job of explaining what it teaches, let alone instruct why it's important to study its tenets.

I think most would agree that if the Bible really were the indisputable word of God, then it would be advisable to find out just what it has to say about our individual conduct.

Perhaps the following basics will help to unveil the mystery surrounding its authenticity...which is the beginning point for trusting its contents.

Where Did We
Get The Bible?

The Old Testament was written by alleged men of God before the birth of Jesus Christ, and the New Testament was written after His death. The King James version (or translation) from the original Jewish and Greek texts is the most widely accepted among conservative scholars. The New American Standard version is another widely accepted translation.

Unfortunately, many other translations have been altered somewhat to reflect the personal beliefs of its translators, and in cases like the version used by the Jehovah's Witnesses, the changes are drastic. What we should seek is a pure translation from the original with minimal theologically interpretive changes.

THE OLD TESTAMENT - There are 39 books found today in the Old Testament of the Protestant Bible which can be grouped into four major categories: (1) Law (2) History (3) Poetry and (4) Prophets. These books were written and compiled from the time of Moses and were revered and adhered to in the Jewish faith for centuries. Conservative scholars believe that they were completed no later than 425 B.C. with the book of Malachi being the last written. Among the conservative scholars, the most widely recognized proof that the Old Testament contains the inspired word of God was the testimony of Jesus Christ, Himself. He recognized the fact in *Matthew 5:18, Luke 24:44, and John 5:39 and 10:34. (see Figures 17.2 & 17.3)*

THE NEW TESTAMENT - The New Testament was written between 50 and 100 A.D. by several of Jesus' disciples and a late convert, the apostle Paul, and by other writers closely associated with the apostles. Luke, for example, was a close companion of Paul and wrote the books of Acts and Luke. The agreed upon books, called the "canon" of the New Testament, consists of only 27 books. [18-1] Many other alleged holy books were written soon after Christ's death, but the "canon" of Scripture recognizes only those authors who were known associates of Jesus. False doctrines have always been, and remain today, a threat to the pure message of the Bible.

How Does the Bible Compare to Other Ancient Manuscripts?

How does the Bible stand up in comparison to other books of antiquity? By definition, this refers generally to documents authored prior to the Middle Ages: 476 A.D. to 1450 A.D. Is the authenticity of the writings of Aristotle and Plato, as an example, more conclusive? How about Homer's Iliad? We certainly accept these writings without question as to their authorship. Why do we challenge the Bible so adamantly? The facts are, the New Testament Scripture is the most preserved text on Earth. If the existence of identical ancient manuscripts helps prove their validity and authenticates authorship, then let's examine the numbers:

Comparison of Surviving Original Documents

Document:	Remaining manuscripts:
Sophocles	193
Plato (Testralogies)	7
Aristotle	49
Caesar (Gallic Wars)	10
Homer (Iliad)	643
The New Testament (Book of Mark, as an example)	24,633

Homer's Iliad is the second most preserved document of antiquity but its numbers don't even come close to the number of authentic replicas of the New Testament's Book of Mark, as an example. The New Testament, then, is by far **the world's most well-preserved document from antiquity.**

The next most important test of the reliability of ancient documents is determined by what time span exists between the writing of the original document and when the earliest existing copy was made. Again, the New Testament is by far the world's most accurate text:

Comparison of Document Time Spans

Document	Date Authored	Date of our Earliest Copy	Interval In Years
Sophocles	496-406 B.C.	1000 A.D.	1,400
Plato (Testralogies)	427-347 B.C.	900 A.D.	1,200
Aristotle	384-322 B.C.	1100 A.D.	1,400
Caesar (Gallic Wars)	100-44 B.C.	900 A.D.	1,000
New Testament (Mark)	**48 A.D.**	**130 A.D.**	**82**

Of all the important books of antiquity, only one can claim to be less than one-thousand years removed from the original. Our earliest copy of the Gospel of Mark was made within a generation of the original. The authenticity of other texts of antiquity aren't even remotely as reliable as the Books of the New Testament. Ironically, it's the New Testament that is most often questioned by certain atheistic skeptics, as well as by "scholarly" clergymen not convinced of its inerrancy.[18-2]

Rediscovered Truths

The Bible has always had it's critics who say the claims made in Scripture are untrue. Some of the very earliest criticism comes from the time of Moses, Abraham and Lot. In Genesis 14:18, mention is made of five cities of the plains near the Dead Sea: Sodom, Gomorah, Admah, Zeboiim and Zoar. It also mentions the names of their kings. Critics have said that no such cities ever existed and that stories about their kings and associated events were historically unreliable because there wasn't one shred of evidence to prove they ever existed.

Then, in the 1970s, a major find rocked the archeological world. The ancient kingdom of Ebla was unearthed in Northern Syria, buried beneath thousands of years of debris, and discovered by two professors. The excavation has been extensive and since 1974 has yielded over 17,000 tablets with vast information on the Ebla Kingdom era. These incredibly well-preserved tablets contained samples of the world's earliest written language.

The discovery of the tablets was particularly crucial because critics had claimed that the first five chapters of the Bible (called the Pentateuch) were purportedly written prior to the time of any known written language. In other words, Moses could not have recorded the Pentateuch because there was no written language at the time he supposedly lived. Not only did the archives of Ebla prove the existence of an earlier written language; it also showed that the civilization existed 1,000 years before Moses recorded the Pentateuch.

As if to add insult to injury, the critics discovered that among the vast information written on the tablets was proof that the five cities mentioned in Genesis existed exactly where the Bible had claimed, and that the very kings mentioned in Scripture were forced to pay tribute to the kingdom of Ebla. Furthermore, all the spellings of these cities and their kings were virtually identical to the Genesis account. [18-3]

Even today, archeological finds are constantly proving the Bible to be 100 percent historically accurate (see *Figure 18.1*). No other religion on Earth can make this claim!

One-third Prophecy

The Bible consists of fully one-third prophecy. What's incredible is that every ancient prediction made has come true with 100 percent accuracy! In fact, four-fifths of these prophecies have already come about and only one-fifth remains yet to be fulfilled. This one-fifth is a very significant portion in that it pertains to the "End Times": that time period the Bible predicts will end in a cataclysmic world war preceded by a series of ecologically devastating events, such as the pollution of *one-third* of the Earth's fresh water and the loss of one-third of the oceans' fish.

When Israel became a nation, it fulfilled a prediction that set the "prophetic time clock" in motion. Many modern Bible scholars, including Hal Lindsey, author of *The Late Great Planet Earth*, (the number one best-selling nonfiction book of the decade of the seventies), agree that we are living in the End Times. Jesus warned us of this perilous time in *Matthew, chapter 24*. More on this in chapter 29 of this book.

Prophetic Odds

When using the laws of probability in examining the Bible, the odds are overwhelmingly in favor of its absolute authenticity.

In a series of experiments conducted by Dr. Peter W. Stoner, noted scientist and mathematician, assisted by over 600 college research students, Dr. Stoner was able to apply the "principle of probability" to Bible prophecy with startling results.

This mathematical principle asserts that if the chance of accuracy is one in X, and the chance of accuracy in another separate event is one in Y, then the chances of both events occurring with accuracy is one in X times Y. Insurance companies use this principle when fixing rates for their policy holders.

Using very conservative estimates, the conclusions achieved in Bible prophecy were very convincing. As an example, the Bible prophet Ezekiel predicted Tyre's destruction (see *Ezekiel 26:3-19*). The current city of Tyre is located in Lebanon but was not built on the ruins of the ancient city. Ezekiel prophesied seven definite events in connection with the destruction of Tyre: (1) Nebuchadnezzer would capture the city (2) other nations would help fulfill the prophecy (3) Tyre would be leveled "like the top of a rock" (4) Tyre would become a place where fishermen would spread their nets on her rocks (5) The city's stones and timber would be laid in the sea (6) other cities would fear because of the destruction of Tyre (7) The city would never be rebuilt at its ancient site.

The chance of all seven events occurring as predicted was estimated by Stoner as **one in 400 million**.

Similar estimates were made for other prophetical schemes, including the destruction of Babylon. Using seven predicted events in connection with the city's demise, Stoner concluded that the odds were:

one in 100 billion. [18-4]

Naturally, there will be those who will say to themselves, "I don't think the Bible was written as early as the 'conservative scholars' claim, therefore, these 'predicted' events could have taken place before it was written, or the text could have been changed over the centuries to reflect the events as they occurred."

If this is your position then I challenge you to read the section on the Dead Sea Scrolls. It may be true that our earliest copy of the Old Testament is dated 150-200 B.C. and the stories of Moses are as ancient, perhaps, as 2000 B.C., but there is one event that was predicted that cannot be disputed: The birth and life of Jesus Christ.

Many theologians say that Christ was just a man. A prophet like so many others. It's an indisputable fact that Jesus Christ was born nearly 2000 years ago. Ancient relics abound that attest to the fact. And the fact that the events of His life were recorded by several men very close to Him make Christ's life the most documented in the annuls of history. Yet, these same "learned" theologians stop short of proclaiming Jesus the Messiah, even though the Scriptures proclaim Him so throughout the New Testament. Old Testament predictions of a coming Messiah are voiced in over three hundred places and the life of Jesus of Nazareth fulfilled *every last one* of those prophecies. How significant should this be to the "sincere" skeptic?

Stoner and his students applied the principle of probability to only eight of those hundreds of events prophesied about Jesus. The eight prophesies were as follows:

1. He would be born in Bethlehem (Michah 5:2)

2. That a messenger (John the Baptist) would tell of his coming (Malachi 3:1)

3. That he would ride into Jerusalem proclaimed the king of the Jews, but riding on a jackass as a lowly person (Zechariah 9:9)

4. That he would have been wounded in the hands by his own kind (Zechariah 13:6)

5. That he would be betrayed for thirty pieces of silver (Zechariah 11:12)

6. That the betrayer (Judas) would give the money away to a potter in a church (Zechariah 11:13)

7. That Jesus would not open his mouth in his own defense when brought before his accusers (Pontius Pilot and the lawyers and Jewish rabbis who tried Christ – Isaiah 53:7)

8. That his hands and feet would be pierced and dogs would lick his wounds (Psalm 22:16)

Many of these prophecies were made 600 years before Christ's birth. Additionally, there had been many other predictions made regarding the events that occurred in the life of Christ, but these were not included in Stoner's formula.

With the principle of probability applied to just these eight incidents, Stoner estimated the odds of their happening, just as predicted, as one chance in ten to the twenty-eighth power (10^{28}).[18-5] In order to grasp the figure let's write it out with numbers. That's one chance out of:

10,000,000,000,000,000,000,000,000,000

Not one chance in a billion. Not one chance in a trillion, or a quintillion, or even a septillion! Here's how you say it:

ONE CHANCE IN TEN OCTILLION!

It's estimated that the whole universe contains two trillion galaxies with each galaxy containing approximately 100 billion stars. Mathematically that would be expressed as ten-to-the-twenty-seventh power or 10^{27}. The chances of the preceding 8 prophecies being fulfilled in one man are greater than picking one special star in all the universe. In fact, the odds would be one chance in ten of our universes! Amazing! In other words, it's totally inconceivable that these prophetical events could have occurred by mere chance. It would take a whole lot more faith to believe that Christ was not the man He said He was, than it would to accept Him as the only begotten Son of God. That's "statistically speaking," of course. It's impossible to imagine the odds if the same principle were applied to all the fulfilled predictions made about Jesus Christ in the Old Testament in over 350 places. It would obviously be wise to listen to all that this proven Messiah has to say about our conduct and His amazing gift.

The Dead Sea Scrolls

In 1947, as Israel prepared for statehood and Kenneth Arnold alerted the world to the phenomenon called flying saucers, several nomadic herdsmen, while driving their stock to grassy highlands near the Dead Sea, were enticed to explore some caves that were seen high up on the face of a cliff.

As they entered the dark recesses of one of the caves they discovered some ancient urns containing several scrolls of deteriorating parchment. Each scroll had a strange series of symbols written clearly across one side.

Little did they realize that they had just made what was to become the most significant archeological discovery of the century. Bible scholars and historians worldwide, naturally, were eager to examine the ancient manuscripts. It was soon learned that the surrounding caves contained parts or fragments of every book of the Hebrew Old Testament with the exception of Esther. They had been faithfully copied by a group of sectarian Jews know as Essenes from a small village called Qumran (pronounced: koom-ran). The Scrolls were sealed in large clay jars and hidden in the caves during a time of religious persecution.

Among the manuscripts still intact was a complete copy of the book of Isaiah. The significance of the find was that the manuscript was virtually identical to the Masoretic Hebrew text, which was the oldest known text in existence – dated A.D. 826. The Dead Sea Scrolls, as they were promptly labeled, predated the existing text by nearly one thousand years. For years, avid skeptics have asserted that the clergy has altered various passages of the Old Testament to make certain events that had already taken place appear to be prophetical revelation. The fact that the Qumran copy of the Book of Isaiah and historians' later copies of the Book were identical has totally discredited the skeptics' claims of alteration. [18-6]

No Other Like It

No other religion in the world can make these claims. If you would research them yourself, you would discover that they simply don't stand up to the light of day. The Hindu's don't know what they worship. There are over 3,000 sects with over 30 million "Gods." Does that sound divine or confused and accommodating?

The Buddhists are basically a spin-off of Hinduism, formed by a man named Gotama under alleged divine inspiration. But Gotama was a man. He has a grave where his bones decomposed. So does Mohammed.

Mohammed, the author of the Muslim religion, embraced the prophets of the Old Testament – even Jesus – as wise men of religion. However, he stopped short of declaring Jesus the only begotten Son of God. Mohammed teaches that it is the Muslim's divine duty to kill all those who will not accept his faith. He also speaks of heaven as a place of human pleasure. As an example, any man (women are sub-standard human beings in the Muslim world) who dies in battle defending the principles of Mohammedism, or Allah, as he calls God, will be taken to heaven and rewarded with scores of sexual orgasms daily! Does that sound divinely or humanly inspired? It would almost be humorous if it weren't for the fact that hundreds of millions of poor misguided humans are willing to die for their Muslim beliefs.

Now, I realize that the "Christian" Crusaders also swept across the Middle East and killed millions of people who would not accept Catholicism (more accurately: the State Church and its doctrines of control). But these men defiled every Christian principle imaginable. Christ had no part in what those men did out of their own volition. Obviously greed and lust for power were their Gods.

I challenge everyone to research the world's major religions for yourselves. There are hundreds of good historical books on their formation and beliefs. Be sure, however, that you don't choose "THE" path to God without first examining what all religions have to say. Find out why they were formed and by whom. It's important that you look at it from the outside and maintain some distance because truths will be distorted by those who have perpetuated the various teachings. Don't believe it just because it sounds good. What's important is that it contain 100% truth…any percentage less is misleading and ultimately destructive. And don't look to religious organizations or individuals as the answer because they'll let you down. Look to the original work and measure its truth. If you are like I was, a marginal Christian, then odds are you'll come full circle back to the undeniable evidence of Jesus Christ's divinity and the authenticity of the inspired Word of God.

* * * * *

Bible's account of city's fate gets backing

By CARLE HODGE
Arizona Republic Science Writer

All King Solomon's men did put Gezer together again.

A University of Arizona archaeologist says his research supports the biblical account of the partial reconstruction of the ancient walled city, which had been obliterated by the Egyptians 10 centuries before Christ.

When the city was rebuilt has been disputed among archaeologists for years. Their versions varied by as much as a millennium.

But William Dever's search through the rubble that remains today, 20 miles northwest of Jerusalem, resolved the riddle. He and eight doctoral students from the UofA spent five weeks spading up the site last summer before striking pay dirt.

They unearthed part of a wall built in a squared-stone architectural style unique to Solomon's reign.

"The excavations dug new trenches against the outer wall and were able to demonstrate that this wall, founded on bedrock and 20 feet high, had two building phases," Dever said.

Their finding came in what the professor described as "the last hours of the last day of the expedition."

"A final push to bedrock proved dramatically that the Solomonic builders of the 10th century B.C. had discovered the stub of a ruined earlier city wall," he said.

Dever said the builders "retrenched" the wall "to check its footings and finally built it up higher by adding eight to 10 new corners and inserting a series of towers into it."

Egypt's pharoah, according to I Kings 9:15-17, "burned Gezer with fire," then ceded the city to Solomon as a dowry. The Israelite ruler married the pharoah's daughter.

Solomon later rebuilt Gezer, the Bible says.

Sprawled across 35 acres near the Aijalon Valley, the city-state flowered for 3,500 years, inhabited in turn by Canaanites, Philistines, Israelites, Assyrians, Babylonians, Persians, Greeks and Romans.

Because of that longevity and its biblical implications, the ruins became among the best known in Israel. They have been relentlessly analyzed by archaeologists. Dever spent 10 years on one such study, sponsored by Hebrew Union College and the Harvard Semitic Museum.

At the finish, in 1973, the scholars concluded the outer wall was erected in about the 14th century B.C., in the Late Iron Age. Gezer then was a powerful Israelite center in an area dominated by Egypt.

The date of the rebuilding was based partly on the known ages of the pottery dug up. But the archaeologists also decided Solomon's engineers had restored much of the outer wall by adding at intervals squared-stone towers.

While their seven-volume report on the excavation shed light, it also ignited fire.

Seven Israeli archaeologists contended the wall actually had been built long after Solomon.

Figure 18.1 – An example of yet another historical Bible claim being substantiated in modern times. *Reprinted from The Arizona Republic Newspaper, January 27, 1985, p. B-4.*

In The Beginning
...God

Created In God's Image

To the fundamentalist Christian, the Bible is the inerrant word of God. The Bible itself declares so:

> II TIMOTHY 3:16 *All scripture is given by inspiration of God, and is profitable for the doctrine, for reproof, for correction, for instruction in righteousness:*

> 17 *That the man of God may be perfect, thoroughly furnished unto all good works.*

According to God, then, how did it all begin? The story of creation and the early history of man is found in the first few books of the Old Testament. Most Bible historians and theologians agree that Moses wrote the first five books of the Bible.

Conservative theologians teach that the Bible was written by God's holy men through the inspiration of the indwelling spirit of God called the Holy Spirit. Moses' writings, as an example, were directly inspired by God.

According to God, the following passage explains why man was fashioned the way he was physically and instructs us that man would dominate all of Earth's creatures intellectually.

GENESIS 1:26 *And God said, Let us make man in our image, after our likeness: and let them have dominion over the fish of the sea, and over the fowl of the air, and over the cattle, and over all the earth, and over every creeping thing that creepeth upon the earth*

This passage clearly states that before man was created, there was more than just one entity in existence: "Let us make man in our image..." Most would explain the meaning of the phrase to include God the Father (Creator) God the Son (Jesus) and God the Holy Spirit (God in us).

Most theologians also believe that the angels of heaven were in existence at the time of the creation of man, including the three main angels, or archangels: Michael, Gabriel and Lucifer.

In addition, these divine beings must all have looked very much like man because man was made in their image. Jesus Himself said:

ST.JOHN 12:45 *"And he that seeth me seeth him that sent me."*

So it's clear that the creatures of heaven look very much like men. Furthermore, God Himself looks very much like a man...rather, we look very much like God because we were made in His image.

At the beginning of our world, God and His man-like creatures called angels were in existence. But what about those strange flying machines that apparently come from another world?

UFOs - Heresy or Mystery?

Is there any evidence of UFOs in ancient biblical Scripture? If UFOs exist today, wouldn't they also have been around even at the very beginning of our recorded history?

I think the answer to these controversial questions is "yes." I also believe that the Bible is full of evidence to support this contention.

I have poured over the Scriptures for answers to these perplexing questions and have concluded the following:

"If God created all things, then He surely created the numerous UFOs spotted around the world by literally tens-of-millions of people."

Incredibly, I've discovered what I think is overwhelming evidence that UFOs did, in fact, exist in biblical times...and, furthermore, in the exact form as they appear today!

Not only did they exist then, but they were always associated with the appearance of God and His angels.

The evidence has been in the Bible for thousands of years, but only in light of present technological knowledge could these mysterious ancient passages be properly interpreted.

I've shown several of these Scriptures to friends and family members who claim they have read the Bible several times. In every case they either did not remember reading the particular passage, or, if they had, they certainly never gave them much thought. In other words, these mysterious passages were simply skipped over for lack of understanding.

The wonderful truths of these passages reveals that the UFO has played a key role in God's past dealings with man and that it will continue to be an integral part of His "Master Plan."

There are, of course, inherent dangers in making such a claim, but the potential benefit to mankind far outweighs the risks, at least in my mind.

To many, the territory into which I am about to embark is sacred, which is to say, traditional teachings and Bible scholars' own interpretation of Scripture is viewed by them as sacred. Dogma is not a pretty word.

There are a few, however, who will bravely reexamine centuries-old preconceptions and give serious consideration to the possibility of what I am about to relay. To those, a whole new understanding will unfold that will undergird their faith. That is my sincere desire and, I hope, purpose.

This is not something that I take lightly and I certainly recognize that the implications are profound. Therefore, I have been careful not to make false assumptions or to deliberately take subject matter out of context in order to better make my case.

Methodology of Interpretation

Probably the single most important thing to bear in mind when reading mysterious passages from the Bible is to keep them in reference to one another. Far too many cults in America have taken bits and pieces of Scripture out of context and have based whole theologies on these carefully chosen pieces of misinformation.

This, naturally, has lead to religions of half truths. To everyone reading this book, I urge you to carefully weigh what is written here and to check it for yourselves with the Scriptures of the King James Version of the Bible.

Space does not permit me to include all of the Scriptures associated with each quoted text, however, I will try to summarize the general scenario of each passage to keep things clearer in your mind.

I am in no way trying to mislead or deceive anyone. Quite the contrary, my whole desire is to shed new light on the subject and thereby strengthen as well as enlighten my readers. The result should be a renewed faith in the Truths of the Bible. And for those who have seen UFOs, it should help preserve your Christian faith in spite of what you've seen or may have heard about the subject.

How the Ancients Viewed the World

When reading ancient accounts of events it is vital to keep in mind the mentality of the day. If we were able to show a light bulb to someone who lived thousands of years ago, most likely their only explanation for the apparatus would be that it resembles a glowing ember of coal or a fire. The words simply would not exist in their vocabulary to explain what they had seen.

Throughout the Bible, accounts are given of ancient prophets who were given glimpses of the future by the angels of God. What a frightening sight it must have been.

Try to put yourself in the place of someone like the Jewish prophet Ezekiel who lived about 600 years before the birth of Christ. How could he explain what he saw if he were given a glimpse of the 20th century? To what could he compare a modern automobile or airplane?

This is precisely what the ancient prophets had to contend with when given their visions of the future. But this is also true for those who were fortunate enough to find themselves in the presence of God, Himself. In what form did God and His angels manifest themselves and what comparisons did the ancients use to describe what they had seen?

Clouds, Fire & Whirlwinds

The Old Testament abounds with accounts of God's appearance and there are several phenomena that are consistently associated with His appearance: clouds, fire and whirlwinds.

God, the Bible says, lives high above the Earth in the heavens where He can look down to see the affairs of men:

> **PSALM 33:13** *The LORD looketh from heaven; he beholdeth all the sons of men*
>
> *14 From the place of his habitation he looketh upon the inhabitants of the earth.*

When He spoke to Job He arrived in what Job described as a whirlwind:

> **JOB 38:1** *Then the LORD answered Job out of the whirlwind...*

It's important not to mistake the whirlwind for God. Remember, God looks like a man but is too glorious to look upon directly, as Moses discovered when God spoke these words to him:

> **EXODUS 33:22** *And it shall come to pass, while my glory passeth by, that I will put thee in a clift of the rock, and will cover thee with my hand while I pass by:*
>
> *23 And I will take away mine hand, and thou shalt see my back parts: but my face shall not be seen.*
>
> **I JOHN 4:12** *No man hath seen God at any time...*

Moses was also privileged to speak directly to God on many other occasions but God always shielded His appearance. Each time that God appeared, He arrived in a "cloud".

> EXODUS 19:9 *And the LORD said unto Moses, Lo, I come unto thee in a thick cloud, that the people may hear when I speak with thee, and believe thee for ever...*

An estimated two to four million Jews saw this cloud descend from out of heaven.

AUTHOR'S NOTE: It's generally recognized that "heaven" can refer to one of three different areas: (1) The heavens directly around the Earth...what we call Earth's atmosphere. (2) The place where Christians will live for eternity in the presence of Jesus: a magnificent city called "The New Jerusalem," "God's holy mountain," "Mount Zion" and a host of other references that we shall explore further in later chapters. Jesus said *"I go* (to heaven) *to prepare for you a place that where I am, you may be also,"* (referring to the New Jerusalem), and (3) the area beyond our atmosphere including all of infinite space and its suns and planets. An area that exists within this heaven is the present place of God's habitation. It is described as a place rather than a planet and its exact location is unknown at present, although there may be hints in the 9th chapter of Job.

On another occasion, God appeared to Moses in a cloud and directed him to build Him a holy dwelling place which would be called the "tabernacle of God." Each time that God wished to speak to Moses, He would descend upon the tabernacle in a cloud:

> EXODUS 40:34 *Then a cloud covered the tent of the congregation, and the glory of the LORD filled the tabernacle.*

> EXODUS 33:9 *And it came to pass, as Moses entered into the tabernacle, the cloudy pillar descended, and stood at the door of the tabernacle, and the LORD talked with Moses.*

EXODUS 40:38 *For the cloud of the LORD was upon the tabernacle by day, and fire was on it by night, in the sight of all the house of Israel, <u>throughout all their journeys.</u>* [Underlines added for emphasis]

The New American Standard version clarifies, "the cloud of the LORD was <u>on</u> the tabernacle by day, and there was fire <u>in</u> it by night, in the sight of all the house of Israel." NOTE: the <u>cloud</u> was 'on' the pillar as a disguise or covering and the <u>fire</u> was "in" the pillar as a glow.

The Jews wandered through the wilderness for forty years before they finally settled in what was to become Israel. When Jerusalem was built, God also instructed the people to build Him a permanent temple to replace the tent tabernacle that Moses had used. As part of God's plan for the Jews, once a year, the people would come to the temple and offer a sacrifice to God and ask for His forgiveness. The sacrificial lamb was a symbol of their sins which the priests would kill, symbolizing that God had killed His memory of their sins. The lamb also symbolized Jesus who was made a sacrifice for our sins.

On this special occasion God, Himself, would descend on the temple in a cloud and speak directly to the high priest. The exact preparation that the priest would make in order to share God's presence was highly secretive and specific. We do know that a protective vapor would fill the temple, most likely to shield the priest from the energy that emanated from the presence of the LORD. This radiant energy is often called the "glory" or the "Shekinah" of the LORD.

I KINGS 8:10 *And it came to pass when the priests were come out of the holy place, that the cloud filled the house of the LORD.*

This particular cloud was different than the "thick cloud" which had descended with God aboard and stood at the door of the tabernacle (see *Exodus 33:9* above).

It was a giant "thick cloud" of God that lead the tribe of Israel through the wilderness for forty years. At night the pillar of cloud would glow brightly and look more like a pillar of fire and its light would shine down on the Lord's tabernacle and illuminate it continuously:

NEHEMIAH 9:12 *Moreover thou leddest them in the day by a cloudy pillar; and in the night by a pillar of fire, to give them light in the way wherein they should go.*

NUMBERS 9:15 *And on the day that the tabernacle was reared up the cloud covered the tabernacle, namely, the tent of the testimony: and at even there was upon the tabernacle as it were the appearance of fire, until the morning*

The prophet Isaiah also described God's method of transportation as a "swift cloud":

ISAIAH 19:1 *The burden of Egypt. Behold, the LORD rideth upon a swift cloud, and shall come into Egypt: and the idols of Egypt shall be moved at his presence, and the heart of Egypt shall melt in the midst of it.*

Jesus, too, was taken up from the Earth by a cloud in the witness of hundreds of people:

THE ACTS 1:9 *And when he had spoken these things, while they beheld, he was taken up; and a cloud received him out of their sight.*

10 *And while they looked stedfastly toward heaven as he went up, behold, two men stood by them in white apparel;*

11 *Which also said, Ye men of Galilee, why stand ye gazing up into heaven? this same Jesus, which is taken up from you into heaven, shall so come in like manner as ye have seen him go into heaven.*

The Bible promises that one day Jesus will return to Earth in a cloud:

ST.LUKE 21:27 *"And then shall they see the Son of man coming in a cloud with power and great glory."*

The Laws of Nature and God

W hen God created the universe He did it with great order and purpose. This is obvious in all that we see around us. The great order necessitates that certain guidelines be established that cannot be violated without devastating consequences.

Einstein proved the consistency of the universal creative force in his mathematical formula $E=MC^2$. He knew that without this perfect order, what many call the "laws of nature", the universe would be in total chaos. All things must adhere to these laws.

So, too, must God adhere to His laws of creation. If He didn't, He would be breaking His own rules, something that He cannot do because God is truth. Therefore, when God appears to men, He must abide by the true laws of physics. We may be in error in some of our limited understanding of these laws and, thus, may misinterpret their effects, but they are laws nonetheless.

It's true that God the Creator is a Spirit Being. We might say that He exists in a higher or tachyon plane or dimension (see the section on Black Holes, chapter 16, p.199), and He is capable of coming into our own plane of existence at will. However, to do so He must adhere to the laws that govern our world, the very laws that He created. That would explain His need to arrive here in a "thick cloud," or "a mountain" as the prophets described His vehicle, or " throne."

DANIEL 7:9 *I beheld till the thrones were cast down, and the Ancient of days did sit, whose garment was white as snow, and the hair of his head like the pure wool: his throne was like the fiery flame, and his wheels as burning fire.*

G od may move about our planet in His "throne," but He always disguises it in a cloud.

JOB 26:9 *He holdeth back the face of his throne, and spreadeth his cloud upon it.*

The whole point of this chapter is to show you that when God revealed Himself to His prophets His appearance was always connected with clouds, fire and/or whirlwinds. However, God the Father has never shown His face to anyone. Jesus said, *"if you have seen me, you have seen the Father, who sent me."* Thus, we must conclude that God the Creator looks just like a man, more specifically, the man called Jesus Christ.

*   *   *   *   *

Image Courtesy NASA / Hubble Directorate

Figure 19.1 – Several galaxies combine to form this magnificent "galactic rose". The distorted shape of the larger of the two galaxies shows signs of tidal interactions with the smaller of the two. It is thought that the smaller galaxy has actually passed through the larger one.

NASA, ESA and the Hubble Heritage Team (STScI/AURA)

Wheel Within A Wheel

UFOs vs. HFOs

As we have established, God has appeared to men in clouds and fire and whirlwinds. But aren't we stretching things just a little (or a lot) to imply that these descriptions may have something to do with the modern UFO phenomenon?

I might question such a contention if it were not for the sheer volume of supportive evidence.

As the following Bible stories are examined with new insight – and devoid of dogma – it becomes undeniably clear that the Word of God is absolutely full of accounts that could very aptly be described in association with what have come to be known as unidentified flying objects.

The only objection that I have for this description is that these phenomena should more accurately be labeled HFOs:

"HEAVENLY FLYING OBJECTS"

The fact that they are identified as objects from heaven containing either the LORD or His creation (the angels) – both obedient AND fallen – automatically eliminates the "unidentified" portion of the acronym UFO.

What we term UFOs in our society have been explicitly described on many occasions throughout the Bible and in other credible- sources from antiquity. The only confusion has existed in semantics. Realizing the limited technological knowledge of the men who wrote the Bible, let's explore some of the more enlightening passages of Scripture.

Ezekiel's Encounter

The story of Ezekiel was the first evidence that I discovered of UFOs in God's Holy Book. Prior to this discovery, I had read several books on the subject of modern-day UFO accounts. I had been convinced that many other people around the world had witnessed the same phenomena that my brother John and I had seen back in 1967.

It was one summer, while staying with a friend, out of work, desperate for some glimmer of hope and in deep depression, that I turned to the Bible for solace. It had been a long time since I had read the Bible. Like many young people growing up in middle-class America, I was introduced to the teachings of Jesus Christ through the church I had attended with my parents. But, as does often happen, I got out of the habit of going to church when I reached the elusive age of accountability. For me, it was my second year in high school.

Well, there I was, lonely, depressed, divorced and out of work, searching for some hope. That's when I stumbled upon Ezekiel's strange encounter that occurred some twenty-five hundred years earlier. The discovery soon changed my life.

There in chapter one of Ezekiel, as well as in chapter 10, was a strange tale of an encounter with God unlike any other in the Bible. Full of symbology and hidden meaning, these chapters seemed to describe the approach and subsequent landing of several flying discs. Ezekiel aptly called them "a wheel within a wheel."

The story of Ezekiel, I feel, makes the best case for UFOs in the entire Bible, therefore, I intend to commit a great deal of time and space to this truly amazing account. The following chapter describes my own translation of Scripture as seen through the eyes of a twentieth (and now, by the grace of God, a twenty-first) century man and someone who has studied the UFO phenomenon extensively.

Let's first establish who Ezekiel was. Ezekiel was a notable Jewish prophet who lived during the reign of King Darius of Persia, around 600 years before the birth of Christ. Ezekiel lived during the same period as another great Jewish prophet named Daniel.

Ezekiel was among the Jews captured when Jerusalem fell to the Persians (modern-day Iran) and was in captivity at the time of his "close encounter of the third kind."

He tells us that he was sitting by the river Chebar in Babylonia. The Chaldeans forced the captive Jews to dig large man-made canals for them and we assume this was why Ezekiel was held captive near the river.

We also assume that Ezekiel, being a priest, was away from the other people one evening in private devotion to the LORD. It must have been evening because he describes part of his vision as appearing like glowing coals. He also makes no mention of anyone else being present when he received his vision.

In the following examination of the first chapter of Ezekiel I want to literally dissect each verse (with the exception of the first several verses which don't really require close scrutiny).

The "Whirling Wheels"

The story begins while Ezekiel is sitting alone by the river Chebar gazing up at the evening sky in prayer. He first describes the approach of a large mother ship coming from out of the north, high in the heavens.

> EZEKIEL 1:4 *And I looked, and behold, a whirlwind came out of the north, a great cloud, and a fire infolding itself, and a brightness was about it, and out of the midst thereof as the colour of amber, out of the midst of the fire.*

As the great glowing object got closer, Ezekiel noticed an amber-colored object (or objects) descend to Earth, each apparently carrying four occupants:

> 5 *Also out of the midst thereof came the likeness of four living creatures. And this was their appearance; they had the likeness of a man.*

Out of these objects came four living creatures. Each had the appearance of a man. I believe Ezekiel was establishing their overall appearance from a distance as looking humanlike. As they got closer, Ezekiel tried to describe how they were dressed and whatever equipment they may have been using during flight.

EZEKIEL 1: 6 *And every one had four faces, and every one had four wings*

Let's momentarily skip over the "four faces" at this point and concentrate on their wings. The introduction here of wings might be interpreted in several ways. The first is that they did indeed have wings which were a part of their physical bodies. I think it highly unlikely because Ezekiel later describes in verse 9 that "Their wings were joined one to another..." and again in verse 11 "...two wings of every one were joined one to another, and two covered their bodies." And again in verse 24 "...And when they went, I heard the noise of their wings, like the noise of great waters..." All of this indicates to me that these wings were, in fact, mechanical devices which might be both life support systems for long space travel (much like Betty Andreasson encountered) and flight equipment for mobility outside of the spacecraft – as we shall explore in detail later.

> 7 *And their feet were straight feet; and the sole of their feet was like the sole of a calf's foot: and they sparkled like the color of burnished brass.*

Here is a description of their feet that could parallel the description of modern boots. *"Their feet were straight feet"* could be the upper portion of boots worn on the outside of the pants.

As described by Betty Andreasson, the aliens she encountered wore high shoes or boots.

"And the sole of their feet was like the sole of a calf's foot." Since people of Ezekiel's time had never seen anything other than bare feet or sandals, it would have been difficult to describe even our society's current footwear. Calf's feet are hard and are visibly different from the rest of the leg, thus, this could be a description that parallels modern boot heels (see *Figure 20.1*).

"And they sparkled like the color of burnished brass." That's a pretty accurate description of modern polished leather or, perhaps, one of the many shiny synthetic materials that have been developed within our lifetime. Although it's not real clear whether Ezekiel was describing just their feet in the preceding passage, or if he was describing the overall shine of their garments, it is clear that the material did not exist in his culture.

EZEKIEL 1: 8 *And they had the hands of a man under their wings on their four sides; and they four had their faces and their wings.*

"And they had hands of a man under their wings..." indicates the humanlike form of aliens prevalent in modern UFO accounts.

9 *Their wings were joined one to another; they turned not when they went; they went every one straight forward.*

As previously suggested, the angels/aliens may have been Siamese quadruplets – joined at the wings – or Ezekiel may have been describing something entirely different. Perhaps this is a description of the four aliens inside of the four spacecraft who were joined together mechanically by space travel life-support systems (see *Figure 20.2*)

"...they turned not when they went; they went every one straight forward." Possibly Ezekiel could look inside the portholes of the spacecraft and see the four aliens attached to their life support systems. Since these spacecraft appeared to be spinning, perhaps Ezekiel is trying to make it clear to us that the creatures or angels inside were not. That's why he says *"they turned not when they went"* even though the outside rim of the craft was spinning.

The third hypothesis for this peculiar verse is that Ezekiel called anything that covered the angels and assisted them in flight their "wings." The possibility of the spacecraft themselves (what he later termed a *"wheel within a wheel")*, being joined to, or touching, one another cannot be ruled out, either.

In the third chapter Ezekiel describes the noise of the "wings" that touched one another and the noise of the "wheels" in the same sentence.

3:13 *I heard also the noise of the wings of the living creatures that touched one another, and the noise of the wheels over against them, and a noise of a great rushing.*

Perhaps he is indicating that the wheels were somehow joined together as they landed. Numerous UFO accounts have described just such an event where several UFOs have appeared to be connected by some sort of arc of light (see *Figure 9.3*). As covered in Chapter 9 under the heading of "Some Rare Phenomena." I speculated that this is a safety device that prevents saucers from banging into one another, especially when descending in tight formation. Their normal falling leaf characteristic while in descent would be disastrous otherwise.

A fourth alternative is that Ezekiel was simply reporting that the two cylinders or compartments of the flight pack were connected together into one unit (see *Figure 20.3*). Whatever the case, the solution to this allegedly mysterious wing formation may have a much more conventional explanation than previously believed.

> **EZEKIEL 1: 10** *As for the likeness of their faces, they four had the face of a man, and the face of a lion, on the right side: and they four had the face of an ox on the left side; they four also had the face of an eagle.*

Here is perhaps the most difficult part to understand of this whole mysterious passage. The confusion is natural and Bible illustrators in the past have served to foster the confusion. I've seen pictures of four-faced heads and four-headed creatures with eagles' wings flapping and whirlwinds spinning over their heads. Strange creatures right out of a fairy tale book!

Perhaps the angels' true identities are not quite as exotic as we have tended to believe. Let's remember that in verse 5, Ezekiel described the appearance of all four aliens with "..the likeness of a man." Therefore, we assume they had four appendages and stood upright.

Now he says that as for their faces, they had the face of a man but also on the right side they had the face of a lion. It's possible that he was simply describing several symbolic patches on the alien's clothing. On the left sleeve they may have worn the ox patch and on their chests an eagle's head.

Betty Andreasson described a uniform worn by the aliens she encounter-ed with an emblem resembling an eagle on their left sleeves (see *Figure 12.4*).

We can't rule out the possibility that Ezekiel is describing several different races of angels. Four human looking forms, four lion like figures, four eagle like and four ox-like creatures, but I think it highly unlikely.

In his book on alien contact from the Pleiades, Eduard Meier claims he was told that 108 different civilizations, at last count, had visited the Earth from distant stars. [20-1] Betty Andreasson, fifteen years earlier, said 70 different races had visited Earth.

> **EZEKIEL 1: 11** *Thus were their faces: and their wings were stretched upward; two wings of every one were joined one to another, and two covered their bodies.*

If the assertion that Ezekiel was describing angelic life-support systems is true, then this verse is fairly clear. Each angel was connected to a common source inside the craft. It would appear to Ezekiel that they were all connected together (see *Figure 20.2*).

It's important to remember that this passage describes one specific incident. Other spacecraft may not require the same type of life support system as described here in Ezekiel. In *UFO Contact from The Pleiades* the aliens returned several times in different types of spacecraft, although all the craft had the same basic saucer shape. [20-2]

> **12** *And they went every one straight forward: whither the spirit was to go, they went; and they turned not when they went.*

The "spirit" was that part of this Godly visitor that communicated with Ezekiel. Since he couldn't differentiate between the wheels and the cherub creatures (aliens) inside, he wanted to make it clear that it was the spirit part of these strange craft that controlled where they went. He further says that they were not the part that was spinning but that they went "straight forward." This verse is really a repetition of the information contained in verse 9 for clarity (see *Figure 20.4*).

> **13** *As for the likeness of the living creatures, their appearance was like the appearance of lamps: it went up and down among the living creatures; and the fire was bright, and out of the fire went forth lightning.*

Obviously mystified and perhaps somewhat confused Ezekiel calls the entire apparition "the living creatures" because they all appeared to have a life of their own. Repeating what he had seen, Ezekiel describes again the discs coming out of the mother ship and appearing like lamps going "up and down" from the main craft to the Earth and back again. As indicated in many reports, UFOs have exhibited strobes or laser types of beacons that periodically shine out from them. This may have been what Ezekiel described as "lightning."

In *Interrupted Journey,* Betty Hill described the object she saw as it traveled across the sky in front of the moon. "It looked at the time like it wasn't close to us. But I could see it outlined in front of the moon. And there were like searchlights rotating around it." The investigator asked her if they were like those you see on police cars. "No. You know what a searchlight looks like?" she replied, "and how it's sort of in a pencil line of light, and it swings around. They were like that." [20-3]

EZEKIEL 1: 14   *And the living creatures ran and returned as the appearance of a flash of lightning.*

As the craft ran head-long into the mother ship and back, they appeared to Ezekiel like lightning because of their tremendous speeds. We can't rule out that other discs were busy about their appointed tasks elsewhere in the surrounding countryside and Ezekiel may have seen these others darting away like lightning.

15   *Now as I beheld the living creatures, behold one wheel upon the earth by the living creatures, with his four faces.*

Perhaps Ezekiel is describing the landing of one of the craft upon the Earth near an already landed angel. Perhaps he is simply describing the same event again. Obviously parts of Ezekiel's explanation is repetitive and apparently out of sequence, consequently, somewhat confusing.

16   *The appearance of the wheels and their work was like unto the color of a beryl: and they four had one likeness: and their appearance and their work was as it were a wheel in the middle of a wheel.*

The word "work" would indicate something that had been crafted by the angels. Insightfully Ezekiel explains that the workings of the wheels, perhaps their power source (engine), was glowing like a beryl. Beryl stones occur in nature in many colors including blues, greens and yellows, which makes it difficult to know exactly what color Ezekiel saw. Perhaps he saw the mechanism change several shades. It's fascinating to see the drawing by Betty Andreasson of the mode of propulsion shown her by her captors. The idea of a wheel within a wheel is clearly portrayed in her sketches and her brief explanation indicates that the mechanism changed from red to blue to green or white (see *Figures 12.1 & 12.2*).

EZEKIEL 1: 17 *When they went upon their four sides: and they turned not when they went.*

Ezekiel now describes a strange movement of the spacecraft that would indicate they had turned up on their "four sides" in a vertical or angled position rather than their normal horizontal position. I would compare this to the "dead leaf" motion of descent, remembering that this occurs with a saucer just prior to it's spinning. He says they "turned not" as they flew.

This erratic movement is described by Betty Hill: 'It would go along straight, and then it would suddenly go right up straight. And then it would flatten out horizontally. And then it would drop down straight. This seemed to be the overall pattern. It wasn't done in an exactly precise way. It would jerk out. It would flatten out. So it was sort of, it wasn't smoothly done. And as they got closer, there seemed to be more of this jumping back and forth in the sky." [20-4] (see *Figure 9.2*)

This characteristic has been exhibited many times by descending UFOs as they near the Earth's surface. Once they have descended to a lower altitude, the occupants apparently engage another part of the flight system which causes the outside rim of the craft to spin. The spinning acts to steady the craft, perhaps much like a gyroscope, for slower more concise movement near the Earth's surface.

As this outer ring is engaged it will give off small points of light. This would explain the next passage:

18 *As for their rings, they were so high that they were dreadful; and their rings were full of eyes round about them four.*

Since the electric light bulb would not be invented for another 2,500 years, it was difficult for Ezekiel to describe what he was seeing. Just as animal eyes glow in the night when approaching a campfire, so too these rim lights appeared to glow in the night.

Ezekiel is moved to fear by the fact that the "rings" could fly up so "dreadfully" high into the heavens.

> **EZEKIEL 1:19** *And when the living creatures went, the wheels went by them: and when the living creatures were lifted up from the earth, the wheels were lifted up.*
>
> *20 Whithersoever the spirit was to go, they went, thither was their spirit to go; and the wheels were lifted up over against them: for the spirit of the living creature was in the wheels.*

Again Ezekiel emphasizes that the "spirit" or communicating part of the creatures was different than the wheels but that they were also inseparable. Wherever the living creatures went, so too went the wheels.

> *21 When those went, these went; and when those stood, these stood; and when those were lifted up from the earth, the wheels were lifted up over against them: for the spirit of the living creature was in the wheels.*

Countless hundreds of people have seen UFOs defy gravity and simply stop in midair. Perhaps Ezekiel is describing just such an event when he says "when those stood, these stood."

> *22 And the likeness of the firmament upon the heads of the living creature was as the colour of the terrible crystal, stretched forth over their heads above.*

The term "firmament" refers to the "sky" or the "expanse" over the creature's heads. It is from this very verse that early Christian artists conceived the idea of a glowing round hallow over the heads of angels. Perhaps what Ezekiel really saw was a helmet worn by these "aliens."

It appeared like the "color of the terrible crystal" which is paraphrased in the Living Bible: "It looked as though it were made of crystal; it was inexpressibly beautiful."

Hundreds of modern-day UFO witnesses have reported seeing aliens wearing what appeared to be space helmets.

> **EZEKIEL 1: 23** *And under the firmament were their wings straight, the one toward the other: every one had two, which covered on this side, and everyone had two, which covered on that side, their bodies.*

This is a repetitive statement but clarifies that each angel had two sets of wings, two on each side that somehow covered either part of, or all of, their bodies.

> **24** *And when they went, I heard the noise of their wings, like the noise of great waters...*

Here, again, the strangeness of the situation totally confused Ezekiel. He is attempting to describe a great and fearsome noise that the "wings" made. Apparently whatever he saw, they possessed two characteristics: (1) The apparatuses allowed the angels to fly. (2) The apparatuses made a noise like rushing water or rushing wind.

Jet packs and other similar devices are used by our own astronauts even now. An attempt to describe them in terms familiar to the people of Ezekiel's day might result in a very similar explanation (see *Figure 20.3*). Notice that the "wings" of the Manned Maneuvering Unit (MMU) appear to cover the astronaut's arms and legs in what might be construed as "pairs of wings". It may very well have been that Ezekiel was describing something quite similar. Again, remember this sighting is from over 2,600 years ago. Perhaps modern alien visitors no longer require this more conventional mode of planetary surface transportation.

> **24** *(cont'd)* *...as the voice of the Almighty, the voice of speech, as the noise of an host: when they stood, they let down their wings.*

Have you ever analyzed the sound of a rushing jet or tried to imitate one? It has a peculiar sound not unlike rushing wind and loud human voices. I think Ezekiel was very perceptive in his description.

Next it says they "let down their wings." The MMU is strapped to the bodies of our astronauts and can be detached whenever desired. Perhaps our angel friends did that very same thing once they had descended out of the spacecraft (whirling wheels) and had landed on the Earth's surface. The cumbersome flight mechanisms were no longer required, so they simply took them off and set them on the ground.

Another possibility is that Ezekiel was simply describing the landing of one of the "wheel within a wheel" vehicles, what he termed their "wings." We must realize that any of several explanations may hold the truth to his experience. Remember that in the introduction I stated that we must remain somewhat open-minded about the interpretation of mysterious passages.

> EZEKIEL 1: 25 *And there was a voice from the firmament that was over their heads, when they stood, and had let down their wings*

As Ezekiel's attention went from the small angelic creatures to the spacecraft from which they had just parted, he noticed a figure seated just inside the doorway:

> 26 *And above the firmament that was over their heads was the likeness of a throne, as the appearance of a sapphire stone: and upon the likeness of the throne was the likeness as the appearance of a man above upon it.*

As Ezekiel stood gazing up at the giant spacecraft, inside he saw another alien who looked like a human. This one was sitting in some sort of chair, perhaps seated at the control board of the craft. It was like a throne in Ezekiel's mind because of the grandeur of the foreign technology. He describes the chair's appearance as glistening blue, like a sapphire stone.

> 27 *And I saw the colour of amber, as the appearance of fire round about within it, from the appearance of*

*his loins even upward, and from the appearance of his
loins even downward, I saw as it were the appearance
of fire, and it had brightness round about.*

The key word here is "within" which tells us Ezekiel was looking into
some object when he saw the throne with a man seated on it. The figure
was bathed in yellowish light that came from inside the object.

EZEKIEL 1: 28   *As the appearance of the bow that is in
the cloud in the day of rain, so was the appearance
of the brightness round about...*

As the angel sat at the control board of the spacecraft he was surrounded
by multi-colored light panels as seen on other occasions in modern UFO
encounters. The only thing Ezekiel could compare the sight with was the
multi-colored bright light of a rainbow.

28 *(cont'd) ...This was the appearance of the likeness
of the glory of the LORD. And when I saw it, I fell
upon my face, and I heard a voice of one that spake.*

As Ezekiel stood gazing at the face of the man seated on the throne he
fell into a trance. As in all alien contact: first eye contact, then mental
contact. Ezekiel establishes this fact in the opening verse of the second
chapter when he says at that point "the spirit entered into me." Why did
he use this carefully chosen phraseology rather than just say, "the LORD
spoke to me?"

EZEKIEL 2:1   *And he said unto me, son of man, stand
upon thy feet, and I will speak unto thee.*

2 *And the spirit entered into me when he spake unto
me, and set me upon my feet, that I heard him that
spake unto me.*

Ezekiel was then levitated to his feet as duplicated in many modern UFO accounts. The angel went on to tell him many things about the future of our planet and warned the people of impending dangers and imparted great wisdom...wisdom that could only have come from a much higher intelligence.

This brief passage in Ezekiel contained undeniable proof (in my mind) of UFOs in the Bible, as incredible as that seemed at the time. But what about other Scriptures of ancient encounters with God? Did others have similar experiences with HFOs? Was the story of Ezekiel just an isolated incident that could be misconstrued to sound like there was some connection between UFOs and HFOs? Or, were there other equally significant accounts of strange encounters with God? The search was on and so was the excitement of discovery that soon consumed me.

* * * * *

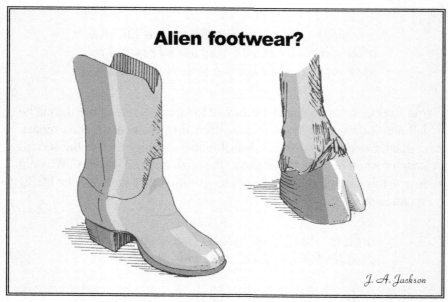

Figure 20.1 – Notice how the heels of modern boots could be likened to a calf's foot. This relatively new footwear, the boot, would have been totally foreign to someone who lived 2,500 years ago.

"Wings" attached one to another

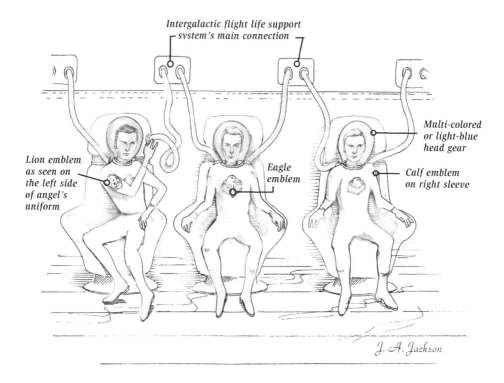

Intergalactic flight life support system's main connection

Lion emblem as seen on the left side of angel's uniform

Eagle emblem

Multi-colored or light-blue head gear

Calf emblem on right sleeve

J. A. Jackson

Figure 20.2 – Perhaps the illustration above somewhat accurately depicts what Ezekiel described as "their wings were stretched upward; two of their wings were joined one to another." (**EZEKIEL 1: 11**) Life support systems are interconnected on most UFOs as seen in *figures 12.7* and *12.8, p.158*. Emblematic patches are also a very common characteristic of NASA flights and military uniforms. Why not on alien/angel uniforms as shown? It takes a lot of the mystery out of the provocative passages in Ezekiel, does it not? The focus should be, rather, on what they represent (*see page 292*). A second scenario can be seen on *page 124, Figure 9.4*.

The fable of the Phoenix Bird has represented Jesus' resurrection since the inception of the Church

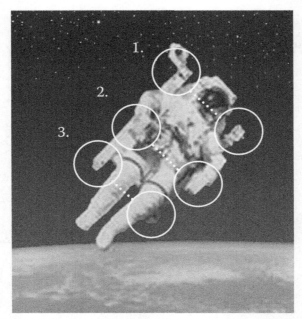

Figure 20.3 – The MMU (manned maneuvering unit) used on current space shuttle flights represents our way of being mobile in a hostile environment. The astronaut's space suit is completely self contained with an Earth-like atmosphere maintained inside. Would it necessarily be any different for an alien visitor? Notice how the MMU unit extends beyond the hands and legs of the astronaut in three perceived "pairs" of protrusions. How would someone living 600 years before the birth of Christ describe this peculiar look into the future? I would never be dogmatic about this explanation, but is it to be dismissed out of hand?

Passenger compartment of a UFO is stable as the outer rim of the craft spins. This may explain Ezekiel's descriptive passage: "And they went every one straight forward...and they turned not when they went." Ezekiel 1:12.

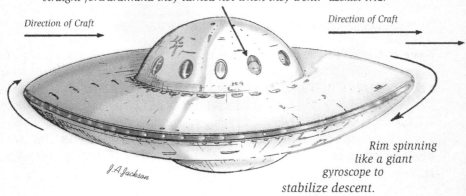

Direction of Craft

Direction of Craft

Rim spinning like a giant gyroscope to stabilize descent.

Figure 20.4 – Usually as a spacecraft nears the Earth's surface, the aliens engage some mechanism that causes the outer ring of the craft to spin rapidly. This device has been likened to a gyroscope because its effect is to stabilize the craft just prior to landing.

HFOs In Other Bible Stories

Abraham's "Furnace"

Other stories of "Heavenly Flying Objects" abound in Bible Scripture. From the very beginning of man's recorded contact with God, mysterious flying objects have been sighted and reported.

When God appeared to Abram, who was later given the name Abraham by God, His appearance was preceded by a mysterious phenomenon. But first, let's give some background to this story.

Abraham was greatly loved by God. So much so that He promised that through Abraham's lineage He would bless the Earth and that his offspring would be as numerous as the sands of the sea. In fulfillment of this promise, Abraham is known as the father of the Jewish and Arab races that inhabit the Middle East area today.

Not only did God greatly bless Abraham, He also gave him and his seed what has become known as the "promised land."

> GENESIS 15:18 *In the same day the LORD made a covenant with Abram, saying, Unto thy seed have I given this land, from the river of Egypt unto the great river, the river Euphrates:*

Naturally, both Jew and Arab lay claim to the promised land. However, it is the Jew that has kept God's word in their hearts and it was through the Jewish lineage that Jesus Christ, the Son of God, was born.

It is the Jewish race, also, that the Bible predicted would one day reclaim the land after being scattered for thousands of years. In 1948,

Israel once again became a nation of Jews by reclaiming the land once given to Abraham by God.

It was during God's visitation with Abram (Abraham) in which He gave him the promised land that the following apparition appeared:

> **GENESIS 15:17** *And it came to pass, that, when the sun went down, and it was dark, behold a smoking furnace, and a burning lamp that passed between those pieces.*

What exactly had he seen? He could only describe the incident in familiar terms. As the sun went down there appeared (we assume in the evening sky) a huge apparatus that Abraham could best describe as a smoking furnace.

There may have been more than one of these glowing masses because he says that there appeared to be a small bright light that passed "between **those pieces.**" His description of the event is mirrored in hundreds of modern sightings, as the following story affirms.

In 1954, literally thousands of witnesses all across Europe saw, as attested to in numerous European newspaper accounts, what appeared to be huge cylinder-shaped objects enshrouded in clouds. Hundreds of witnesses saw small brightly lit objects (when viewed at night) drop out of one end of these huge vertical columns and streak off at tremendous speeds only to return later and re-enter the "cloud."

As one witness said: "In my opinion it was not a real cloud, for it stayed motionless and kept its shape while other clouds were gliding away very fast above it, toward the horizon." 21-1

The whole apparatus would then appear to tilt into a horizontal position and slowly move away, eventually disappearing over the horizon.

When viewed at night, these "gigantic glowing cigars" were seen by their own luminosity and hence not compared to clouds. However, the discs that exited from them were described with precision, resembling in every detail the commonly described saucer UFO. 21-2

The following account is taken from the excellent book by French scientist and mathematician Aim'e Michel called *Flying Saucers and the Straight-Line Mystery*.

Here he describes one eye witness' account:

"It was about five in the afternoon. I was working in the fields with my men when all at once, emerging from the thick layer of clouds that looked like a storm coming up, we saw a sort of luminous blue-violet mist, of a regular shape something like a cigar or a carrot. Actually, the object came out of the layer of clouds in an almost horizontal position, slightly tilted toward the ground and pointing forward (like a submerging submarine).

"This luminous cloud appeared rigid. Whenever it moved (and its movements had no connection with the movement of the clouds themselves) it did so all of a piece, as if it were actually some gigantic machine surrounded by mists. It came down rather fast from the ceiling of clouds to an altitude which we thought was perhaps half a mile above us. Then it stopped, and the point rose quickly until the object was in a vertical position, where it became motionless.

"During this time the dark clouds went on scudding across the sky, dimly lighted from underneath by the violet luminosity of the object. It was an extraordinary sight, and we watched it intently. All over the countryside other farmers had also dropped their tools and were staring up at the sky like us.

"All at once (by now we had been watching for several minutes) white smoke exactly like a vapor trail came from the lower end of the cloud. At first it pointed toward the ground, as if spun from an invisible shuttle falling free, then it gradually slowed down while turning around, and finally rose up to describe around the vertical object an ascending spiral which wound it up in its coils. While the rear of the trail was dissolving rapidly in the air, carried off by the wind, the beginning got sharper and finer all the time, as if it were gradually drying up at its source, but without any slowing down of the unseen object that was continually spinning it into the air.

"It thus went on up, turning around, up to the very top of the vertical object, and then started to come down again, turning in the other direction. Only then, after the smoke trail had vanished entirely, could we see the object that was 'sowing' it; a little metallic disk, shinning like a mirror and reflecting, in its rapid movements, flashes of light from the huge vertical object.

"The little disk almost immediately stopped turning around the luminous cloud and went down toward the ground again, this time moving away. For quite a few minutes we could see it flying low over the valley, darting here and there at great speed, sometimes speeding up, then stopping for a few seconds, then going on again. In this manner it flew in every direction over the region between St-Prouant and Sigournais, villages about four miles apart. Finally, when it was almost a mile from the vertical object, it made a final dash toward it at head-long speed, and disappeared like a shooting star into the lower part where it had first come out. Perhaps a minute later, the 'carrot' leaned over as it began to move, accelerated, and disappeared into the clouds in the distance, having resumed its original horizontal position, point forward. The whole thing had lasted about half an hour." 21-3

The existence of similar large columnar-shaped UFOs is substantiated in the Bible in another well-known story:

Moses and the HFO

Moses was the Jewish leader who led the tribe of Judah out of Egypt around 1,200 to 1,500 B.C. The Jews, also called Hebrews from the Egyptian word *Habiru* meaning 'slave', were once favored by a former Pharaoh (king) who made the Jewish slave, Joseph, the second in command in all of Egypt because he was able to accurately interpret the Pharaoh's dreams. Joseph had also saved Egypt from famine because God warned him in a dream of the impending disaster. Through Joseph's leadership Egypt's wealth increased ten-fold during the famine by selling food to others. In return, Pharaoh freed the Jews from slavery and gave them the choicest land in the Nile delta called Goshen in which to attend their sheep. But that had all changed in the time of Pharaoh Ramses, the 18th reign of Pharaoh (or possibly the 19th reign of Ramses II). He had long forgotten the promises to Joseph, and the previous Pharaoh had reintroduced slavery among the Jews. Rameses (commonly spelled Ramses) also coveted the choice land that his distant predecessor, Pharaoh Apopis, had given to the decendants of Joseph.

Our greatest hint that Ramses was Rameses II is given in Isaiah 52:4 "My people went down aforetime into Egypt to sojourn there; and the Assyrian oppressed them without cause." It has been established that Rameses II had Chaldean or Assyrian blood lines.

Because of pressure applied by God, in the form of many plagues and infestations, the Pharaoh begrudgingly allowed the Jews to leave. However, shortly after they had gone, he had a change of heart and decided to send his armies to overtake Moses and kill all the Jews. I think it was most likely that Pharaoh saw it as an opportunity to rid himself of the Jews, once and for all, without having to do a house-to-house search of all of Egypt. He waited a few days before sending his army, thus assuring that the stench of decaying carcasses would not foul the main cities' air quality. He knew his troops could easily catch up to the Hebrews in a far away desert. His way of getting even for all the death and mysery that the Jewish God, Yaveh, had inflicted on the stubborn, unbelieving king and his people.

Most Americans, as children in Sunday school, have learned the story of Moses and the parting of the Red Sea or recall the film, *The Ten Commandments,* and its great special effects. As the fleeing Jews attempted to escape from the Pharaoh they came upon the Red Sea and were fearful that they would die at the hands of the closing Egyptian army.

If you read the account given in the Bible you'll find that it differs significantly from the film version portrayed by Cecil B. DeMille. The Israelites were in reality preceded by a huge pillar of cloud. When they got to the Red Sea and saw Pharaoh's army approaching, they cried out to Moses saying, "better we should have stayed slaves than to die in this barren, God foresaken wilderness." But Moses knew God's plan. He told the people, "Don't be afraid, for God is going to fight for you today. Be still and watch the salvation of the Lord." The people watched as the huge cloud of the Lord maneuvered:

> **EXODUS 14:19** *And the angel of God, which went before the camp of Israel, removed and went behind them; and the pillar of the cloud went from before their face, and stood behind them:*

Note that it's not called "a pillar of cloud" but, rather, referred to as the (solid) pillar "of the cloud", inferring the cloud or vapor was simply a cloaking mechanism to hide the appearance of the cylinder, or pillar. Deuteronomy 33:2 tells us this pillar physically held over 10,000 angels. (see *Figure 21.15*).

> **20** *And it came between the camp of the Egyptians and the camp of Israel; and it was a cloud and darkness to*

*them, but it gave light by night to these: so that the one
came not near the other all the night.*

The sight was so awesome that the Egyptian army was hesitant to attack the Jews. As the night drew near the object gave off an enormous light that lit the entire camp of over 1 million Jews, as well as the Egyptian army.

It was during that tense night that Moses stretched out his hand and the sea parted, but it was not an instantaneous occurrence as portrayed in the film. It took all night to dry out the seabed:

> **EXODUS 14:21** *And Moses stretched out his hand over
> the sea; and the LORD caused the sea to go back by a
> strong east wind all that night, and made the sea dry
> land, and the waters were divided*

Then in the early morning hours the tribe of Israel escaped through the parted waters:

> **EXODUS 14:22** *And the children of Israel went into the
> midst of the sea upon dry ground: and the waters were
> a wall unto them on their right hand, and on their left.*

As daylight approached, the Egyptians were able to see that the Jews were escaping. Pharaoh's general certainly must have been a tremendous leader because he was able to talk his army into pursuing the Israelites through the walls of the huge, nearly ten-mile wide body of water. It must have been an awesome and fearful sight (see *Figure 21.1*) :

> **EXODUS 14:23** *And the Egyptians pursued, and went in
> after them to the midst of the sea, even all Pharaoh's
> horses, his chariots, and his horsemen.*

Now when the Egyptians had traveled well into the sea path, the Lord caused the chariot wheels to fall off, ensuring that none would escape:

> **EXODUS 14:24** *And it came to pass, that in the morning
> watch the LORD looked unto the host of the Egyptians
> through the pillar of fire and of the cloud, and troubled
> the host of the Egyptians,*

25 *And took off their chariot wheels, that they drave them heavily: so that the Egyptians said, Let us flee from the face of Israel; for the LORD fighteth for them against the Egyptians.*

As they fled back to shore Moses stretched out his hand again and the sea water came crashing in on the Egyptians and the entire army was killed.

I sincerely believe that God had Moses stretch out his hand as a symbolic gesture. He wanted the people to think that Moses was somehow responsible (of course, he was in a sense) for the way the giant cloud (the "angel" of the Lord) had demonstrated its awesome ability.

Now, as the tribe of Judah traveled farther into the wilderness the people began to complain about the lack of food. God heard their complaints and sent a huge cloud which dropped manna (angel's food) on the camp. Each morning, with the exception of Sundays, the cloud would appear and would drop enough manna for the entire camp to eat. The strange substance was ground up and made into cakes of bread which tasted like "wafers made with honey." This practice continued throughout their entire forty-year journey (see *Exodus chapter 16*).

The Ten Commandments

Moses and "the children of Israel," as they were called, were a special people to God, therefore, He demanded that they live by certain rules and regulations, all of which were meant to enrich the quality of their lives.

It soon became evident that the people had short memories because they impulsively returned to their former pagan rituals, once out of Egypt.

To help simplify matters the Lord decided to introduce ten basic rules of conduct.

To ensure that everyone knew these rules came directly from God, Moses was told that the Lord would appear to the whole tribe of Judah in a huge mountainlike cloud:

EXODUS 19:9 *And the LORD said unto Moses, Lo, I come unto thee in a thick cloud, that the people may hear when I speak with thee, and believe thee for ever. And Moses told the words of the people unto the LORD*

10 *And the LORD said unto Moses, Go unto the*
people, and sanctify them to day and to morrow, and
let them wash their clothes,

This is a strange request. The Lord asked the people to sanctify themselves (translates: cleanse themselves) not only once but for two days in a row.

This practice is reminiscent of the action taken by the aliens that abducted Betty Andreasson. If you recall, she was exposed to something she called a "cleansing thing." She explained that she thought the device was being used to rid her body of any germs or contaminating bacteria... something that may have been harmful to her captors.

EXODUS 19:11 *And be ready against the third day: for the*
third day the LORD will come down in the sight of all
the people upon mount Sinai.

There was probably some significance, symbolically, in the fact that the Lord appeared on the third day. When Jesus died it was on the third day that He arose from the dead. The number three also represents the Trinity.

EXODUS 19:12 *And thou shalt set bounds unto the people*
round about, saying, Take heed to yourselves, that
ye go not up into the mount, or touch the border of
it: whosoever toucheth the mount shall be surely put to
death:

May I ask, "How do you set bounds around a mountain? Where does a mountain begin so that you can be sure that you are not touching it?" If we stretched ropes around a mountainous area to define the area, would we not still be touching the mountain by walking on the Earth as we approached the boundary? The only logical explanation is that the mountain that is referred to here is the mountain of the Lord. More graphically: the huge metallic spacecraft obscured by clouds; most likely the "pillar of cloud by day and the column of fire by night."

Again, the only familiar terminology that Moses could use to describe the huge solid object would be to call it a "mountain."

And why the stiff penalty for just touching something? Obviously there must have been great inherent danger in the thing itself.

As we have learned in the first half of this book, UFOs often leave traces of harmful radioactivity. Could this stiff penalty imposed by Moses simply have been for the people's own protection?

So that they might better understand the peril, Moses emphasized the urgency of following the LORD's instructions by putting it into terms that the people could relate to:

> EXODUS 19:13 *Thee shall not an hand touch it, but he shall surely be stoned, or shot through: whether it be beast or man, it shall not live: when the trumpet soundeth long, they shall come up to the mount.*

Note that this passage simply instructs the people to come "up to" (approach) the object, not to come "into" the object as Moses would later be instructed to do.

Moses was apparently up on Mount Sinai in the presence of the Lord when he received his directions:

> EXODUS 19:14 *And Moses went down from the mount unto the people, and sanctified the people; and they washed their clothes.*

Here we clearly see what God meant by sanctify...He was telling the people to cleanse themselves physically as well as spiritually.

> 15 *And he said unto the people, Be ready against the third day: come not at your wives.*

> 16 *And it came to pass on the third day in the morning, that there were thunders and lightnings, and a thick cloud upon the mount, and the voice of the trumpet exceeding loud; so that all the people that was in the camp trembled.*

The "thick cloud" floated over the top of mount Sinai (another word for thick is solid). The solid mass surrounded in clouds, rumbling and shooting out sparks like lightning, settled down over the top of the mount.

Next, the huge object let out a fierce blast that sounded like a trumpet. It was so loud that the people actually shook in fear.

It truly must have been loud to alert up to four million people who, no doubt, were spread out over a tremendously large area. The city of Phoenix contains less than 1.5 million people and any horn we have – I don't care how loud it is – would never alert people from one end of the city to the other. Can anyone say, "Sky Trumpets?"

> **EXODUS 20:18** *And all the people saw the thunderings, and the lightnings, and the noise of the trumpet, and the mountain smoking: and when the people saw it, they removed, and stood afar off.*

Visibly shaken, Moses had to coax the people into approaching the fearful mountain of God:

> **EXODUS 19:17** *And Moses brought forth the people out of the camp to meet with God; and they stood at the nether part of the mount.*

Moses brought the people forth and had them stand under the huge object. "Nether" means "down under," as the nether world would indicate a place under the Earth.

> **EXODUS 19:19** *And when the voice of the trumpet sounded long, and waxed louder and louder, Moses spake, and God answered him by a voice.*

The object that descended was a gigantic pillar of cloud, likely the same pillar that led them out of Egypt.

> **PSALM 99:7** *He spake unto them in the* cloudy pillar: *they kept his testimonies, and the ordinance that he gave them.*
>
> **20** *And the LORD came down upon mount Sinai, on the top of the mount: and the LORD called Moses up to the top of the mount; and Moses went up.*

Apparently, near the center of the huge craft was an entrance which was used to usher Moses up into it. Once inside, the Lord instructed Moses to go back out and warn the people not to attempt to enter into the mount because they would be killed. Moses had been prepared by the Lord to withstand the atmosphere inside, but the rest of the people hadn't.

No doubt, when the people saw that Moses was able to enter into the craft they began to lose their fear. Like people everywhere, curiosity got the best of them. They were just about to break through the man-made boundary, possibly a rope-and-stanchion-type barrier, to attempt to get nearer to the source, when Moses came back out and pleaded with them to obey his instructions:

> **EXODUS 19:21** *And the LORD said unto Moses, Go down, charge the people, lest they break through unto the LORD to gaze, and many of them perish.*

> **EXODUS 19:22** *And let the priests also, which come near to the LORD sanctify themselves, lest the LORD break forth upon them*

Once again, we see God asking for the special preparation of cleansing before allowing any humans to approach Him.

Spiritual cleansing played a major part in preparing the priests for God's presence. In addition, they may have been provided a protective shield in the form of special clothing or otherwise. The special garments may have been utilized to protect them from radioactive emissions from the craft, as well as the "face" of god.

The ritual of sanctification continued throughout Old Testament times by the Jewish high priest who came before God in the temple once a year during the Day of Atonement festival. He was set aside for fasting and prayer, to be made worthy of the presence of the Almighty and was given special garments to wear on this occasion which were provided by God:

> **LEVITICUS 16:4** *He shall put on the holy linen coat, and he shall have the linen breeches upon his flesh, and shall be girded with a linen girdle, and with the linen mitre* [head piece] *shall he be attired: these are holy garments; therefore shall he wash his flesh in water, and so put them on.*

Notice it says "the" holy linen should be worn. It was a very specific garment who's design God had provided.

And what did the priests and elders of Moses' camp see when finally allowed to look inside of God's mountain?

> **EXODUS 24:10** *And they saw the God of Israel: and there was under his feet as it were a paved work of a sapphire stone, and as it were the body of heaven in his clearness.*

This is the description Moses used when describing his visit to the throne of God. He took Aaron, Nahdab and Abihu: his high priests; and seventy of his elders with him. What they saw was a "man-made" (paved) work, or substance, that looked like a bright-blue sapphire. The last part of verse 10 reads: "in his clearness" in the King James version of the Bible. However, the word "his" was added by the interpreters for clarification. If you eliminate what has been added to the original Hebrew text it makes more sense. It now reads: "and as it were the body of heaven in clearness." It's now clear that the paved platform of the craft was a luminescent, sky-blue color, exactly as Ezekiel had described in Ezekiel 10:26 (see chapter 20).

Whether or not they actually saw the Creator of the universe is unlikely. As we have already established, it is impossible for mortal man to look directly at the face of the Lord because of His powerful radiant energy.

Perhaps they were able to look at one of the Lord's angels as he sat inside the luminous interior of the craft. In my opinion, it was often impossible for the Bible's authors to differentiate between the Lord and the craft that brought Him to Earth. In the story of Ezekiel it is very clear that he had that very problem. He called the "wheel within a wheel" the Lord, and he also called the being who sat "on a throne" (in today's terminology: a seat) inside of the craft the Lord, not choosing to differentiate between the two. To him, both were equally mysterious and wondrous sights.

Perhaps this confusion, although not detrimental to the overall integrity of the Word, led to misidentification on several occasions.

Remember that the men who interpreted their visions were technologically primitive. For thousands of years their advanced technology consisted of the wheel and sword. Chariots were the equal of today's armored tanks.

It's fairly simple for us to conceive of a race of people in outer space who might be more technologically advanced than us. But for men in biblical times the sight must have staggered their imaginations. All they could say is that it must be God, whether man or machine.

Elijah knew better than to mistake the outward results of God's presence for God's actual bodily self:

> I KINGS 19:11 *And he said, Go forth, and stand upon the mount before the LORD. And, behold, the LORD passed by, and a great and strong wind rent the mountains, and brake in pieces the rocks before the LORD; but the LORD was not in the wind: and after the wind an earthquake; but the LORD was not in the earthquake.*

Back to the story of Moses and The Ten Commandments: As with the description given by Abraham, the LORD was described further as appearing like a smoking furnace, indicating a glowing object covered in clouds:

> EXODUS 19:18 *And mount Sinai was altogether on a smoke, because the LORD descended upon it in fire: and the smoke thereof ascended as the smoke of a furnace, and the whole mount quaked greatly.*

The Real Mount Sinai – in Saudi Arabia

In 1988, two American explorers concluded that the traditional site of Mount Sinai was geographically incorrect. It was not in northeastern Egypt on the Sinai Peninsula, but, rather, in Saudi Arabia (see *Figures 21.6-7*). Galatians clearly makes that distinction:

> GALATIANS 4:22 *For it is written, that Abraham had two sons, the one by a bondmaid* [Hagar], *and the other by a freewoman* [Sarah].

GALATIANS 4: 23 *But he who was of the bondwoman was born after the flesh; but he of the freewoman was by promise.*

By way of explanation, Ishmael is the father of today's Arab/Moslem people. It's interesting to note that the Muslim Law, called the Sharia, is an extensive set of do's and don'ts of personal and societal conduct. Their clergy is consumed with applying their Law to the people, even by force if necessary. They do not believe that Jesus is the only begotten Son of God, nor do they believe He was God's promised Savior.

The other son, Isaac, was the lineage to King David who's descendant produced Mary, the mother of Christ. She bore a son immaculately because of God's promise. And because of the promise that Jesus brings, we do not have to live under the bondage of the Law, but rather, we have freedom in Christ's sacrifice. It is simply available for the asking, but we shall get into that later.

24 *Which things are an allegory: for these are the two covenants; the one from the mount Sinai the Law, which gendereth to bondage, which is Agar* [Greek spelling Hagar, who birthed Islam's lineage through Ishmael – see *Exodus Chpt. 21*].

25 *For this Agar is <u>mount Sinai in Arabia</u>, and answereth to Jerusalem which now is, and is in bondage with her children.*

26 *But <u>Jerusalem</u>* [Mt. Zion: God's holy mountain] <u>*which is above*</u> *is free, which is the mother of us all.* [and home to God the Father, Jesus Christ, and the angels & saints – see *Hebrews 12:22-24.* – Underlines added for emphasis]

Mount Sinai is not on the Sinai Peninsula where tradition has mistakenly placed it, but in Saudi Arabia. If it were on the Sinai Peninsula that would have required Moses and the Jews to cross either at the Reed Sea (or one of its tributaries), or at the western finger of the Red Sea, called the Gulf of Suez today. Crossing the waste-deep Reed Sea would not require much of a miracle and has been a favorite target for skeptics who claim a "typo" in the Bible. What is written "Red" should have been labeled "Reed," they say. Crossing the thousand-foot-plus deep Gulf of Aqaba (see *Figure 21.2*) invited skepticism. It's easy to see how critics would doubt the parting of a thousand foot wall of water. It would be a monumental task, even for angels. Remember God created the laws of physics and even the angels have to obey them.

Bob Cornuke and Larry Williams, the aforementioned explorers, have discovered that a natural land bridge – covered in only 50 feet of water – connects the southern tip of the Sinai Peninsula with the mainland of northwestern Saudi Arabia. Directly across this bridge, and just north, is a secret Saudi (Islamic) archaeological site guarded by soldiers and enclosed in 15-foot-high fencing topped with razor-wire (see *Figure 21.12*).

The fencing prohibits access to a large 8,000 foot high mountain called Jabal al Lawz – known locally as the "Mountain of Moses". It could also be interpreted the Mountain of the Law. The double-peaked formation has a natural amphitheater between its peaks (see *Figure 21.11*).

Cornuke and Williams claim this is the true Mount Sinai because it fits all the requirements, primarily that it is in Saudi Arabia. That means that Moses would likely have crossed over the shallow Reed Sea, but that is not where the miracle of the parting of the waters took place. The miracle actually occurred near the second inlet of the Red Sea, now called the Gulf of Aqaba (see *Figures 21.2 & 21.6*).

Additionally, when Cornuke and Williams managed to sneak by the guards at night and dig under the fence, they surveyed the area and found what appeared to be a large altar constructed from stacked boulders. On some of the rocks they found 8 foot tall petroglyphs of cattle, something that resembled those found in Egypt, but not in Saudi Arabia where they'vehistorically kept mainly sheep. Cornuke and Williams speculate this is the site where the tribe of Israel erected their pagan idol: the golden calf, fashioned after the Egyptian bull god, Apis (see *Figures 21.13 & 14*).

Further exploration revealed the remnants of twelve huge columns constructed in a single row, each about 18 feet in diameter and spaced 5 feet apart, just as described in the Bible (*Exodus 24:4*).

As they ascended the mountain, they noticed the rocks got blacker. It is the only mountain in the area with such a feature. The rocks and boulders appeared as dark as coal, almost volcanic, but when they broke some specimens open they discovered their centers were normal, light-colored granite as in the surrounding geography. These rocks had apparently been blackened by an outside source of tremendous heat, supporting the description Moses gave of the "sight of the glow of the Lord...like a devouring fire on the top of the mount..." (*Exodus 24:17*) (see *Figure 21.11*).

They also found an ancient dry stream bed "...the brook that descended out of the mount" (*Deuteronomy 9:21*), and suitable vegetation to feed large numbers of livestock. Moses, we know, had kept sheep at Mount Sinai several years prior (*Exodus 2:21, 3:1*). In fact, it's where he met his wife. When he returned with the Israelites, they camped there for eleven months, requiring sufficient food and water for their sizeable herds and millions of people. Only the Saudi site possessed the necessary components to support such a multitude. 21-4

* * *

For emphasis, the Lord inspired the writers of the Bible to repeat certain events. The story of Moses and the mountainous cloud of the Lord is mentioned many times throughout both the Old and the New Testaments and, as such, represents a very significant message to mankind.

Some years later, as told in Deuteronomy, Moses admonished the people to keep the Lord's Commandments.

As is human nature, the people began to stray away from God's teachings. Moses reminds the people of the awesome experience they had when they saw God's evidence first-hand:

> **DEUTERONOMY 4:11** *And ye came near and stood under the mountain; and the mountain burned with fire unto the midst of heaven, with darkness, clouds and thick darkness.*

God's mountainous craft "burned" with such force that it charred all the rocks beneath it. It was so large that, as the people looked up at the "mountain," it appeared to extend "unto the midst of heaven." New evidence confirms the intense heat produced by God's mountain, including the charred rocks on top of mount Sinai (Jabal al Lawz) found by explorers Cornuke and Williams, as previously discussed.

> **DEUTERONOMY 4:12** *And the LORD spake unto you out of the midst of the fire: ye heard the voice of the words, but saw no similitude; only ye heard a voice.*
>
> **13** *And he declared unto you his covenant, which he commanded you to perform, even ten commandments; and he wrote two tables of stone.*

Verse 11 clearly states that the people stood "under" the mountain of the Lord. Most Bible scholars have interpreted this to mean that the people were so afraid that they hid in caves at the foot of mount Sinai. How could that be? How could an estimated two to four million Jews find caves large enough to hide them all? Neither the traditional site, nor the newly discovered site of Mt. Sinai, have enough caves near the size required to hide the mass of people in the Jewish camp (see *Figures 21.3 & 21.4*). In fact, they haven't any large caves at all.

> **DEUTERONOMY 5:3** *The LORD made not this covenant with our fathers, but with us, even us, who are all of us here alive this day.*
>
> **4** *The LORD talked with you face to face in the mount out of the midst of the fire,*
>
> **5** *(I stood between the LORD and you at that time, to shew you the word of the LORD: for ye were afraid by reason of the fire, and went not up into the mount;) saying,*
>
> **6** *I am the LORD thy God, which brought thee out of the land of Egypt, from the house of bondage.*

The Lord spoke to them face-to-face. In other words, directly to them from out of the mountain. How could He do so if they were all hiding in caves?

Moses also says that the people were afraid to go up "into" the mountain because of the bright light or "fire."

> **EXODUS 24:15** *And Moses went up into the mount, and a cloud covered the mount.*
>
> **16** *And the glory of the LORD abode upon mount Sinai, and the cloud covered it six days: and the seventh day he called unto Moses out of the midst of the cloud.*
>
> **17** *And the sight of the glory of the LORD was like devouring fire on the top of the mount in the eyes of the children of Israel.*

18 *And Moses went into the midst of the cloud, and gat him up into the mount: and Moses was in the mount forty days and forty nights.*

If Moses was already on Mount Sinai when the cloud descended why did the cloud "gat him up into the mount?" Clearly, there are two mountains being spoken of here. One is mount Sinai and the other is the mount of the Lord. But a possible third object is called "the cloud."

And what did the smaller cloud look like that took Moses up into the Lord's mountain? Perhaps we can get a clue from the shape of the covering used on the clay jars containing the Dead Sea Scrolls.

I visited Israel myself to find answers to these many baffling questions. During my tour I was taken to the Shrine of the Book in Jerusalem. A few blocks away from the Israeli Knesset building (their parliament) stands the monument housing replicas of the Dead Sea Scrolls. One is taken aback by the striking shape of the building (see *Figure 21.20*). There, rising before your eyes, is a saucer-shaped dome, uncannily similar to a disc-shaped UFO.

"Why this shape?" was the first question that came to my mind. Our tour guide told me that it was shaped like the covering on the jars containing the scrolls. The shape of the lid has likely been passed down from the time of Moses as have the Hebrew texts of the Old Testament.

Why this shape? Is it merely coincidence that the symbolic covering over God's Word is in this form? Could it be that the priests of the Lord have preserved a likeness of "God's Cloud" from the beginning, only we have not been able to recognize the significance of the shape? The same cloud that covered the temple at certain times during Moses' reign? The same cloud that took Moses up into the mount? And the same type of cloud that took Jesus into heaven?

The exodus of the Jew from a hostile land and God's preservation of a special race of people is such an incredible story! In light of present knowledge, the story of Moses and the Ten Commandments, as well as many other Bible stories, has taken on special meaning.

Enoch & Elijah - Beamed Up!

The biblical accounts of Elijah and Enoch have something in common. Both relate that they were translated: taken up into heaven, without ever experiencing death.

Webster's defines the word "translation" as follows: (1) Motion in which every point of the moving object has simultaneously the same velocity and direction of motion. (2) To change something into another form.

Enoch

HEBREWS 11:5 *By faith Enoch was translated that he should not see death; and was not found, because God had translated him: for before his translation he had testimony, that he pleased God.*

6 But without faith it is impossible to please him: for he that cometh to God must believe that he is, and that he is a rewarder of them that diligently seek him.

The opposite of faith is fear. By overcoming fear through faith in God, Enoch was taken out of this world and never died. He was instantly changed into a creature of the heavenly realm.

Betty Andreasson was "chosen," according to her own testimony, because of her faith. Could it be that she, too, had pleased God just as Enoch had? Most people would have panicked if they had seen little green men coming through the kitchen door. Not Betty. She offered to feed them and kept her mind on God, remembering the following Scripture:

HEBREWS 13:1 *Let brotherly love continue.*
2 Be not forgetful to entertain strangers: for thereby some have entertained angels unawares.

Elijah

Elijah is the only other human mentioned in Bible Scripture who was translated into heaven before his death:

> II KINGS 2:11 *And it came to pass, as they still went on, and talked, that, behold, there appeared a chariot of fire, and horses of fire, and parted them both asunder; and Elijah went up by a whirlwind into heaven.*

There appeared to Elijah and his young friend, Elisha, a large glowing craft with several smaller objects accompanying, and apparently preceding it. The formation was graphically described by Elisha as a flaming chariot and horses of fire. Sound familiar? How about a large mother ship preceded by several glowing discs, in classic formation?

One of the objects appeared to spin in a circular pattern like a "whirlwind" as it dropped down to the Earth to pick up Elijah. When it did, it caused the two men to be separated (parted asunder) so it could take Elijah aboard and depart into the sky.

Daniel's "Holy Mountain"

Daniel was another great Jewish prophet who lived at the time of Ezekiel. He was also a captive of the Chaldeans but was held in the city of Babylon.

Daniel, the son of King David, was a faithful follower of the laws of God even while in captivity and was blessed by Him with the gift of prophecy.

His prophetic utterances, as recorded in the book of Daniel, tell of the End Times when Jesus will return to Earth. Others of his predictions told of coming world powers including the Roman and Grecian Empires and predicted their eventual demise, along with the fall of the Babylonian Empire, itself.

His ability to interpret King Nebuchadnezzar's dream led to his eventually being made the third in command over the whole Babylonian Empire. As you can see, Daniel was a great man in history with the equivalent office of a Secretary of State or Chief of Staff.

As a priest of the Hebrew faith, Daniel was familiar with the accounts of Moses, including, no doubt, the sanctification process that Moses was directed to employ when making preparations for his face-to-face encounter with the LORD of Israel.

It was while fasting and executing a special prayer to call forth God's "holy mountain", that Daniel was rewarded with a special visitation.

> DANIEL 9:20 *And whiles I was speaking, and praying, and confessing my sin and the sin of my people Israel, and presenting my supplication before the LORD my God for the holy mountain of my God;*
>
> 21 *Yea, whiles I was speaking in prayer, even the man Gabriel, whom I had seen in the vision of the beginning, being caused to fly swiftly touched me about the time of the evening oblation.*

The Bible gives special reference to the fact that the angel Gabriel (who looks like a man) "flew swiftly" before presenting himself to Daniel. Just how he was able to fly is a matter of speculation. I would imagine you can guess what kind of transportation I think he used. Remember, Daniel was calling forth God's holy mountain.

One of the angels that Daniel saw is described in verses 10:5-6 and appears to be clothed much the same as Ezekiel's cherubs. This is Gabriel, however, the archangel who's appearance is more magnificent than the lower ranking angels.

The "Star" Of Bethlehem

The star of Bethlehem which marked the spot where the infant Christ was born, in all likelihood was an HFO. How can we explain such a bright object so close to Earth that remained stationery after Christ's birth? If it were an ordinary star, I doubt the uneducated shepherds could have distinguished it from all the other stars, as they did (see *Figures 21.19 & 21.20*).

The object (more likely, objects) was unique enough to attract the attention of the "wise men" from as far away as Persia which is some 1,200 miles distant. A later legend says that they were kings and names them Melchior, Caspar, and Balthazar. And then it was said that these three kings came from the three continents of Asia, Africa, and Europe. It is a beautiful tradition, symbolizing the kings of the earth from all directions and races gathered to pay homage to the newborn King of the Jews. The wise men, however, were all from the east (as stated in *Matthew 2:1*), probably from Persia, where ancient astrologers believed that stars heralded the birth of human beings destined for greatness. Luther thought that the wise men were neither kings nor princes but "merely honorable men like our professors and preachers."

The Magi visited the baby Christ at least several months after His birth (it may have taken up to two years, which would explain why King Herod The Great ordered the death of all Jewish boys 2 years or younger) because they were carried there by camels and horses. Tehran is roughly a thousand miles away, as the crow flies, but the Magi would likely have taken the merchant trade routes, extending the distance up to several hundred miles. As speculation, 1,000 miles would have taken a very long time to travel on horseback especially in the company of a kingly entourage. Most experts speculate such travelers at the time would have only gained around 6 to 10 miles a day.

Some have speculated that several "stars" actually lead the wise men from their native lands. Each Magi may have followed a separate HFO, which in turn, may have joined the Bethlehem mother ship at some point. When they all arrived in Jerusalem they lost sight of their star and asked the people where they could find baby Jesus. King Herod found out and sent for them and asked them to tell him where Jesus was so he could go there and worship him, too (a lie):

ST. MATTHEW 2:9 *When they had heard the king they departed; and lo, the star, which they saw in the east, went before them, til it came and stood over where the young child was.*

10 *When they saw the star, they rejoiced with exceeding great joy.*

11 *And when they were come into the house, they saw the young child with Mary his mother, and fell down, and worshipped him: and when they had opened their treasures, they presented unto him gifts; gold, and frankincense, and myrrh.* [Underlines added for emphasis]

Clearly, this was no ordinary star. This star moved and "*went before them, til' it came and stood...*" If the light had been visible, such as a comet would be as some have speculated, surely the King could see it for himself and send his assassins to do his dirty work. Another key passage is that baby Jesus is no longer in a stable's manger at an Inn-keeper's establishment, but in His own home with His parents. This incident clearly has taken place some time after Jesus' birth.

After they departed, an angel appeared to them and warned them that King Herod actually planned to kill baby Jesus. Once the wise men found Jesus and had given Him their gifts, they departed another way back to their own countries. At that time, the star of Bethlehem disappeared and King Herod, obviously, never found the infant Christ. In fact, Herod went insane and died within months.

Jesus And The "Cloud"

In addition to Jesus being taken up by a cloud after His resurrection, there exists another account of Jesus and a mysterious cloud or HFO.

This particular event took place several days prior to Jesus' crucifixion in Jerusalem.

ST. LUKE 9:28 *And it came to pass about an eight days after these sayings, he took Peter and John and James, and went up into a mountain to pray.*

29 *And as he prayed, the fashion of his countenance was altered, and his raiment was white and glistering.*

30 *And, behold, there talked with him two men, which were Moses and Elias:*

31 *Who appeared in glory, and spake of his decease which he should accomplish at Jerusalem.*

32 *But Peter and they that were with him were heavy with sleep: and when they were awake, they saw his glory, and the two men that stood with him.*

33 *And it came to pass, as they departed from him, Peter said unto Jesus, Master, it is good for us to be here: and let us make three tabernacles; one for thee and one for Moses, and one for Elias: not knowing what he said.*

34 *While he thus spake, there came a cloud, and overshadowed them: and they feared as they entered into the cloud.*

35 *And there came a voice out of the cloud saying, This is my beloved Son: hear him.*

36 *And when the voice was past, Jesus was found alone. And they kept it close, and told no man in those days any of those things which they had seen.*

Peter, John and James had either fallen asleep or were induced into a sleep-like trance just prior to the appearance of Moses and Elias (Greek for Elijah). Apparently whatever they discussed was not to be divulged to any other person including the other apostles. We assume it was evening because they were able to detect Jesus' countenance change. It may have been light from the mysterious "cloud" of God that reflected off of Jesus as the apostles gazed at Him in the distance.

As the Bible passage continues, we read that apparently Moses and Elias walked away from Jesus and then Peter and the others rushed up to Jesus and said "let's build a monument to this holy event," but God had other ideas.

His holy cloud came down and overshadowed them. Matthew 17:5 called it a "bright cloud."

Apparently they watched as Moses and Elias "entered into the cloud", at which point the disciples fell down on their faces in fear.

God spoke to them out of the cloud and told them to follow the instructions of His beloved Son. This mysterious incident is depicted in the central apse mural inside the Church at Gethsemane on the alleged site where Jesus prayed. His time of prayer is portrayed, as an angel descends from a strange object looking very similar to a modern-day UFO which is engulfed in pink and blue clouds (see *Figure 21.21*).

> **MATTHEW 17:6** *And when the disciples heard it, they fell on their face, and were sore afraid.*
>
> *7 And Jesus came and touched them, and said, "Arise, and be not afraid."*
>
> *8 And when they had lifted up their eyes, they saw no man, save Jesus only.*
>
> *9 And as they came down from the mountain, Jesus charged them, saying, "Tell the vision to no man, until the Son of man be risen again from the dead."*
>
> [Underlines added for emphasis]

Why was the appearance of the mysterious cloud such a closely guarded secret? Could it have been that Jesus did not want any interference by anyone when the angels would come back to His grave site to assist Him after His death at Calvary? Perhaps He was concerned that the apparition would have taken the focus away from the truly important event that was about to take place on Calvary hill when He would be crucified and rise from the dead three days later.

Clearly, HFOs have played an important role in God's plan for the ages. The paramount question has to be, "are the HFOs of biblical vintage the same as those objects currently referred to as UFOs?"

*   *   *   *   *

> **EXODUS 14:21** *And Moses stretched out his hand over the sea; and the LORD caused the sea to go back by a strong east wind all that night, and made the sea dry land, and the waters were divided.* [Underlines added for emphasis]

Figure 21.1 – "And the angel of God, which went before the camp of Israel, removed and went behind them; and the pillar of the cloud went from before their face, and stood behind them: And it came between the camp of the Egyptians and the camp of Israel; and it was a cloud and darkness to them, but it gave light by night to these: so that the one came not near the other all the night."

EXODUS 14:19-20

It's interesting to read that the object was able to direct its light so that it lit the Hebrew camp but was darkness and cloud to Pharaoh's forces. [NOTE: Moses was actually on the opposite shore we see here when the sea parted for the Hebrews. In order for this artwork to be accurate he would have to race to the other shore, perhaps on horseback, to be in position to lower his hand and have the sea walls collapse, thus drowing the forces of Pharaoh, some 250,000 strong.]

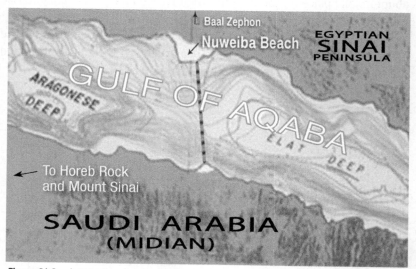

Figure 21.2 – A natural underwater bridge occurs at Nuweiba Beach which makes for a more manageable miracle for God's angelic "pillar of fire" to part the waters and create dry land for the estimated 2-3 million Hebrews to cross over.

Traditional Mount Sinai -- authenticity is challenged by new satellite imagery of Sinai Peninsula

Traditional Mt. Sinai

Figure 21.3 – Traditional Mount Sinai on the central-southern Sinai Peninsula of Egypt. New evidence disputes this site (see pp. 257-263) which was arbitrarily chosen by Roman Emperor Constantine's mother, long after the actual Exodus, and has little in common with the facts of Moses' journey to Midian (Saudi Arabia). This site has become a highly trafficked tourist destination and,naturally, church officials want to keep its designation as the true site of the deliverence of the Ten Commandments.

Figure 21.4 – St. Catherine's Monastery at the foot of the traditional site of Mt. Sinai, located in Egypt's central-southern Sinai Peninsula, has become a top tourist attraction

Recently discovered site of Mount Sinai in Saudi Arabia

Actual Saudi site includes the rock of Horeb near the base of Jebel el Lawz (Moses' Mountain to the locals).

Figure 21.5 – On the western or back side of Jebel el Lawz is Rephidim where Moses and the Children of Israel first encamped before reaching Mt. Sinai. It was here that Moses struck the rock, above, which split in half and gushed forth large quantities of water. The giant 60 foot rock, known as The Rock of Horeb, is on a 300-foot-tall hill, and has obvious signs of water erosion, yet it is located in a desert region. The fissure in the rock is so large that you can easily walk through the space. A 20 foot square man-made altar with hewn rectangular stones is also at this Saudi site, preserved in its original form (Exodus 17:15), which was built after the Children of Israel defeated the Amalakites (Deuteronomy 25:17-19). *The Amalakite territory covered "An area south of Judah and probably extended into northern Arabia" -- Encyclopedia Britanica.*

New discoveries challenge Moses' path to Mt. Sinai

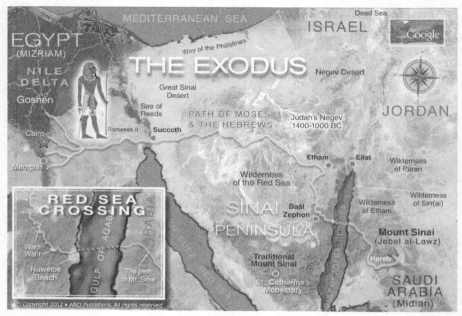

Figure 21.6 – Explorers Bob Cornuke and Larry Williams have revealed the likely route taken by the tribe of Israel which differs substantially to the traditional route to the lower Sinai Peninsula (above) where the Catholics have built St. Catherine's Monestary. The route further north can be traced by today's technology, I used Google Earth to reconstruct the likely route following existing Wadis (or dry basins), to a canyon that ends at Nuweiba Beach.

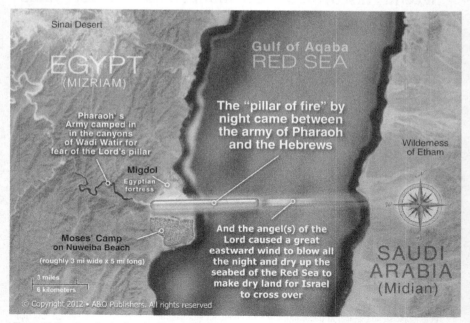

Figure 21.7 – Nuweiba is short for Nuwayba'al Muzayyinah in Arabic which means "waters of Moses open" is a clear indication that this is the right place for the Hebrew's crossing. The steep, impassable canyons following the Wadi Watir (water gully) has impassable cliffs on either side making it the perfect place for Pharoah's army to to trap the Hebrews. But the Lord had other plans and positioned his column of fire between the two camps until the seabed was dry enough for Moses to pass over.

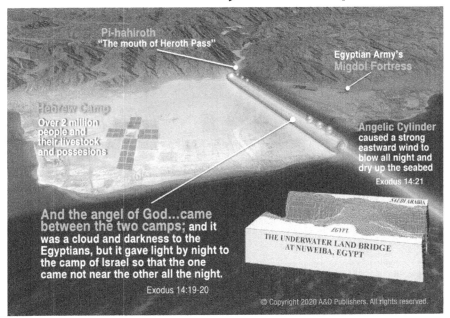

Figure 21.8 – And the angel of God came between the two camps and it was a cloud and darkness to the Egyptians; but gave light by night to the camp of Israel to prevent a surprise attack from the army of Pharoah 250,000 strong. Meanwhile, it created a strong eastward wind to blow all night and dry the seabed.

Figure 21.9 – And when the Hebrews came near to Mount Sinai they ran out of fresh water, so the angel of the Lord instructed Moses to strike the rock at Horeb and it split in two and a river gushed forth with enough water to satisfy the million plus people and all their livestock. Because Moses struck the rock in anger and set a bad example as God's representative before his people, HE was never allowed to set foot in the "promised land".

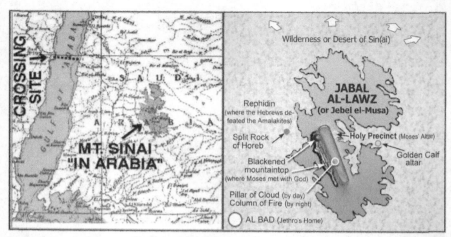

Figure 21.10 – Above/Left - Details of the route taken by Moses to Mount Sinai. Above/Right - Area where God descended on Mt. Sinai in burning heat. The Saudi site sports a mountaintop with blackened stones, suggesting it had been subjected to intense heat which penetrated the outer layer of the rocks permanently.

Figure 21.11 – The top of the Saudi mountain is abnormally dark, like obsidian; the rocks look almost like coal. It appears as if the localized area has been scorched or exposed to extremely high temperatures from some outside force powerful and large enough to cause the entire top of the mountain to be discolored. The discoloration has penetrated at least one-quarter inch into the actual rock from the unkown influence.

Figure 21.13 – 8 foot Egyptian petroglyph of a (golden?) calf found at the base of the Saudi site attests to the influence of a foreign culture that once resided there. Native representations of cattle are markedly different to this highly sylized primitive artwork.

Figure 21.12 – Fencing guards the site called Jabal al Lawz - or "Mountain of The Law." It is also known as "The Mountain of Moses" to the local Bedouins. This outcropping is where the petroglyph of a calf was found (See figure 21.11) & is likely the altar for golden calf. Site is now closed to the public and protected by a garrison of the Saudi military in the staunchly Moslem country.

Figure 21.14 – Example of artwork from Egypt featuring the bull god Apis. Same basic image as that shown above, except this more sophisticated design was done by the finest artisans in Pharoah's court.

Moses' pillar of cloud by day, and column of fire by night would have been hundreds of times larger than this artist's rendering of a column-shaped mothership

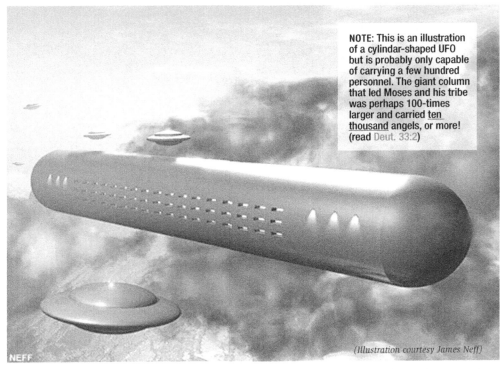

NOTE: This is an illustration of a cylindar-shaped UFO but is probably only capable of carrying a few hundred personnel. The giant column that led Moses and his tribe was perhaps 100-times larger and carried ten thousand angels, or more! (read Deut. 33:2)

(Illustration courtesy James Neff)

Figure 21.15 – "The giant "pillar of cloud" by day and "column of fire" by night took up position between the two opposing camps: Pharaoh's army and Moses' Tribe of Israel. The fearsome sight kept the Pharaoh from attacking during the night because of the cylinder's awesome radiant light. The giant craft, which held 10,000 angels according to Deuteronomy 33:2, caused "a great east wind to blow all night" and I speculate the exhaust dried the seabed for the Jews to cross over – the reason it took 8 or 10 hours to accomplish – and produced, perhaps, a type of force field which caused the waters of the sea to be held in place. Given what we perceive as extremely advanced "alien" technology, it wouldn't have been that hard for them to achieve. Read Exodus 14:19-21.

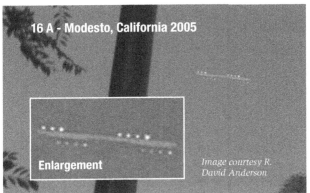

16 A - Modesto, California 2005

Enlargement

Image courtesy R. David Anderson

16 B - Giant carrot-shaped UFO recorded over Auxerre, France airport in 2008.

Figure 21.16 A&B – Cylinder UFO seen in Modesto, California in 2005. It appears to have 15 attached spherical objects. Docked UFOs of a smaller class?

Shrine of The Book in Jerusalem: UFO shape (below) represents covering on clay jars that contained the Dead Sea Scrolls

Figure 21.17 — The Israeli Shrine of The Book, housing documents called the Dead Sea Scrolls, which were discovered in 1948. It features a complete copy of the book of Isaiah. Notice the unusual shape of the shrine. It was fashioned after the shape of the lids of the clay vessels which housed the ancient relics. Is the shape mere coincidence, or does it represent the shape of the "cloud of the Lord" that covered the holy temple during the time of Moses? I speculate its shape may represent a symbolic covering over God's holy Word.

Figure 21.18 — The elevated central display inside the Shrine of The Book Museum is designed to look like a giant scroll handle with the original book of Isaiah — found in Qumran Cave One — on display. Fragments of other scrolls are displayed around the circular outer wall of the unique structure.

The "star" of Bethlehem

277

Illustration courtesy James Neff

Figure 21.19 – The "star" of Bethlehem poised over the manger, as an angel of the Lord announces to the local shepherds, "Glory to God in the highest, and on earth peace, good will toward men." *St. Luke 2:8-15*

Nativity by GIOTTO di Bondone 1310 Fresco North Transept, Lower Church, San Francesco, Assisi

Figure 21.20 – This representation of the Nativity by Giotto is from St. Luke's account of how the Shepherds were led to Christ's birthplace. Note that two "stars" are present. One directly overhead pointing its rays toward the baby Jesus. The other is a star that is moving across the horizon, obviously guiding the shepherds to the Nativity site, and clearly denoting movement.

Apse mural in The Church at Gathsemane

(Photo by J. Allen Jackson – Copyright 2012, A&O Publishers. All rights reserved.)

Figure 21.21 – The central apse mural from The Church at Gethsemane, also called The Church of All Nations, located at the base of the Mount of Olives just outside the Eastern Gate of Jerusalem where Christ will first set foot on planet Earth at His return. Notice the angel descending from a large saucer-shaped object which is surrounded by pink and blue clouds. Is this a mere coincidence of artistic style? Are there coninicidences with God?

Miracles, Apparitions and "Dancing Suns"

Miracle At Fatima

The Catholic Church has embraced several visions of the Virgin Mary as attested to by young Catholic children. With one notable exception, these "miracles" must be accepted with a great deal of faith because no other witnesses, other than the children, were able to see anything that could be considered proof of an apparition.

The one exception occurred in 1917 near a small town in Portugal called Fatima. The incredible sight witnessed by over 50,000 people has been called "the day the sun danced." This holy apparition ranks second only to the miracle at Lourdes in importance to the Catholic Church.

Each year thousands of people visit the holy site at Fatima. Many have claimed miraculous healings after visiting the shrine that has been erected at the site.

On May 13, 1917, as three small children stood tending their family's sheep near a natural amphitheater called the Cova da Iria, a "lady of light" appeared. She told the children she had come from heaven and that she wanted them to return to the exact same spot on the 13th of each month for six consecutive months.

"In October (the sixth month) I will tell you who I am and what I want."

Lucia , who was then 10 years old, and her two younger cousins Francisco (a little boy) and Jacinta Marto ran home to tell of their strange visitation. Most did not believe them, but a few curious villagers decided to follow the children on their next visit to the holm-oak tree where the apparition first appeared.

It was reported that only Lucia was able to see and speak to the "girl" but the villagers heard a "soft buzzing sound" and saw the branches of the oak tree bend downward suddenly as Lucia waved goodbye to the vision.

By the third visit there were over 5,000 people present to witness the "holy vision of the Virgin Mary." Again, it was Lucia who spoke to the lady:

> **Lucia:** Who are you? Will you tell me your name and work a miracle so that everyone will believe?
>
> **Lady:** Continue to come here every month. In October I will tell you who I am and what I want. In October I shall work a great miracle so that everyone will believe you.[22-1]

Lucia was told other "secrets" by the Lady of Light including prophecies about Russia and the end of World War I. She was also given a terrifying vision of hell. This time as the visitation ended there was a thunderous explosion that even shook a triumphal arc that had been erected at the site by the reverent villagers.

When the local Governor heard of the tremendous reaction by the people to this "so-called" miracle, he was outraged. He was an avowed atheist and certainly skeptical of the children's wild story. The situation was getting out of hand he felt, so he attempted to frighten the children into admitting the whole thing was a lie. Even though he threatened to "boil them in oil," the children faithfully stuck to their story.

Word of the miracle spread quickly and by the next month over 20 thousand people had gathered at the Cova. But the children had been forcibly taken to the nearby town of Ourem by the sub-prefecture of police. The crowd did hear an explosion, however, even though the children were absent. The explosion was followed by a bright flash of light.

On August 13, the crowd had grown slightly to between 20 and 30 thousand people. Obviously, the governor's ploy did little to discourage the crowd or the children from attending the prearranged meeting.

This time many thousands in the crowd saw a luminous globe cross the sky and disappear. Ten minutes later, as the vision ended with the children under the oak tree, the crowd, who had gathered on the surrounding hills, began to point up at the sky. The same luminous globe reappeared directly overhead.

Among those who saw the HFO were Father Joao Quaresma:

> "To my great astonishment...I saw, clearly and distinctly, a luminous globe coming from the east to the west, gliding slowly and majestically through space. With my hand I motioned to Monsignor Gois who was standing next to me, and who had been making fun of me for coming. Looking up he too had the good fortune to see this unexpected vision.

> "Suddenly this globe, giving off an extraordinary light, disappeared from my sight and Monsignor Gois, also, saw it no longer. But there was a little girl near us, dressed like Lucia and of about the same age, who continued to cry happily, 'I see it, I see it! Now it's coming down towards the bottom of the hill.' " [22-2]

The object was described by many as being oval in shape and, as it left, it discharged small white "flakes of snow," except they were round and slightly luminous. The particles disappeared as soon as they touched the ground.

This discharge phenomenon has been reported in association with several UFO sightings throughout the world. The most notable occurred in 1954 in Oloron, France. On Friday, October 17, the townspeople reported seeing an enormous cylinder-shaped cloud floating high overhead, moving toward the southwest. The ominous cloud was preceded by about thirty smaller red spheres surrounded by a yellowish ring of vapor (each shaped much like the planet Saturn with its ring). These saucers traveled in pairs in the same trajectory as the huge cylinder. Each of the objects moved in a series of rapid zigzag patterns. Several hundred people reported seeing the strange formation which occurred in broad daylight (see *figure 22.1*).

As the procession passed overhead, "All these strange objects left an abundant trail behind them, which slowly fell to the ground as it dispersed. For several hours, clumps of it hung in trees, on the telephone wires, and on the roof of houses," said M. Yves Prigent, the superintendent of Orloron high school.

The material looked like long fibers of hair and were quickly labeled "angel's hair" by the local townspeople and press. The discharge was of a gelatinous consistency and was gathered by several witnesses, only to have the material slowly vaporize and completely disappear without a trace within minutes. The whole procession, showering the entire countryside with these strange filaments, soon disappeared over the horizon.

Reports flooded in from across the area including sightings by several astonished hunters in the countryside. [22-3]

Back to our story in Fatima. By October 13, the day of the purported last and most significant visit by "The Lady of Light," an estimated 70 to 100 thousand people had come from all around the country. The previous month's vision had generated a great deal of interest and the thousands of witnesses gathered for as many reasons. Some came to be healed, some came to worship, others came to jeer the gullible crowd. Even the press showed up in sizable numbers. One skeptical journalist was an avowed atheist and editor of the Socialist newspaper *O Seculo* (The Century). He gave the following impartial account of the incident:

> "At 10:00 the sky was covered with black clouds and the rain fell heavily; but nobody thought of going home. Photographs taken on that day graphically show the crowd covered by a forest of umbrellas. A little before the customary time of the appearance of the 'Lady', and although the weather had only slightly improved, Lucia asked people to shut their umbrellas; the request, passed round from mouth to mouth, was rapidly carried out.
>
> "At 13.30, official time, but mid-day by local time, the clouds began to disperse. The children fell in ecstasy; the usual white mist formed and rose round them three times. In a few moments Lucia cried out loudly: 'Look at the sun!' Surprised, the people, who had been watching the evergreen oak anxiously in the hope of seeing something or

someone, turned round. The wonder that was announced then took place.

" 'I could see the sun,' wrote one of those present, 'like a disc with sharp edges luminous and brilliant, but not in any way hurtful to the eyes. I heard people comparing it to a disc of matt silver; but I did not think this was quite correct as it was of a brighter colour, vivid and rich, shimmering like a pearl. This disc did not look in the least like the Moon, which looks transparent and pure at night: it looked like a living star. It was different from the Moon in another way, it was not spherical, it looked like a flat and polished disc which had been cut from the pearl in a shell...and was clearly seen to have a ridged edge like a drawing board.'

"But this silvery sun, flat and disc-shaped, could not have been very high up, for in the words of another witness, 'the light clouds which crossed the sky from east to west did not hide the brightness of the star and as a result one gained the impression that these clouds passed behind the Sun and not in front of it.' The 'star' was, therefore, at that moment, between the clouds and the Earth.

"Suddenly the Sun shuddered and rocked, and then began to turn round and round sending out bundles of light-beams which changed colour at regular intervals. The whole landscape was affected by these colours, 'But Senhora, you've turned yellow!' cried one of the witnesses, before the lady turned in succession green, blue and then crimson at the same time as everyone else. After two or three minutes, the disc seemed to hang motionless for several seconds, then it began its gyratory movements, changing colour all the time.

"Finally, becoming blood-red it began to come down in a series of zigzagging leaps, each of which brought it nearer the Earth, where the temperature rose sharply. Finally, after a final swing, much more slowly, the disc rose rapidly up to the heavens – at that moment completely bare of clouds. Then everything suddenly reverted to normal; the Sun, motionless in the sky shone with its customary dazzling light, preventing the crowd from looking at it any further.

"The clothes of those who, since the morning, had been drenched by the rain were now completely dry." [22-4]

Doctor Domingos Pinto Coelho from the newspaper *Ordem* wrote:

"The sun, at one moment surrounded with scarlet flame, at another aureoled in yellow and deep purple, seemed to be in an exceedingly fast and whirling movement, at times appearing to be loosened from the sky and to be approaching the earth, strongly radiating heat."

In a letter written by another witness laboriously named Don Maria do Carmo da Cruz Menezes we get the following account:

"Suddenly the rain stopped and the sun broke through, casting its rays upon the earth. It seemed to be falling on that vast crowd of people and it spun like a firewheel, taking on all the colours of the rainbow. We ourselves took on those colours, with our clothes and even the earth itself. One heard cries and saw many people in tears. Deeply impressed, I said to myself, 'My God, how great is your power!' " [22-5]

This truly amazing, well-documented account describes, without question, the appearance of an object that must be classified as a typical UFO (In this case, however, I would label the apparition an HFO: a Heavenly Flying Object).

The Dancing Sun In Yugoslavia

Beginning in June of 1981, in Medjugorje (Med·jew·gor'·yah), Yugoslavia (since divided into Bosnia-Herzegovina, Serbia, Kosovo, Slovinia, Montenegro and Croatia) several children began having purported visions of the Virgin Mary who has called her people to conversion, prayer, penitence and fasting with an emphasis on peace in the world. She consistently has asked her followers to look to Jesus, her Son, as Savior and example. These apparitions, which continued for at least 9 years, have been embraced by literally millions of sincere people from around the world. Many have claimed to have seen the sun dance and quiver and give off different colors of light as it apparently turned into a silver-like disc.

Other visitors have witnessed a glowing sphere descending upon the village. Wayne Weible, author of *Medjugorje: The Message* – and interestingly enough, a Protestant Lutheran – has seen these apparitions himself (with the exception of Mary, whom only the chosen children can see). In his excellent book he takes a close look at the effects of the daily appearances of Mary. The tiny village of some 400 Croatian families in central Yugolsavia has been dramatically changed by the events. There has been a renewed commitment to Jesus Christ by the people and prayer groups are springing up throughout the world, mainly in answer to Mary's pleas. The one overriding message has been a call to conversion, prayer and fasting because we are living in the End Times, according to the vision of Mary. [22-6]

Miracles At Lubbock

In 1988 three parishioners of St. John Neumann's Catholic Church in Lubbock, Texas, claimed to have heard from the Virgin Mary. Her messages forecast a miracle during the celebration on the feast of the Assumption of Mary into heaven, a traditional Catholic mass. On August 15 at about 6:10 p.m. a crowd, estimated at over 12 thousand, had gathered. "Many in the crowd began to applaud and point to the sun, which was going behind a cloud. Some described the sun as pulsating and changing colors as light streamed through the edge of the cloud." [22-7]

286

As had been predicted by the three parishioners, it began to rain even though no rain was forecast for that day. As the sun re-emerged from behind the cloud it took on a special character. "...most said they saw it pulsate and were able to look directly into the sun without it hurting their eyes...some saw a round object spinning before the sun, while the sun grew larger and smaller behind it. Many saw beautiful beams of light coming from the clouds and falling on the people," according to the editor of Today's Catholic. Many claimed to have seen visions of Mary, Christ and angels in the clouds.

Visions of the sun were reported to have occurred at the Oblate Shrine in San Antonio on the feast day and are reportedly taking place in Nicaragua, Guatemala, Chile, Russia, the Ukraine, in Africa and elsewhere. Mary's messages "...are a call for conversion, prayer, fasting and reconciliation. They are an invitation to...pay attention to the signs of the times." [22-8]

* * * * *

The Miracle at Fatima

Figure 22.1 – The miracle at Fatima, Portugal is also called "The Day The Sun Danced" by the Catholic Church. The reoccurring vision by three children was accompanied by a classic UFO which changed colors and was witnessed by over 70,000 people on one occasion. The Blessed Virgin called for a return to her Son, Jesus, and repentance by the people.

Angels

What Is An Angel?

The Bible describes angels as heavenly creatures who carry out the affairs of God throughout the universe. The time of their actual creation is uncertain, but most Bible scholars agree that they existed long before God created man and likely the Earth, itself. They are eternal creatures, they never die, because they are spirit beings.

We might describe them as "tachyon" creatures, able to come into our plane of existence and interact with men and then return to their own heavenly dimension, according to God's will.

However, not all angels are eager to obey the will of god, as we shall see.

Their Order In The Hierarchy Of Intelligences

The Bible puts God at the head of all creatures, naturally, and the Triune God manifests Himself in God the Father (the Creator), God the Son (when He came to Earth in the form of Jesus to teach and dwell among us as an example), and God the Holy Spirit (God present within us).

Next, would be the archangels which include Michael and Gabriel, and at one time, Lucifer.

Twenty four elders are also mentioned who are likely some of the holy prophets described in the Bible, although that is unclear. They are positioned nearer the throne of God which likely indicates they hold places of special favor in heaven. Then there are the "normal" angels, if you will.

Differing Degrees of Honor

ST. MATHEW 11:11 *"Verily I say unto you, Among them that are born of women there hath not risen a greater than John the Baptist: notwithstanding he that is least in the kingdom of heaven is greater than he."*

This verse is very significant in that it establishes the fact that there are differing levels of importance in heaven. In saying the "least" in heaven is greater than John the Baptist (while still a mortal on Earth) Jesus implied that there are greater and lesser angels in heaven.

Possibly on equal footing with the angels, although not clearly defined in the Bible, are the creatures called the "beasts" in the Book of Revelation.

After these spiritual beings, come the "firstfruits" of God: Man, himself, and the Saints who were once men but have been changed into spirit beings (like angels) after their physical deaths. There is a hierarchy of the saints, too, who have been judged and rewarded "according to their works" on Earth. (*Rev. 22:12*)

Although man has dominion over the beasts of the Earth, there is no reference to animals having a special place in heaven (*Genesis 1:26*). We do know that there will be animals in heaven, however, that reside in perfect harmony in the Garden of Eden.

Where Do They Live?

The angels dwell in heaven in the presence of God:

PSALM 80:1 *Give ear, O Shepherd of Israel, thou that leadest Joseph like a flock; thou that dwellest between the cherubims, shine forth.*

Whether they came from another world similar to ours or from a place significantly different than ours is not known.

Their Appearance

Angels have appeared, for the most part, in the form of a human male.

Daniel, in describing a visiting angel, clearly states: "...one like the appearance of a man"(*Daniel 10:18*).

Abraham entertained three angels not knowing they were angels (*Genesis, chapter 18*). Manoah and his wife also entertained an angel not realizing it until he disappeared in a flame (*Judges, chapter 13*).

Other names for angels are "cherubim" and "seraphim" and there is some indication that they can appear in forms other than man-like.

Seraphim

The word seraphim is used to describe the messengers of God in only one incident in the entire Bible and it describes creatures with "covering wings" as with Ezekiel's cherubim.

> **ISAIAH 6:2** *Above it stood the seraphims; each one had six wings; with twain he covered his face, and with twain he covered his feet, and with twain he did fly.*

In the original Hebrew the word is seraph and means "fiery" or copper-colored. Isaiah is simply describing the Lord's angel as a glowing, orange-colored creature or object. It stands to reason, then, that the term "saraphim" should more properly be used as an adjective (descriptive) rather than a noun (person, place or thing) and be used in conjunction with the noun: angel.

Wing in Hebrew also simply means "extremity" or can mean to "project laterally." Twain in Hebrew also means to "disguise."

With optional Hebrew words placed in this Scripture, let's read it again. "Above it stood the fiery objects: each one had six extremities that projected them laterally; the disguise covered his face, the disguise covered his feet and the disguise caused him to fly.' Quite a different picture emerges from this interpretation, doesn't it?

Cherubim

In the original Hebrew, cherub meant "imaginary figure." Cherubim is the plural form of cherub. The term cherub and angel were interchangeable in the *Old Testament* and the last place where cherub is mentioned is in the Book of Ezekiel. We might say that Ezekiel has the last word on cherubim.

It's interesting to note that Ezekiel mentions the four cherubim as looking like four separate creatures. In *chapter 1, verse 10,* he says they had the faces of a man, a lion, an ox and an eagle. Yet, in *chapter 10, verse 14*, he says they had the faces of a man, a lion, a "cherub" and an eagle. We know that he is speaking of the same creatures because in *verse 20* of *chapter 10* he says that they were the same creatures that he saw by the river Chebar, the previous incident mentioned in *chapter 1.*

He saw the messengers of God on two separate occasions and described these creatures as looking both like a cherub and an ox (I hope you're still following me, because this is very important). Therefore, we must deduce that the cherub (or angel) he saw was similar in appearance to an ox.

In describing these same living creatures, the apostle John, in *Revelation 4:7*, said they had the appearance of a man, a lion, a "calf" and an eagle. By comparison:

Book, Chapter and Verse Comparison		
EZEKIEL		**REVELATION**
1:10	10:14	4:7
MAN	MAN	MAN
LION	LION	LION
OX	CHERUB	CALF
EAGLE	EAGLE	EAGLE

In examining the third item in each column you can see a clear view of a second type of angel emerge called a cherub and looking like an ox to one prophet and a calf to another.

CHERUB = OX = CALF

The face of a cherub resembles either an ox or a calf. Perhaps it's stretching my imagination, but I can see a resemblance between a calf's head and the head of a typical small humanoid alien (see illustration).

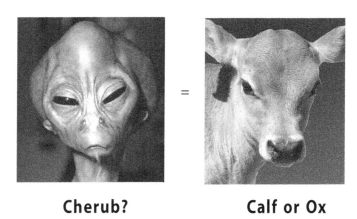

Cherub?   **Calf or Ox**

I don't want to totally discredit the possibility of the existence of the two other creatures mentioned here: the eagle and the lion. It may very well be that two other creatures exist in God's heavenly corp of servants that resemble these two animals.

There is some evidence for hairy creatures in UFO accounts, although extremely rare, that may be analogous to the lion's face mentioned in connection with cherubim. These accounts are so rare and questionable that I doubt their validity. However, I know of no eagle-like or feathered creatures ever reported by credible UFO witnesses. The only mention of a bird is the Phoenix Bird that Betty Andreasson saw and it was, I believe, largely a symbolic apparition produced by God representing the magnificent resurrection of Jesus Christ.

Betty's aliens wore the symbolic patch of an eagle with its wings spread out. It's interesting to note that the symbol for America, the last bastion of Christianity in the world, is also an eagle.

If, as I am inclined to believe, the eagle and lion were symbolic patches on the clothing of the angels that Ezekiel encountered, then what do they represent?

As previously mentioned, the fable of the Phoenix Bird, who arises from its own ashes to become a magnificent creature, symbolizes the resurrected, immortal Christ in early Christian art and literature.

Betty Andreasson's ox-like creatures all had the emblem of an eagle emblazoned on their left shoulders. It's notable that the Phoenix Bird is always represented as an eagle arising out of flames.

So, too, the lion represents the triumphant Christ. Christ is called the "lion of Judah" in *Revelation 5:5*

Symbolized in Ezekiel and Revelation, then, are the immortal, resurrected and triumphant Christ.

Angel's Clothing

Obviously, the angels that came to minister to men, who were mistaken for men themselves, must have worn the fashionable attire of the society they were visiting. However, several accounts are given of angels dressed in other types of garments.

Archangels dress differently than others perhaps to denote rank. Daniel encountered the archangel Gabriel dressed in green colored fine linen (representing the finest kind of cloth available at that time) with a golden belt. His arms and feet were covered with something that resembled polished brass (*Daniel 10:5-6*).

Many have interpreted this descriptive to mean that the archangel actually had brass colored legs and arms. However, I think Daniel is more likely describing parts of the angel's clothing. In *Revelation 1:15 and 2:18* John speaks of his vision of the resurrected Jesus with his feet "like unto fine brass." Obviously Jesus' feet were not colored like brass, as all his disciples would attest, when He visited them after His resurrection. He looked very much like a normal man except He was in His glorified (tachyon) body. Most likely John is describing whatever foot apparel Jesus was wearing.

Clothing Of The Saints

We know that the resurrected saints are dressed in white, according to *Revelation 3:5*

The angel that rolled back the stone covering of Jesus' grave also was dressed in a glowing white garment:

> MATHEW 28:1 *In the end of the sabbath, as it began to dawn toward the first day of the week, came Mary Magdalene and the other Mary to see the sepulchre*
>
> *2 And, behold, there was a great earthquake: for the angel of the LORD descended from heaven, and came and rolled back the stone from the door, and sat upon it.*
>
> *3 His countenance was like lightning, and his raiment white as snow:*
>
> *4 And for fear of him the keepers did shake, and became as dead men*

Even the rugged Roman soldiers who were left to guard the tomb of Jesus were terrified by the sight of God's powerful angel. Either they fainted, played possum, or were induced into a trance-like state much like Betty Andreasson's family had been during their visitation.

When Jesus was resurrected into heaven in a cloud, two angels in "white apparel" stood nearby.

> ACTS 1:9 *And when he had spoken these things, while they beheld, he was taken up; and a cloud received him out of their sight.*

ACTS 1:10 *And while they looked stedfastly toward heaven as he went up, behold, two men stood by them in white apparel;*

Popular Misconceptions About Angels

All angels have wings - There are several misconceptions about angels that stem from early representations in art. Artists from the primitive Byzantine and Early Christian art periods translated Scripture in terms familiar to them. Since angels flew, they represented them as having wings like an eagle. It's highly unlikely that Abraham, Manoah and others would mistake angels for ordinary men if they were trailing eagle's wings behind them!

Cherubs are baby angels - Another inventive idea of artists of that period is the naked baby cherub. Cupid is supposedly a cherub but the fable has no basis in Christian theology. It's interesting, however, that cherubim are represented as "small" human-like figures.

All angels wear white robes - Angels, too, are usually thought of as wearing the long flowing garments and sandals as was stylish in Jesus' day. No doubt, angels have appeared to many in traditional white robes because they were mistaken for ordinary men. But there is no basis in believing that robes are standard angelic apparel.

Other types of garments have been described by biblical personalities on many occasions. When the prophets were given visions of the future, for instance, prophesying angels have been dressed in completely different attire. Polished brass coverings for their feet and arms and glowing colored garments are just some of the apparel described by our ancient ancestors such as Ezekiel, Daniel and the disciple John. In these cases the angels were sent directly to these specific men and did not need to disguise themselves in carrying out their assignments.

Cornelius saw an angel that appeared in glowing, or brightly colored, clothing, as did many others:

ACTS 10:30 *And Cornelius said, Four days ago I was fasting until this hour; and at the ninth hour I*

*prayed in my house, and, behold, a man stood before
me in bright clothing,*

Angels have floating halos - The concept of round glowing halos
suspended over the tops of angel's heads is also one of primitive
interpretation.

Ezekiel's description of his encounter with angels probably gave early
artists their inspiration. He writes:

EZEKIEL 1:22   *Over the heads of the living beings there
was something like an expanse, like the awesome
gleam of crystal, extended over their heads.*

(NAS)

As I have explained in the chapter on Ezekiel, this is an extremely accurate
description of a clear space helmet as seen worn by many aliens in current
UFO accounts.

It's interesting to note that the earliest illustrations of Christ,
discovered in the catacombs and painted during the Christian Period of
Persecution, always show Him as either a teacher or a shepherd.

Not until Christianity became the official state religion of the Roman
Empire did the artists begin to depict Christ with a glowing halo or wearing
purple robes denoting the special status of rulership.

The halo, then, was originally only an apparatus connected with angels
and the earliest examples look clearly like a helmet. Not until much later
did artists detach the halo and portray it as a loose ring floating over the
tops of the heads of various biblical personalities.

The earliest depiction of a halo over the heads of diety was actually
fashioned after the pagan goddess Isis. The winged Egyptian goddess
predates Christianity by over three thousand years. She was depicted with
a sphere over her head which was a representation of the Egyptian sun
god Ra (their top diety), as opposed to the Son of God, Jesus the Christ.
The sphere also represented fertility. The winged, haloed goddess was the
precursor of the modern errantly depicted winged female angel, which
has little to do with the Bible's account. [23-1]

*   *   *   *   *

UFOs/HFOs in Ancient Artworks

Detail

Detail

Figure 23.1 - The Annunciation of St. Emidus by Carlos Crivelli, 1486 AD, depicts an object representing God which looks strangely familiar to UFOlogists. The dove descending the object, repre-senting God's Holy Spirit, is seen over the woman's head after passing through the solid-stone wall. The influence of HFOs is prevalent in early Christian artworks.

Angels' Abilities & Powers

Angels in the Bible

The following brief descriptives accurately portray the vast powers of God's angelic host. Pay close attention and you'll notice their powers and abilities closely parallel those described in modern alien accounts.

Clouds, Fire & Whirlwinds, too – Angels, too, are associated with the appearance of clouds, fire and whirlwinds. In most cases when the LORD comes in these forms, He also brings with Him His angels. John speaks of a mighty angel that came down from heaven "clothed with a cloud" and a "rainbow upon his head." (*Revelation 10:1*)

Appear and Disappear - Angels are clearly different than men. They exist in another "dimension" called the heavenly realm in the Bible. This is an unseen universe that apparently parallels our own material world. Angels are able to change their existence in the heavenly realm and materialize into our earthly realm to interact with men. Although at times they appear as men, on other occasions their physical difference is quite noticeable. Again, Ezekiel presents the best example of an angel appearing in a form quite distinguishable from an ordinary man.

Move On a Beam of Light - Several mysterious accounts exist in the Bible of angels transporting themselves in unusual ways. Sampson's parents describe an encounter in the following passage:

> JUDGES 13:20 *For it came to pass, when the flame went up toward heaven from off the altar, that the angel of the LORD ascended in the flame of the altar. And Manoah and his wife looked on it, and fell on their faces to the ground.*

> 21 *But the angel of the LORD did no more appear to Manoah and to his wife. Then Manoah knew that he was an angel of the LORD.*

Perhaps what they saw was the angel descending into heaven on a beam of light, centered over the altar they had built to God.

Move On Ladders - Jacob described an encounter with angels:

> GENESIS 28:12 *And he dreamed, and behold a ladder set up on the earth, and the top of it reached to heaven: and behold the angels of God ascending and descending on it.*

Modern UFO witnesses have also recounted stories of aliens using ladder-like apparati.

In 1975 George O'Barski, who owns a liquor store in the Chelsea district of Manhatten, had just closed the store and was on his way home in North Bergen, New Jersey. It was around two a.m. when he noticed a brightly lit object pass by his car slightly overhead and about one hundred yards to the left.

The thirty foot disc was now hovering about 10 feet above the ground over North Hudson Park in Manhattan. George watched intently as the craft approached the neatly manicured lawn in the baseball field not far from the road. It had several evenly spaced, vertical windows approximately one foot by four feet that circumscribed the object.

Suddenly a ladder-like apparatus emerged from between two of the windows and was lowered to the ground.

"The ship settled to within four feet of the playing field, and immediately a group of small figures appeared and, one after the other, descended to the ground."

"They came down this ladder thing like kids coming down a fire escape. Fast. No wasted motion," said George.

The small humanoid creatures wore helmets and light-colored one piece jumpsuits. "They looked like kids in snowsuits," he said. One by one they dug into the turf with spoon-like apparati, putting the samples into small bags of some sort that they carried with them. Within minutes, having obtained their samples, they were back inside the craft and the object ascended and moved away to the north. The whole thing lasted no more than four minutes.

Several witnesses were later located in the area who had seen a strange luminous object hovering over the park, lending more credibility to the otherwise incredible account. [24-1]

Walk Through Walls - Creatures who come from the heavenly realm, with their "glorified" bodies are able to pass through earthly matter without being affected.

Jesus, when He appeared to His disciples in His resurrected body, was able to pass through the closed doors and appear before them (*St. John 20:26* and *Luke 24:36*). That included his clothing.

When Betty Andreasson was ushered out of her home, she was able to pass through the door just as her hosts did. [24-2]

Let's remember that she was in close proximity to the main spacecraft. As she stood between the aliens the whole group was transported automatically into the spacecraft.

I would hypothesize that the aliens possess the technology that allows them to rearrange the molecular vibration of matter within a given perimeter. The "atom exciter" causes matter to vibrate at speeds beyond the speed of light and, thus, not to be hampered by earthly physical matter. If you recall, there is a vast universe of space between the nucleus and revolving electrons of all atomic structures. Certainly enough room for other "vibrating" particles to pass through without being affected.

All of this, of course, is purely hypothetical and is mentioned only to help stimulate an openness to the possibility of such a phenomenon as passing through walls.

Move Men About at Will - As mentioned, Betty Andreasson was moved without any effort on her part. In fact, she was "controlled" by an unseen force which kept her from exercising any freedoms with her extremities (arms & legs).

Many UFO abductees have experienced similar episodes. Frequently the aliens make mental contact, usually telephathically, with the subject after which they are able to gain control of their physical bodies. At that time they are transported into an awaiting craft, often levitated by an unseen force.

As would be expected, the witnesses have resisted the fearful control the aliens had over them, but always to no avail.

Are there any accounts that parallel this strange phenomenon in the Bible? When Ezekiel was taken aboard the "whirling wheels" this is what he recounted:

> **EZEKIEL 3:14** *So the spirit lifted me up, and took me away, and I went in bitterness, in the heat of my spirit; but the hand of the LORD was strong upon me.*

Evidently Ezekiel reacted as any other human would and resisted with "bitterness." No matter how hard he resisted, the power of the spirit moved him about easily.

Another similar situation occurred when Daniel encountered his angels:

> **DANIEL 8:15** *And it came to pass, when I, even I Daniel, had seen the vision, and sought for the meaning, then, behold, there stood before me as the appearance of a man.*
>
> **16** *And I heard a man's voice between the banks of Ulai, which called and said, Gabriel, make this man to understand the vision.*
>
> **17** *So he came near where I stood: and when he came, I was afraid, and fell upon my face: but he said unto me, Understand, O son of man: for at the time of the end shall be the vision.*

18 *Now as he was speaking with me, I was in a deep sleep on my face toward the ground: but he touched me, and set me upright.*

Daniel, too, was levitated to his feet and ushered away with angels to see visions of the future. Notice that there is another element present in the preceding passage: induced unconsciousness.

Angels Can Induce Unconsciousness - Gabriel put Daniel into a trance-like state which he described as a deep sleep. In the following separate incident, the angel Gabriel appeared and frightened away Daniel's companions. Apparently they were so afraid of the awesome visitor that they literally shook in their boots with a "great quaking."

DANIEL 10:7 *And I alone saw the vision: for the men that were with me saw not the vision; but a great quaking fell upon them, so that they fled to hide themselves.*

Once again, the angel established mental contact with Daniel first, at which time he caused him to lose consciousness:

DANIEL 10:9 *Yet heard I the voice of his words: and when I heard the voice of his words, then was I in a deep sleep on my face, and my face toward the ground.*

In similar testimony by UFO witness Barney Hill, he described being controlled by several aliens as he was assisted aboard their craft. The following disoriented testimony comes from the tape of one of the hypnotic sessions he underwent to uncover the event locked deep inside his subconscious:

"I felt very weak. I felt very weak, but I wasn't afraid. And I can't even think of being confused. I am not bewildered, I can't even think of questioning what is happening to me. And I am being assisted.

> *And I am thinking of a picture I saw many years
> ago, and this man is being carried to the electric
> chair. And I think of this, and I think I am in this
> man's position. But I'm not being carried to the
> electric chair. And I think of this, and I think I'm
> in this man's position. But I'm not, but I think
> my feet are dragging, and I think of this picture.
> And I am not afraid. I feel like I am dreaming."*

Half-conscious and being escorted into the craft, he fluctuates between a normal state of panic and one of assuring calm, no doubt induced by his captors. His mind wanders back to a memory of a film he had seen as a child where a man was dragged off to the electric chair. Just as this thought is about to disturb him, he is reassured that everything is okay, that he should not be afraid, that he will not be harmed. The whole incident felt "like a dream" to him. [24-3]

Daniel was awake when the angel Gabriel first appeared but was put into a "deep sleep on his face" after the voice was heard. Again, first mental contact then a loss of consciousness.

Barney Hill's wife, Betty, also experienced being put into a deep sleep by her captors:

> *"I'm thinking I'm asleep...I'm asleep, and I've got to
> wake up! I don't want to be asleep. I keep trying...
> I've got to wake myself up...I try...and go back again...
> I keep trying...I keep trying to wake up..."* [24-4]

No matter how hard she resisted, her mental faculties were being controlled by the "voices" of the aliens.

Communicate Via Mental Telepathy - In the preceding account notice that Daniel says he "heard the voice," without saying the angel actually spoke to him.

Ezekiel, too, describes communication with angels in an unconventional manner:

> EZEKIEL 2:1 *And he said unto me, Son of man, stand
> upon thy feet, and I will speak unto thee.*

2 *And the spirit entered into me when he spake unto
me, and set me upon my feet, that I heard him that
spake unto me.*

When Ezekiel says *"the spirit entered into me"* he is accurately describing
the very common experience of mental telepathy that modern-day UFO
witnesses have repeatedly related. Notice this usage is lower case "s" in
"spirit," i.e. not denoting the Holy Spirit.

Betty Hill described the type of communication her captors used:

Betty:	*I knew what they were saying.*
Doctor:	*You knew what they were saying?*
Betty:	*And they knew what I was saying.*
Doctor:	*Well...do you think that was some form of thought transference?*
Betty:	*It could have been. But if it was, I knew what they were thinking.*
Doctor:	*You knew what they were thinking. You rather liked this leader, didn't you?* (The doctor aptly perceived an affectionate tone in Betty's voice)
Betty:	*I was afraid of him at first.*
Doctor:	*But afterwards?*
Betty:	*I...you know...began to feel that they weren't going to harm me.* [24-5]

Communication between the aliens and their captives was always friendly
and didn't require the verbalization of thoughts. Somehow they exchanged
ideas simply by thinking them. This would certainly eliminate hiding
anything from them.

Ezekiel, too, informs us that the LORD knows what we are
thinking:

EZEKIEL 11:5 *And the Spirit of the LORD fell upon me,
and said unto me, Speak; Thus saith the LORD;
Thus have ye said, O house of Israel: for I know the
things that come into your mind, every one of them.*

Contact With Angels Can Produce Tingling Sensations - Another phenomenon associated with alien contact has been a tingling sensation felt by the manipulated witnesses. The feeling has often been compared to a slight electrical shock and is accompanied by total debilitating control by the aliens.

This indicates at least two types of control being exerted by the alien. First, the use of mind control. If an alien had to direct his attention to other matters, however, he could not, in many situations, allow the witness the freedom to move about at will. Therefore, another "freezing" device would be required. Most likely it would involve a mechanical or physiological device of some kind.

Several accounts exist of witnesses approaching UFOs and attempting to touch the objects. When this occurs, the witnesses are either stopped short of the craft or knocked down by a beam of light discharged from the object.

The smaller drone class of UFOs seem to have an extremely strong electrical force around them. The buzzing sensation felt by approaching curious humans usually serves as adequate warning and they will refrain from attempting to touch the object.

When the LORD appeared to Saul of Tarsus, who was later to be renamed Paul the apostle, he experienced what might be described as an electrical force field. The experience terrified him:

> ACTS 9:3 *And as he journeyed, he came near Damascus: and suddenly there shined round about him a light from heaven:*
>
> 4 *And he fell to the earth, and heard a voice saying unto him, Saul, Saul, why persecutest thou me?*
>
> 5 *And he said, Who art thou, Lord? And the LORD said, I am Jesus whom thou persecutest: it is hard for thee to kick against the pricks.*

As incredible as the following exposition may sound, I have never heard of a more plausible explanation for this incident than one analogous to a typical alien encounter.

The Greek translation for "pricks" is "sting." And the word "kick" translates: refuse to obey, to be in stubborn opposition.

Paul was fighting against the stinging, tingling sensation that overcame him when Jesus, Himself, came and spoke to him.

Paul, like most of us would, fought this supernatural and fearful experience. God had to literally "hold him down" to give him His message.

Paul was a great persecutor of Christians at the time and had sentenced many to die when he was a Pharisee of the Jewish faith. The incident changed his life completely. Instead of persecuting the Christians, he became one of the greatest followers of Christ in history. Paul eventually authored First and Second Thessalonians, Galatians, First and Second Corinthians, Romans, Philemon, Colossians, Ephesians, Philippians, and both epistles (letters) to Timothy.

Angels Can't Be Killed or Injured - Angels are eternal spirit beings and, as such, cannot be harmed by men. Many times throughout the Bible angels are credited with interaction among humans; eating, talking, and sometimes struggling with them at will. They have even carried out God's instructions and destroyed whole armies of evil intentioned men without being harmed.

Current aliens have also withstood some rough treatment from humans with little or no effect.

The evening of August 21, 1955, near Hopkinsville, Kentucky, a group of people were terrorized by several small creatures with large heads and large cat-like eyes. Dressed in silvery colored jumpsuits that glowed in the dark "like the lettering on a radium painted watch" and wearing helmets, several of these creatures attempted to make contact with the terrified people huddling inside their small farm house.

The creatures held their arms high over their heads in a surrender-type gesture but the people mistook the gesture as an attack posture because of their frightening appearance. [24-6]

On several occasions the small humanoid creatures approached the darkened home, only to be repelled by shotgun blasts and bullets from a .22 pistol. As the witnesses recalled in their official report to investigators: "Whenever it was hit, it would float or fall over and scurry for cover... The shots when striking the object would sound as though they were hitting a bucket. The objects made no sound...while jumping or walking or falling. The undergrowth would rustle as the objects went through it...There was no sound of walking. The objects were seemingly weightless as they would float down from trees more than fall from them." [24-7]

Although repelled, the creatures were persistent. In all, over fifty shots were fired at them and the "attack" may have lasted for over two hours.

An interesting side note to this experience is that several members of the group, which included 8 adults and 3 children, had gone to a church meeting that evening at Trinity Pentecostal Church. As skeptics described:

"They had become worked up into a frenzy, becoming very emotionally unbalanced." [24-8]

I would speculate that it was precisely because of this religious experience that the group was visited. Perhaps the aliens were on a mission to communicate something to certain members of the group, only to be misunderstood as attacking monsters. It's unfortunate, I feel, that these people weren't able to experience what the aliens had planned for them. Fear, the Bible tells us, is the opposite of faith and the fear that the group displayed eventually caused the aliens to give up and leave. If they had only maintained the trust in God that they obviously felt earlier in the evening, who knows what they may have experienced.

Weapons of Fire - Angels possess a weapon that is able to destroy. Ezekiel saw the awesome weapon in his vision of the future when the angels of the LORD come to deal out God's justice to the wicked of the Earth:

> EZEKIEL 9:1 *He cried also in mine ears with a loud voice, saying, Cause them that have charge over the city to draw near, even every man with his destroying weapon in his hand.*

When Gideon had prepared a meal for an angel of the LORD, the angel instructed him to put the gift on a nearby rock:

> JUDGES 6:21 *Then the angel of the LORD put forth the end of the staff that was in his hand, and touched the flesh and the unleavened cakes; and there rose*

*up fire out of the rock, and consumed the flesh and
the unleavened cakes. Then the angel of the LORD
departed out of his sight.*

David, too, saw the awesome destructive power of the angel's weapon:

I CHRONICLES 21:26 *And David built there an altar
unto the LORD, and offered burnt offerings and
peace offering, and called upon the LORD; and he
answered him from heaven by fire upon the altar of
burnt offering.*

*27 And the LORD commanded the angel; and he put
up his sword again unto the sheath thereof.*

*28 At that time when David saw that the LORD had
answered him in the threshing floor of Ornan the
Jebusite, then he sacrificed there.*

*29 For the tabernacle of the LORD, which Moses
made in the wilderness, and the altar of the burnt
offering, were at that season in the high place at
Gibeon.*

*30 But David could not go before it to enquire of
God: for he was afraid because of the <u>sword of the
angel of the LORD.</u>*

The awesome sight of the weapon so frightened David that he refused to
go to Gibeon in fear he might have to face the angel again!

Notice that at first David says that "the LORD" beamed down the
destructive force from "heaven." He then clarifies what he meant by
saying that an angel was actually instructed to use his powerful "sword"
of fire.

In another incident we see a similar offering consumed by God's
"fire." Moses ordered Aaron to make a sacrifice to the LORD according

to God's specific instructions. The LORD wanted to show the people a sign so that they would remember Him and keep His commandments:

> **LEVITICUS 9:24** *And there came a fire out from before the LORD, and consumed upon the altar the burnt offering and the fat: which when all the people saw, they shouted, and fell on their faces.*

When Aaron's sons on another occasion defied God's specific instructions they were abruptly punished:

> **LEVITICUS 10:2** *And there went out fire from the LORD, and devoured them, and they died before the LORD.*

In these particular cases the "fire" was shot directly from the LORD's cloud. In the following incident the fire came from high overhead and its source was apparently unseen.

When Elijah needed a sign from heaven that his God was the one true god, the LORD answered his request much to the dismay of the nonbelieving heathens that accompanied him:

> **II KINGS 1:12** *And Elijah answered and said unto them, if I be a man of God, let fire come down from heaven, and consume thee and thy fifty. And the fire of God came down from heaven, and consumed him and his fifty.*

Angels Have Their Own Language - Paul speaks of the language of angels as being different from that of men:

> **I CORINTHIANS 13:1** *Though I speak with the tongues of men and of angels, and have not charity, I am become as sounding brass, or a tinkling cymbal.*

As described previously, aliens have been overheard speaking to one another in very odd languages. Sometimes even clicking or low guttural sounds emanate from them when addressing one another. These same creatures are then able to communicate with humans in their own earthly language.

Angels Bring Power of Conception - One of the stranger verses in Bible Scripture speaks of angels cohabitating with earthly women and bearing them children *(Genesis chapter 6)*.

It's obvious from this account that angels possess the ability to interact with the human species in a very intimate way.

Angels have announced to several Biblical families a forthcoming birth. Among those who experienced such an announcement were the parents of Isaac, Sampson and Jesus.

Sarah, the mother of Isaac, was ninety years old at the time and the birth was truly miraculous.

Manoah's wife bore Sampson who became the strongest man in the world, another miraculous birth. And, of course, Mary bore Jesus even though she never lay with her husband, Joseph.

I wouldn't go so far as to state that the angels who announced these births had also had intimate relations with these women, but I cannot rule it out, either.

Power To Blind Men - When two angels came to Lot's home in the wicked city of Sodom, they were spotted by the lusty populace. A crowd of homosexuals and whores surrounded his house and demanded that Lot *"bring them out...that we may know them."* *(Genesis 19:5)*

Lot, in a desperate attempt to save the angels from such a wicked ordeal, offered his two young virgin daughters to the crowd in their place. But the crowd would have no part of it. They wanted the two handsome young men. What an evil place Sodom must have been. It's no wonder God destroyed it.

The angels grabbed Lot and pulled him inside the house and closed the door quickly behind them.

The crowd pressed forward and tried to break the door down. That was a mistake they would soon regret:

> GENESIS 19:11 *And they smote the men that were at the door of the house with blindness, both small and great: so that they wearied themselves to find the door.*

The angels then instructed Lot to gather up his family and his possessions and leave the city.

GENESIS 19:12 *For we will destroy this place, because the cry of them is waxen great before the face of the LORD; and the LORD hath sent us to destroy it.*

Again, the LORD used His angels to deal out His justice:

GENESIS 19:24 *Then the LORD rained upon Sodom and Gomorah brimstone and fire from the LORD out of heaven;*

If the LORD sent the angels to destroy the cities, it was they who were above the city bombarding it with their awesome, destructive weapons.

Angel's Food - Angels that appear in man-like form have often dined with humans. Several cases exist in the Bible where men have fed angels regular earthly food. But angels have their own food as the following account of Elijah will attest:

I KINGS 19:5 *And as he lay and slept under a juniper tree, behold, then an angel touched him, and said unto him, Arise and eat.*

6 And he looked, and behold, there was a cake baken on the coals, and a cruse of water at his head. And he did eat and drink, and laid him down again.

7 And he arose, and did eat and drink, and went in the strength of that meat forty days and forty nights unto Horeb the mount of God.

This "super food" lasted him for forty days without the need for any other nourishment.

When the tribe of Israel was wandering through the wilderness, following the pillar of cloud, there were times when food supplies from the surrounding countryside were scarce, so the angels of the LORD provided a perfect, grain-like food substance that the people would gather off the ground, grind into flour and make into small cakes. The LORD fed an estimated four million Jews every day for forty years with what became known as manna:

EXODUS 16:14 *And when the dew that lay was gone up, behold, upon the face of the wilderness there lay small round thing, as small as the hoar frost on the ground.*

15 *And when the children of Israel saw it, they said one to another, it is manna: for they wist not what it was. And Moses said unto them, This is the bread which the LORD hath given you to eat.*

16 *This is the thing which the LORD hath commanded, Gather of it every man according to his eating, an omer for every man, according to the number of your persons; take ye every man for them which are in his tent.*

The LORD specified an allotted amount for each to gather. Since God's supply is not limited, why did He specify a limit for the camp of Israel? Could it have been because the angels had limited cargo space for shuttling food to the Israelites?

Jesus, in His glorified form, ate the food of humans when He dined with the disciples after His resurrection. The glorified body, therefore, has the power to take matter from our earthly dimension and transport it into the heavenly realm. This has not only occurred with foodstuffs but with living men, as well. Several prophets have been transported to heaven and back.

Angels Are Super Intelligent - They are filled with the knowledge and presence of God Almighty and are far superior to men in intelligence. Their tremendously advanced technology uses laws of matter and/or anti-matter that defy modern scientific dogma.

Angels Perceive the Past & Future - Living in a dimension where time has no relevance, angels have often foretold major world events. Many of the passages containing these prophecies use a form carefully designed to hide the meaning from all but those enlightened souls who have the faith to search for their hidden meaning. Four-fifths of Bible prophecy has already come to pass with 100% accuracy. The remaining one-fifth deals with the "End Times" when Christ returns for the Church. As we shall see, we are living, without question, in the End Times.

*   *   *   *   *

Figure 24.1 - The classic depiction of an angel is routed in early christian-era interpretations of Scripture which added bird-like wings and halos, likely based on the influence of images of the Egyptian goddess Isis. To that vision they added the prevalence of feminine angels. However, nowhere in the Bible do the authors describe a female angel, as an example, yet the misrepresentation continues because the image seems softer and gentler, I suppose. I certainly do not dismiss the existence of female angels, but I do strongly question the flapping wings and halos thing.

Angels' Purpose & Activities

Always On The Move!

Contrary to the popular misconception, angels do not simply sit around on clouds strumming harps and eating grapes. Angels are extremely active and serve an irrepressible purpose. We are, naturally, speaking of God's obedient angelic force. The following brief descriptions give a general idea of the various categories of activity but the actual enactment of duty is as diverse, no doubt, as can possibly be imagined. What a tremendously interesting and fulfilling existence angels must live. Their purposes and activities include:

To Worship God - Angels live in the presence of God in heaven and worship and glorify Him at all times.

To Obey God's Will - Angels are not capable of, or at least don't have the desire to resist the will of God. When they do their works on Earth it is always with God's direction.

Act as Ministering Spirits - It may be true that angels worship God when in His presence, but I can assure you that it is not their job to sit around, strum harps and sing songs. Angels have a purpose and a job that is extremely important.

> HEBREWS 1:13 *But to which of the angels said he at any time, Sit on my right hand, until I make thine enemies thy footstool?*

14 *Are they not all ministering spirits, sent forth to minister for them who shall be heirs of salvation?*

When the Bible says angels worship and obey God it no doubt entails doing the heavenly will of the Father. These duties are vast, and include assisting the Christians of the Earth (heirs of salvation).

To Protect the Faithful - God's angels have protected His people on numerous occasions. Guardian angels are ministering angels who have charge over righteous men. Angels can be summoned from heaven to assist a righteous man whenever he is faced with dangers on Earth.

Famed evangelist Arthur Blessitt recounted a spine-tingling story in his book, *Arthur a Pilgrim: an autobiography,* and has added detail to the experience in appearances on TBN (Trinity Broadcasting Network). Please be advised that I do not ascribe to all the tenets taught on TBN, but I relate this story simply because I think it's relevant to this dissertation. In fact, the management of this network regularly promote the errant concept that all UFO encounters are of the devil, a concept based in a lack of understanding that perhaps this book will clarify. Here's the story: Arthur Blessitt described an event that took place in war-torn Nicaragua in 1978. Arthur and two minister companions, acting as driver and interpreter, were traveling the Pan American Highway just south of Leone during the time of political upheaval. They were warned by the local people not to stop along the highway at night because it was too dangerous. Gangs of marauders were known to brutalize travelers during the cover of darkness.

Arthur, because of his belief in a protective God, was not one to be intimidated by anything, so he ignored the warnings of impending danger. They parked their motor home at a roadside stop that evening just as they had always done and depended on the LORD to protect them.

Around 2:00 A.M. they heard a truck pull up outside their caravan. Several Spanish speaking soldiers banged on their door and demanded to see Arthur. These were hardened soldiers who pulled Arthur outside of his trailer and lined him up against his truck. They formed a line and prepared to execute him on the spot.

Back in America the wife of the founder of the Christian television network, TBN, was roused from her sleep. Deep anxiety gripped her as she knew in her heart that something was wrong with her beloved friend, Arthur. Not knowing exactly what the problem was, she was obedient to her instincts and awoke her husband. Paul and Jan Crouch knelt at their bedside and prayed for Arthur's deliverance. Jan asked specifically that twelve angels be sent to protect him. As they prayed, a calm came over Jan's spirit and she was able to rest in the knowledge that their friend had been delivered from danger.

Arthur was determined not to die without his beloved Bible in his hand. "Better yet," he thought, "I'll give a Bible to each of these men." He was determined to get to the box of Bibles locked inside his truck. As he reached in his pocket and grabbed his keys, his fingers instantly picked the right key. The soldiers hesitated for a second. That was all he needed... immediately he made a head-long dive for the locked door. Somehow the key went in the slot on the first pass and Arthur was grabbing the box off the seat before the soldiers could stop him. Out came the box and down went Arthur. Frantically he tore at the heavy strapping tape that bound the box. *If I can just get to these Bibles and give them a copy, I'll be all right,* he thought to himself.

Quickly the soldiers gathered around him and pulled at his arms impatiently trying to make him stand so they could carry out their gruesome task.

Meanwhile, inside the camper, Arthur's two friends were terrified. They knew their friend was in trouble, but they also knew if they tried to help him they too would likely be shot. If Arthur were critically wounded, who would help to save his life? This was an obvious moment for fervent prayer. As the two knelt and plead with God for mercy, they suddenly heard what sounded like flesh-against-flesh punches. Someone was fighting off the soldiers, they thought. Perhaps they were beating Arthur before they shot him. *But it sounds like a whole crowd of people scuffling. What's going on?* one admitted thinking.

Arthur was determined to get that stubborn box open. All he could think of and all he saw was his struggle with the strong strapping tape. Whatever else was going on did not concern him. He wanted that box open! Finally it gave way and he ripped several Bibles out. As he stood to give the soldiers a copy of his beloved Book, he noticed they were no longer standing over him.

Oddly, the men were scattered all about him, some knocked completely out, others holding broken noses and jaws. What had happened? One poor guy was unconscious and hanging out of his truck feet-first!

The soldiers looked at Arthur in terror in the darkened clearing. "No... senior!...No!...(speaking in Spanish)...we don't want to mess with you, Sir.

No more, Senior!" The terrified men quickly gathered themselves, picked up their wounded comrades, threw them into their truck and sped off.

What had happened? Arthur knew that a miracle had just taken place even though his preoccupation with getting the box open prevented him from seeing anything happen to his assailants. He began to weep and praise God for his deliverance.

A miraculous and mysterious thing occurred that night, yet no one really saw what happened. The only thing that was reported was a strange appearance in the evening sky. The local people related that God had visited their village that night and that He "descended from the sky in a bright glowing sphere of light." [25-1]

To Convey the Mandates of God - As messengers of God, angels are used to convey the mandates of God. It was an angel who appeared to Moses in a bright beam of light from behind a bush when God told him it was time to lead the captive Jews out of Egypt.

> EXODUS 3:2 *And the angel of the LORD appeared unto him in a flame of fire out of the midst of a bush: and he looked, and, behold, the bush burned with fire, and the bush was not consumed.*

The bright light could only be compared to fire in Moses' mind. Obviously the bush wasn't really on fire because it "was not consumed": it didn't burn.

It was an "angel of the LORD" that is credited with leading the tribe of Israel to the promised land, riding in a pillar of cloud by day, and a pillar of fire by night.

Time and again, whenever God has made contact with man, it has been His angels who have carried out His great works, either directly, or as accomplices with the LORD, Himself.

Execute Punishment on Their Adversaries - Angels have fought for Godly men in earthly battles on many occasions. When the kings of Assyria were planning to attack Judah, King Hezekiah prayed and asked God to intervene:

ISAIAH 37:36 *Then the angel of the LORD went forth, and smote in the camp of the Assyrians a hundred and fourscore and five thousand: and when they arose early in the morning, behold, they were all dead corpses.*

There are modern accounts of battles being won by vastly outnumbered troops even today. The Six Days War that Israel fought in 1967 is full of "miraculous" victories. In 1982 when Israel invaded Lebanon the Syrian Air Force was almost completely destroyed, while the Israelis didn't lose a single aircraft. It's no wonder that Israelis are hailed as the best fighting men in the world. Their ability to plan and execute military maneuvers is known throughout the world. What is not so widely known (or accepted) is the fact that they, no doubt, have "unseen allies" in many of their battles.

Serve as Instruments of God's Displeasure - God uses angels to punish even His own chosen people when they return to their wicked ways.

Loose the Seven Seals - In the Book of Revelation, angels are used to loose the great plagues and curses upon the Earth during the terrible Tribulation Period.

Will Fight the Final Battle & Gather God's Elect - Angels from "one end of heaven to the other" will one day deal out God's justice. In a final battle called Armageddon the angels will gather together the "elect" (believers in Christ) and destroy the wicked, sending their evil souls to a place called hell, where they shall suffer separation from God and His light for eternity.

Billy Graham On Angels

As a respected representative of the conservative Christian community, Billy Graham speaks with great authority. Doctor Graham recognizes the similarities between angels and aliens in his excellent book, *Angels: God's Secret Agents.* In it he states:

"Some Christian writers have speculated that UFOs could very well be a part of God's angelic host who preside over the physical affairs of universal creation. While we cannot assert such a view with certainty, many people are now seeking some type of supernatural explanation for these phenomena. Nothing can hide the fact, however, that these unexplained events are occurring with greater frequency around the entire world and in unexpected places.

"Japan recently witnessed a typical example of unexplained objects that appeared in the night skies. On January 15, 1975, a squadron of UFO-like objects, resembling a celestial string of pearls, soared silently through the evening skies over half the length of Japan. As government officials, police and thousands of curious citizens stared at the sky in wonder, from fifteen to twenty glowing objects, cruising in straight formation, flew over Japan inside a strange misty cloud. Further, they were sighted and reported in cities seven hundred miles apart in less than an hour.

"Hundreds of frantic telephone calls jammed switchboards of police stations and government installations as the spectacular formation sped south. 'All the callers reported seeing a huge cloud passing over the city. They said they saw strange objects inside the cloud moving in a straight line,' recalled Duty Officer Takeo Ohira. Were they planes? 'No,' said Hiroshi Mayazawa, 'because no planes or natural phenomena appeared on my radar. It was an exceptionally clear night. To me the whole thing is a mystery.'

"Professor Masatoshi Kitamura watched the dazzling display in the night sky from the Control Room of Tokyo's Meteorological Bureau station near the airport. He said, 'I was mystified. Nothing showed up on my radar. I reported my sighting to the airport control tower and they told me nothing showed on their radar either.' (Author's note: I would speculate that the strange misty cloud surrounding the objects also prevented radar from detecting them.)

"Hundreds of similar events are being reported every year on every continent. A scientist at the atomic laboratory research installation at Los Alamos told me that for every one in twenty of these UFOs that have been investigated no scientific explanation exists. The highly imaginative and speculative theories of some men simply will not do." [25-2]

Dr. Billy Graham

* * * * *

Massive hovering UFO causes Chinese officials to close airport

Three views of a gigantic cylinder
UFO seen over China airport in 2010.

Image 25.1 – DATELINE: July 9, 2010 - A cigar-shaped UFO seen hovering over East China's Zhejiang Province around 9 p.m. on Wednesday evening caused massive flight delays at Xiaoshan International Airport after air traffic controllers shut down the airport for one hour, the China News Service reported Thursday. Control tower officers detected the unidentified flying object with long-range visual instruments. They immediately ordered several incoming flights to land at airports in neighboring Ningbo and Wuxi, delaying passengers for nearly four hours, the report said. Stunned witnesses reported seeing a comet-like fireball in the sky and a number of local residents took photos of the strange column of light which was visible for nearly an hour.

Image 25.2 –
(Right) Strange
formation of lights in
(1) Guido Reni and
(2) Luca Giordano
paintings from 1627
and 1692.

Image 25.3 – The Annunciation by Alamanno
-15th Century

Image 25.4 – Baptism of Jesus by Aert De
Gelder painted in 1710 AD.

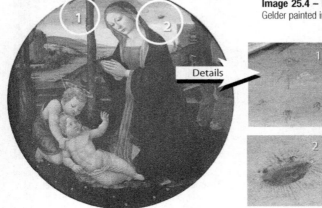

Image 25.5 – Madonna and child with infant St. John by Sebastiano Mainardi - 15th Century. Provocative
background images portray a metallic glowing disc with a dome or turret which is being observed by a man
and his dog, and on the left is a star or object with what appears to be three sparkling objects that precede it.

26

Warning: Satan is a Fallen Angel

Don't be Deceived by What You Hear

Not everytthing you read or hear about UFOs is true. As explained previously, the UFO phenomenon has a tendency to attract some very strange people, indeed. Many seek to benefit financially or to gain national notoriety. Others, like some gossip newspapers, simply fabricate stories weekly to cash in on the sensationalism. It's vital to weed through these obvious fakes and substantiate those that appear to be true. It's harmful to believe every UFO encounter because it's detrimental to the phenomenon's credibility. However, there is another danger that exceeds one's being deceived by phonies and nuts. A far more subtle deception is evident even within credible witness accounts.

Satan's UFOs

Do not be mistaken. There are, without doubt, evil aliens in some of the UFOs spotted in our skies even today.

The Bible tells us that God uses evil angels to punish disobedient earthlings:

> **PSALMS 78:49** *He cast upon them the fierceness of his anger, wrath, and indignation, and trouble, by sending evil angels among them.*

Satan has great power in the Earth and in the atmosphere around our planet:

> **EPHESIANS 2:2** *Wherein in time past ye walked according to the course of this world, according to the prince of the power of the air, the spirit that now worketh in the children of disobedience.*

Satan is called "the prince of the power of the air." And he is the leader of the fallen angels, (also known as demons). We must always be on guard against the temptations these evil creatures will bombard us with:

> **EPHESIANS 6:12** *For we wrestle not against flesh and blood, but against principalities, against the rulers of the darkness of this world, against spiritual wickedness in high places.*

It's clear in this passage that these creatures exist in an unseen realm, what the Bible calls the spiritual world, and they rule from "high places."

Satan, as well as his army of angels, I believe, has the same appearance as any other angel:

> **II CORINTHIANS 11:13** *For such are false apostles, deceitful workers, transforming themselves into the apostles of Christ*
>
> **14** *And no marvel; for Satan himself is transformed into an angel of light.*

Of course, Satan's appearance and powers, as the leader of evil, is probably somewhat greater than his cohorts.

Do they have all of the abilities that good angels do? Almost. They appear as normal angels and have enough power to battle God's forces, but there are at least three notable differences:

1. They are confined to Earth and its atmosphere
2. They cannot defeat God's forces (which include men living a Godly life as instructed in the Bible)
3. They are restricted in their interaction with mankind

Satan's Fall

The Bible teaches that Satan enlisted one-third of heaven's angels to be his agents here on Earth. In the beginning, it was Satan who tempted Adam and Eve and thus corrupted mankind. And Satan and his followers still have great power on Earth today. His powers are evidenced in chilling reality throughout the world.

Just what did Satan do to deserve his bad reputation? Originally, he was the most magnificent creature that God had ever created, one of only three special archangels with great wisdom and power. What was his downfall? In a word: vanity. Satan got so caught up in his own greatness that he thought he could rival God:

> **ISAIAH 14:12** *How art thou fallen from heaven, O Lucifer, son of the morning! how art thou cut down to the ground, which didst weaken the nations!*

> **13** *For thou hast said in thine heart, I will ascend into heaven, I will exalt my throne above the stars of God: I will sit also upon the mount of the congregation, in the sides of the north:*

> **14** *I will ascend above the heights of the clouds; I will be like the most high.*

This, of course, not only angered God, but broke His heart. His most beloved creation had turned against Him even after all the special favor that He had bestowed upon him:

EZEKIEL 28:13 *Thou hast been in Eden the garden of God; every precious stone was thy covering, the sardius, topaz, and the diamond, the beryl, the onyx, and the jasper, the sapphire, the emerald, and the carbuncle, and gold: the workmanship of they tabrets and of thy pipes was prepared in thee in the day that thou wast created.*

14 *Thou art the anointed cherub that covereth; and I have set thee so: thou wast upon the holy mountain of God; thou hast walked up and down in the midst of the stones of fire.*

15 *Thou wast perfect in thy ways from the day that thou wast created, till iniquity was found in thee.*

16 *By the multitude of thy merchandise they have filled the midst of thee with violence, and thou hast sinned: therefore I will cast thee as profane out of the mountain of God: and I will destroy thee, O covering cherub, from the midst of the stones of fire.*

17 *Thine heart was lifted up because of thy beauty, thou hast corrupted thy wisdom by reason of thy brightness: I will cast thee to the ground, I will lay thee before kings, that they may behold thee.*

From this revealing passage we can analyze Satan's personality and see his shortcomings. He was heaven's musician and especially gifted with tabrets and pipes (musical instruments). He was also heaven's chief defender. The Scripture says he was the cherub that covereth. The term covereth in the original Hebrew meant to cover over or defend. Satan was apparently in charge of the defense of heaven. He was perfect in all his ways in the beginning, but something happened to him that caused him to fall from favor. It says he was turned to violence because of all his possessions ("the multitude of thy merchandise"). His love of wealth and his vanity ("thine heart was lifted up because of thy beauty") corrupted his wisdom. He only wanted to please himself and said in his heart, "I don't need God. I'm as great as God. I can do anything I put my mind to. I'll be my own God and all my admirers will look to me because I'm the richest and brightest and best looking. Who needs God?"

Self-indulgence, arrogance and greed. Sound familiar? It's the same thing that motivates millions today.

Because of his sin, Satan was kicked out of heaven and sentenced to confinement in and around planet Earth. In what form did Satan arrive on Earth? According to Jesus, he came from the sky like a shooting star or lightning:

> **ST. LUKE 10:18** *And he said unto them, "I beheld Satan as lightning fall from heaven."*

Satan Wasn't Alone

Satan wasn't alone when he was cast down to Earth. He brought one-third of heaven's tachyon creatures with him; evil angels who loved their own fleshly lusts and possessions more than God.

Most of these angels are doing their evil works throughout the Earth today, causing great misery and pain wherever they can get a foothold. However, those who are true followers of Christ are protected from these evil entities, provided they stay in the Word.

> **JOB 1:6** *Now there was a day when the sons of God came to present themselves before the LORD and Satan came also among them.*

> *7 And the LORD said unto Satan, Whence comest thou? Then Satan answered the LORD, and said, From going to and fro in the earth, and from walking up and down in it.*

> *8 And the LORD said unto Satan, Hast thou considered my servant Job, that there is none like him in the earth, a perfect and an upright man, one that feareth God, and escheweth evil?*

9 *Then Satan answered the LORD, and said, Doth Job fear God for nought?*

10 *Hast not thou made an hedge about him, and about his house, and about all that he hath on every side? thou hast blessed the work of his hands, and his substance is increased in the land.*

Because of his faithfulness, Job had been protected from Satan and blessed with great material wealth.

But even Godly men are tempted by Satan and his band of spiritual pirates. God promises in His word that He will provide guidance and power to overcome these thugs if men will heed His commands. Those who are caught up in their own little vanity trips will not be so fortunate.

Intermarriage With Angels?

As stated before, angels have the power to at least bring the power of conception to earthly women. There is evidence that they not only possess the knowledge to induce pregnancy, but they are able to engage in sexual intercourse with earthlings.

However, this is one of the restrictions forced on angels by God, Himself, and there is probably no danger of an angel impregnating a human today, unless, of course, there is some truth to the wild stories put forth by Bud Hopkins (as we shall discuss shortly).

In the early history of mankind, however, several of Satan's evil astronauts apparently violated this restriction:

GENESIS 6:1 *And it came to pass, when men began to multiply on the face of the earth, and daughters were born unto them,*

2 *That the sons of God saw the daughters of men that they were fair; and they took them wives of all which they chose.*

NOTE: "sons of God" always refers to angelic beings in the Old Testament.

Giants In The Land

From this union of angels (sons of God) and daughters of men, were born mighty people. They were superior in many ways except one: they were evil by heritage.

GENESIS 6:4 *There were giants in the earth in those days; and also after that, when the sons of God came in unto the daughters of men, and they bare children to them, the same became mighty men which were of old, men of renown.*

5 *And God saw that the wickedness of man was great in the earth, and that every imagination of the thoughts of his heart was only evil continually.*

6 *And it repented the LORD that he had made man on the earth, and it grieved him at his heart.*

7 *And the LORD said, I will destroy man whom I have created from the face of the earth; both man, and beast, and creeping thing, and the fowls of the air; for it repenteth me that I have made them*

7 *But Noah found grace in the eyes of the LORD.*

13 *And God said unto Noah, The end of all flesh is come before me; for the earth is filled with violence through them; and, behold, I will destroy them with the earth.*

Evil Angels Bound in Hell

Satan's plan may have been to pollute God's creation by interbreeding and producing a race of earthlings loyal to his evil way of life. Apparently the plan was working because when God looked down He saw that mankind was totally corrupt. It was the corruption of His creation that prompted God to destroy the whole mess and bring the flood.

He decided to start over with the seed of the only man in the world who would listen to Him and obey: Noah. Furthermore, God decided to punish the angels who had bred with Earth's women:

> **JUDE 1:6** *And the angels which kept not their first estate, but left their own habitation, he hath reserved in everlasting chains under darkness unto the judgement of the great day.*

These angels of Satan who once were free to interact with humans are chained up in total torment now as a warning to any others who might be tempted to do the same.

In order to make sure we understood just who these angels were, the apostle Peter tells us it was the same group that was around prior to the great flood:

> **II PETER 2:4** *For if God spared not the angels that sinned, but cast them down to hell, and delivered them into chains of darkness, to be reserved unto judgement;*
>
> *5 And spared not the old world, but saved Noah the eighth person, a preacher of righteousness, bringing in the flood upon the world of the ungodly;*
>
> **(King James version)**
>
> *6 and if He condemned the cities of Sodom and Gomorah to destruction by reducing them to ashes, having made them an example to those who would live ungodly thereafter;*
>
> *9 then the LORD knows how to rescue the godly from temptation, and keep the unrighteous under punishment for the day of judgement.* **(NAS)**

Many scholars think that the angels of Satan did more than just breed with Earth women. They claim it's a perversion strange flesh, a total abomination in the eyes of God, equal to homosexuality. They further speculate that Noah was one of the few, and perhaps only, earthling who was of pure Adamic lineage, i.e. without any angelic blood in his heritage. The main reason that Noah remained faithful to God was because his bloodline had not been corrupted by these evil angels.[26-1]

Battles in a Parallel Universe

If angels, either good or evil, are eternal spirit beings, then their destruction is impossible. Since Satan could not be destroyed by God, He did the next best thing and restricted him to a certain region of the universe. Satan is the prince of the air (or atmosphere) around the Earth and, as such, He and his troops have the power to battle with God's holy angels here on special assignment.

When Daniel prayed to God to ask for the meaning of a dream that had come to the king of Babylon, God sent his special messenger Gabriel to Earth to give him special insight. But Gabriel was detained by Lucifer (referred to as the prince of Persia).

Poor old Daniel just about starved to death waiting for an answer, fasting and praying for an answer for 21 days. When the angel finally arrived, he told Daniel that his prayer had been heard from the first day but that he had been detained:

> **DANIEL 10:13** *But the prince of the kingdom of Persia withstood me one and twenty days: but, lo, Michael, one of the chief princes, came to help me; and I remained there with the kings of Persia.*
>
> **14** *Now I am come to make thee understand what shall befall thy people in the latter days: for yet the vision is for many days*
>
> **20** *Then said he, Knowest thou wherefore I come unto thee? and now will I return to fight with the prince of Persia...*

Here is a prime example of God working within the laws of nature (His own). It would be natural for us to ask "Why didn't God just wipe out Satan and let Gabriel fly to Daniel immediately?" Obviously, that's not the way God works. He will not defy His own laws, because that would make Him a law-breaker, something He cannot be. It is critical to recognize that _God works through men and His angels_, and they are subject to certain rules that govern the universal forces of nature. Satan still has power and he will do everything he can to thwart the plans of God. But he will always lose to God's messengers. Satan's victories are only due to people who allow him to work his evil in them, either through their lack of knowledge, or their evil desires. People who don't realize their own power through Jesus Christ are easy targets.

Just as UFOs can suddenly appear and disappear, so too can the angels of God. The heavenly struggle is going on all around us, I firmly believe, it's just that it's a battle in the tachyon dimension. These tachyon (spiritual) creatures can come into our dimension and affect the affairs of men if instructed to do so by God. A prime example is the story of Elisha in the Old Testament.

Elisha the prophet had warned the king of Israel about impending dangers on at least three occasions, telling him that the king of Syria was going to attack. The Israelites would then flee the Syrian army, something that made the king of Syria furious. When the Syrian king heard through his spies that Elisha had warned the Israelites, he made plans to kill him.

Late one night the Syrian army encircled the town where Elisha lived and made plans to attack. It didn't take long for word to get to Elisha. A young man from his camp came and told him that they were surrounded and outnumbered and asked "What shall we do?" Elisha just said, "Relax, the army of God is with us and they far outnumber our enemies." He then asked God to open the young man's eyes so that he could see them. What he saw was described as glowing chariots of fire.

> **II KINGS 6:17** _And Elisha prayed, and said, LORD, I pray thee, open his eyes, that he may see. And the LORD opened the eyes of the young man; and he saw: and, behold, the mountain was full of horses and chariots of fire 'round about Elisha._

Captain of God's Host

Joshua was given the privilege of seeing a warring angel near Jericho. The angel made it clear that he was not on either his or his adversaries' side. Most likely he was there on an unknown mission locked in battle with unseen evil forces.

It's very likely that the angel had something to do with knocking down of the walls of Jericho. Some have claimed that evidence indicates the walls of Jericho weren't really knocked down in a literal sense but were actually pushed down into the ground. Only God's alien astronauts would be capable of such a "supernatural" feat.

> **JOSHUA 5:13** *And it came to pass, when Joshua was by Jericho, that he lifted up his eyes and looked, and, behold, there stood a man over against him with his sword drawn in his hand: and Joshua went unto him, and said unto him, Art thou for us, or for our adversaries?*
>
> **14** *And he said, Nay; but as captain of the host of the LORD am I now come. And Joshua fell on his face to the earth...*

An Angel's Laser

Just what kind of force do these warring angels use? In a battle described in II Samuel, God came to Earth in a thick cloud that glowed like kindled coals and fought in behalf of king David. The weapons are described as arrows of lightning. Might they now be described as laser weapons?

> **II SAMUEL 22:10** *He bowed the heavens also, and came down; and darkness was under his feet.*
>
> **11** *And he rode upon a cherub, and did fly: and he was seen upon the wings of the wind.*

12   *And he made darkness pavilions round about him,*
dark waters, and thick clouds of the skies.

13   *Through the brightness before him were coals of*
fire kindled.

14   *The LORD thundered from heaven, and the most*
High uttered his voice.

15   *And he sent out arrows, and scattered them;*
lightning, and discomfited them.

Hailstones or Heaven's Stones?

As Joshua, the mighty conqueror, pushed across the region after destroying Jericho and Ahi, word came to him that one of his allies was under siege from the Amorites, one of Israel's mortal enemies. He and all his thousands of mighty warriors descended on the city with great confidence, for God had told Joshua He would help him in the battle.

As the huge army came down out of the mountains, the Amorites tried to escape:

> **JOSHUA 10:11**   *And it came to pass, as they fled*
> *from before Israel, and were in the going down to*
> *Bethhoron, that the LORD cast down great stones from*
> *heaven upon them unto Azekah, and they died: they*
> *were more which died with hailstones than they whom*
> *the children of Israel slew with the sword.*
>
> 12   *Then spake Joshua to the LORD in the day when*
> *the LORD delivered up the Amorites before the children*
> *of Israel, and he said in the sight of Israel, Sun, stand*
> *thou still upon Gibeon; and thou, Moon, in the valley*
> *of Ajalon.*

13 *And the sun stood still, and the moon stayed, until the people had avenged themselves upon their enemies. Is not this written in the book of Jasher? So the sun stood still in the midst of heaven, and hasted not to go down about a whole day.*

14 *And there was no day like that before it or after it, that the LORD hearkened unto the voice of a man: for the LORD fought for Israel.*

Could this "sun" have been a huge HFO glowing brightly over the battlefield during the night illuminating the countryside and appearing more like a "moon" or flat metallic sphere during the daylight hours? If the Earth stood still while the sun glowed brightly why would there be any mention of a moon? Moons are associated with nighttime and there wouldn't have been any nighttime if, in fact, the Earth had really stood still. This particular moon is mentioned as appearing in an area called Ajalon which was just north of Gibeon, the place where the battle took place. (Gibeon was six miles northwest of Jerusalem).

We should well remember the miracle at Fatima and how it was titled "the day the sun danced." Even though it was a classical UFO sighting, the object was described in terms more acceptable to the astonished onlookers.

Satan Can Win-But Only if We Let Him

There's no question that Satan is a powerful prince. The prince of the dark side. His abilities are far greater than ordinary men. However, he or his followers are only able to do with men what they themselves allow. Satan's followers have the power to alter earthly matter including inducing such phenomena as levitation, sickness and even death.

These "miracles" can only be effective where ignorance or evil prevails. If those being affected by this black magic knew their own powers, through Jesus Christ, they could totally disarm any of Satan's workers. The practice of voodoo, witchcraft and other mystic exercises only overpower unwary souls. God gave all Christians power over the forces of darkness long ago through Jesus Christ:

> **PHILIPPIANS 4:13** *I can do all things through Christ which strengtheneth me.*

Power to Tempt

Satan has limited rights in dealing with men. First, he isn't allowed to manifest himself in his true form for all of humanity to see. He and his angels remain in the spirit realm except on occasions when his followers "conjure" him up or on rare occasions when he manifests himself to believers in an attempt to manipulate or intimidate.

Again, God won't allow a faithful Christian to be tempted or intimidated beyond that which he can endure. "Resist the devil and he will surely flee."

Satan also cannot tell the truth. He and his fallen angels are liars. They are the masters of subtle deception, in addition to being the authors of all open deceit.

As previously stated, these beings (until recently, perhaps) are forbidden to have sexual contact with humans, but there is biblical, as well as modern, evidence that they can inhabit the minds and/or bodies of certain human beings.

Once an individual has been indwelled by the evil spirit, he can only be freed by a process called the "casting out" of demon spirits. All spirit-filled, knowledgeable Christians have the power to conduct this exorcism by the authority of Jesus Christ. A note of caution is needed here: unless one knows the Scriptures well, and his/her place in God's kingdom, it is dangerous to confront an evil spirit and attempt an exorcism.

One of the areas where Satan is free to do as he pleases is that of temptation. Even Christians are subject to this constant barrage of evil suggestions. However, as God said, He will never allow a Christian to be tempted beyond that which he can endure:

I CORINTHIANS 10:13 *There hath no temptation taken you but such as is common to man: but God is faithful, who will not suffer you to be tempted above that ye are able; but will with the temptation also make a way to escape, that ye may be able to bear it.*

How are We to Recognize Evil Aliens?

Since Satan is the master of deception, it is important to know how to recognize one of his agents.

There is no question that many UFO contacts being made today are of the devil. Since the appearance of good and evil angels are identical, one could easily be deceived.

Jesus told us not everything is as it seems. The fruits of one's work gives a truer indication of one's motivation. He said, "You'll know a tree by the fruit it bears." That's a pretty good method to determine whether the UFO story you read is of Satan or of God. If it lifts up and glorifies Jesus, you can be sure it's of God, provided it's the Jesus as described in the pages of the New Testament, not a new or better Jesus like some cults promise.

If the contactee claims that these creatures spoke to him of an invasion in which all of humanity will be enlightened, watch out! The Bible speaks of a similar invasion of God's angels, but only the elect shall be saved i.e. only true believers in Christ. The wicked will be killed and their spiritual bodies will be cast into hell along with Satan and his angels (demons).

As mentioned, Satan is the master of subtle deception. Subtle deception employs half-truths: false pretenses grounded in partial truth. The idea of an alien invasion is the "true" part of the equation, however, an invasion in which "all" of mankind will be saved and/or enlightened is simply not Scriptural.

Another key deception is the concept of a God of "forces." To represent God as a force and not as the Holy Trinity is vintage Lucifer. Beware of aliens who speak of a Universal Consciousness or the "forces" of good and evil. Many fundamentalist Christians have seen this dangerous concept presented in the *Star Wars* series of films. We all remember Luke Skywalker saying, "May the Force be with you." Some say that the nation has been taken in through this most subtle of methods: masking the lie in a fairy tale film. There may be a great deal of merit in what they say.

The Bible says the Antichrist will worship the "God of forces:"

> **DANIEL 11:38** *But in his estate shall he honour the God of forces: and a god whom his fathers knew not shall he honour with gold, and silver, and with precious stones, and pleasant things.*

The Antichrist will reduce the concept of God down to the human level of relativity. God is just a neutral creative force which is neither good, or evil, and to have His blessing depends upon the situation. It's proponents will have to answer directly to God one day:

> **ZEPHANIAH 1:12** *And it shall come to pass at that time, that I will...punish the men that are settled on their lees: that say in their heart, The LORD will not do good, neither will he do evil.*

This philosophy is called "situational ethics", the concept that "good" is dependent upon the situation. This philosophy is preached by Marxist-Leninist communism. There is no absolute right or wrong, as decided by an Omnipotent God. If it promotes communism, then it is good. All else is evil. Moral "absolutes" do not exist. It's the very foundation of communism. That's why it isn't immoral for the Russian army to invade Afghanistan or Poland or to drop toy-shaped bombs, if it deems it necessary, to maim poor defenseless children of the resisting villagers as a means of striking terror in the people's hearts. Many horror stories involving Soviet war practices have filtered out of Afghanistan in recent years.

It also explains why the Russians have violated the rules of every major arms treaty ever made with America. Their only concern is for total world dominance by whatever means available to them. Remember that any communist leader of a major nation, no matter his line of rhetoric, has stepped over the corpses of thousands of foes to rise to his position of power. Ovations of peace are always masked by strategic battle plans and the forced economic failures of such an oppressive system. But don't take my word for it. Read your history. Find out how communism has enslaved nations and killed more humans in 70 years than all the world's wars combined. You may be rudely awakened! And just because they may have changed their label in recent years, it doesn't mean that the spirit of communism is dead in Russia. In fact, it is my discovery that all of the political "isms" are grounded in deception and deceit. Communism, socialism, Marxism and, yes, Mohammedism. Move over Solmon Rushde.

So the message is clear: Beware these wild stories of alien visitation. Don't believe everything you hear, for it may be a part of Satan's subtle deception. No doubt Satan will use every method available to him to deceive the nations. On the other hand, just because the concept of UFOs doesn't fit into your chosen paradigm of reality doesn't mean they don't exist and it certainly doesn't mean that all UFOs are of the devil. In fact, these strange glowing spheres in our atmosphere may be playing a much more significant part in our futures than we had ever imagined, as we shall see.

DECEPTION ALERT: I wanted to include a short explanation about the Billy Meier photos (see *pp. 112-114* and *figure 8.4*) and the scientific proofs presented to validate them. This may be among the most clever deceptions to date. I'll admit I was taken in at first, as you may have been. The first book on the sightings by the one-armed Swiss farmer, called *UFO - Contact from the Pleiades*, said little about controversial subject matter, other than to reveal that many types of aliens exist and are currently visiting our planet. After more research, I discovered that Eduard "Billy" Meier had, indeed, made many claims that challenged the biblical view of Creation and Universal Order.

As an example, he claimed to have had many previous, as well as subsequent, visits from several entities and gave them names like Semjase, Quetsal and Ptaah. Further, he contended these benevolent aliens were here to prevent mankind from destroying the ecosystem of the Earth and beyond. Semjase claimed that there really is no difference between Jesus and Buddha and Mohammed, as they were all more highly evolved offspring of alien intervention, all with a common message.

These are commonly accepted New Age viewpoints which warn that man is destroying the planet with pollution and overpopulation. That the nature of man and his penchant for war has prevented him from expressing a fuller cosmic revelation. These are all common to the satanist's view of mankind and future as well. But the claims don't end there. They get stranger and farther from biblical truth the closer you look. When their stories are challenged, proponents of the Meier contact phenomenon simply change the message. As an example, one gentleman who makes the regular Meier/UFO speaker's circuit explained that the reason a certain photo was so much more detailed than the others, "...was because the FBI had played around with it and enhanced it by photo manipulation in an effort to gain more knowledge..." about how the saucer was powered. "Billy never got that close to them to get such a clear photo," he retreated.

Meier has also claimed there are several other "secret" planets in our solar system, as yet undiscovered, with names like 'Transpluto' and 'Vulcan' and 'UNI' or 'Nibiru' One has an orbit exactly behind the sun so we will never detect it ...never mind our recent space probes that have gone to that area and detected no such secret planet.

Other claims are that Earth's different ethnic races are the result of breeding with different alien races thousands of years ago. That one alien race still lives underground near the Gobi Desert called the blue people... and so it goes, getting stranger and farther out the more you dig, but all the time selling books and CDs for its promoters.

This is a prime example for my warning not to believe everything you see and hear about the UFO phenomenon. All these claims must be judged by the Word of God, and if there are contradictions then don't believe them. In fact, run away as fast as possible. They are, indeed, of satanic inspiration and origin. But, I might add, the photos may be very real.

*   *   *   *   *

27

Why Are Aliens Visiting the Earth?

What Can be Their Motivation?

There appears to be convincing evidence to support the theory that aliens and angels may, in fact, be one in the same. We've studied their physical attributes and we've shown how similarities abound between angel's powers and abilities and those of our alien visitors.

But what of their motive? Aliens seem to be strangely detached from human activity, unlike their angelic counterparts. How do we explain the strange scientific examinations given to numerous human "specimens?" It seems as though there almost exists a dichotomy of motivation between angels and aliens. Angels express "Godly" intentions, while aliens usually exhibit purely scientific fact-finding resolve.

As we proceed to the chapters ahead, I think you'll begin to see a clearer picture emerge of the overall plan of our alien visitors. Furthermore, a correlation will be made between alien activity and the purpose of God's angels, as spelled out in the Bible.

Always Emit Love & Compassion

We have no way of knowing just exactly what kinds of attitudes are displayed by all UFO occupants, but for those few fortunate enough to have made contact with aliens, their behavior has been described as very friendly.

In almost every case, witnesses have reacted with total panic when first confronted with saucer occupants. There is no basis for this fear, however, because no one has ever been maliciously mistreated by any alien captor (ignore sensational false stories to the contrary).

On initial contact, the alien will invariably attempt to establish eye contact with the witness first. Once this contact has been established, the alien is able to communicate their intent, usually via mental telepathy.

Reassuring feelings of friendship, even to the point of love, emanate from these creatures. The first words the captive will "hear" are: "Don't be afraid, we won't hurt you, we are your friends," (or words to that effect). The transmission is so convincing that most people relax immediately, loosing all fear, and actually end up talking to the aliens with casual candor.

As the aliens proceed with their examinations, the attitude of those aliens assisting in the details appears utilitarian. An almost elusive attitude pervades. This detachment may be, in fact, intentional. Could it be they are making a concerted effort to interfere as little as possible with the mental processes of their human guests?

Planting Seeds?

There has been some speculation that the purpose of alien physical examinations has been to implant devices into the witnesses for future use. This is merely hypothetical but might explain the consistent stories of probes being inserted into the witnesses' heads via the nostrils. Several witnesses have described such seemingly terrible ordeals.

Although it sounds cruel and painful, modern Earth medicine has begun to employ techniques of surgery with uncanny similarities.

In one operation a laser fiber .2 millimeters wide (approximately the thickness of 2 sheets of printer paper) is used to reach kidney stones lodged in the urinary tract. The tiny glass tube is inserted into the ureter to the point of the blockage and the doctor simply pulverizes the stone with a laser light blast and the small pieces are later naturally passed out of the body.

A similar device is used by doctors today to stop bleeding ulcers by inserting the tube down the throat into the stomach. In addition, ailments such as blocked arteries, detached retinas, glaucoma, hemorrhoids, lung and bladder tumors and a whole host of other disorders can be corrected with laser surgery. This form of surgery is highly favorable for several reasons. The laser's light beam is so intense and hot that the objectionable tissue is vaporized while surrounding blood vessels are seared shut by the intense heat. This provides a simple and "clean" procedure for surgeons, far superior to the knife, or through the use of drugs which often have harmful side effects.

Remember, these techniques represent current developments in medicine. Over 45 years ago, when Betty and Barney Hill were penetrated by similar fiber optic instruments, the possibility of such techniques in Earth medicine were only hopeful speculation.

If the aliens have actually implanted some sort of device in their human specimens, perhaps they'll be triggered at the opportune time to produce a predetermined response. So far, there is no evidence that any UFO witness has responded to any of this "higher calling," although their responses may have gone unnoticed by the larger population.

Don't Be Deceived by the Latest Craze

AUTHOR'S UPDATE: There has been a great deal of talk about a theory put forth by author and self-taught hypnotist, Bud Hopkins. He claims that several witnesses have made startling revelations while under hypnosis. These alleged abductees claim that aliens have taken ovum and sperm samples during their medical examinations, or "experimentation," as Hopkins labels the process. During subsequent abductions, the aliens have shown these supposed witnesses small hybrid infants with both human and alien characteristics. Hopkins hypothesizes that the aliens are systematically breeding these hybrids to inhabit a dying alien world, or perhaps to breed a super race of aliens (or humans) for reasons unknown. This, Hopkins claims, is their purpose for visiting our planet.

His theory, however, totally ignores the facts that aliens have systematically charted the planet and have shown special interest in our military installations and power systems (explained further in the next chapters). Other critics also question why aliens would bother to individually extract ovum or sperm on repeated abductions. As scientifically advanced as they obviously are, one would certainly agree that aliens could easily biogenetically create whatever type of species characteristics that they desire using a one-time storehouse of genetic ingredients. Recent successes with cloning animals by our own scientists suggest this is much easier than once thought.

The fact that Bud Hopkins has acted as an "unbiased" hypnotist in these cases presents a crucial conflict of interest. In the abduction cases that I detail in this book, the hypnotist's credentials are impeccable and unprejudiced. Can we make the same assumption of an author of UFO books, as is Bud Hopkins, who has become a self- taught hypnotist? The possibility of his purposely, or even unintentionally, guiding his subject's responses is just too great to give their testimony much credibility.

The same holds true of Whitely Strieber, a "science fiction" writer who was advanced one million dollars by his publisher to recount his avowed true story of alien abduction in the popular book *Communion*. I just don't find these men very credible. Not too surprisingly, both of these men hold a New Age view of the world.

The purported alien breeding of a half-human species is, to say the least, far out. My first reaction is to ask that these supposed "abductees" take lie detector tests and extensive personality disorder tests by a neutral third party. Provided they pass such tests of their truthfulness, I would put forth a theory of my own.

The Bible teaches that in the early history of life on Earth, Satan's cohorts bred with the daughters of men producing a race of super humans or "mighty men of old...men of renown" *(Genesis 6:4)*.

Jesus said "as it was in the days of Noah, so shall it be in the time that He returns." *(Matthew 24:37)*. Could it be that Satan's followers are up to their old tricks, taking the daughters of men at their own discretion to breed a race of defiled humans that will wreak havoc on humanity during these latter times? Please don't fear, however, because this book will show you how to avoid loosing any such confrontation with evil agents.

In the nearly 200 cases that Hopkins has explored, only a few have related such experiences. The vast majority have had simple examinations and were released. I would suggest that the aliens are mostly of the good (God's friendly angels) variety and they are seeking humans who qualify to go the full distance in their "spiritual encounter" with human beings, as did Betty Andreasson, and many of the prophets of the Old Testament, as well as apostles John and Paul in the New Testament.

During a typical abduction the first thing that is done to the subject is his/her exposure to a "cleansing device", ostensibly to rid the body of harmful bacteria and other microscopic predators. Next, comes a very thorough physical examination in preparation for the long journey ahead. Any diseased organs or sensitive areas of the human body would likely require either medical treatment, or that extra precautions be taken to protect the potential space traveler.

Lastly, but most important, I think the aliens search the 'heart' of each individual to ensure that their motives are pure. Cooperation with the "alien" entities is vital. I don't think they would violate our will if we chose not to go on their exciting journey.

I realize this explanation rates high on the "oddity scale", but it does explain the strange goings-on with abductees (especially those like Betty Andreasson) in terms consistent with biblical prophecy, as we shall see.

* * * * *

The Advent of The Halo

Figure 27.1 – Halos In Early Christian Art first appeared in the fourth century and artists were likely enfluenced by the "nimbus" or "aureole" of the Greeks (see god Neptune above right) which predates Christianity by several centuries. Also the Egyptians used spheres to represent their sun god (inset: goddess Isis with sphere suspended over her head, often also winged). The earliest halos represented in Christian art looked much more like glass helmets as the Early Byzantine mosaic (above) illustrates. They eventually evolved to simple ovals or flat discs over the heads of deity.

By the Renaissance period, halos were not reserved just for deity and angels, but were applied to the apostles (bottom right) and Mary and other biblical characters and eventually church officials and notable good citizens. I think there is evidence for halos in the Bible, but not as envisioned by most artists. Revelation 10:1 describes an angel clothed in clouds and a "rainbow" over his head. The angels that visited Ezekiel had what he described as "something like an expanse, like the awesome gleam of crystal, extended over their heads." *Ezekiel 1:22* (NAS) That could very possibly be describing a glass-like helmet.

Possible evidences of "alien" contact since the dawn of time?

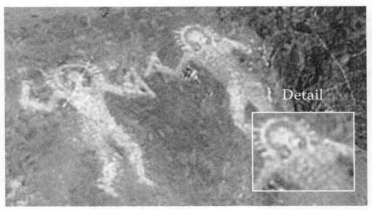

Figure 27.2 – Cave painting from Val Camonica, Italy, of mysterious figures with glowing helmets in protective suits holding strange implements and appearing to float, circa 10,000 BC. Note figure on the right has extremely large eyes (see detail above).

Figure 27.3 – Sumerian God figurine with large cat-like eyes, circa 6,000 BC.

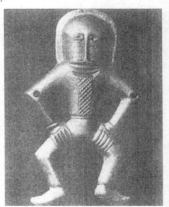

Figure 27.4 – Strange suited figure found in Kiev. It dates to around 4,000 BC.

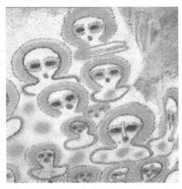

Figure 27.5 – Wandjina petroglyphs from Kimberley, Australia. The images are about 5,000 years old and strongly resemble helmeted alien beings.

Figure 27.6 – Small humanoid figurine made during the late Jomon period of Ancient Japan, circa 1000-400 BC.

UFOs Are Ready to Invade!

They've Already Charted Our Planet!

U FOs have been engaged in a systematic survey of our entire planet, many experts have claimed. Air Force scientists and intelligence officers have confirmed this finding in several past secret investigations which have since come to public attention.[28-1]

Step-by-step, it appears, UFOs have carefully guided their craft along strategic routes designed to encompass the entire planet.

One distinguished scientist in France, Dr. Aime Michel, has gone to great pains to map out the 1954 UFO flap using information collected from newspaper articles and through first-hand investigation of literally thousands of purported sightings. In his excellent book *Flying Saucers and The Straight Line Mystery*, Michel has concluded that all of Europe was systematically visited by the strange flying machines.

His scenario went like this: At first there were several eye-witness accounts of a huge cloud-like apparatus in an area, usually rather isolated (not over heavily populated places like large cities). The huge cigar-shaped cloud would descend in a horizontal fashion with the leading end tilting down toward the ground slightly. When it was about one-half to two miles above the Earth, the cloud would stop, tilt into a vertical position and remain stationary, often for hours. Once this position was taken, small saucer or disc-shaped objects would free-fall from the lower end of the column. These much smaller craft, estimated at around 20 to 30 feet wide, would race off in different directions, often darting back and forth at tremendous speeds, sometimes stopping abruptly with no apparent slow-down and then would resume their seemingly unorthodox flight path.

As nighttime approached, the huge column would lose its cloud-like appearance and begin to glow faintly with a greenish cast. The smaller discs would appear as brilliantly lit objects or lights, often changing color as they traversed a given area.

The whole episode would conclude with the return of the smaller craft which would race head-long into the lower end of the mother ship, in single file, and disappear. The huge object, with its passengers safely aboard, would then tilt back into its angled horizontal position and slowly move away up into the clouds, or night sky, or simply disappear over the horizon.

This episode was repeated hundreds and even thousands of times as reported across many parts of Europe.

What Doctor Michel discovered, when he plotted the times and locations of eyewitness accounts, was truly amazing. He found that the smaller discs left a pattern of sightings from their main distribution point (the huge cigar cloud) which radiated outward like the spokes of a wheel. He could almost predict where another sighting would occur once he had established the location of the main cloud and a nearby sighting of a disc.

He would simply draw a straight line from the two connecting points outward until a population center (town or village) was located along the path. Usually investigation would net several accounts of the strange discs in that area just minutes after the original sighting.

Michel had proven that a systematic well-planned surveillance of Earth had been undertaken by these mysterious guests. [28-2]

In March of 1967 a similar conclusion was revealed by a leading Greek physicist and engineer, Dr. Paul Santorini. During WW II, Dr. Santorini was instrumental in the development of fuses for the atomic bomb and also helped to develop the guidance system for the NIKE missile. It seems that in 1947 the Greek government had become alarmed at the existence of strange objects invading their air space. Dr. Santorini, at the Army's insistence, lead a group of top engineers in investigating the phenomenon. When the Greek Army contacted the

U.S. Defense Department about the strange objects, they were quickly pressured into dropping their investigation. Santorini later concluded that these strange craft were systematically surveying the Earth "possibly for an invasion," but government pressure kept his conclusion from being made public. Governments around the world, he claimed, were afraid to admit they were defenseless against the alien invaders. [28-3]

I'm unaware of any investigation in the U.S. of equal magnitude, however, the appearance of a tremendous number of mysterious objects over our defense and power systems is undeniable.

Strategic Military Installations

The late forties and early fifties were a time of numerous UFO reports. Since the Air Force had not yet put their debunking efforts into full gear, there still remains a great number of good reports within UFO archives from these years. These reports deal with the presence of UFOs near military installations and weapons systems. Strange silvery discs were sighted by ground personnel and airplane pilots near many strategic military bases while ground radar tracked the unidentified craft. They had been seen near White Sands, N.M.; the Hanford Atomic Plant in Washington; the Army's secret lab at Fort Monmouth, N.J.; near the A-Bomb test site in Levelland, Texas; the Muroc Test Center, during test shots of the Polaris missile and V-2 rockets as well as during a great majority of the American manned space flights (covered in chapter 3). [28-4]

As Major Ruppelt, head of the AF's Project Blue Book, reported: "UFOs were seen more frequently around areas vital to the defense of the United States. The Los Alamos-Albuquerque area, Oak Ridge and White Sands Proving Ground rated high. Port areas, Strategic Air Command bases, and industrial areas ranked next. UFOs had been reported from every state in the Union and from every foreign country." [28-5]

Dr. Hynek revealed some startling news in the February, 1985 issue of OMNI Magazine. He was quoted:

> "...The government did classify many of the unexplained sightings, and CAUS (Citizens Against UFO Secrecy),

wielding the Freedom of Information Act, managed to discover a number of things. The most important material concerned the Strategic Air Command (SAC) bases.

"CAUS learned that in the fall of 1975, there had been a spate of sightings at the Loring Air Force Base, in Maine; the Wurtsmith Air Force Base, in Michigan; the Malmstrom Air Force Base, in Montana; and the Falconbridge Air Force Base, in Canada. In each case, according to classified government documents, the nuclear-weapons storage area was penetrated by UFOs. One helicopter pilot sent in to look at the Malmstrom UFO even claimed that it had manipulated the computer, changing guidance directions on intercontinental ballistic missiles." [28-6]

Interested in Our Power Systems

Another key observation is that UFOs show an unusual affinity to high power transmission lines. There have been an alarming number of incidents reported where alien craft have been observed flying along power lines, often just a few feet above. In his excellent book Incident at Exeter, John Fuller noticed that most of the reported UFOs were typically seen either near air bases, civilian atomic power plants or over major electrical power lines. [28-7]

Several accounts described a device that extended from the underside of the craft and actually touched the power lines. [28-8]

Joseph Jalbert was looking at the evening sky near his home in Fremont, New Hampshire one day in 1965 when he sighted a strange object in the sky. The following excerpt is taken from *Incident at Exeter:*

"...Joseph had recently noticed a reddish cigar-shaped object in the sky, high over the power lines. It hovered there motionless for several minutes – exactly how many he did not know because he was so absorbed with watching it. After a considerable length of time, a reddish orange disk emerged apparently from inside the object, and began a slow, erratic descent down toward the power lines. As it reached a point within a quarter mile of them, it leveled off, then moved over the wires until it reached a point several hundred feet away. It then descended slowly until it was only a few feet above the lines. Then a silvery, pipelike object came down from the base of the disk and actually touched the lines, remaining there for a minute or so."

The protrusion then slowly retracted into the body of the object, and it took off at considerable speed – exactly how fast, Joseph could not estimate then rejoined the reddish cigar-shaped object and disappeared inside it.

Joseph's mother reported seeing a similar occurrence some 20 miles away, near Manchester. The only difference in their descriptions was that the protrusion extending down from the object she observed, in the separate incident, was reddish, rather than silver colored. [28-9]

The Great Blackout of '65

It was shortly after 5:00 p.m. the afternoon of November 9, 1965, when the lights went out in New York and parts of eight other states including Connecticut, Massachusetts, Main, New Hampshire, New Jersey, Pennsylvania and Vermont. The power failure also extended up into Canada.

At precisely the same moment huge fireballs or glowing spheres were seen by several witnesses throughout the area. Among the list of qualified eyewitnesses were several pilots in separate sightings. At the head of the credible list was the director of the FAA, himself. Dozens, if not hundreds, of reports from upper New York and Canada, to as far away as Philadelphia, flooded into the authorities describing the appearance of these mysterious fireballs.

Without warning, and for no apparent reason, something had happened that the utility companies had sworn to Congress could never happen. Multiple millions of dollars had been spent by the twenty nine utilities affected to prevent just such a giant blackout. [28-10]

A huge area covering some eighty thousand square miles with over 36 million people (nearly one-fifth of the nation's population) was suddenly without power. The outage lasted for eight hours in New York City. Authorities were completely baffled by the giant electric grid's failure. Isolated outages had occurred before but they were always localized and caused by equipment malfunction or failure. This one was different. When the power finally came back on, the same equipment that had failed for the entire night was suddenly in perfect working condition. It was as if nothing had happened, with the exception of a few tripped circuit breakers.

The mysterious failure that night received tremendous press coverage and most older Americans today can recall the incident. What is not commonly known is that over the next several months much of the nation would be affected by similar blackouts or something labeled "brown outs." The term refers to a condition where power is not totally lost but seemingly drained from the system, causing lights, for instance, to dim to a fraction of their normal brightness.

Within the next several months mysterious blackouts were reported in various parts of the world including England, Italy, Peru, Brazil, Argentina, Finland and Mexico and all were accompanied by reports of strange glowing objects in the sky. [28-11]

On November 16, blackouts were reported in several parts of Great Britain. By November 26, two sections of St. Paul, Minnesota, were blackened while strange orbs flew overhead. December 2nd was marked by the sudden loss of power in parts of Texas, New Mexico and Mexico which affected nearly one million people. Three days later 40,000 homes were darkened mysteriously in east Texas. During the month of December, alone, power outages affected huge population centers in Saudi Arabia, Mexico, Finland, Argentina and America.[28-12]

Within six months the power failures repeated themselves in Italy, Peru and England and had darkened huge portions of Wyoming, Utah, Nebraska and Colorado. [28-13] Never before had the world experienced such massive power failures.

The original blackout of November 9th resulted in a rather surprising reaction in America. As ABC's Edward P. Morgan related in candlelight from their darkened NY studio, the whole affair was accepted with great composure "...a marvel of calm and cooperation." [28-14]

There were a few panicked people caught in darkened subways and elevators, to be sure, but the overall self-control of the isolated millions of people was truly amazing. Had they known of the numerous UFOs spotted in the skies that night, their reactions may have been quite different.

On the evening of the great blackout in the northwest, *Syracuse Herald-Journal* reported that the Deputy City Aviation Commissioner had seen a strange object over the main power lines leading to the generating plant at Niagara Falls. Robert C. Walsh had just landed his aircraft near the darkened city at the Syracuse Airport which had switched to emergency backup power. As he and several friends stood on the runway discussing the power outage, they were astounded by the sight of a huge red fireball that rose swiftly into the air and disappeared. Several minutes later a second fireball was seen by several witnesses from the airport. The same thing was viewed from the air by a flight instructor and his student who estimated the globe to be about one hundred feet across. They calculated the object was at the point where the New York Power Authority's two 345,000 volt power lines pass over the New York Central's tracks, known as the Clay Substation. This was precisely where power authorities would lay blame for the power failure later that evening.

At 10 p.m. the announcement came that the power failure was centered over the remote controlled Clay Substation, a key part of the power companies' "superhighways" of power distribution feeding electricity into New York City from the Niagara Falls area. Subsequent inspections failed to pinpoint the cause, however, and the country was looking for an explanation for the mystery. [28-15]

At the time, photographs of several glowing spheres were taken by several sources including a *LIFE* photographer, Arthur Rickerby, and published by *TIME* and the *Herald-Journal* . Stories began to surface in the press hinting at a possible connection between the UFOs and the power failures.[28-16]Several network news reports mentioned the existence of the UFO accounts even as the chairman of the Federal Power Commission, Joseph C. Swindler stated: "The Northeast blackout may never be fully explained, and there is no guarantee it will not happen again." [28-17]

Authorities knew of the danger in the spreading "rumor" and issued a hurried statement to squelch the wild speculation: "All the trouble had been caused by a simple broken relay, a circuit breaker, in a Canadian power plant," they explained.

Although hundreds of safety devices had been installed to prevent just such a huge outage on the multi-billion dollar grid, somehow they had all failed. The explanation was unconvincing but was good enough to satisfy the press and prevent any further investigation into the cause. The only problem was, the story was also false.

According to the power industry's own publication called Power, the Adam Beck Plant Number 2 in Ontario had simply been tripped by an unexplained overload. It was not broken and, in fact, returned to normal operation the next day. A huge mysterious surge of power, lasting only four seconds, had wrecked havoc on the entire grid causing some plants to blow open boiler safety valves. Several plants without emergency stand-by equipment were forced to remain shut down for hours. The whole system was not able to function normally until the next day when adjustments had been made to equipment affected by the huge power surge. [28-18]

What had caused the power surge and its resultant blackout is still a mystery.

Perhaps the reason for the massive blackout can be explained by the alien who spoke through Betty Andreasson while in a hypnotic trance. When a group of specialists investigating her claims asked her if the aliens had been responsible for the great blackout of '65, and if so, what their purpose may have been. She responded:

"It was to reveal to man his true nature. Man seeks to destroy himself. Greed, greed, greed, greed. And because of greed, it draws all foul things. Everything has been provided for man. Simple things. He could be advanced so far, but greed gets in the way. Freely it will be given to those who have loved." [28-19]

What Do They Want?

As the preceding chapters have attested, the similarities between angels and aliens are astounding. In every aspect of angel's powers and physical make-ups there exists strangely similar UFO documentation.

These similarities cannot simply all be dismissed as coincidence or deception. If there is an attempt at deception by the aliens, how can we explain their unusual behavior? Evidence overwhelmingly describes a visitor who's interactions are totally friendly, if not loving. Recent reports of human-snatching aliens is very suspect and profit motivated, in my estimation (see *Author's Update* pp. 335-337 in *chapter 27* for more).

One has to ask the question, since the aliens are making isolated contact with men, what are their motives? What do they want? Perhaps the answer lies in a motivation almost unknown to modern civilization. Maybe they don't "want" anything. Better stated: Perhaps they are simply biding their time, trying not to interfere with the daily activities of mankind and are, in fact, here to assist us in unseen ways if only we know how to engage their help.

It All Fits a Pattern

Is there an overall pattern of logic in all this? Why would these aliens chart our world and cause blackouts and not just come out with their intentions? If they are planning an invasion, why haven't they done so already? Goodness knows, we couldn't stop them. The answer, as always, is in the Bible.

Scripture states that Christ will return one day for His Church (the believers) but the exact time is known only to God. Even His angels don't know when:

MATTHEW 24:36 *But of that day and hour knoweth no man, no, not the angels of heaven, but my Father only.*

Therefore, the angels must be prepared to make their assault on the Earth at any given moment. To do so, they would have to carefully chart out the Earth's surface and assign certain areas to specific craft to avoid any collisions or duplication of effort.

I know it sounds almost sacrilegious to some to speak about "supernatural" angels in this way. But, if you think about it, it makes perfect sense in light of what's going on in the world.

We would all agree that even the angels must obey the laws of God when doing His work. And those laws include our planet's laws of nature (at least the ones we have correctly defined). Any outside matter, including God's angels, that interacts with our world must observe what we call the "laws of physics."

That's not to say our visitors don't have superior technology. Obviously the UFOs have that. But God, Himself, must work within the framework of these universal rules or He would be breaking His own law. As noted theologians have confirmed, a Boeing 747 would have flown at the time of Adam. It's not the laws of nature that have changed. It's our knowledge of how to deal with God's laws that has evolved. The aliens obviously have an advanced knowledge of intergalactic space travel as well as a thorough knowledge of Earth's physics.

Angels, then, must be prepared to interact with the world's system, as it actually exists, at the time of their invasion.

That's why it was necessary for them to come into our atmosphere and manipulate the computer guidance system on one (or more) of our nuclear-tipped missiles, as a precautionary test of their ability to do so during their all-out invasion.

This would also explain the systematic "updating" of their records every six to ten years. We call them "flaps." In reality, the world changes rapidly, and the angels need to keep abreast of our major developments.

AUTHOR'S NOTE: The following data was collected and noted by me in 1985. The patterns have since been repeated, but space dictates that I refrain from trying to cover too much material. Some notable sightings have been the Phoenix sightings of March 13, 1997, and the wave of sightings from South America and Mexico occuring to this very day. And there have been many others too numerous to cover in this work. Plenty of books exist documenting the recent influx of sightings.

The last major flap occurred in 1973-74. Evidence would indicate that another flap should begin within the next three years, if they remain true to their recent historical pattern. There is some evidence that this is beginning to occur. In the last several months there have been two mysterious power outages that have affected several western states.

On Wednesday, February 28, 1984, a huge power failure blacked out nearly three million people's homes for up to 2 hours. It spread across 6 western states including California, Arizona, Nevada, Utah and parts of Texas. Officials said, "The precise cause of the blackout may never be known." [28-20]

On Tuesday, October 2, 1984, another massive blackout affected nearly one million customers in Arizona and California. [28-21] The power failure was later blamed on high winds that blew two lines together in a remote California region. Authorities speculated that when the two lines blew together it caused the system to malfunction. That would also cause the two lines to disintegrate, would it not? In both cases the equipment returned to normal function immediately afterward (see *Figures 28.2 & 28.3*).

In addition, The Center for UFO Studies, now located in Phoenix, reports in a story datelined October 1, 1984, in the Arizona Republic that over a thousand UFO sightings had been made in recent months in upstate New York. It represented the largest flap in recent history according to Dr. Hynek, the Center's director. [28-22]

On March 25, 1985, thousands of startled spectators from "Chattanooga, Tenn., to as far south as Orlando, Florida," reported seeing a strange fireball. As it descended in the evening sky it changed from red to green to orange. Authorities claimed it was a giant meteor but I am unaware that meteors change colors as they descend. This particular "meteor" came straight down much to everyone's astonishment (see *Figure 28.4*). [28-23]

Two strange green lights were reported in California and Arizona on May 25, 1985. The FAA attributed the mysterious orbs as being two Navy missiles "which came from Point Magu, California." However, Lt. Cmdr. Thomas Mitchell, the command duty officer in charge at Point Magu would not comment on whether any missiles had been fired from the base or not (see *Figure 28.5*). [28-24]

The latest flap at the time of this writing has occurred, incredibly enough, 90 miles from where I sit. Tucson has reported the most unusual sighting of its kind. Over 60 UFOs were tracked on radar at Tucson International Airport in wave after wave of 3 or 4 craft groupings. The UFOs flew at normal speeds around 300 mph and, thus, registered on the radarscopes. For over 90 minutes the phenomenal formations were tracked by radar and nearby military bases denied that any jets were in the area. "We stop flying jets by 10:30 p.m.," said Lt. Julie Fortenberry, base spokeswoman for Davis-Monthan Air Force Base only four miles away from the civilian airport (see *Figure 28.6*). [28-25]

Planning an Invasion!

If the aliens aboard these UFOs are planning an invasion, they would do exactly what's been done. Especially if this invasion corresponds with the Christian event known as "The Rapture" where millions of chosen people will be suddenly taken out of the world. This would require knowing where every individual on Earth was in order to make a quick "harvest" of certain individuals (more on the Rapture in *chapter 30*).

The first action that would be taken by the aliens would be to chart out the entire planet and record precise locations of all potentially hostile forces. Then they would make plans to render them inoperative. They would also locate all dangerous zones to avoid any accidents. All this information would be fed into huge computer banks and a master plan devised. Only subsequent updates would be required to allow them to be on constant stand-by readiness. The computer used by the aliens to keep track of all this must be even more sophisticated than the one in Brussels, Belgium, which is used by the World Bank. I understand it's capable of recording vast amounts of information on every human alive on the face of the Earth!! I wonder how much memory the "intergalactic computer" has?

The alien scenario goes like this:

Systematic Charting of the Planet - Would avoid any mid-air collisions when maneuvering untold billions of craft near the Earth's surface. It would also eliminate random searches and duplication of effort by ensuring that all areas of the planet would be covered in one sweep. The operation could be done quickly, something that would be important to those left behind when the power goes off. Getting back to normal power would be especially important in hospitals and wherever people are attached to life support systems.

Control Our Power Systems - The ability to cut the world's electrical power would effectively disable most of the planet. Electromagnetic power, such as that used by automobiles, would also be cut off. This would cause panic and confusion, but the loss of life would be minimal from auto accidents and equipment left unattended. These systems would all come back on after the aliens leave, as if nothing had happened (with the exception of those machines left unattended, which the aliens could easily switch off before leaving).

Disable Our Military Installations & Weapons Systems - These would be key areas to incapacitate. Obviously, the craft couldn't afford to be shot at or blown apart by our crude weapons while they were materialized in our plane of existence. Back-up power systems utilized by the armed forces would require special attention once the main power utilities had been disabled.

Guard Our Atomic Plants & Missile Bases - These installations have garnered special attention from UFOs. First, I imagine, because they want to keep abreast of our latest technological developments. Second, they would need to make sure that no accidents occurred at these strategic installations. A melt down at an atomic plant or the explosion of a nuclear missile would kill hundreds of thousands of people, something that angels are instructed not to do until the final battle of Armageddon (more on this, also, later).

Evidence that the aliens are planning the actions just listed are overwhelming. Any diligent student of the UFO phenomenon can compile information showing that these are the precise actions being taken by our friendly visitors. We could be invaded at any moment and be totally incapable of reacting. Plans have been laid, it seems, and all that the aliens are waiting for is the final order to invade!

Do Flaps Relate to Major Events?

In analyzing major flaps of the past thirty years, a pattern emerges that may be more than mere coincidence. Although 1947 is given historically as the year of the first major sighting of "flying saucers", others do exist that precede 1947.

During WW II, the first modern UFOs were identified by Allied fighter pilots. The sight of tiny alien craft accompanying Allied, as well as enemy, maneuvers was so common that they were given the nicknames of "foo fighters" and "Kraut fire balls," depending upon which theatre of the War they were spotted in. These strange silvery balls or discs accompanied pilots on bombing runs to Japan and one was reported descending near the exploding city of Hiroshima by an Air Force crew just after they dropped the first A-Bomb. [28-26] Apparently these small craft are the unmanned probe type and are as small as several inches across. Stephen Spielberg portrayed one of these small lighted orbs when he showed one accompanying a group of UFOs following a roadway at night in his film Close Encounters.

Kraut fire balls were also seen over major ground battles and near the German V-2 bases as they launched the world's first self-propelled rockets aimed at London. [28-27]

Obviously the sight of "friendly" objects in the sky took a back seat to the business at hand of winning a war. The whole affair was dismissed by the Allied war machine as hallucinations and battle fatigue.

Then came the 1947 incident which gained notoriety in the annals of UFO history because it caught the imagination of the press. "Flying saucers" was an imaginative description which was really created to lampoon the idea of things from outer space.

The significance of the year 1947 to UFO occupants is speculation, however, it was the formative year for the nation of Israel. It may not have been happenstance that the UFOs would make themselves evident as this key event was about to unfold. The Bible had predicted 2,000 years earlier that Israel would become a nation, once again, and that the event would mark the beginning of the end as it pertains to prophetic Scripture.

1952 through 1954 were peak years of UFO activity, as well. These were crucial times in the U.S. war with Korea. 1957 was another major season for UFOs. It was also the time that the Russians launched the world's first satellite, Sputnik I. Apparently the space race is of particular interest to the aliens.

The next major flap didn't occur until 1965. By August the Air Force had 262 reports for the month even after debunking and discrediting the large majority of reports it had to process. Through 1967 UFO activity was extremely high and the phenomenon gave rise to several popular TV shows including *Star Trek, Lost in Space* and *The Invaders.* [28-28] This was at the height of the Vietnam War and the nation was incredibly alive with social unrest including the demonstrations on college campuses accompanied by mass violence. Hippies and anarchists and communes...the whole country was in a mess. And the world was on the brink of a major war. Amid all this, the U.S. had pressed ahead with its space exploration program and was gearing up for a landing on the moon.

The Congressional hearings of 1968 came just as the UFO wave was winding down. By the time the Condon Committee made their final appeal for their non-existence, the UFO wave had, for all practical purposes, ended. Very good timing, indeed, for the Air Force.

When the next major wave began in late 1972 there was no one to call if you saw a UFO. The Air Force had ended its investigation after the Condon Report and was "out of the UFO business." Nixon had announced in the fall that the war in Vietnam was about to end and our troops evacuated en mass in 1975 under the direction of Gerald Ford. By the winter of 1972, the UFO flap was in full swing and lasted through the end of 1974. It was the last major wave but it was also the largest wave ever seen. One researcher recorded over 500 UFO sightings in the state of Pennsylvania alone. [28-29]

UFO activity has since subsided and many have forgotten the significant part they played in our lives in past years. But I predict the phenomenon will resurface in the coming years as never before.

AUTHOR'S UPDATE: The new wave began in 1985 (see *Figure 28.6*) and has continued through to the present time in alarming proportions! Most of us are aware of some of these attention-getting stories. New York has become a hotbed of UFO activity. The prophet Joel warned us in the second chapter of Joel that "there will be signs in the heavens and in the earth"...including "pillars of smoke" (or cloud) just before the coming of Christ. Crop circles have appeared all over the world, simultaneously, and with no fanfare in the beginning. Of course, there have been many counterfeiters who get a kick out of mocking the true apparitions, another sign of the "last times" (*Jude 1:18-19*). Reports come in from Japan, Mexico, Europe, Russia and elsewhere across the globe on a regular basis (see *Figure 9.5* near the end of *chapter 9*). What major Earth-changing event(s) is the recent influx of heavenly apparitions portending?

God's Eyes Are Watching!

D o Scriptures indicate any connection between major historical events and the appearance of HFOs? The following passage may hold the key:

> **ZECHARIAH 6:1** *Now I lifted up my eyes again* [gazed skyward] *and looked, and behold, <u>four chariots were coming forth from between two mountains; and the mountains were bronze mountains</u>.* [gigantic metallic objects]
>
> 7 *<u>When the strong ones went out, they were eager to go patrol the earth.</u> And he said,* "Go, patrol the earth."*So they patrolled the earth.*
> [Underlines added for emphasis]   **(NAS)**

These "patrols" are obviously meant to systematically watch over the affairs of men. "Patrol" means to "make a regular and repeated circuit of an area in guarding or inspecting."

Daniel called these patrollers the "watchers" of God. He described a vision given to king Nebuchadnezzar in which an angel came down from heaven who's duty was to watch:

DANIEL 4:13 *I saw in the visions of my head upon my bed, and, behold, a watcher and a holy one came down from heaven;*

DANIEL 4: 17 *This matter is by the decree of the watchers...*

Let's look at the New American Standard version of the Bible for a more in-depth look at Zechariah's visitation: (from the NAS version for clarity)

ZECHARIAH 4:13 *So he answered me saying, Do you not know what these are?" And I said, "No, my lord."*

14 *then he said, "These are the two anointed ones, who are standing by the Lord of the whole earth."*

ZECHARIAH 5:1 *Then I lifted up my eyes again and looked, and behold, there was a flying scroll.*

2 *and he said to me, "What do you see?" And I answered, "I see a flying scroll; its length is twenty cubits and its width ten cubits."*

3 *Then he said to me, "This is the curse that is going forth over the face of the whole land; surely everyone who steals will be purged away according to the writing on one side, and everyone who swears will be purged away according to the writing on the other side.*

4 *"I will make it go forth," declares the LORD of hosts, "and it will enter the house of the thief and the house of the one who swears falsely by My name; and it will spend the night within that house and consume it with its timber and stones."*

ZECHARIAH 6:1 *Now I lifted up my eyes again and looked, and behold, four chariots were coming forth from between the two mountains; and the mountains were bronze mountains.*

2 With the first chariot were red horses, with the second chariot black horses,

3 with the third chariot white horses, and with the fourth chariot strong dappled horses.

4 Then I spoke and said to the angel who was speaking with me, "What are these, my lord?"

5 And the angel answered and said to me, "These are the four spirits of heaven [calf, lion, eagle and man? see Rev. 4:6-7], *going forth after standing before the Lord of all the earth,*

6 with one of which the black horses are going forth to the north country; and the white ones go forth after them, while the dappled ones go forth to the south country.

[POSSIBLE INTERPRETATION: sounds like the chariots, or battle groups, are carried into strategic position in four regions by four motherships – each which are apparently color-coded – where they will dispense the legion of smaller craft]

7 "When the strong ones went out, they were eager to go to patrol the earth." And He said, "Go, patrol the earth." So they patrolled the earth.

8 Then He cried out to me and spoke to me saying, "See, those who are going to the land of the north have appeased [Note this is past tense] *My wrath in the land of the north."* [Russia is the "land of the north," as established elsewhere – see Ezekiel 38:15. When Christ returns at His 2nd Coming He will have already orchestrated the destruction of five-sixths of the Russian army – see *Ezekiel 39:1-2, 11*]

In the preceding mysterious passage, Zechariah relates an experience which is unequalled in Scripture. During his visitation he was given a glimpse of the future when God would deal out His judgement on mankind with great wrath. Earlier in *chapter 4* we find who is leading the charge. The archangels Michael and Gabriel are God's anointed captains of His heavenly hosts. In *verse 14* we gain the knowledge that they are "standing by" the Lord, awaiting His marching orders.

In *chapter 6* we see that they have special vehicles which will bring them to the various assigned areas of the earth. God uses the lexicon of the day when He calls them "chariots" to make the point that they are riding in swift and powerful modes of transport. Chariots were the Abrams A-1 tank, or Apache helicopter gunships, of the day. These "chariot drivers" are definitely of God, even though they are called a "curse" in *chapter 5, verse 3*, by those who receive God's judgement.

Note in *chapter 5* how the translators took liberty with the descriptive "flying roll" from the King James version and now call them flying "scrolls." In the original Hebrew, one use of the word is simply "cylindrical hallow object." These translators also added the idea of writing on two sides of the "scroll." Their prejudices corrupt the original passage and, therefore, substantially – even if unintentionally – change its prophetic meaning.

In *chapter 6, verse 1*, the smaller objects come out from between two larger, mountainous metallic, or bronze-colored, objects.

We see in *chapter 6, verse 7*, that these spirit creatures (angels) have been assigned a duty to "patrol the earth." These patrols are obviously meant to systematically watch over the affairs of mankind. Again, patrol means to "make a regular and repeated circuit of an area in guarding or inspecting." Daniel called these patrollers the "watchers" of God.

Clearly, there are angels who's task it is to keep watch over the Earth. The meaning of the word watch is "to be on alert; be on the lookout," and anything that would effect the future and safety of God's creatures would be watched carefully. Wars, armaments and technological breakthroughs would most certainly be carefully monitored.

"God's eyes run to and fro through the whole Earth," according to *Zechariah 4:10*. HFO activity and purpose is clearly defined in Scripture and represents an obvious effort to keep God and His angels posted on the affairs of men.

This angelic activity strongly parallels with the systematic charting of our planet by our "alien" visitors every few years. The Bible, once again, presents the only logical explanation for the pattern of UFO activity experienced in modern times, therefore, its warnings of impending dangers should not be taken lightly.

* * * * *

Image Courtesy NASA / Hubble Directorate

Figure 28.1 – M64 The "Black Eye" Galaxy

Huge blackout hits area from California to western Texas

Utilities uncertain of blackout cause

By Sam Stanton
Republic Staff

Utility officials were scrambling Thursday to determine what caused a power outage that began in northern California and plunged more than 2.6 million people in six Western states into darkness Wednesday.

However, the officials said the precise cause of the blackout may never be known.

The blackout, which spread in a chain reaction from California to Arizona, Nevada, New Mexico, Utah and El Paso, Texas, posed no serious problems, other than some computer difficulties.

"We still don't know what happened," Pacific Gas & Electric spokesman Greg Pruett said from his San Francisco office.

Pruett said investigators know the trouble occurred in one of two 500,000-volt transmission lines that provide PG&E with hydroelectric

Portions of the six shaded states were affected by the power outage on Wednesday.

Kee Rash/Republic

2.6 million in 6 states hit; users of computers reported most problems

power from Oregon. The line consists of a series of 2¼-inch-thick braided aluminum cables that may have touched each other, causing the short.

"There was something on that line that interrupted the flow of electricity," Pruett said. "It could be something as simple as high winds blowing some lines together and shorting things out."

The interruption of electricity began on a line between the Malin substation in Oregon and the Round Mountain substation in northern California, Pruett said.

That failure immediately set off a series of automatic relays that shut off power throughout California and tripped more relays that blacked out portions of five other states.

Pruett estimated that 2 million of PG&E's 3.5 million customers were without power at some point.

Bob Dintelman, assistant administrative manager of the Western Systems Coordinating Council in Salt Lake City, estimated that at least 2.6 million customers — and probably more — were affected in the six states.

Utah state and city police officials reported Wednesday night that they knew of no outages in their state, but Dintelman said some minor blackouts had occurred in the southern portion of Utah.

Dintelman, whose council represents 56 power companies in 14 Western states and two Canadian provinces, said a task force of officials

— Blackout, B7

Blackout

Continued from B1

from utilities is investigating the outage but that PG&E officials are leading the hunt for the problem.

The relays are designed to shut down power in selected areas as a means of protecting equipment from burning up, utility officials said. The system helps utilities prevent a blackout similar to the 1965 outage that left New York City and much of the Northeast in total darkness.

In Arizona, more than 400,000 customers were plunged into darkness Wednesday as power plants in central and northern Arizona shut down automatically.

Arizona Public Service Co. lost one-third of its generating power, Salt River Project lost about half of its normal electrical supply, and Tucson Electric Power Co. lost two-thirds of its power, spokesmen said.

Backup systems were put into use immediately, and hundreds of technicians were sent out to flip manual switches that had been shut off by the power outage.

The blackout lasted only a few minutes in many areas, and only a tiny number of homes were without power for more than three hours.

APS and SRP officials said the problem shut down power generation at the Navajo Generating Station near Page, the Cholla plant near Holbrook and the Four Corners plant in northern New Mexico. All three are coal-fired plants.

"We immediately began bringing on some oil-fired plants here in the Valley and also began heavily using the hydroelectric power from the Salt River," SRP spokesman Howard Alexander said.

Some natural-gas-fired plants were brought on line but were shut down by Thursday morning. The oil-fired Santan station southeast of Gilbert was kept in operation, Alexander said.

A pump in one of the water-boiling units at the Navajo station went out when the electricity surged, knocking out some power at one of the three generators.

"It has not caused the unit to stop generating but has curtailed it down to half-load," Alexander said. "It'll be out for three to five days."

Despite the extent of the blackout, police departments reported few problems other than traffic jams caused by malfunctioning stoplights.

The biggest problems apparently were felt by computer users, officials said.

Figure 28.2 - *Reprinted from the Arizona Republic, March 2, 1984.*

Waves of UFOs cruise air over Tucson, FAA reports

TUCSON (UPI) — UFO enthusiasts have a new case to ponder: waves of unidentified craft cruising the night sky over Arizona's second largest city.

About 60 objects were tracked by radar at 12:15 a.m. Monday and were monitored for 90 minutes, said Patrick O'Sullivan, air traffic manager for the Federal Aviation Administration at Tucson International Airport.

"We've been studying these things for 33 years and we've never had anything like this anywhere in the world," said Coral Lorenzen of Tucson-based Aerial Phenomena Research Organization.

"I don't know what they were," O'Sullivan said.

Davis-Monthan Air Force Base, only four miles away from the civilian airport, stops flying jets by 10:30 p.m., said Lt. Julie Fortenberry, base spokeswoman.

No military flights were known to be in the area, she said.

Figure 28.3 – *October 9, 1985.* UFO reports are now so common that little is mentioned in mainstream media at this point. They've returned to "It can't be, therefore, it isn't."

'Think tank' says world is entering great crisis

Report warns of peril in resource depletion, population increases

United Press International

WASHINGTON — Mankind is plunging into the "worst crisis since the Great Depression" as the pressure of overpopulation depletes Earth's oil, forests and soil, a major research institute warned in a report Saturday.

The lengthy study by Worldwatch Institute, a Washington-based "think tank," noted that in a time of dwindling resources, global military expenditures climbed to $663 billion in 1983, a 20 percent increase from 1979.

"Third World countries now spend more on the import of arms than on the import of grain," said institute President Lester Brown. "As a result, many Third World populations, though poorer and hungrier, are better armed."

The failure of national leaders to deal with deteriorating conditions means that "the belated U.S. economic recovery in 1983 notwithstanding, the world economy is in the worst crisis since the Great Depression," the report concluded.

Brown, chief author of the study *State of the World — 1984,* said its basic finding is that "existing economic, agricultural and population policies are not working very well."

The crisis is prompting many nations to pile up enormous budget deficits as they fail to adjust policies to shrinking resources, the institute said.

"By the end of 1983, developing countries owed some $700 billion," it said. In the United States, budget deficits during the course of the Reagan administration "will increase the federal debt by an estimated $692 billion ... closely approaching those of all previous administrations."

The roots of worsening economic problems "lie in the depletion of resources," the study declared. This involves:

● Soil — A net loss of 7 percent of the world's topsoil per decade, or about 23 million tons annually.

"The unprecedented doubling of world food supplies over the last generation was achieved in part by adopting agricultural practices that led to excessive soil erosion that is draining the land of its productivity."

● Forests — "As a result of overcutting and clearing for farming and grazing, the world's forests are shrinking by nearly 1 percent per year."

● Oil — Depletion of oil reserves "is the most immediate threat to world economic stability." Although oil dependence has been reduced since the 1973 Arab oil embargo, proven reserves will only last 37 years at 1983 production levels.

● Fish — "The world fish catch, which had tripled between 1950 and 1970, has increased little since then."

● Grasslands — "Between 1950 and 1976, the world's grasslands sustained a doubling of beef output, but since then, there has been no growth at all."

Brown said a key to attacking the problems is to slow population growth. In 1970, world population increased by 70 million, but in 1983, it jumped 79 million.

He suggested family-planning expenditures be quadrupled worldwide.

Figure 28.4 – *December 2, 1984.* Doomsday prophets have always been with us.

When You See These Signs

The End Times

The Bible says there will come a time in the future of mankind when the world, as we know it, will be changed. The ultimate New Paradigm. The years preceding this Earth-shattering event will see the world reeling with turmoil. Diseases and ecological poisons will threaten the lives of millions of Earth's inhabitants. This foreknowledge of impending doom is not lost on the secular world, either. The current preoccupation with global warming is nothing new. Prophets of doom have been warning of such an outcome for decades, if we don't "come to the rescue" of the planet (see *Figure 28.4*). We are told that nations will be at war with one another to such a degree that it will require the intervention of God, Almighty, to prevent them from totally annihilating the human race. Jesus told His disciples of this time:

> MATTHEW 24:22 *"And except those days should be shortened, there should no flesh be saved: but for the elect's sake those days shall be shortened."*

The "elect" refers to those left on Earth who have (re)committed themselves to Christ's teachings during these troublous times.

This period of history is known as "the End Times" in fundamentalist's circles. It's conclusion will result in the final battle between the wicked armies of the Earth and the intervening "heavenly hosts" led by Jesus Christ.

This period of time can be recognized by certain "signs" or clues which God will arrange to warn the faithful. As we study these signs it will become evident that we are, indeed, living in the End Times, something that may be quite frightening for those who are unsettled in their theological position. Let's examine the first sign:

The Rebirth of Israel

The key event that started God's time clock ticking was the reappearance of a homeland for the Jews. In 1948 Israel became a nation, once again, as predicted in the Bible thousands of years earlier.

> **EZEKIEL 29:25** *Thus saith the LORD God; when I shall have gathered the house of Israel from the people among whom they are scattered, and shall be sanctified in them in the sight of the heathen, then shall they dwell in their land that I have given to my servant Jacob.*

> **JEREMIAH 23:3** *And I will gather the remnant of my flock out of all countries whither I have driven them, and will bring them again to their folds; and they shall be fruitful and increase.*

> **EZEKIEL 34:13** *And I will bring them out from the people, and gather them from the countries, and will bring them to their own land, and feed them upon the mountains of Israel by the rivers, and in all the inhabited places of the country.*

Since the early 90s the former Soviet Union loosed its policies and allowed massive numbers of Jews to leave their nation for Israel. Estimates are staggering at how many immigrants are expected in Israel over the coming years. Ethiopia recently experienced massive social upheaval and Israel airlifted tens of thousands of "falashas," or black Jews, in the world's largest single airlift operation to that point. The tied e gates have been opened, it would appear, and Israel is gathering its Jewish brothers and sisters at a rate that is alarming to their Arab neighbors.

AUTHOR'S UPDATE: Vladimir Putin, the ex-KGB Russian president has rescinded the loosening of immigration policy – along with increasing State control over many areas of his "democratized" society – and it is, once again, very difficult for Jews to escape their Russian oppressors.

Russia and Her Allies

Examined on its own, the formation of the nation of Israel seems insignificant and coincidental. "After all," we say, "those industrious Jews were bound to get together again sooner or later." However, other events that have occurred in the past few years make one stand up and take notice.

The prophet Ezekiel described an alliance of nations that would exist in the "End Times" who's main goal would be world dominance *(Ezekiel, chapter 38)*. This alliance of nations, according to Ezekiel, will descend upon the newly formed nation of Israel and sweep through that country on their way to the continent of Africa. News from the north and east will trouble the leader of this alliance and cause him to send his troops back up into Israel where five-sixths of his army will be destroyed in the Valley of Megiddo. This will eventually lead to the great "Battle of Armageddon" as described in many places in the Bible.

How does this relate to today's headlines? The alliance that Ezekiel spoke of is being formed so quickly and accurately that it's hard to imagine how anyone could have predicted it, so exactingly, 600 years before the birth of Christ. Just who is a part of this powerful End Times alliance and what has it to do with the world today? I think the answer will shock many.

According to *Ezekiel, chapter 38*, a great leader shall arise whom the Bible calls "Gog" from the land of Magog (may'gog).

To further clarify who this leader is and his country, Ezekiel says he is the "chief prince of Meshech and Tubal." Meshech and Tubal were the grandsons of Noah. Historians tell us that Meshech and his family, as they proliferated over the years into a nation, settled in an area known as Russia. In fact, many top historians and Bible scholars believe the name Moscow (the capitol of Russia) is a derivative of the name Meshech.

Likewise, Tubal and his family grew and became a mighty tribe of people. His descendants settled in the area of the world once known as the nation of Siberia. It's believed the Siberian city of Tobolsk got its name from Tubal and his descendants. It's interesting to note in the Baltic Sea's Gulf of Finland, there are two large islands guarding the entrance to Leningrad called Gogland and Moshcnvy (Gog & Magog).

In 1922, Siberia and Russia joined forces and became known as the U.S.S.R. (Union of Soviet Socialist Republics), today's Russia.

Ezekiel further defines this End Times alliance and points out that several other nations will be allied with Gog, including Persia (the area where Iran and parts of Iraq exist today), Ethiopia and Libya (names these nations still possess). Also Gomer and Togarmah and all their bands will join with Gog. Gomer was another grandson of Noah whose descendants settled in the Eastern European area. This area includes the current Eastern European block of East Germany, Poland and Czechoslovakia. Togarmah, another grandson of Noah, settled in the part of the world we know as Bulgaria, Romania and Turkey.

As incredible as it seems, nearly every nation just mentioned has allied with Russia (Magog).

The only nations who are not currently a part of this alliance, that Ezekiel described 600 years before Christ, are Iran and Egypt (Egypt's alliance with Gog is foretold in *Daniel, chapter 11*. Called "the king of the south," the Egyptian leader will join the Russian/Arab alliance in an attack against Israel, according to the prophet Daniel).

Are Iran and Egypt soon to be a part of the Russian alliance of nations? In 1984, Egyptian president Mubarak opened up diplomatic relations with the Soviets which had been broken off by Anwar Sadat. The death of Sadat has almost ensured the eventual realignment of Egypt with their Arab brothers. This will probably lead to a military alliance with the Russians (or whatever new title they may have adopted as a nation) in the near future. Iran, the other missing piece of the prophetic puzzle, has taken a much more moderate stance since the death of the Ayatollah Khomeini. President Hashemi Rafsanjani re-established diplomatic ties with the Russians during his first month of office and an unprecedented meeting with then Soviet President Gorbachev took place in Iran.

When these two nations join Russia's alliance the entire puzzle will be completed for the fulfillment of Ezekiel's prophetic message. What's even more disturbing is that these last two nations could conceivably be forced into the Russian camp, virtually overnight, and the end of Western civilization, as we know it, could happen shortly thereafter.

AUTHOR'S UPDATE: Current Iranian President, Mahmoud Ahmadinejad, has strengthened ties to Russia in his bid to own a nuclear bomb, and the Arab Spring uprisings have positioned extremist Muslim Brotherhood forces, traditional allies of Russia, to take over in Egypt after Mubarak's overthrow.

Jesus Gave Us Clues
of the End Times, too

Jesus was asked by His disciples in Matthew 24 when the end would be, when He would return to Earth as the reigning Messiah. His answer is paraphrased here:

1. When you hear of wars and rumors of wars, don't be worried because that must happen in the course of history.

2. But when you hear of many wars and famines and diseases and earthquakes all around the world, that is a sign that the great troublous times are beginning.

Wars - "Many wars, famines, diseases and earthquakes." These are the beginning signs of the End Times. Today, scores of wars are ragging throughout the globe, far more than at any time in history. The Earth is preoccupied with the thought of a nuclear holocaust between the two superpowers. Small children are so frightened that most don't believe they will even live to be 30 years old before the the human race destroys itself in war.

Famines - Thirty-five thousand people die every day due to hunger related causes. 13 to 18 million people die every year, mostly children. One out of every 5 people on this planet, more than one billion, are chronically hungry. More people have died from hunger in the past two years than were killed in World Wars I and II combined.

The current world population of 6.54 billion is expected to double in the next 40 years. That can only mean an unprecedented increase in worldwide famines. 29-1

The following chart shows the dramatic increase in major world famines this century. Note the major jump in the 40s, the decade that Israel became a nation.

Frequency of Major National Famines

Decade	Famines
1950-59	4
1960-69	7
1970-79	11
1980-89	19
1990-99	22

The world will have 100 million extra hungry people by 2015, scientists say. They were speaking at the annual meeting of the American Association for the Advancement of Science (AAAS). Despite great improvements in food availability in the 1960s and 1970s, these trends are reversing in many developing countries, they say. [29-2]

Many in the year 2012 (as of this writing) are predicting that food crises will be the element that pushes the world into global anarchy. Already shortages have led to the "Arab Spring" uprisings in the Middle East, and Greece is teetering on the brink of insolvency driven by the high costs of food. Their financial stability is only being propped up by other nations in the EU, primarily Germany. Should their system collapse, it is highly likely to lead to a domino effect causing global markets to crash. President Obama continues to put America into deeper debt, unimpeded by warnings of dire consequences. The globalist bankers will "ride to the rescue" with stern regulations imposed as solutions to the worldwide instability, and One World Government will be established as the only answer to the crisis.

Diseases - A.I.D.S. has surfaced in the last few years as a terrifying new disease. Herpes is epidemic and syphilis is running rampant in our land. In fact, in the U.S. one in four teenage girls (14 to 19) has a sexually transmitted disease according to a CDC study on March 12, 2008.

The personal physician to former Prime Minister Margaret Thatcher of England was recently quoted after Mrs. Thatcher asked for a special report on the status of the disease. He said, "A.I.D.S. is in motion like a time-bomb waiting to explode. It's far worse than the Black Plague of the Middle Ages where half the world's population was wiped out. It'll make the Black Plague look like measles!" He estimated that millions of individuals are currently infected and don't know it and are spreading the disease at an alarming rate. The only solution is a quarantine of the suspected carriers, only it's probably too late now to do anything like that effectively. [29-3]

The A.I.D.S. virus is believed to have originated through sexual contact with monkeys in Africa. Many of these nations are so perverse that individuals have an average of 150 to 250 sexual encounters...per year! They are far from monogamous in their sexual practices. The Bible tells us to choose a partner carefully and remain married for life.

In America, A.I.D.S. virus carriers are predominantly homosexuals (over 80%) and most scoff at the thought that the disease may have anything to do with Bible's prophetic warning of an End Times plague.

I only know one thing: The disease will produce a more moral America, unless cured in the next few years (something that is highly unlikely since most major diseases have required over 20 years of research time in order to find cures). UPDATE: I was wrong in my prediction.

Earthquakes - In the decade of the '70s, alone, the world experienced six of the thirteen most destructive earthquakes of all time. According to the U.S. Geological Survey, earthquakes are, indeed, increasing in both frequency and magnitude as never before. The following chart shows the frightening pattern of earthquakes registering 5.0 and 7.0 or higher on the Richter scale. [29-4]

Worldwide Frequency of Earthquakes. [29-4]

10-Year Period	5.0 plus	7.0 plus
1940-1949	43	33
1950-1959	47	29
1960-1969	58	28
1970-1979	41	25
1980-1989	47	9
1990-1999	56	31
2000-2009	369	117

Wow! ✓

The past decade has produced earthquake rates that are off the charts and the trend is continuing. Something is definitely out of the ordinary.

For a real-time graphic look at worldwide earthquakes, go to: *http://www.iris.edu/seismon/*

3. Many false prophets will try to deceive you with half truths and blatant lies. False Christs shall arise with great powers to deceive even the brightest and most sincere.

False Prophets: Who can forget the awful incident in Jonestown, Guyana, where over 900 people followed the "holy" order of their "religious" leader, Jim Jones, and committed mass suicide. The Reverend Moon claims to be "The Christ" on Earth today. Maitreya also claims to be "The Christ" who has come to usher in the "New Age" (see *Figure 29.1*). The list goes on and on with literally dozens around the world claiming to be the Christ, many more than at any time in history. I suspect this trend will intensify in the days ahead.

> *4. But the gospel of Jesus Christ shall be preached in all the world so that those who want to know the truth can have an opportunity to hear it.*

Films, satellite TV, radio and the Internet have made this a possibility. Hopefully, Christian programming will cover the entire planet in a very short time.

According to an angel who spoke to Daniel, knowledge shall be greatly increased in the end times and people will go to and fro around the Earth with great ease.

> **DANIEL 12:14** *But thou, O Daniel, shut up the words, and seal the book, even to the time of the end: many shall run to and fro, and knowledge shall be increased.*

Who can deny that the human race has taken tremendous steps in the past few decades? Jets and cars allow people to move great distances in just a few hours, something beyond the comprehension of anyone living 500 years before Christ. Daily newspapers, and radio and television newscasts inform Americans of the latest breaking events in every corner of the globe. The Internet has exploded our knowledge base with instant informaiton on any subject you can imagine. What the average citizen knows today would stagger the imaginations of people living just one hundred years ago, let alone 2,500 years ago. Prior to this century it took hundreds of years for collective world knowledge to double. World knowledge now doubles every three years. Incredible!

> *5. Don't believe them when they say that Christ is in the desert - don't go to him to join his forces. If they say he is hiding in a secret chamber, don't believe it, for Jesus Christ shall come in the sky in great light.*

*Like thelightning that shines from the east to the west,
so shall the coming of Christ be. So massive that it
covers the entire heavens.*

Christ shall one day return to Earth and all His angels with Him, "riding
in a cloud."

LUKE 21:27 *"And then shall they see the Son of man
coming in a cloud with power and great glory."*

Signs in The Heavens

Beginning with the formation of Israel in 1947-48, the modern era of
UFO sightings has emerged. These great and mighty sights have been
misunderstood, even by the Church of Jesus. Intellectual man simply
reasons away these manifestations of God and classifies them along with
other "miracles" closer to home. Healings can be documented all across
our nation, yet most Americans scoff at the "divine power" that Christ
exhibits in His followers. "Americans are much too sophisticated to believe
in such absurd claims," we say, " let alone, a connection between UFOs
and religion." People are much more inclined to believe in UFOs as long
as they think they come from another planet somewhere "out there."

Not all societies share our skepticism, however. In 1965 in Kazakstan,
USSR, the Communist Party was forced to issue a series of articles
debunking the UFO phenomenon. Several Communist Party officials were
rushed to the area, including former Soviet Premier Breshnev, personally,
to deliver official answers to the people because of the "breakdown in
Communist morale."

It seems the citizens were so frightened by what many thousands
had seen in the skies over Kazakstan, that it induced a massive revival of
religion in the area. Interpreting these sightings as signs from God, the
people were seeking guidance from Above. This return to Godly ethics
caused the Communist Party great concern, and prompted them
to take "corrective measures." [29-5]

ST. LUKE 21:10 *Then said he unto them, "Nation shall
rise against nation, and kingdom against kingdom:"*

11 *"And great earthquakes shall be in diverse places,
and famines, and pestilences; and fearful sights and
great signs shall there be from heaven."*

God Will Reveal The Truth

This whole scenario of the End Times will not be a mystery to the entire world because many will sound the warning. If you are reading this book, you are one of the fortunate ones who will be given an opportunity to understand these events as they begin to unfold.

Jesus said that the whole world will hear His message before the end comes (*Mark 24:14*).

God, speaking through his prophet Joel, said many people will be enlightened and given insights into these coming events, even those of lowly social status:

> **JOEL 2:28** *And it shall come to pass afterward, that I will pour out my spirit upon all flesh; and your sons and your daughters shall prophesy, your old men shall dream dreams, your young men shall see visions:*
>
> **29** *And also upon the servants and upon the handmaids in those days will I pour out my spirit.*

To those who will listen, God has promised to warn them beforehand so they don't harbor fears about these earth-shaking events:

> **AMOS 3:7** *Surely the LORD GOD will do nothing but he revealeth his secret unto his servants the prophets.*

I wouldn't be so presumptuous as to call myself a prophet, but I do think that I've been blessed – through hard work, I hasten to add – with a new understanding of the events leading to Christ's return.

There is no question that Jesus plans to return to Earth. Just when will that be? Let's allow Jesus to answer for Himself:

> **MATTHEW 24:36** *"But of that day and hour knoweth no man, no, not the angels of heaven, but my Father only."*
>
> **44** *"Therefore be ye also ready: for in an hour as ye think not the Son of man cometh."*

* * * * *

The Arizona Republic   Sunday, April 25, 1982

THE WORLD HAS HAD *enough*... OF HUNGER, INJUSTICE, WAR.

IN ANSWER TO OUR CALL FOR HELP, AS WORLD TEACHER FOR ALL HUMANITY,

THE CHRIST IS NOW HERE.

HOW WILL WE RECOGNIZE HIM?

Look for a modern man concerned with modern problems—political, economic, and social. Since July, 1977, the Christ has been emerging as a spokesman for a group or community in a well-known modern country. He is not a religious leader, but an educator in the broadest sense of the word — pointing the way out of our present crisis.

We will recognize Him by His extraordinary spiritual potency, the universality of His viewpoint, and His love for all humanity. He comes not to judge, but to aid and inspire.

WHO IS THE CHRIST?

Throughout history, humanity's evolution has been guided by a group of enlightened men the Masters of Wisdom. They have remained largely in the remote desert and mountain places of earth, working mainly through their disciples who live openly in the world. This message of the Christ's reappearance has been given primarily by such a disciple trained for his task for over 20 years.

At the center of this "Spiritual Hierarchy" stands the World Teacher Lord Maitreya known by Christians as the Christ. And as Christians await the Second Coming, so the Jews await the Messiah, the Buddhists the fifth Buddha, the Moslims the Imam Mahdi and the Hindus await Krishna. These are all names for one individual. His presence in the world guarantees there will be no third World War.

WHAT IS HE SAYING?

"My task will be to show you how to live together peacefully as brothers. This is simpler than you imagine. My friends, for it requires only the acceptance of sharing."

"How can you be content with the modes within which you now live: when millions starve and die in squalor; when the rich parade their wealth before the poor; when each man is his neighbor's enemy; when no man trusts his brother?"

"Allow me to show you the way forward into a simpler life where no man lacks; where no two days are alike; where the joy of Brotherhood manifests through all men."

"Take your brother's need as the measure for your action and solve the problems of the world."

WHEN WILL WE SEE HIM?

He has not as yet declared His true status, and His location is known to only a very few disciples. One of these has announced that soon the Christ will acknowledge His identity and within the next two months will speak to humanity through a worldwide television and radio broadcast. His message will be heard inwardly, telepathically, by all people in their own language.

From that time, with His help, we will build a new world

WITHOUT SHARING THERE CAN BE NO JUSTICE;
WITHOUT JUSTICE THERE CAN BE NO PEACE;
WITHOUT PEACE THERE CAN BE NO FUTURE.

This statement is appearing simultaneously in major cities of the world

| TARA CENTER 40 UNIVERSITY PL NEW YORK NY 10003 USA | TARA CENTER P.O. BOX 6001 N HOLLYWOOD CA 91603 USA | THE TARA PRESS 49 DARTMOUTH PARK ROAD LONDON NW5 1SL ENGLAND | INFORMATION CENTER AMSTERDAM P.O. BOX 41877 1009 DB AMSTERDAM HOLLAND |

Locally sponsored by
UNIVERSARIUN
P.O. Box 1188, Sedona, AZ 86336

Figure 29.1 — The headline tells it all. Jesus told of this End Times sign in Matt. 24:24.

Reprinted from the Arizona Republic, April 25, 1982.

'Cashless' retail purchases to get test

2 banks, 4 chains are joining in 'point of sale' pilot project

By IRA FINE
Assistant Economics News Editor

A major experiment in use of bank cards for "cashless" retail purchases — with money transferring directly from a customer's bank account to a store's account at the time of sale — will be conducted in the Phoenix area starting next month.

Valley National Bank and First Interstate Bank of Arizona will conduct the pilot project through all Phoenix-area Circle K convenience stores, 10 Diamond's department stores, five Bashas' supermarkets and 80 Exxon service stations.

Details of the project are to be announced in early May, but some aspects surfaced Tuesday at a Phoenix conference of the National Automated Clearing House Association.

The Exxon stations and five Circle K stores already are using the point-of-sale system; by the end of May, 1,200 terminals are scheduled to be operating in the Valley.

Customers of the two banks will be able to use their plastic "debit" cards instead of cash to make purchases at the participating stores. The amount of the transaction will be deducted directly from their bank account.

The card will be inserted into a terminal, which will "read" the magnetic coding and, through a telephone link, check the card against a list of those that have been lost, stolen or canceled.

An alternative plan would have the store clerk type data from the card into the computer-linked cash register.

"This approach has great promise," Paul W. Finch, vice president for systems research and development at Valley National Bank, told the conference.

"About 95 percent of all consumer cash transactions occur within 50 miles of their homes," Finch said. "We believe our approach can eventually account for a significant proportion of those purchases."

The experiment will determine two major questions on the point-of-sale program: whether customers and retailers will accept it, and how much it will cost per transaction.

The point-of-sale method will have no direct cost for the consumer, Finch said, adding that system designers hope to get the per-transaction cost down to between 5 cents and 7 cents.

Philip Martinelli, vice president in charge of the program at First Interstate Bank, indicated that retailers will have to be convinced of the program's success — and low expense — if point of sale is to gain wide acceptance.

He indicated the banks and retailers probably would share the cost, rather than one or the other paying the whole cost.

Advantages to consumers and retailers are the security of not having to handle cash. The banks presumably would benefit by having to handle fewer checks and credit-card transactions if customers used point of sale instead.

Anita Best, electronic services manager for the Phoenix-based Circle K Corp., said her company expects the point-of-sale program to increase sales to the average customer "since they won't be concerned with the amount of cash" in their wallets.

The average Circle K transaction now is $2.40 and the average cash transaction is $2.15, she said. That figure should grow with point of sale, she said, indicating Circle K's participation in the pilot project will last at least six months.

Martinelli said First Interstate's preliminary studies "have shown that people don't like to write checks, so they will use the card. They're also not concerned about the direct debit from their account.

"But they are concerned about forgetting to write down the transaction" in their records so they know how much is in their account.

"But we feel the overall convenience will win out," he said.

Finch said banks still are studying whether to use signatures, photos or personal identification numbers as authorization for card use.

Jim Darcy and Dawn Masters, both of Phoenix, watch as a "debit" card is processed at a Tempe Circle K by manager Betty Payne. Circle K's participation in the project will last at least six months.

Figure 29.2 — When the Debit Card was first introduced it was considered a dramatic departure from check writing and was resisted by many. Today, cashless cards come in all denominations and flavors, including long-distance prepaid cards, and even cashless food stamp cards in many states. A prime example of slowly cooking a frog. Bill Gates is a big proponent of a national ID tattoo, and REAL ID which replaces a normal drivers licence is being implemented nationwide by 2021. Cash will soon become a thing of the past.

Christ Returns for His Church

The Tribulation Period

The 'Tribulation Period' is described in the Bible as a seven-year period in history when the 'Antichrist' will arrive on the world scene and eventually rule the masses. At first, he will bring peace and prosperity to a confused world, but after three and one-half years this great leader will change. The Bible says he will be indwelled by Satan, himself, and will disrupt the entire planet with his evil intentions.

The Bible also describes a battle between the forces of the Antichrist and an alliance of nations headed by the leader of what was formerly known as the Soviet Union, as previously explained. Prior to this battle the Russian/Arab alliance will sweep through Israel and conquer many nations. There is much debate within the fundamentalist's circles as to whether the battle between Israel and the Russian/Arab alliance will be prior to, or somewhere during, the seven years of the Tribulation Period. Many have labeled this battle World War III.

Whatever chronological time frame this battle falls into is relatively insignificant. Much more important to the Christian is something labeled the 'Rapture', and how it fits into future events.

The Rapture

This event is described as the time when Christ will return for His Church (His faithful followers) so that they may escape the terrible catastrophes that befall the wicked inhabitants of the Earth.

The word "Rapture" is not mentioned in Scripture in its modern nomenclature, but this is the title used by many Bible students today to describe this great "catching away" of the Church. The actuality of an all-out invasion on mankind by the heavenly realm, however, is mentioned in Scripture in many places. The chronological time frame of the catching away of the Church has been debated in many quarters, but I see the event clearly in Scripture. It must happen prior to the seven year Tribulation Period in order for the following passage to have validity. Jesus said:

> ST. LUKE 21:34 *"And take heed to yourselves, lest at any time your hearts be overcharged with surfeiting, and drunkenness, and cares of this life, and so that day come upon you unawares.*
>
> 35 *"For as a snare it shall come on all them that dwell on the face of the whole earth.*
>
> 36 *"Watch ye therefore, and pray always, that ye may be accounted worthy to escape all these things that shall come to pass, and to stand before the Son of man."*

Clearly, those who are judged worthy shall escape the Tribulation curses.

The Tribulation Period is described as such a destructive time that it is impossible to imagine Christians living in its midst and not recognizing it as such. In order for a people to be caught by surprise, the time preceding the Rapture must be one of relative peace and well-being.

Isaiah described events surrounding the Rapture of the Church in the following passage:

> ISAIAH 5:26 *And he will lift up an ensign to the nations from far, and will hiss unto them from the end of the earth: and, behold, they shall come with speed swiftly:*
>
> 27 *None shall be weary nor stumble among them; none shall slumber nor sleep; neither shall the girdle of their loins be loosed, nor the latchet of their shoes be broken:*

28 *Whose arrows are sharp, and all their bows bent,*
their horses' hoofs shall be counted like flint, and
their wheels like a whirlwind:

29 *Their roaring shall be like a lion they shall roar*
like young lions: yea, they shall roar, and lay hold of
the prey, and shall carry it away safe, and none shall
deliver it.

30 *And in that day they shall roar against them*
like the roaring of the sea: and if one look unto the
land, behold darkness and sorrow, and the light is
darkened in the heavens thereof.

To paraphrase Isaiah's message: he is saying that the LORD will show the people of the Earth a great sign (ensign) from far out in space just prior to His invasion. The invading armada will sound like a hiss from deep space, but as the billions of craft near the Earth's surface they will sound more like roaring lions. In verse 28, the Hebrew term for "counted" can also mean "be like" or "fabricated from". Isaiah is really saying that the whirlwind-like transportation used by the angels will appear to be fabricated from a hard substance that looks like flint. Why flint? Flint is a gray-colored rock and gives off sparks when purposely struck for making fires. I think there is a deliberate revelation here.

At this point, the angels of heaven will swoop down in their metallic or "flint-like whirlwinds" to carry away the righteous from the Earth. This will include untold millions of Godly Earth dwellers and will require so many HFOs (heavenly flying objects) that the sun will be blotted out. Notice that no mention is made of God destroying the wicked of the Earth at this point. You might want to read this passage again carefully with the new insight I've just shared.

The Great Restrainer

I believe the Antichrist is alive today, living somewhere on this planet. Why don't we know who and where he is? Because the time has not yet come for him to reveal his true identity. The Bible says the only thing holding back the Antichrist from power is the Church, itself. Christians are well-schooled in recognizing this deceitful leader and if he began to make certain moves on the world scene, he would, undoubtedly, be recognized and exposed by knowledgeable Christians.

Once the Church is gone, however, the Antichrist will be free to work his evil plan. The Earth will erupt into global war and misery during this seven year Tribulation Period, the Bible predicts, because nothing is here to prevent the wicked men of Earth from doing their thing. The Gospel addresses this in the following passage:

II THESSALONIANS 2:7 *For the mystery of iniquity doth already work: only he who now letteth will let, until he be taken out of the way.*

8 *And then shall that Wicked be revealed, whom the LORD shall consume with the spirit of his mouth, and shall destroy with the brightness of his coming:*

The "he" who now letteth refers to the Holy Spirit of God which lives in the hearts of good Christian people around the planet. Without God's love, the world would be full of only wicked people.

If you recall, the alien who spoke through Betty Andreasson said that "...man is very arrogant and greedy...he thinks all worlds revolve around him."

"Not all men think this way," the investigators stated quickly in defense of mankind.

"Only because love is present," replied the alien. [30-1]

Only God's love, living in Christian's hearts has prevented the Antichrist from revealing himself. The word "Wicked" is capitalized in *verse 8* of *Second Thessalonians*, because it refers to a person: namely, the Antichrist. Once the Christians are "taken out of the way," then the Wicked one will come into full power almost overnight and thus will begin human suffering on an unprecedented scale.

The Rapture of the Church will usher in the seven-year Tribulation Period.

Tribulation Plagues

The Tribulation Period will be a time of unparalleled human suffering. Many plagues and curses, as mentioned in the Book of Revelation, will nearly destroy the inhabitants of the Earth.

So terrible are these men-induced tragedies that it's been estimated that only around 30 million people will be left alive when it's all over.

The prophet Joel spoke of mighty sights during this period that paralleled the events of a nuclear explosion:

> JOEL 2:30 *And I will shew wonders in the heavens and in the earth, blood, and fire, and pillars of smoke.*

A nuclear explosion produces a blinding flash of light and a red ball of flame, and then a giant mushroom cloud, just as Joel described. He then continues:

> JOEL 2:31 *The sun shall be turned into darkness, and the moon into blood, before the great and the terrible day of the LORD come.*

This accurately describes the aftermath of several nuclear exchanges between the world's Super powers. Notice that it says this will happen before the day of the LORD. The "day of the LORD" is different than the Rapture. It's commonly referred to as Christ's Second Coming, a time when Jesus returns to punish the wicked of the Earth and to set up His kingdom here (more on this later).

There is evidence that Palestine, or the area where Israel and Jordan now lie, will one day be attacked by the forces of Satan:

> ISAIAH 14:29 *Rejoice not thou, whole Palestina, because the rod of him that smote thee is broken: for out of the serpent's root shall come forth a cockatrice, and his fruit shall be a fiery flying serpent.*

A "fiery flying serpent" is a colorful description of a nuclear tipped missile that would no doubt be used in an all-out war between the powers of the Middle East.

They Shall be Changed
–or–
Taking On Tachyon!

As you recall, those who are judged worthy will be raptured, or taken away, by Christ and His angels prior to the Tribulation Period.

Just what happens to the believer at this moment? The Bible says he will be changed in a moment, in the twinkling of an eye, and the natural or earthly body will take on a new dimension called the "spiritual body."

> I CORINTHIANS 15:44 *It is sown a natural body; it is raised a spiritual body. There is a natural body, and there is a spiritual body.*
>
> 48 *As is the earthy, such are they also that are earthy; and as is the heavenly, such are they also that are heavenly.*
>
> 49 *And as we have borne the image of the earthy, we shall also bear the image of the heavenly.*

I refer back to my explanations in the sections labelled Parallel Universes and Black Holes. As you recall, the possibility of matter existing parallel to our universe, or resonating faster or slower than our known elements, has been strongly supported by scientific speculation.

The Bible says that it's a fact. When Jesus and His angels return for the Christian, they will be changed into that dimension which allows them to be immortal and to live in the presence of God.

Even though the atoms of our bodies will be changed, our general appearance will not. We will have the same "earthly image" that we bore while in this life. The major difference is, it will be a perfected body without disease or blemish. That's a promise from God!

We Will Not All See Death

Just when the saints will be changed into this spiritual being? I've tried to examine existing accounts of near death incidents and compare them to what the Bible says about it.

The Apostle Paul wrote to both the Corinthian and Philippian churches that he expected to be with Christ as soon as he died:

PHILIPPIANS 1:23 *For I am in a strait betwixt two, having a desire to depart, and to be with Christ; which is far better:*

How does this compare to modern documented cases of near death? In his excellent book, *Beyond Death's Door*, Dr. Maurice Rawlings describes, first hand, several near death incidents. Unlike the authors of several popular books on near death experiences who interviewed their witnesses several months, or even several years after their experience, Dr. Rawlings bases his conclusions on facts gathered sometimes within seconds after clinical death and subsequent revival. This is a key element, as we shall see.

Rawlings concluded that death experiences fall into two categories: (1) Either a pleasant, heavenly, out-of-body experience or (2) a horrible, terrifying and painful one. Some of his patients experienced both on subsequent bouts with death, but in these cases the hellish experience always preceded the pleasant ones. These grateful patients felt as if they had been given a second chance by God.

Heavenly Near-death Experiences

Those who remembered their experiences with the greatest of ease were the ones who had pleasant experiences. Oftentimes the witness would see himself or herself as they left their "earthly" bodies behind. Accurate descriptions of events surrounding their deaths leaves others in disbelief. Many have described detailed conversations that people in the room have held while the patient was totally unconscious and clinically dead. The "dead" person sees and feels himself floating above the scene, suspended by some unseen force, observing the whole affair with simple detachment. Exactly how a dead person can know who entered the room, what they were wearing and what was said...while unconscious and in total heart arrest...is a great mystery but these strange accounts abound.

As the person slips further into his/her death experience, they feel themselves being floated through a long tunnel ascending up into the outer atmosphere of the Earth. They usually recall being accompanied by a friendly intelligence who's presence is only sensed. There is a communication between the deceased and their companion via mental telepathy and the being has often been described as an "angel of God."

As strange as it sounds, this experience has been repeated around the world by many others, even those in diverse cultures.

The subject is mysteriously drawn to a glorious, beautiful and somehow loving light that shines in the distance at the other end of the tunnel. Ofttimes deceased loved ones are in the tunnel to greet the person as he nears the light.

Each person is so drawn by this incredible light, so soothed by its love and compassion, that they simply do not want to return to earthly life. But a voice speaks to them within and tells them that their time has not yet come...that they must return (or words to that effect). [30-2]

One witness I saw interviewed on a local television show said he was very depressed that he had to come back to his earthly existence. It was difficult to explain to his wife, whom he loved dearly, that he wished he were still dead. The experience was so wonderful that all he could do was make the following comparison: "Imagine the most wonderful moment of your life. An event or experience that you still remember with great fondness...where you had 'the time of your life.' If you take that feeling and multiply it by a hundred billion, it still doesn't even come close to the love and joy I felt by being in the presence of that light"

Hellish Near-death Experiences

The other side of the coin is represented by hellish death experiences. These descriptions vary somewhat depending apparently on where in hell the victim is taken. Some have seen the "Lake of Fire" described in Revelation 1:9-11 and 21:8. Many have described descending down a totally blackened corridor or cave into a place where other humans in tormented agony can be seen in the dim light. The place has been described as red hot, some seeing actual flames leaping up around its inhabitants, others seeing more of a smoldering atmosphere like molten rock. Consistent, however, is the total fear and despair that grips these unfortunate souls. Hell has become to them a very real and terrifying place.

Usually these people are escorted into this place of torment by some other life form, often a grotesque creature. Some have said they didn't look upon the creature because of the terror of the experience or that their presence was only sensed because of the darkness of the corridor.

Forgotten Hell

Pleasant near death experiences have been recorded by several authors as noted previously, but only Dr. Rawlings' accounts have included hellish experiences. He noted that these hellish encounters were usually recalled by only a few who'd had near death experiences. In fact, many of his own patients exhibited terror from hellish experiences when first summoned back from death, only to totally forget the incident within a few days. He hypothesizes that these hellish experiences are so traumatic that the human mind forces itself to forget the terror of it all. Perhaps God designed the human mind to forget these experiences so that those who have gone through such terror can continue to cope with the demands of daily life. Obviously, the mind is a fragile thing and God is a merciful God. [30-3]

Spirit Bodies Have the Image of Earthly Bodies

In all these experiences both hellish and heavenly, the persons see themselves as they actually are in earthly life. Some heavenly observers have noticed that their bodies and clothing have a faint glow. Loved ones who have died before them are instantly recognized because of their form.

Christ's Second Coming

Even though those who were judged worthy have escaped the mess on Earth, there will be many left behind who will come to a saving knowledge of Christ after the Rapture. Marginal believers will, no doubt, finally understand what has happened and what they must do to be taken on the "second ship." God, in His infinite mercy, will allow them one final opportunity to change their wicked ways.

It's quite evident to me that the Church will be taken out of the Earth at the Rapture. The Holy Spirit, which Jesus left with us as a comforter, will no longer live among us. This will mean that mankind's link to heaven will be temporarily shut off. Those who die during the Tribulation Period will have to wait to join Christ because there will be no angels available to escort them to heaven during this period. But this will be a unique time in Earth's history.

During the seven year Tribulation Period untold millions of people will be persecuted for their religious beliefs. Those who die in witness for Christ during this time will have their spirits awakened when Christ, Himself, and all His angels with Him, descend upon the Earth. They will have come to collect those faithful followers who have managed to escape into the mountains or have been hidden in secret chambers by relatives and friends. This is about the only way Christians can escape the persecution perpetrated by the Antichrist and his thugs. But first those newly converted Christians who died during the Tribulation Period (after the Rapture) will have their tachyon (or spirit) bodies "beamed aboard."

Next it will be the turn for the remaining living Christians to meet them "in the air."

HFOs will descend upon Earth looking like falling stars:

> **MATTHEW 24:29** *"Immediately after the tribulation of those days shall the sun be darkened, and the moon shall not give her light, <u>and the stars shall fall from heaven</u>, and the powers of the heavens shall be shaken:"*

30 *"And then shall appear the sign of the Son of man
in heaven:* (author's note: at this moment their shapes
shall be recognized as mechanical devices rather than just
falling stars) *and then shall all the tribes of the earth
mourn, and they shall see the Son of man coming in
the clouds of heaven with power and great glory."*

31 *"And he shall send his angels with a great sound
of a trumpet, and they shall gather together his elect
from the four winds, from one end of heaven to the
other."*

Lastly, Christ and His angels will totally destroy the wicked plague from
the face of the Earth. Those unfortunate, evil, self-important people will
also be turned into spirit creatures (more accurately, shed their earthly
bodies, ergo die) and cast into hell to endure eternal damnation and
suffering.

I CORINTHIANS 15:22 *For as in Adam all die, even so in
Christ shall all be made alive.*

23 *But every man in his own order: Christ the
firstfruits; afterward they that are Christ's at his
coming.*

24 *Then cometh the end, when he shall have
delivered up the kingdom to God, even the Father;
when he shall have put down all rule and all
authority and power.*

God's rescue plan in summation: (1) first, the "firstfruits" or those
raptured believers and resurrected saints in Christ who died prior to
the Tribulation Period will go to be with Him. Next, those who became
Christians during the Tribulation Period are taken up at His Second

Coming. Lastly, Christ and His army will destroy the wicked and will set up His rule over this planet and will reward His faithful servants.

This Generation Will See it All!

Christ summed up the 'End Times' scenario by revealing this startling bit of good news:

MATTHEW 24:32 *"Now learn a parable of the fig tree; when his branch is yet tender, and putteth forth leaves, ye know that summer is nigh:*

33 *"So likewise ye, when ye shall see all these things, know that it is near, even at the doors.*

34 *"Verily I say unto you, This generation shall not pass, till all these things be fulfilled."*

> This is the generation
> That will see all of
> These events fulfilled!

Does that sink in? The signs are all around us. Daily news accounts relay stories that foretell of these things happening. I can scarcely watch the evening news, surf the Web, or read a newspaper anymore without seeing some event that is directly related to Bible prophecy. The time is now and the message is urgent...

** LOOK UP! **

* * * * *

What Will The World Say?

What Will the World Say When Millions Disappear?

an you imagine the utter chaos that would ensue if all the professing evangelical Christians were taken out of the world? By definition, evangelical Christians include all those who believe the Bible to be the inspired word of God. Those who believe that Jesus rose from the dead and is alive for eternity. Those who trust every word in the Bible and try to live by its principles and example.

Obviously, not all of those who profess to be good Christians really are. The Bible says that many will cry out to God when He returns saying "LORD, LORD," but God will say, *"Depart from me, for I knew you not" (Matthew 7:21-23)*. But, for the sake of illustration, let's say that all who profess to be Christians are taken in the Rapture.

This would include untold millions from around the planet. Very likely, the United States would be hardest hit. Perhaps Presidents, along with many cabinet members and Congressmen – people from all levels of government – would suddenly vanish. Heads of large corporations, doctors, lawyers, lawmakers and law keepers of every known variety and color would simply have disappeared.

That would leave the world in the hands of selfish, arrogant, godless tyrants and their minions. The United States would be reduced to a second rate power overnight. The stock market would collapse, the banks would fold, and panic would sweep this country. Who could help a world in total chaos? The monetary system of the world would be destroyed because it relies on faith in the future. What kind of future exists when no one knows what happened to hundreds of millions of people?

Slowly, the world would try to regain its composure. Those in churches would try to explain to their congregations that it was the work of the devil. But the wisdom of church leaders will be misguided and misleading. The Bible says the true knowledge of God's word (His law) will not be in the hearts of those who call themselves His servants.

> **EZEKIEL 7:25** *Mischief shall come upon mischief, and rumour shall be upon rumour; then shall they seek a vision of the prophet; but the law shall perish from the priest, and counsel from the ancients.*

The deception would run deep because the egos of the wicked clergy, naturally, would try to explain what has happened to them in terms that are self aggrandizing. The traditional biblical explanation put forth in this book would certainly not be considered.

If you recall, Satan, himself, roams the Earth with his band of fallen angels even now *(Eph. 6:12, I Peter 5:8)*. What a field day it will be for demons. The Bible says that these spirits will indwell the leaders of the world *(Rev. 16:14)*. These leaders will preach self-righteousness and self-preservation, but lust and greed will be their motivators *(James 4:1-3)*.

A Leader Emerges

Out of this dismal situation will arise a great leader. He will speak of love and peace, while in his heart planning his eventual total control of the planet. The Bible calls him the "Antichrist," the "Wicked one" and "the Beast."

The world will hail him as a great man. His economic solutions will save the world's destroyed economies. What will his economic solution include?

The Mark of The Beast

The Antichrist will require everyone to have an identification mark applied to or implanted into their right hands. For amputees it will be placed on their foreheads *(Rev. 15:16)*. The Bible calls it "the mark of the Beast." No one can buy or sell without this identification mark and cash purchases would soon be eliminated as a trading vehicle by the forces of the Antichrist.

The Bible warns that anyone who takes this mark will not be allowed entrance into the kingdom of heaven. This mark will seal your fate. Eternal damnation will be your reward *(Revelation 14:9-11)*.

But most will ignore this warning and simply be fooled by this "perfectly harmless" and logical solution. It won't be an overnight thing either. It doesn't require an overactive imagination to realize that the groundwork has already been laid for just such a cashless system.

Every day we move closer and closer to the eventuality. Television commentators bring us news constantly of new advances toward a cashless society. Newspapers carry stories of new credit techniques and future plans for the eventual elimination of cash (see *Figure 29.2*).

We all should recognize the familiar USP mark on each of the products we buy at the grocery store. This series of small bars is configured for holographic laser light scanners to read the product's description and to enter a price automatically into the computerized cash register.

Not long ago, the debit card was introduced by several banks. Participating merchants now let you make purchases with plastic "debit cards" which looks exactly like a credit card. It uses computer technology to access your bank account immediately. This ensures that you have the funds on hand, and helps transfer funds instantly from your account into their own. It's only a matter of time before all purchases are made this way. It protects the merchants from being defrauded by customers who don't have the cash in their accounts to pay for their merchandise. Checks will soon become obsolete.

The other problem that now needs solving is the lost billions of dollars incurred from stolen credit (and now debit) cards. So what's next?

394

It's only _one small step_ to require everyone to have an identifying code either implanted as a computer or within what's called the Quantum Tattoo or, alternatively, to use laser technology to painlessly burn a code (probably your social security number) onto your flesh. This invisible mark will prevent anyone, other than the rightful owner, access to your unique account. And the code can easily be recorded by those laser scanners already in place in thousands of stores across this nation. But first comes an app on your cell phone which can be scanned instantly. This is already being implemented in venues across the USA and the world, including China. [31-1]

When the Antichrist implements a worldwide system of cashless purchases it will certainly require a centralized base of operation. The central headquarters of the World Bank in Brussels, Belgium, now has an array of computers with enough memory to allow the processing of vast amounts of financial transactions. The multi-nation network of supercomputers is managed from its Brussels centralized location. The network's capacity is so massive that it can process the lifetime monetary transactions of every human on the face of the planet. [31-2]

In 2013 the US government opened a data storage facility of its own in Bluffdale, Utah (see _Figure 31.7_). The National Security Agency's Utah Data Center in Bluffdale is a top-secret data warehouse that holds as many as 1.25 million 4-terabyte hard drives, built into some 5,000 servers to store the trillions upon trillions of ones and zeroes that make up your digital fingerprint. The facility is over one million sqaure feet in size. Cray XC30 Supercomputers serve the facility, running up to 1 million Intel Xenon core processors all at once, with speeds as fast as 100 petaflops per second. One petaflop is about one thousand trillion calculations per second. This would make the system three times faster than the world's fastest supercomputer. It is slated to be the "first facility in the world expected to gather and house a yottabyte". [31-3]

The data center is alleged to be able to process "all forms of communication, including the complete contents of private emails, cell phone calls, and Internet searches, as well as all types of personal data trails – parking receipts, travel itineraries, bookstore purchases, and other digital 'pocket litter'," for every human on the face of the planet.

Modern computing has made extraordinary increases in capability in recent years with the introduction of Quantum Computers. Using something called qubits, they are besting conventional computers in speed by many factors. IBM has 18 quantum computers currently under testing. Google has a series of 5 quantum computers currently in operation. Their Sycamore QC, with 54 qubits, took complex exascale datasets and processed them in 200 seconds.. [31-4] The same amount of data processing would have taken the world's most powerful conventional high-performance computers (HPC) ten thousand years to achieve! At the moment the most powerful Quantum Computer is operated by Honeywell. "Our quantum computer will get 100,000 times faster by 2025," Honeywell claims. [31-5] The original 5-qubit systems are now at 53-qubits and increasing exponentially, according to IBM (as of July 1, 2020). Although quantum computing is not in practical use yet, the short-term future for the ability to track and record lifetime events for the entire world's populations is inescapable.

Daniel 12:4 *But thou, O Daniel, shut up the words, and seal the book, even to <u>the time of the end</u>: many shall run to and fro, and <u>knowledge shall be increased</u>.*

Social Security numbers are currently assigned to citizens as young as 5 years old, and there is great support to enforce assignment at birth. Children who receive social welfare benefits must currently be assigned a social security number before they can receive any benefits. The eventuality of every citizen being assigned a mark in a cashless society is not idle speculation, it's an alarming fact that is taking place rapidly. And it appears ID2020 is the final step in assigning a new identity code to every human on planet earth. A worldwide group of globalists are planning your future, with or without your permission.

In their own words, "Approximately one-sixth of the world's population cannot participate in cultural, political, economic and social life because they lack the most basic information: documented proof of their existence. Establishing identity is critical to accessing a wide range of activities, including education, healthcare, voting, banking, mobile communications, housing, and family and childcare benefits. The goal of ID2020 is to make digital identity a reality through a technology-forward approach that will leverage secure and well-established systems." [31-6]

The increased actions of terrorists and worldwide pandemics like COVID-19 will soon require that such identification be made mandatory. It will be a matter of life and death and you will have no choice as to whether to participate.

2016 marked the year that all credit cards went from magnetic strip to computer chip, as it has been in Europe, the UK and elsewhere for several years. Dogs are now implanted with grain-sized chips for GPS tracking. Bill Gates has implemented what he calls the Quantum Tattoo with plans to use it during the next pandemic as a universal identification mark. ID2020 is replacing our driver's licenses with a state-mandated new identification card in the name of safety and security. [31-7] The world is in turmoil and changes are coming, just ask the "peaceful demonstrators" who are tearing down our historical monuments in an attempt to erase our history; and burning major cities where allowed to force their will on the innocent masses. If you don't get that we are in the Last Days, you just haven't been paying attention.

> **1 Thessalonians 5:3** *For when they are saying, 'Peace and safety,' then sudden destruction will come on them, like birth pains on a pregnant woman; and they will in no way escape,"*

The process of setting up the system of a cashless society has been a clever and slow one up to now, but it will soon come to a full boil. Like the analogy of the method used for cooking frogs: If you throw a frog into a pot of boiling water it will jump out immediately because it recognizes the danger. However, if you put the frog in cool water first and then slowly heat it to boiling, the frog will stay calm in his surroundings, not sensing the fact that his secure environment is slowly cooking him to death.

So, too, the world is being conditioned for the eventual takeover by the forces of the Antichrist. It's not just coming, it's here NOW!

The Spirit of the Antichrist is Already Here

In this given End Times scenario it won't take long for evil men to come to power. With the Christians out of the way they will make inroads into the world's power structures within weeks. They'll be aided by misguided supporters from a whole myriad of secular organizations who simply do not understand the magnitude of the situation. This network of organizations already exists today and is staffed by earnest, well-meaning individuals for the most part. It's doubtful most realize just what their organizations really represent because the deception of Satan is so subtle. These organizations all have one thing in common. They deny the deity of Jesus Christ. If they are not of Christ, the Bible says, then they are "Antichrist."

> I JOHN 4:3 *And every spirit that confesseth not that Jesus Christ is come in the flesh is not of God: and this is that spirit of Antichrist, whereof ye have heard that it should come; and even now already is it in the world.*

These "New Age" organizations are masked in appealing rhetoric and pretend to promote the good of mankind. World hunger and peace initiatives are among their favorite causes. But their leaders deny the God of the Bible. They are instead (mis)guided by "Spirit Guides" or "Ancient Masters" conjured in their own minds.

The following excerpt from New Age astrologer Virginia Kay Miller candidly explains their true position:

"...the world is in the midst of a massive upheaval.

"...many people believe that humankind is on the verge of an evolutionary break-through and we are standing on the threshold of a New Age.

"Called the 'Aquarian Age,' it will bring about a new world order in which individuals will realize their true spiritual being and their interconnectedness with all life.

"To survive...as a planet, we must...develop the Aquarian consciousness, which recognizes that we are all linked together as members of the human race and as inhabitants of planet Earth. We must network..." [31-8]

The God of Forces

The "spirit" of Antichrist is alive and growing as never before in Earth's history. These New Age organizations profess that God is a "God of forces," not a personal God represented by the Trinity in Holy Scripture. They deny what they have labeled the "antiquated fables" of the Bible and instead preach a modern version of God. A God for the modern man – a God within that's a part of a "Universal Consciousness."

The rhetoric is appealing and sounds very Godly, but it is far from Scriptural. It's masked in the original sin of Satan. "I will be God," he said in his vanity, and "all others will worship me." That's the line he used on Adam and Eve. "You can know what God knows, you can be like God. God only wants to keep you in ignorance for selfish reasons. Go ahead, eat the fruit...If it feels good, do it!" With that act of disobedience, the human race lost its direct fellowship with God.

The leaders of the New Age Movement are numerous. Some openly admit worshipping Satan, while others are much more subtle in their deception.

The Aquarian Gospel of Jesus Christ by Levi (Leo Dowling) claims that one may enter the spirit of "the God of Force." According to Christian writer Constance Cumby:

"New Agers do not believe in a personal transcendent (superior) God to whom we are all accountable. They believe that God is a 'neutral Force' which can be manipulated either for good or evil." [31-9]

Dr. Charles S. McCoy, a professor at the Graduate Theological Union of Berkeley openly says:

"The pluralistic Faiths around the globe and the surges of oppressed peoples in all cultures toward liberation dissolve the limited conceptions of God, Jesus Christ, and history, transmitted to us by our Christian past and open us to widened perspectives and an emerging consummation hidden in God." [31-10]

Here's what the Bible says:

I JOHN 2:22 *Who is a liar but he that denieth that Jesus is the Christ? He is Antichrist, that denieth the Father and the Son.*

It's no coincidence that many UFO contactee stories profess a coming Messiah. Christian author Dave Hunt writes:

"The Mark-Age MetaCenter in Miami, Florida, has published voluminous teachings received from the space brothers: about the God-Self within, known as the Christ or I-Am Self; that God is not personal, but a Force of which every atom and person is a part." [31-11]

The theme of a God of Forces has been echoed in popular films such as *Star Wars, E.T., and Independence Day* (and a host of others).

The Bible says this is exactly the philosophy of Godhood that the Antichrist will profess:

DANIEL 11:37 *Neither shall he regard* [respect] *the God of his fathers, nor the desire of women, nor regard any god: for <u>he shall magnify himself above all.</u>*

. . .

38 *But in his estate shall he honour the <u>God of forces</u>: and a god whom his fathers knew not shall he honour with gold, and silver, and with precious stones, and pleasant things.* [NOTE: Underlines added for emphasis]

The New Age Movement Has an Answer

What will the world make of these flying messengers of God who came to take away the Christians? Obviously, some kind of explanation will be accepted by the majority of Earth's remaining skeptics.

The very teachings that exist today, espoused by New Age leaders, is most likely the explanation the world will embrace.

Constance Cumby in her excellent book *The Hidden Dangers of the Rainbow* observes that the New Age Movement leaders have stated in their writings that those of us who refuse to accept their brand of religion will "be sent to another dimension other than physical incarnation, out-of-physical embodiment, to another level of vibration where they will be happier." [31-12]

She also states:

"The New Agers believe that a 'cleansing action' will be necessary to rid the world of 'evil' (defined as anything that causes separation. Separation is defined as caused by God-fearing religions - Jews, Christians, and orthodox Moslems)." [31-13]

The Antichrist's explanation for the strange disappearance of millions of people is already mirrored in the teachings of New Age guru David Spangler:

"Furthermore, it is not really important to know where the old pattern will go; we are assured that it is shepherded by the Christ and will be fully ministered to by this cosmic presence...

"However, there are a few words which can be said about where the old world and those attuned to it will go. Throughout creation there are infinite spheres of environment representing and educating all stages of consciousness development. Some of these are physical planets, like earth; others exist on higher dimensional levels. It is possible that many from earth will find themselves attracted to such other spheres or planets within the universe which are at a stage of growth comparable to what earth has moved out of.

"There is another pattern, though, which is more likely. Earth is really like a vast mansion with the ground floor representing the physical plane. Only a small percentage of the souls associated with earth evolution are ever on the physical plane at once; they tend to travel together like groups, like classes in university which move together as a wave through the various levels and all graduate together...It would not be without precedence for them to be withdrawn into the inner worlds, to live in an 'upstairs' room which would reflect the needs of their consciousness and minister to those needs. In other words, the planet or plane or level to which they will go through the law of attraction, may not be 'somewhere else.' It may be another level of earth's own consciousness where they can be contained and ministered to until such time as they can be released into physical embodiment again...

"Whether this is indeed the pattern, or whether these ones shall be moved entirely out of the earth pattern...the main point is that they

will lose for the time being, their access to the etheric planes of power and the ability to control or influence the developments upon earth." (*Revelation, Birth of a New Age*, pp.163-164). [31-14]
[NOTE: Underlines added for emphasis]

This massive "planetary initiation" is what shall herald in "The New Age" as professed by Alice Bailey, Benjamin Creme and David Spangler, all avowed Satan worshippers and leading spokespersons and initiators of the New Age Movement. [31-15]

"UFOs Have Helped The World to Evolve," They'll Say

This "cleansing action" will be credited to UFOs. UFOlogy is already embraced by the New Age Movement in a distorted self-serving way. Several publications insult their readers with absurd claims.

Here are a few headlines from stories and ads in *The UFO Review* and *Inner Light* publications:

MYSTERY PLANTS LEFT BY ALIENS

NUMEROLOGY CAN MAKE YOU RICH

ETs OPERATED ON ME AND CURED MY BODY OF CANCER

A VOICE FROM SPACE OFFERS SALVATION

(notice how subtle this deception is...the "salvation" offered here is far from biblical)

JIMI HENDRIX - SPACEMAN!

STRANGE UNKNOWN FACTS
ABOUT THE LIFE OF JESUS
MORE IMPORTANT THAN THE
DEAD SEA SCROLLS [31-16]

These absurd vehicles have ads that offer their readers books on numerology, astrology and reincarnation. They offer to sell I Ching Cubes that tell the future, Amazing "Telecrystals" that open up telepathic channels and heal those who wear them around their necks, and dozens of other equally ridiculous gadgets. [31-17]

Intermingled with the absurd are probably some valid stories by very sincere UFO witnesses. But the association with obvious fakers and opportunists simply misleads the sincere observer. It wouldn't surprise me if the U.S. agency in charge of debunking the UFO phenomenon is behind some of these publications. It certainly serves them well in their desire to embarrass and discredit all UFO witnesses.

Even the Church Says UFOs are Not of God

For those who are left behind at the Rapture and aren't familiar with the biblical explanation...the world will give them assurances that they are really the lucky ones. The view that UFOs are of Jesus Christ will be totally discredited. I fear the "experts" will point to Christian fundamentalist's own teachings to make their point in many cases. Most evangelical Christian teachers believe that if UFOs do exist, they are the deception of Satan. In fact, very little credence is even given to the UFO phenomenon, at this point, in Christian circles.

Popular Christian author, Dave Hunt, links messages from "space brothers" to those of the "spirit guides" of Eastern occultic practices. He also cites messages received through the practices of automatic writing, seances, drug trips, Ouija boards, TM or other forms of Yoga, and hypnotic trances as all being of the same family as the UFO phenomenon. [31-18]

He further discredits hypnosis as the central tool of the New Age's proponents and researchers in "orchestrating a clever deception for its own purposes." [31-19]

It's no wonder he thinks this way since all the information he cites in referring to the UFO phenomenon has been supplied by the very ones he attempts to expose: the New Age philosophers.

It's no secret that the New Age occultic so   embraced the UFO phenomenon as its own. Mark Albrecht   ks Alexander (New Age leaders) are quoted as saying:

"Science itself is being dragged kicking and s   into the realm of parapsychology. Ultimately, the sheer weigh   es of psychic evidence and experience, the likes of which th   as never seen before, will cause the alteration (or collapse) of   s we know it.

"The emphasis on data and facts will give w   exploration of 'consciousness' (i.e. subjectivity) as a means of co   eality; psychic phenomena, especially UFOs, will receive the imprimatur of scientific respectability." [31-20] [Underlines added for emphasis]

UFOs will be studied by science all right. But it may be a hands-on experience, as I shall explain later.

Mr. Hunt comes very close when he says E.T.s (extraterrestrials) are "either angels or demons" but goes on to say that all have been identified as demons by what they espouse. [31-21] With a little more research I hope that hard lines like these will be softened enough to allow for an open-minded discussion of the hypothesis outlined in this book.

AUTHOR'S CRUCIAL POINT:

It is widely espoused in Fundamental Christian circles that Satan is the great counterfeiter of God's truths. For every major truth that God asserts, Satan has a distorted counterpart. If Satan is counterfeiting these phenomena, then the paramount question is, "what reality is he distorting?"

How To Spot A Fraud

This Christian fear of the UFO phenomenon is not totally unfounded. In fact, most contactee stories do espouse a New Age philosophy. Many stories claim the aliens will one day invade the Earth to save all of humanity from destroying itself. The key here is the claim that all will benefit from this contact. This scenario totally conflicts with the biblical account of the return of Christ.

As Satan has always done, he will use the goodness and truths of Almighty God to fool unwary souls through clever deception. Be on guard to the occult world's misuse of this phenomenon.

Even though most of these misleading accounts have been fabricated by people with ulterior motives (profit, fame or misinformation) there is a real danger that Satan and his crew of evil angels (aliens) are deliberately attempting to distort God's plan for mankind.

It's false if:

1. Claims are made that they do not represent any God.

2. Claim to represent God as a "Universal Consciousness" or a "Force."

3. Deny the three-person trinity of Christianity: God the Father, God the Son (Jesus Christ) and God the Holy Spirit.

4. Claim to love and offer to unconditionally help all of humanity no matter what their nature or beliefs.

5. Plan to invade Earth for the good of all.

6. Any other occultic or non-Scriptural claims.

As stated, most published reports on UFOs will be efforts to debunk the subject. They would imply that those who see UFOs are simply kooks. Even supposedly serious newspaper reports will always have some mention of a conventional explanation, giving the reader the opportunity to conclude that claims of UFO validity are actually misleading or false. Stories abound about evil-intentioned aliens or plans for global intervention on the part of the aliens. These reports are far from truthful and are in the minority. Any diligent student of the UFO phenomenon will find countless stories about a benevolent, non-interfering outsider who's chief purpose remains a mystery. The overwhelming majority of credible UFO witnesses present absolutely no conflicting evidence of the biblical account of creation or the future as foretold by its prophets, contrary to popular belief.

They'll Believe a Lie

No person that has been left behind at the Rapture will happily accept the fact that they may be bound for hell. The very thing that kept them from going in the first place, greed and vanity, will very likely be the thing that will make them reject the biblical explanation.

It's only natural that the vast majority will be attracted to the New Age explanation saying they are the chosen people of the "Universal Christ Consciousness." The Bible validates this probability in the following passage:

> II THESSALONIANS 2:9 *Even him, whose coming is after the working of Satan with all power and signs and lying wonders,* [the Antichrist]
>
> ...
>
> 10 *And with all deceivableness of unrighteousness in them that perish; because they received not the love of the truth, that they might be saved.*
>
> ...
>
> 11 *And for this cause God shall send them* strong delusion, *that they should believe a lie:*
>
> ...
>
> 12 *That they all might be damned who believed not the truth, but had pleasure in unrighteousness.*

The Antichrist will possess great power to deceive the people. He'll show them his "supernatural" abilities and comfort them with lies about what has happened. "They are the enlightened ones," he'll tell them, and he'll set the example as an "evolved" human being living in the New Age of spiritual enlightenment.

They Will Curse the Saints

A world without the Godly will be a place of incredible evil. Greedy, self-indulgent masses will devour the Earth.

Even the people of God's holy nation Israel will gloat in their own pride. They'll probably play the New Age theme to its hilt. Not fearing the God of Israel they'll say, "…there is no God. The poor masses who have left us have simply transcended to another level where they'll be more comfortable. Good riddance to the dummies!"

EZEKIEL 9:9 *Then said he unto me, The iniquity of the house of Israel and Judah is exceeding great, and the land is full of blood, and the city full of perverseness: for they say, The LORD hath forsaken the earth, and the LORD seeth not.*

In fact, all the Earth's religions will be ridiculed along with Christianity:

II CHRONICLES 32:19 *And they spake against the God of Jerusalem, as against the gods of the people of the earth, which were the work of the hands of man.*

In their false confidence and misguided rejoicing they'll look forward to the return of the spacecraft. "At last," they'll say, "we've entered the Age of Aquarius. New and glorious things await us 'on the other side' of this plane of existence."

But God has different plans. "The meek shall inherit the Earth," the Bible says. In that final day those who have been persecuted and killed by the evil, self-seeking opportunists will have the last laugh:

AMOS 5:8 *Seek him that maketh the seven stars* [the star cluster Pleiades] *and Orion, and turneth the shadow of death into the morning, and maketh the day dark with night: that calleth forth the waters of the sea, and poureth them out upon the face of the earth: the LORD is his name:*

...

9 That strengtheneth the spoiled against the strong, so that the spoiled shall come against the fortress.

...

10 They hate him that rebuketh in the gate, and they abhor him that speaketh uprightly.

...

11 Forasmuch therefore as your treading is upon the poor, and ye take from him burdens of wheat: ye have

built houses of hewn stone, but ye shall not drink
wine of them.

...

12 For I know your manifold transgressions and your
mighty sins: they afflict the just, they take a bribe, and
they turn aside the poor in the gate from their right.

...

13 Therefore the prudent shall keep silence in that
time: for it is an evil time.

...

18 <u>Woe unto you that desire the day of the LORD!</u>
<u>to what end is it for you? the day of the LORD is</u>
<u>darkness, and not light.</u> [Underlines added for emphasis.]

New Agers will rejoice in the "Age of Aquarius" and welcome the return of
their "space brothers." But God says they are fools to hope for His return.

New Age Symbols & Organizations

So that you may be aware of the organizations that profess all – or at
least some – of the doctrines of this New Age philosophy, I wanted to
include a partial list of this worldwide "Network." They include:

EST, The Unification Church of Reverend Moon,
Lifespring, Silva Mind Control, Scientology, Arica and
many, many more.

The Rev. Jim Jones of the infamous Jonestown massacre,
and the Heaven's Gate cult were at one time members in
good standing with the N.A. leadership. [31-22]

Groups and movements such as Findhorn Foundation,
Theosophical Society, Rosicrucians, Lucis Trust,
Amnesty International, Greenspeace, Children of God,
Zero Population Growth, and the Sierra Club (*I'll bet
that surprises a few well-meaning, but uninformed
individuals*). [31-23]

Their members include those involved in Secular Humanism of every description including proponents of the Humanist Manifesto, Holistic Movement, Humanism, Humanistic Psychology, Transpersonal Psychology, New Thought, Third Wave, Third Force, The Third Way, The New Spirituality and Holistic Medicine. [31-24]

Many millions of people involved in these movements and organizations are totally unaware of any New Age attachment, or its even more cleverly disguised alliance with the God of Forces: Satan, himself (*Daniel 11:38*). We all remember the Star Wars character, Obi-wan-kenobi, saying "May the Force be with you Luke Skywalker." The Bible clearly states many times that God is a person in human form, not merely a creative force.

New Age proponents employ techniques such as Yoga, TM, meditation, self-hypnosis, encourage the use of psychedelic drugs like LSD and peyote.

They embrace occultic deities with names like Kali, Lilith, Pan, Lucifer and Shiva – all synonyms for Satan. [31-25]

They use terms like Universal Consciousness, the God within, Self-realization, self actualization, visualization, Spirit Guides, Grand Masters, psychotechnologies, transformation, experiential religion and many others.

New Age symbols include: The rainbow, the unicorn, Pegasus (the flying horse), the all-seeing eye of freemasonry, the pyramid, 666 or any configuration using triple sixes, the swastika and others. [31-26]

For a more thorough list of these groups see Constance Cumby's *The Hidden Dangers of the Rainbow*. Do your homework and find out who started these organizations and why they are directly or indirectly linked to satanic philosophy. It's your duty, especially if you are an uninformed member of one of these organizations.

Many Will Preach The Gospel

Even though the Church is raptured away, there will be plenty of activity among newly converted Christians.

DANIEL 11:32 *And such as do wickedly against the covenant shall he* [the Antichrist] *corrupt by flatteries: but the people that do know their God shall be strong, and do exploits.*

...

DANIEL 11 33 *And they that understand among the people shall instruct many...*

Many Will Be Saved

The Bible says there will be countless numbers of people who return to their Godly ways and profess a new relationship with Jesus Christ. None will take the "mark of the beast" and for that, many will be killed by the Antichrist's secret police and military militias.

You can still be saved if you wait until after the Rapture of the Church, but the consequences will be grim. Be prepared to die defending your beliefs, or at least suffering untold hardships because that's what it will take to survive this brutal regime, one that will make Nazi Germany pale by comparison.

Power To War With The Saints

The Antichrist will possess great powers. Some of his miracles will parallel those of Jesus Christ. He'll be able to call fire down out of heaven. And he'll have the technology to battle with a returning Christ.

The Bible predicts that his technology will be so advanced that he will be able to stand up to the powers of God Almighty. I didn't write the plot. It's written in the Bible. Therefore, I must believe its every word:

DANIEL 8:25 *And through his* [the Antichrist's] *policy also he shall cause craft to prosper in his hand; and he shall magnify himself in his heart, and by peace shall destroy many: he shall also stand up against the Prince of princes* [Jesus]; *but he shall be broken without hand.*

The Book of Revelation describes the final battle of Armageddon with Christ and His army riding "on white horses, clothed in fine linen, white and clean" *(Rev. 19:14)*. His angels will fill the air like "fowls that fly in the midst of heaven." But that won't intimidate the kings of the Earth. They'll have the power to stand and fight God's mighty "HFO Air Force."

> **REVELATION 19:19** *And I saw the beast* [the Antichrist], *and the kings of the earth, and their armies, gathered together to make war against him that sat on the horse, and against his army.*

The one sitting on the horse is wearing clothing that has "KING OF KINGS, AND LORD OF LORDS" written on them (see Revelation 19:16). This Scripture says that the Antichrist will be able to make war with Christ and His army of angels. In fact, they will shoot some of the heavenly hosts out of the sky during the final battle between good and evil, as explained here in the Book of Daniel:

> **DANIEL 8:9** *And out of one of them came forth a little horn* [the Antichrist], *which waxed exceedingly great, toward the south, and toward the east, and toward the pleasant land.*
>
> ...
>
> **DANIEL 8: 11** *And it waxed great, even to the host of heaven; and it cast down some of the host and of the stars to the ground, and stamped upon them.*
>
> [Underlines added for emphasis]

The word "hosts" in this context refers, in the original Hebrew, to "a mass of people, organized for war." Interestingly, God says that not only does Satan cast down the angelic soldiers, but also their HFOs or "stars."

We've discussed previously the fact that Satan has the power to detain God's angels (see *"Battles in a Parallel Universe"* in chapter 27 of this book) and that a heavenly battle rages all around us in the heavenly realm (tachyon dimension). It stands to reason that if Satan indwells the spirit of the Antichrist, he could also give him the knowledge to utilize heaven's technology. Or it may very well be that a saucer or two will fall into the hands of the Antichrist and he and his scientists will be able to duplicate some of their capabilities, including their weapon systems. Just when this happens is a matter of conjecture.

There have been several accounts of aliens apparently repairing disabled craft. The Reverend Gill case is one of particular interest (see chapter 9, *"Other Details"*). Others have seen alien beings busying themselves with tasks that appear to require mechanical tools of a sort. Although it's hard to know, witnesses were sure that whatever these aliens were doing, it was necessary repair or maintenance to ensure proper flight for the object.

The point is, these craft are capable of breaking down and, although the occupants can't be threatened with death – being eternal creatures – it's possible that their equipment can be confiscated or destroyed. The Bible may indicate just such a scenario in the previous mysterious passage in Daniel.

* * * * *

The "flaming shields" over Jerusalem recorded by historian Flavius Josephus

Figure 31.1 – Roman shield designs give credence to Flavius Josephus' description of HFOs over Jerusalem appearing like "flaming shields" shortly before the Roman legion destroyed the city.

See page 430 for the complete story.

Claims of the "World's Fastest Supercomputer"

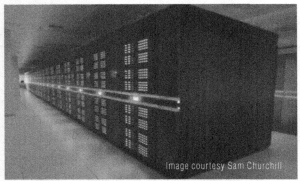

Tianhe-2 Chinese supercomputer formerly fastest in the world in 2015.

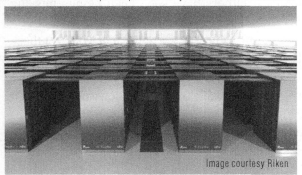

Fugaku — the most powerful supercomputer on the planet as of July 2020 built by Fujitsu of Japan. It's 2.8x faster than IBM's Summit, previously #1.

Figure 31.2 — Petascale High-Performance Computing (HPC): The current most powerful supercomputers in the world are petascale HPC. Petascale refers to a computer system capable of reaching performance in excess of one petaFLOPS, i.e. one quadrillion, calculations per second.

Figure 31.3 — Exascale HPC: The next generation of super-computers is exascale HPC11, a supercomputer operating at 1,000 petaFLOPS or greater. The US, China, Japan, Russia, India and the EU have declared the development of exascale technology to be a strategic priority and are investing heavily into R&D programs to achieve this target.

Figure 31.4 — Blue Gene (above) is an IBM project that created three generations of supercomputers. The aim of the project was to design supercomputers that could reach operating speeds in the petaFLOPS range with low power consumption. America's next-generation exascale supercomputer, dubbed Aurora, is expected to be operational by 2021 and is competing with Cray's "Frontier", also due to arrive in 2021, for the title. It is being built by Intel at Argonne National Laboratory for the Department of Energy, according to Rick Perry, U.S. Secretary of Energy.

Quantum Computing and Beyond

Figure 31.5 — Quantum Computing is the latest development in a quickly accelerating competition toward "Quantum Supremacy". Honeywell is currently the speed champion of the field, as of July 2020, with its H1 machine (above), but IBM, HP, Cray, Google and others are racing to surpass their efforts. Although the technology in theory is very fast, it is not geared toward doing multiple tasks like conventional computers, but is better at solving very complex single challenges requiring extremely fast linear solutions.

Figure 31.6 — Photonic computing is another promising technology for future consideration. Rather than using electrons, as in current chip technology, this plasmon light chip will use single photons of light to transmit instructions to the central processing unit of a photonic computer and speeds could be exponentially faster than electrons. There are many challenges to the development of this technology so don't look for a photonic computer any time soon.

The NSA's Secret Data Center in Bluffdale, Utah

Figure 31.7 — One million square foot NSA Utah Data Center in Bluffdale is the world's largest, most sophisticated spy database.

414

Gates Foundation's Quantum Tattoo vaccine application & tracking technology

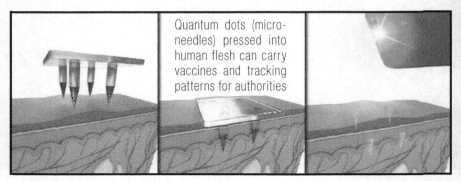

Figure 31.8 — A pattern of 1.5-millimeter microneedles that contain vaccine and fluorescent quantum dots are applied as a patch. The sugar-based needles dissolve under the skin, leaving the encapsulated quantum dots. Their pattern can be read to identify the vaccine that was administered. The project was co-led by Rice University bioengineer Kevin McHugh during his time at MIT. (Credit: Second Bay Studios)

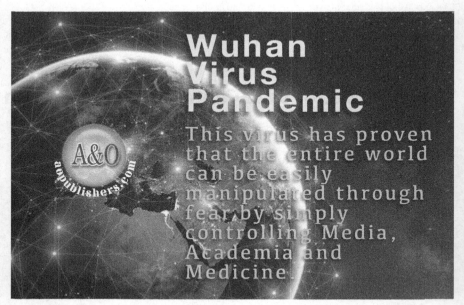

Figure 31.9 — Americans, along with the populations of the world, are being conditioned to accept sweeping government mandates (enforced by stiff penalties) which are allegedly for the common good. It seems that most are seeking a leader with a worldwide system of control which guarantees peace and safety among the nations. Antichrist will offer a system that promises to eliminate terrorists, riots and pandemics, and which guarantees equality for all based on a universal identification mark in the flesh of every man, woman and child on the face of the planet.

The Church Returns

The Proud and Mighty

The reason I've spent the past four years of my life reading, researching and writing this book is to try to reach the people of this Earth. I know untold millions are borderline believers. Many others have never heard the TRUE message in the Bible. They've mistakenly associated theological doctrines and religions of people with the message of Christ and have "thrown out the proverbial baby with the bath water." I can understand that. I lived that way for 30 years, not really knowing for sure if there was anything to this "God business." It took several traumatic events in my life to motivate me to really search for the truth. But I was one of the fortunate ones.

Our society emphasizes the importance of good looks and money and power. Too many people get caught up in doing what feels good. Self-indulgence and pleasure are what most people strive for. "If you've got looks and money, you've got it all." That's the message broadcast to our youth all day, every day. To the more "mature" Americans the gauge of success is intelligence and power…money and possessions are the natural result.

But that's not it…Christ said:

LUKE 12:15 *"Take heed, and beware of covetousness* [greed]*: for a man's life consisteth not in the abundance of the things which he possesseth."*

It would be tremendously difficult to be blessed by extremely good looks and not get caught up in the thousands of vanity trips available. We forget that anything, or anyone, besides ourselves exists.

The same holds true for those who are born with the good fortune of a strong body and sound mind. If you always feel great and have a lot of energy you tend to be satisfied with the pleasures of self- abuse. Drinking and partying take priority. This is particularly prevalent among our youth.

Perhaps the most destructive, however, is a superior intellect. If you get consumed by the self-importance of your thought processes, it's hard to give credit to anyone, or anything else. This particular malady runs the gamut of society. From psychologists to actors, mathematicians to musicians, the gift of superior talent and intellect usually spells the death of any spiritual aspirations. It's rare that an "intellectual" will discover the spiritual laws governing our universe.

In order to understand Spiritual matters you first have to discard your superior attitude. The ego has to go. If finding the truth were a natural outgrowth of basic intellect – all the brightest and most talented of Earth's creatures would also be the most Godly.

> **I CORINTHIANS 1:27** *But God hath chosen the foolish things of the world to confound the wise; and God hath chosen the weak things of the world to confound the things which are mighty;*
>
> ...
>
> **29** *That no flesh should glory in his presence.* [Take the credit themselves]

God doesn't force anything on us. He wants us to make a choice based on His divine kindness and forgiveness. That's why so many of those following God's laws are considered by society to be inferior. They recognize that it's not what you have or how smart you are, but what's inside your heart...your attitude and desires...that's what really matters. The world calls them foolish.

> **I CORINTHIANS 3:20** *And again, The LORD knoweth the thoughts of the wise, that they are vain.*
>
> ...
>
> **HEBREWS 12:14** *Follow peace with all men, and holiness, without which no man shall see the LORD:*

To aspire to wealth and position simply goes against the teachings of Christ. Wealth and position can come as a result of a righteous existence but <u>so much more</u> than that can come from living a Godly life.

> **PROVERBS 28:1** *The wicked flee when no man pursueth: but the righteous are bold as a lion.*

There is no paranoia for the righteous, no worry about who's following you, or if the IRS is going to catch up with you…only peace of mind.

Perversion Has No Place

Too many self-deceiving intellectual "experts" mislead people with their lustful instructions of self-indulgence. This is particularly true in today's entertainment and advertising industries. The proud and haughty intellect debased by sexual perversion has no place in the Kingdom of God:

> **ISAIAH 5:21,23** *"Woe unto them that are wise in their own eyes, and prudent in their own sight! Which justify the wicked for reward, and take away the righteousness of the righteous…*
>
> …
>
> **II PETER 2:18** *For when they speak great swelling words of vanity, they allure through the lusts of the flesh, through much wantonness, those that were clean escaped from them who live in error.*
>
> 19 <u>*While they promise them liberty, they themselves are the servants of corruption: for of whom a man is overcome, of the same is he brought in bondage.*</u>

[Underlines added for emphasis]

Especially during the Tribulation Period, a world full of perverse and proud people will try to intellectualize their lack of morality. Even today, the theme echoes out…"Whatever turns you on!"

JUDE 1:7 Even as Sodom and Gomorah and
the cities about them in like manner, giving
themselves over to fornication, and going after
strange flesh, are set forth for an example,
suffering the vengeance of eternal fire. [God sent
fire down from heaven and destroyed them]

8 Likewise also these filthy dreamers defile the flesh,
despise dominion, and speak evil of dignitaries. [angels]

...

10 But these speak evil of those things which
they know not: but what they know naturally,
as brute beasts, in those things they corrupt
themselves.

11 Woe unto them! for they have gone in the
way of Cain, and ran greedily after the error of
Balaam for reward...

Christ warns a wicked world:

ST.LUKE 11:23 *"He that is not with me is against
me: and he that gathereth not with me scattereth."*

The law of the perverse says there is really no right or wrong. Things
are right only in a given situation (depending upon the circumstances).
Some are born with unnatural desires, so for them unnatural fulfillment
is perfectly fine. It's called situational ethics and it's the same system of
logic that pervades all man-made philosophies, including the litany of
"isms," such as communism, fascism, and socialism.

Everywhere you look there is proof of universal truths. The very
basic building blocks of all matter recognize this fact. Particles are
either positively or negatively charged or dormant (neutral). What would
happen if the positive suddenly became negative at random? Or negative
shifted to positive at a whim? Obviously, utter chaos would ensue. There
would be no absolute order of things. The whole world would exist in

one form one second and in another the next...or not, or maybe, maybe not...and so on.

There are laws of the universe and they exist for a reason. In exactly the same way, there are rights and wrongs for the conduct of a peaceful, harmonious and fulfilling life. Jesus showed us what it would be like to live the life that God intended for man. And what did man do to repay the favor? They ridiculed and brutally murdered Him. Christ will return one day soon to deal out His Father's justice to the unjust. On that you can depend. To the wicked, the event will be a "curse" from God.

The Curse Goes Forth

Throughout UFOlogy the most commonly seen craft fall into the 20- to 40-foot range. Of course, most information comes from witnesses who can only estimate their size. One notable exception is that of Billy Meier of Switzerland. If you recall, he claims to have taken hundreds of photos and 8mm films of several alien craft. Close examination of these photos by the world's most technically advanced scientific equipment has revealed that they are, indeed, authentic.

In the book that tells his story and shows many of the incredibly clear photographs, is a section on their size. Each craft that held three passengers is purported to be about 21 feet in diameter. Four different craft are diagrammed, with two being 10 feet tall at their center points and two approximately 8 feet tall. [32-1]

How does this descriptive compare to biblical evidence? The following passage holds one of the most exact descriptions in the entire Bible of the appearance of God's HFOs when they return to Earth to destroy the wicked.

ZECHARIAH 5:1 *Then I turned, and lifted up mine eyes, and looked, and behold a flying roll.*

2 And he said unto me, What seest thou? And I answered, I see a flying roll; the length thereof is twenty cubits, and the breadth thereof ten cubits.

Aliens & In-laws

ZECHARIAH 5: 3 *Then said he unto me, This is the curse that goeth forth over the face of the whole earth: for every one that stealeth shall be cut off as on this side according to it; and every one that sweareth shall be cut off as on that side according to it.* [Underlines added for emphasis]

As incredible as it sounds, here is the biblical description of God's curse during the final battle with the wicked. Zechariah describes them as flying, oblong, cylindrical objects, approximately 30 feet long and 15 feet tall. They'll divide those dishonest thieves of men's souls from those who have sworn allegiance to Christ.

They'll cover the entire planet, flying to-and-fro at will, and are called "the eyes of God:"

ZECHARIAH 4:10 *...they are the eyes of the LORD, which run to and fro through the whole earth.*

These chariots of fire will bump into one another in their zeal to capture the wicked in their all-out invasion and dart about the planet like lightning:

NAHUM 2:4 *The chariots shall rage in the streets, they shall justle one against another in the broad ways: they shall seem like torches, they shall run like the lightnings.*

The HFOs will fly like clouds, following the wicked men into their very own homes to destroy everything including the stones with incredible force:

ZECHARIAH 5:4 *I will bring it forth, saith the LORD of hosts, and it shall enter into the house of the thief, and into the house of him that sweareth falsely by my name: and it shall remain in the midst of his house, and shall consume it with the timber thereof and the stones thereof.*

Other prophets were given glimpses of these vehicles and gave even more details. Nahum called them the "shields" of the angels, these mighty chariots will have the power to destroy like flaming torches:

NAHUM 2:3 *The shield of his mighty men is made red, the valiant men are in scarlet: the chariots shall be with flaming torches in the day of his preparation, and the fir trees shall be terribly shaken.*

Joel tells us that God's avenging angelic force will be given a pre-determined "path" or corridor to stay in. As they sweep across the planet, everyone will be assigned to a specific time and place to avoid any accidents, or duplication, even though He explains further that no one will be harmed, i.e. there will be no accidents:

Joel 2:1 *...for the <u>day of the LORD</u> cometh, for it is nigh at hand;*

2 ...<u>A day of darkness</u> and of gloominess, a day of clouds and of thick darkness, as the morning spread upon the mountains:

...

4 The appearance of them is as the appearance of horses [the modern mode of transportation at the time]... *so shall they run like mighty men...*

5 Like the noise of chariots <u>on the tops of mountains shall they leap</u>...

...

7 ...and they shall march every one in his ways, and they shall not break their ranks:

8 Neither shall one thrust [wound] *another; they shall walk <u>every one in his path</u>; and when they fall upon the sword* [if someone should get in a lucky shot] *they shall not be wounded.*

[Underlines added for emphasis]

The Weapons of God

These magnificent craft that Zechariah likens to whirlwinds will have the power to shoot out bursts of high energy, like bolts of lightning:

> ZECHARIAH 9:14 *And the LORD shall be seen over them, and his arrow shall go forth as the lightning: and the LORD GOD shall blow the trumpet, and shall go with whirlwinds of the south.*

Isaiah gives us a similar description:

> ISAIAH 30:30 *And the LORD shall cause his glorious voice to be heard, and shall shew the lighting down of his arm, with the indignation of his anger, and with the flame of a devouring fire, with scattering, and tempest, and hailstone*

The power of God's lightning-like weapons are so great that when David saw one used by an angel it scared the wits out of him. This angel (Remember: in the original Hebrew it means "messenger") was stationed in the lower atmosphere over the city of Jerusalem with an awesome weapon being displayed for David's benefit:

> I CHRONICLES 21:16 *And David lifted up his eyes, and saw the angel of the LORD stand between the earth and the heaven, having a drawn sword in his hand stretched out over Jerusalem.*

I speculate that it was a beam of light much like the laser beams our scientists are currently trying to perfect into weapons. Coincidentally, PRAVDA, the state press of the former Soviet Union, lambasted the "Star Wars" idea of having a laser weapon stationed in space to protect America from nuclear attack; part of President Reagan's Space Defense Initiative (S.D.I.). They said it could be used as "a sword of destruction cutting apart cities from high overhead." Obviously, they think the development of such a weapon is a distinct possibility and they gravely fear its destructive potential.

The weapon David described was deadly accurate because the angel was able to direct it to an altar that David had built *(I Chronicles 21:26-27)*.

The sight of this weapon so frightened David that he decided not to go before the LORD with sacrifices for quite awhile. He didn't want anything more to do with God's mighty "sword" *(I Chronicles 21:29-30)*.

Although I know of no passage where it says the angels will do hand-to-hand combat with the men of the Earth, there are Scriptures that describe an awesome hand-held weapon displayed by the angels.

Ezekiel was given a glimpse of the future and encountered several angels with these "destroying weapons." They were guarding the temple in Jerusalem after the LORD's return:

> EZEKIEL 9:1 *He cried also in mine ears with a loud voice, saying, Cause them that have charge over the city to draw near, even every man with his destroying weapon in his hand.*

> 2 *And, behold, six men came from the way of the <u>higher gate</u>, which lieth toward the north, and every man a slaughter weapon in his hand...*

Perhaps the "higher gate" being referred to is the entrance into the New Jerusalem (home of the Saints) which will be stationed over Old Jerusalem as a protective fortress (more on this later).

As In Times of Old
God Will Fight for His People

Godly intervention in the affairs of men is not without precedent. Many times in the past God has chosen to defend His people.

> II CHRONICLES 20:15 *And he said, Hearken ye, all Judah, and ye inhabitants of Jerusalem, thou king Jehoshaphat, Thus saith the LORD unto you, Be*

not afraid nor dismayed by reason of this great
multitude; for the battle is not yours, but God's.

...

22 *And when they began to sing and to praise, the*
LORD set ambushments against the children of
Ammon, Moab, and mount Seir, which were come
against Judah; and they were smitten.

...

24 *And when Judah came toward the watch tower in*
the wilderness, they looked unto the multitude, and,
behold, they were dead fallen to the earth, and none
escaped.

King Jehoshaphat and his people sat around singing songs of praise while
God and His army of angels defeated their adversaries.

So shall it be when Jesus returns to deal out God's justice during
Earth's final battle:

ZECHARIAH 14:3 *Then shall the LORD go forth, and fight*
against those nations, as when he fought in the day of
battle.

We Shall be as Angels

When the Church is raptured (beamed up) it will be gloriously
transformed into a body of tachyon creatures. We will be equal to God's
heavenly angels. Jesus assured us of that when His disciples questioned
Him about marriage in heaven:

LUKE 20:36 *"Neither can they die any more: for they are*
equal unto angels; and are the children of God, being
the children of the resurrection."

He further emphasized that all will be equal in His eyes. Male and female will take on equal rank (they already do in the eyes of God) and marriage will be abolished:

> MATTHEW 22:30 *"For in the resurrection they neither marry, nor are given in marriage, but are as the angels of God in heaven."*

If you think that angels are to be worshipped because of their special position with God – guess again. John found that out when he was so over-whelmed by his visions of the future presented by an angel of the LORD:

> REVELATION 19:10 *And I fell at his feet to worship him. And he said unto me, See thou do it not: I am thy fellowservant, and of thy brethren that have the testimony of Jesus: worship God: <u>for the testimony of Jesus is the spirit of prophecy.</u>*

> [Underlines added for emphasis]

Our First Tour of Duty

Douglas MacArthur may have said it first, but the promise is ours: "We shall return." The facts are: God said He will return along with all His mighty angels to destroy the wicked off the Earth and to save His elect. Those returning will include not only the original angels, but also raptured Christians and all the saints from the beginning of the creation of mankind.

> MATTHEW 25:31 *"When the Son of man shall come in his glory, and all the holy angels with him…"*
>
> …
>
> II THESSALONIANS 1:7 *…when the LORD Jesus shall be revealed from heaven with his mighty angels,*

II THESSALONIANS 1: 8 *In flaming fire taking vengeance on them that know not God, and that obey not the gospel of our Lord Jesus Christ:*

God will gather together His mighty angelic force from one end of heaven to the other. His great and valiant leaders from other worlds, as well as from our own. Moses, Isaac, Jacob, David and all the prophets and kings of old who served Him so mightily. Michael, Gabriel and all the holy angels mentioned in Scripture.

MALACHI 3:16 *Then they that feared the LORD spake often one to another; and the LORD hearkened, and heard it, and a book of remembrance was written before him for them that feared the LORD, and that thought upon his name.*

17 And they shall be mine, saith the LORD of hosts, in that day when I make up my jewels; and I will spare them, as a man spareth his own son that serveth him.

18 Then shall ye return, and discern between the righteous and the wicked, between him that serveth God and him that serveth him not.

[Underlines added for emphasis]

Clearly, those who are loved like a son by God because they have served Him well will be spared the Tribulation sorrows and then will return to pass judgement on the remnant of Earth's people.

God's Army Fills the Heavens

They'll descend on the Earth with an awesome roar, untold billions of them, ready to use their weapons of destruction. The people of the Earth will tremble at the sight. The whole heavens will fill with the cloud of Christ's army and the sun and moon and stars will be blotted out.

ISAIAH 13:3 *I have commanded sanctified ones, I have also called my mighty ones for mine anger, even them that rejoice in my highness.*

4 The noise of a multitude in the mountains, like as of a great people; a <u>tumultuous noise</u> of the kingdoms of nations gathered together: the LORD of hosts mustereth the host of the battle.

5 They come from a far country, from the end of heaven, even the LORD, and the weapons of his indignation, to destroy the whole land.

6 Howl ye; for <u>the day of the LORD</u> is at hand; it shall come as a destruction from the Almighty.

7 Therefore shall all hands be faint, and every man's heart shall melt:

8 And they shall be afraid: pangs and sorrows shall take hold of them; they shall be in pain as a woman that travaileth: they shall be amazed one at another; their faces shall be as flames.

AUTHOR'S NOTE : the glow of the spacecraft will reflect off their faces just as it did at Fatima (see *Chapter 22 of this book*).

9 Behold, <u>the day of the LORD</u> cometh, cruel both with wrath and fierce anger, to lay the land desolate: and He shall destroy the sinners thereof out of it.

ISAIAH 13: 10 *For the stars of heaven and the constellations thereof shall not give their light: the sun shall be darkened in his going forth, and the moon shall not cause her light to shine.*

11 *And I will punish the world for their evil, and the wicked for their iniquity; and I will cause the arrogancy of the proud to cease, and will lay low the haughtiness of the terrible.* [Underlines added for emphasis]

An Eerie Light Envelopes the Earth

As the armada nears the Earth's surface, their sheer numbers will cause the sun and moon to be blocked out, but the glow of the HFOs themselves will give off an eerie light so that even the nighttime will be dimly lit:

ZECHARIAH 14:6 *And it shall come to pass that day, that the light shall not be clear, nor dark:*

7 *But it shall be one day which shall be known to the LORD, not day, nor night: but it shall come to pass, that at evening time it shall be light.*

[Underlines added for emphasis]

The Trumpets of God

The tremendous noise of billions of spacecraft, combined in one gigantic sweep of the planet, will be deafening. Although most modern UFO encounters attest to only a humming or buzzing noise – imagine this noise multiplied millions of times across the entire planet by spacecraft for as far as you can see in any direction. The terrifying sound, in my opinion, is referred to in Scripture as the "final trumpet" announcing Christ's return. In the original Greek translation, the word "trump," or trumpet of God, refers to a loud "vibrating or quavering," a very accurate and graphic description of the sound that would undoubtedly be made by these great numbers of HFOs.

The maneuvering of so many craft near the Earth's surface will represent quite a feat, but don't worry, God doesn't make mistakes. These soldiers and pilots will be well-trained. The spirits of those who died during the Tribulation Period for Christ's witness will be resurrected to be with Him, and then those living persons who have remained faithful to the Gospels during the Tribulation Period will be gathered up, unharmed, but the wicked shall be destroyed. That's a promise from God:

I THESSALONIANS 4:13 *But I would not have you to be ignorant, brethren, concerning them which are asleep [dead], that ye sorrow not, even as others which have no hope.*

14 *For if we believe that Jesus died and rose again, even so them also which sleep in Jesus will God bring with him.*

...

I CORINTHIANS 15:51 *Behold, I shew you a mystery; We shall not all sleep, but we shall all be changed,*

52 *In a moment, in the twinkling of an eye, at the last trump: for the dead shall be raised incorruptible, and we shall be changed.*

53 *For this corruptible must put on incorruption, and this mortal must put on immortality.*

...

I THESSALONIANS 4:15 *For this we say unto you by the word of the LORD, that we which are alive and remain unto the coming of the LORD* [i.e. after the pre-tribulation Rapture] *shall not prevent them which are asleep.*

I THESSALONIANS 4: 16 *For the LORD himself shall descend from heaven with a shout, with the voice of the archangel, and with <u>the trump of God</u>: and the dead in Christ shall rise first:*

17 *Then we which are alive and remain shall be caught up together with them in the clouds to meet the LORD in the air: and so shall we ever be with the LORD.*

18 *Wherefore comfort one another with these words.*

[Underlines added for emphasis]

We'll Ride In Chariots of Fire and Be As Stars

What does the Bible say will be the appearance of this angelic force? Chariots of fire, just like the ones that took Elijah into heaven, spinning like the whirling wheels that Ezekiel described:

ISAIAH 66:15 *For, behold, the LORD will come with fire, and with his chariots like a whirlwind, to render his anger with fury, and his rebuke with flames of fire.*

Although many cities will be destroyed, God will protect His holy city of Jerusalem:

ISAIAH 31:5 *As birds flying, so will the LORD of hosts defend Jerusalem; defending also he will deliver it; and passing over he will preserve it.*

...

ZEPHANIAH 1:12 *And it shall come to pass at that time, that I will search Jerusalem with candles* [HFOs?], *and punish men that are settled on their lees* [beds]:

(more)

that say in their heart, <u>the LORD will not do good,</u>
<u>neither will he do evil.</u>

This is a very accurate description of the New Age's god of forces, a force which is neutral to all.

The angel that will lead the charge is the archangel Michael, God's "Twelve-star General:"

> DANIEL 12:1 *And at that time shall Michael stand up,*
> *the great prince which standeth for the children of thy*
> *people: and there shall be a time of trouble, such as*
> *never was since there was a nation even to that same*
> *time: and at that time thy people shall be delivered,*
> *every one that shall be found written in the book.*
>
> *2 And <u>many</u> of them that sleep in the dust of the*
> *earth shall awake, some to everlasting life, and some*
> *to shame and everlasting contempt.*

Note that it doesn't say "all shall awake," because He is only speaking about those who died during the Tribulation Period. That will include some of the special 144,000 chosen to be witnesses for Christ during the Tribulation Period. (See *Revelation, chapter 7*).

> *3 And they that be wise shall shine as the brightness*
> *of the firmament; and they that turn many to*
> *righteousness as the stars for ever and ever.*

When Christ returns, those who have died as a witness for Him shall be resurrected into eternal tachyon beings and rule with Him a thousand years on Earth.

Now here's the best part: those that turn many to Christ will shine like stars. Could this mean that they'll be given a commission as royal commanders in God's HFO Air Force? I like to think so!

MATTHEW 13:43 *"Then shall <u>the righteous shine forth</u> <u>as the sun</u> in the kingdom of their Father. Who hath ears to hear, let him hear."*

Are there other descriptions in the Bible that refer to God's angels looking like stars? Certainly. In fact, when God's angelic forces fought the battles of men in the past they appeared as "stars" in the heavens:

JUDGES 5:20 *They fought from heaven; <u>the stars</u> in their courses fought against Sisera.*

[Underlines added for emphasis]

Sisera was a general in the army of king Jabin of the ancient Canaanite region called Hazor. He had over 600 iron chariots in his army, an awesome force in those days, and had held the Israelites in subjection for 20 years. Sisera, historians tell us, was probably intent on conquering all of Palestine – including Israel – when God intervened.

HFOs Over Israel

Just what did the author mean when he said, "the stars in their courses fought against Sisera?" Another account may more clearly answer that question:

This account is told to us by noted historian Flavius Josephus. Josephus was born in 37 A.D. and actually accompanied the Roman legion prior to their destruction of Jerusalem in 70 A.D. His accounts come from firsthand knowledge, or from individuals who witnessed these events. Josephus was an impeccable scholar trained by his contemporaries as an ascetic and Sadducee before becoming a loyal Pharisee at the early age of 19. His writings were pronounced "reliable and accurate" by Vespasian and Titus, both who held the highest rank in Roman politics.

Josephus, himself a Jew, tells in his book, *The Jewish War,* of a strange series of events which led up to the destruction of Jerusalem. Around 69 A.D. there had appeared a large star over Jerusalem looking "very much like a broadsword," or the shape of a cross. [32-2] He also mentions a comet, which would indicate an object that trailed sparkling light and transversed the night sky. He said these objects remained for over a year. [32-3]

I am reminded of a fairly recent sighting near San Francisco in Petaluma, California. On May 22, 1986, around 4:30 a.m., a radio news director named Arlette Cohen reported spotting an object while on her way to work. The series of green-, white- and orange-colored lights were in the shape of a large cross. "At first I thought it was an airplane, but then it came overhead and I saw that it wasn't. It seemed almost to stop over the highway," she said. Her report was verified by several other witnesses including a California Highway Patrol Officer. [32-4]

The flying cross incident seen over Jerusalem was followed by another strange occurrence. Josephus tells us, "Then before the revolt and the movement to war, while the people were assembling for the Feast of Unleavened Bread, on the 8th day of Xanthicos at 3 a.m. so bright a light shone round the Altar and the Sanctuary that it might have been midday. This lasted half an hour."

Next, the gigantic East Gate of the inner court of the temple mysteriously "...opened of its own accord – a gate made of bronze so solid that every evening twenty strong men were required to shut it; it was fastened with iron-bound bars and secured by bolts which were lowered a long way into a threshold fashioned from a single slab of stone. The temple-guards ran with the news to the Captain, who came up and by a great effort managed to shut it." The opening of the gate was perceived by the learned as "√a portent of desolation." [32-5]

A few days later a "...supernatural apparition was seen, too amazing to be believed," according to Josephus. "What I have to relate would, I suppose, have been dismissed as an invention, had it not been vouched for by eyewitnesses and followed by disasters that bore out the signs. Before sunset there were seen in the sky, over the whole country, chariots and regiments in arms speeding through the clouds and encircling the towns. Again, at the Feast of Pentecost, when the priests had gone into the inner court of the Temple at night to perform the usual ceremonies, they declared that they were aware, first of a violent movement and a loud crash, then a voice as of a multitude shouted: 'Let us go hence (away).' " [32-6]

And so it was that God's protective angelic army was taken away from Israel and her destruction by the Romans, led by Titus, happened shortly thereafter, just as had been prophesied by Jesus Christ thirty-seven years earlier.

AUTHOR'S UPDATE : Starting sometime in early 2011 a new phenomenon began occurring in the upper atmosphere around the world:

"Sky Trumpets"

As odd as it sounds – no pun intended – this new phenomenon is happening around the globe and has caught the world by surprise, including me. Not yet widely accepted, most of the recorded sounds come from cell phone movies that have been uploaded to YouTube, making its authenticity questionable in some minds. But there are also local newscasts reporting the phenomena with town mayors affirming their existence. [32-7] And there was also a recorded incident on national television of the sounds interrupting a baseball game between The Tampa Bay Rays and the Detroit Tigers on August 23, 2011. [32-8] Strange blasts that fill the countryside, apparently coming from the sky with vibrations as strong as a fleet of B-52 bombers, is sounding the alarm that Christ is about to return, in my opinion. Get ready... God's trumpets are sounding!

We'll Deal Out God's Justice

Let's remember that the mercy of God far surpasses His wrath. It's so easy to accept a ticket aboard His star fleet. The admission was paid for by His own Son. Why wouldn't everyone want to take this fantastic voyage into eternity? It's beyond me how anyone can resist once they get the colorful abridgement offered in this book and, of course, full details in His Book.

Seriously, God has plans for us, as incorruptible spirits, that are so exciting and rewarding that it boggles the imagination. His love transcends all obstacles. He has promised forgiveness for every bad thing we've ever done...and I mean everything! And He will never bring it up again. You may. Or your enemies might. But God says His remembrance of these past errors are as far from His mind as the east is from the west. Since they go in opposite directions for eternity, I think we can pretty safely say He has total forgiveness. And His patience is disquieting. He'll wait until you're 95 (God willing you should live so long) and on your death bed and still forgive you. Of course, too many premature deaths don't really make this option all that attractive.

He's given the world so many chances and all He really wants is for us to choose a lifestyle that will bring us the greatest happiness possible. But, by the same token, He must keep His word. He is truth and if He said He will destroy the wicked, you can take it to the bank!

Here are His words:

NAHUM 1:3 *The LORD is slow to anger, and great in power, and will not at all acquit the wicked: the LORD hath his way in the whirlwind and in the storm, and the clouds are the dust of his feet.*

...

5 The mountains quake at him, and the hills melt, and the earth is burned at his presence, yea, the world, and all that dwell therein.

God can't break His own rules. He can't let any little electron that chooses, to randomly depart from its normal course...all hell would break loose. So, too, must He keep His word even in judgement, but He does so with great regret. It gives Him no pleasure:

LAMENTATIONS 3:33 *For he doth not afflict willingly nor grieve the children of men.*

34 To crush under his feet all the prisoners of the earth,

As His keepers of the universe we have to be trustworthy. I really believe that He will send us on missions to other worlds, if we are faithful.

As Paul wrote to his friends after they had discussed getting a legal opinion on matters that pertained to the church:

I CORINTHIANS 6:1 *Dare any of you, having a matter against another, go to law before the unjust, and not before the saints?*

2 Do ye not know that the saints shall judge the world? and if the world shall be judged by you, are ye unworthy to judge the smallest matters?

3 Know ye not that we shall judge angels? how much more things that pertain to this life?

That's right! We will one day judge angels...since this thing goes on for infinity, I'm sure that includes future generations of saints throughout the entire universe. Hope you like to travel.

We Must Warn the Entire World!
(Especially Friends and Loved Ones)

This next subject may not be so pleasant. It's easy to sneer at a stranger in a strange land. How about eliminating your own friends and family members? The gospel warns us that if, as Christians, we don't warn them...we'll have to take their lives at Christ's Second Coming. It's not always pleasant to witness to friends...but, of course, it's not nearly as unpleasant as spending eternity in hell, as those who ignore you will be forced to do:

> EZEKIEL 3:18 *When I say unto the wicked, Thou shalt surely die; and thou givest him not warning, nor speakest to warn the wicked from his wicked way, to save his life; the same wicked man shall die in his iniquity; but his blood will I require at thine hand.*
>
> 19 *Yet if thou warn the wicked, and he turn not from his wickedness, nor from his wicked way, he shall die in his iniquity; but thou hast delivered thy soul.*
>
> 20 *Again, When a righteous man doth turn from his righteousness, and commit iniquity, and I lay a stumblingblock before him, he shall die: because thou hast not given him warning, he shall die in his sin, and his righteousness which he hath done shall not be remembered; but his blood will I require at thine hand.*
>
> 21 *Nevertheless if thou warn the righteous man, that the righteous sin not, and he doth not sin, he shall surely live, because he is warned; also thou hast delivered thy soul.*

It clearly says here that if a man (meaning any person) turn from his Godly ways he will also lose his future in the presence of God. Obviously, even though once considered saved (righteous), this guy isn't headed for heaven. **Consider yourself warned!**

The Wicked Sent To Hell

All the wicked people of the Earth will be killed and their tachyon bodies will be sent to a place of eternal torment known as "the furnace of fire" and "the pit of hell."

> MATTHEW 13:39 *"The enemy that sowed them is the devil; the harvest is the end of the world; and the reapers are the angels."*
>
> ...
>
> 41 *"The Son of man shall send forth his angels, and they shall gather out of his kingdom all things that offend, and them which do iniquity;"*
>
> 42 *"And shall cast them into a furnace of fire: there shall be wailing and gnashing of teeth."*

The pit of hell has been described as a place somewhere in the bowels of the Earth. During the final battle of Armageddon I think the Earth will split open and untold millions will run for their lives as God's angels execute His final round-up. Hordes of people will be driven to the precipices of hell, a very real and physical place:

> ISAIAH 24:18 *And it shall come to pass, that he who fleeth from the noise of the fear shall fall into the pit; and he that cometh up out of the midst of the pit shall be taken in the snare: for the windows from on high are open, and the foundations of the earth do shake.*

God's Remnant
Will Repopulate the Earth

Note that in *Mathew 13:39-42*, it simply states that those who offend and do iniquity shall be gathered and cast into hell. Undoubtedly, there will be those left in the world who are not an active part of the warring nations and are not totally wicked. Likely, they will be spared to inhabit the Earth at Jesus' Second Coming and Millennial Reign.

Zechariah was told that two out of every three would die on the day of the LORD. That would leave one-third alive to repopulate the planet. Although this represents only a fraction of those alive today, the numbers should still be in the tens of millions:

> **ZECHARIAH 13:8** *And it shall come to pass, that in all the land, saith the LORD, two parts therein shall be cut off and die; but the third shall be left therein.*

> **9** *And I will bring the third part through the fire, and will refine them as silver is refined, and will try them as gold is tried: they shall call on my name, and I will hear them: I will say, It is my people: and they shall say, The LORD is my God.*

Satan Bound In the Pit

Satan's biggest problem is he thinks he's neat. He has a big head. In his vanity he has sought power and tried to fulfill the lusts of his flesh. But the big shot will get knocked down to size come Judgement Day. The nations of the world will look on this pitiful creature and wonder how he could have caused such turmoil:

> **ISAIAH 14:12** *How art thou fallen from heaven, O Lucifer, son of the morning! how art thou cut down to the ground, which didst weaken the nations!*

> **13** *For thou hast said in thine heart, I will ascend into heaven, I will exalt my throne above the*

stars of God: I will sit also upon the mount of the congregation, in the sides of the north:

14 *I will ascend above the heights of the clouds; I will be like the most High.*

15 *Yet thou shalt be brought down to hell, to the sides of the pit.*

16 *They that see thee shall narrowly look* [with circumspect or cautious distance] *upon thee, and consider thee, saying, Is this the man that made the earth to tremble, that did shake kingdoms;*

17 *That made the world as a wilderness, and destroyed the cities thereof; that opened not the house of his prisoners?*

As ruler of the heavenlies around Earth, Satan and all his fallen angels have had a heyday. But that will all end one day soon when Christ and all His powerful saints return to punish the fallen angels residing above the Earth and the wicked leaders living on the Earth:

ISAIAH 24:21 *And it shall come to pass in that day, that the LORD shall punish the host of the high ones that are on high, and the kings of the earth upon the earth*

22 *And they shall be gathered together as prisoners are gathered in the pit, and shall be shut up in the prison...*

23 *Then the moon shall be confounded, and the sun ashamed, when the LORD of hosts shall reign in mount Zion, and in Jerusalem, and before his ancients gloriously.*

Satan and his followers will be cast into hell and The King of Kings will establish His headquarters in Jerusalem in His holy mountain called Mount Zion, the New Jerusalem, and He will rule the affairs of all Earth with His unmatched wisdom. By the way, we'll be able to visit all those exotic destinations we've never had time for, or been able to afford, both here and on other worlds. In fact, our time will be infinite and our transportation will be better than a new Farari or a Princess cruise liner. Brilliant!

* * * * *

An Amazing Update

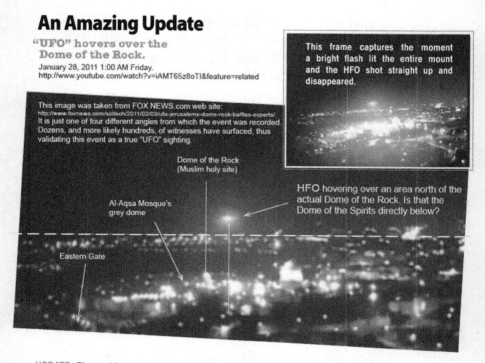

"UFO" hovers over the Dome of the Rock.

January 28, 2011 1:00 AM Friday.
http://www.youtube.com/watch?v=iAMT65z8oTI&feature=related

This frame captures the moment a bright flash lit the entire mount and the HFO shot straight up and disappeared.

This image was taken from FOX NEWS.com web site:
http://www.foxnews.com/scitech/2011/02/03/ufo-jerusalems-dome-rock-baffles-experts/
It is just one of four different angles from which the event was recorded. Dozens, and more likely hundreds, of witnesses have surfaced, thus validating this event as a true "UFO" sighting.

Dome of the Rock
(Muslim holy site)

Al-Aqsa Mosque's grey dome

HFO hovering over an area north of the actual Dome of the Rock. Is that the Dome of the Spirits directly below?

Eastern Gate

UPDATE: **Figure 32.1** – Another amazing event heralding Christ's return occurred the very same day that the Arab Uprising in Egypt grew violent and gave notice to the world of perilous times to come. To underscore God's concern, the Lord sent a special sign to the very Temple Mount to which both Arab and Jew lay claim. The president wrongly called these series of uprisings the "Arab Spring" and "democracy at work", but hard-liner extremists of the Muslim Brotherhood are now taking control and are anything but democratic. This UFO/HFO was filmed from at least three different angles by American, Israeli and Arab witnesses and videos were posted on YouTube the next morning. One video shows an entire formation of very faint spheres directly over the Jerusalem site which stayed for over ten minutes, but no mention was made in the press.

Above - I rotated the video slightly to give a truer horizon line (dotted line) for a clearer reference of the HFO's position when it produced a gigantic burst of light and disappeared. I think it was a clear sign from God and all the world took notice, including all the major television networks in America, but without making any connection to the UFO over the Dome and the current Arab Muslim unrest throughout the Middle East.

Space Station Jerusalem

Advances In America's Space Program

America's space program has taken some large strides in the last few decades with the introduction of the (now retired) space shuttle and International Space Station (who's life has been extended to 2033).

Few Americans, however, realize the potential of such valuable tools in our space arsenal. Their usefulness extends beyond delivering payloads into space. Already science is benefiting from the myriad of experimentation allowed in zero gravity. New processes for producing high-quality products in the weightlessness of space are promising. Several medical serums have been manufactured in their purest form because of the lack of contaminates in space. Valuable industrial products, such as purer silicon crystals for computer use and development of light-weight composites, promise to make the space venture a profitable one.

It's no doubt true that the space shuttle program has also benefited our nation militarily. Not too long ago, Rockwell International Corporation was awarded a contract to build a new satellite navigational system for use by the Pentagon in calculating the location of ships, airplanes, tanks and troops. The space shuttle has delivered scores of such navigational satellites into space and the military has plans for 6,100 Earth receivers to be manufactured in the near future.[33-1] Many other top-secret military missions have already been flown with payloads delivered.

Power Satellites

Another key use of future space shuttles will include the eventual construction of power satellites. With the cost of energy doubling and tripling since the early '70s, an alternative source of energy is desperately needed by the U.S. Our dependence on foreign oil imports, and a lack of effective energy alternatives, may one day force us to look to outer space for solutions. The major American corporations and the best minds in the country are currently working on creating something called power satellites or POWERSATS.

The concept includes the erecting of huge solar panels in geosynchronous orbit to collect the sun's readily available energy. Geosynchronous orbit is 22,236 miles above the Earth's equator and is the area in space where an object travels the same speed around the planet as the planet is spinning. In other words, anything placed in this orbit will remain stationary in relation to the Earth. This is the area of space our current communications satellites occupy. Utilization of this orbit has made transcontinental broadcasting possible. These communications relayers are placed in an exact position where ground stations can bounce television or radio transmissions from them to a receiving station halfway around the world. That's why we are able to watch the Olympics, as an example, live from anywhere in the world.

Colonizing the Moon to Create Energy Reserves on Earth

Plans have already been drawn-up to build giant solar collectors, some as large as Manhatten Island, with materials extracted from the moon. It would be more economical to shuttle raw materials from the lunar surface than from the Earth because the moon has so little gravity. Gravity is the force that requires our rockets to expend such great quantities of energy in order to reach and maintain desired altitudes. The overwhelming majority of storage space on shuttle flights is used by costly fuel. Very little fuel would be required to escape the gravitational force of the moon.

The plan is to position these giant solar panels over major U.S. cities to supply most of their energy needs. They will basically collect sunlight (solar energy) and convert it into relatively harmless microwave beams and then transmit these focused beams to an Earth receiving station. [33-2]

On Earth, the rectenna (receiving antenna) would collect the microwave beam and reconvert it into usable electricity which would then be fed into the sponsoring power company's power grid and eventually into individual homes and businesses.

This sounds like an exotic and expensive proposition, but given the alternatives it appears to be the most efficient method available. By comparison, nuclear energy is extremely expensive and disposing of its by-products (radioactive waste) is a real problem. In addition, the danger of a nuclear melt-down became much more of a perceived threat after the Three Mile Island incident in 1979, not to mention the more recent disaster in Chernobyl, USSR, and the Tsunami in Japan. Expansion of nuclear facilities in this country has come to a virtual standstill.

Other energy sources, windmills and Earth-stationed solar collectors, produce very little electricity for the expenditure. Coal-fired plants release dangerous fumes into the atmosphere and the cost of "cleaning up" these plants is incredibly expensive.

The best source for the massive amounts of energy needed for American cities appears to be powersats. They require little or no maintenance because there is no weathering in outer space and their energy source, the sun, won't be depleted for millions of years.

Space planners can envision work stations above the Earth manufacturing powersats with the help of thousands of workers, much like the work force used in the construction of a nuclear power plant. Their home base would be the moon and its man-made colonies. Inside giant terrariums erected on the lunar surface, workers would grow their own food and create their own artificial Earth-like atmosphere. Arizona is home to new experimentation involving an enclosed biosphere in the desert near Tucson where eight volunteers will spend two years in complete isolation to Earth's atmosphere. They will produce their own food and oxygen and maintain several ecosystems within the two acre container including a miniature rain forest, ocean and marsh. Space Biospheres Ventures, the developer, hopes to demonstrate how to build a "self-contained, self-sustaining world that could serve as a model for bases on the moon or Mars." [33-3]

Again, low energy consumption in traveling from the powersat to the moon and back, and the availability of inexpensive building materials would be the main motivation for colonization of Earth's natural satellite.

The point of this whole explanation is to show you that space colonization is not some kind of science fiction dream. It is a realistic and feasible direction for the future of our country.

The Hilton In The Sky

Hotel entrepreneur Barron Hilton (son of Conrad) once said that if the cost of shipping freight were reasonable enough, he would build a giant hotel in lower Earth orbit. Can you imagine taking a space shuttle to the "Milky Way Hilton" and staying in a room with a view? What an exciting experience (see *Figures 33.1 & 60*). The huge superstructure would be constructed in a giant double-donut shape and then induced to spin slightly. The spin would create artificial gravity through the application of centrifugal force. Each room would have a view of the sunrise every 90 minutes as well as an unobstructed view of the Milky Way. Whew! The rooms would be arranged on the outer ring of the donuts for passenger comfort, but near the center of each ring would be an area for recreation. Weightless flying would attract thousands to the hotel's center every morning. Can you imagine the flying games that might be invented without the interference of gravity? [33-4]

The excitement generated by the thought of such an experience is probably equal to that of our ancestors when they imagined they might one day fly through the sky in giant metal birds!

Flying American Cities

It's not too bold a step, once you conceive of the idea of a space hotel in the not-too-distant future, to imagine large free-flying space colonies. These self-sufficient cities would be created to explore the planets and beyond.

Famed architect and visionary futurist Paolo Soleri of Arizona has conceptualized giant, self-contained cities on Earth to prevent the destruction of the natural resources of our planet. His massive and populous city structures would produce their own food, oxygen, rain, heating and cooling just as a miniature model of the Earth might. No doubt many of the same principles utilized in Soleri's enclosed cities could be used by giant intergalactic mobile space colonies of the future. [33-5]

The correlation between what is possible in the minds of our scientists and what exists in UFOlogy logs is apparent. All that these giant, self-contained space cities need is a method of propulsion that allows instant acceleration to, or near, the speed of light, and you likely have created a vehicle similar to those giant devices recorded on radar cruising Earth's extreme upper atmosphere.

Moses accurately described one of these giant cities when he told us of the large "mountain" that visited the Jewish people thousands of years ago. The Bible tells us that God's giant column of cloud carried at least ten thousand angels (see *Deuteronomy 33:2*).

God's Space Station Jerusalem

What is heaven? The Bible says that God has gone to prepare us a place where we can dwell with Him forever. What does that mean?

To most Americans, heaven is an etherial plane or place of existence where good men go when they die. Its location is a mystery and its description is far too glorious for anyone to try to explain. All we know is that it's "up there" somewhere.

The Bible, however, refers to heaven as being three distinct regions.

First, it refers to the area directly around our planet: our atmosphere. Satan is the ruler of this region.

Second, is the place where the faithful reside: an actual self-contained city built by God.

Third, is the "third heaven" that Paul refers to in *II Corinthians, Chapter 12*. The third heaven is called paradise and is a place apparently somewhere in deep space. This third heaven is also what many refer to when they speak of heaven as being out in the distant galaxies: the heavenlies, as it were. It is the location in deep space where all the spirits of the Saints dwell in the presence of Christ and it's where the city of God (the Second Heaven) is currently located.

We shall deal with the second heaven in the following pages, and examine the actual place that I like to refer to as "space station Jerusalem." What does the Bible call this giant, self-contained city of the Saints?

God's Tabernacle

We do know one thing for sure. The heaven where the faithful will live for eternity is a place where they'll dwell in the presence of God. There will be no more pain, death or sorrow. It'll be a place of eternal joy and happiness:

> REVELATION 21:3 *And I heard a great voice out of heaven saying, Behold, <u>the tabernacle of God is with men</u>, and he will dwell with them, and they shall be his people, and God himself shall be with them, and be their God.*
>
> *4 And God shall wipe away all tears from their eyes; and there shall be no more death, neither sorrow, nor crying, neither shall there be any more pain: for the former things are passed away.*

Mount Zion:
God's Holy Mountain

The prophet Zechariah called the place the "holy mountain of the Lord:"

> ZECHARIAH 8:3 *Thus saith the LORD; I am returned unto <u>Zion</u>, and will dwell in the midst of Jerusalem: and Jerusalem shall be called a city of truth; <u>and the mountain of the LORD</u> of hosts <u>the holy mountain</u>.*
> Underlines added for emphasis.

The "Thick Darkness"

Solomon was instructed that God dwells in "the thick darkness." Somewhere inside of this thick darkness is a place where the LORD is preparing permanent dwellings for His faithful:

I KINGS 8:12 *Then spake Solomon, The LORD said that he would dwell in the thick darkness.*

13 *I have surely built thee an house to dwell in, a settled place for thee to abide in for ever.*

The "Thick Cloud"

What is this "thick darkness" that Solomon spoke of? Moses was also approached by God in a "Thick Cloud:"

EXODUS 19:9 *"...Lo, I come unto thee in a thick cloud..."*

When Moses later recalled the experience he spoke of this same thick cloud as follows:

DEUTERONOMY 4:11 *And ye came near and stood under the mountain; and the mountain burned with fire unto the midst of heaven, with darkness, clouds, and thick darkness.*

From this description we realize that both Moses and Solomon were speaking about an object that was thick and dark like a mountainous rock, but also glowed in the dark like molten rock or fire.

Two Separate Mountains

Mountains carrying God, therefore, are mentioned in several places in the Bible. The thick cloud or mountain of God that visited Moses, however, was not the same as mount Zion. To make that clear to us, Paul wrote the following passage to his Christian friends instructing them as to where their resurrected spirits would go after their deaths:

HEBREWS 12:18 *For ye are not come unto the mount that might be touched, and that burned with fire, nor unto blackness, and darkness, and tempest,*

19 And the sound of a trumpet, and the voice of words; which voice they that heard entreated that the word should not be spoken to them any more:

20 (For they could not endure that which was commanded, And if so much as a beast touch the mountain, it shall be stoned, or thrust through with a dart:

21 And so terrible was the sight, that Moses said, I exceedingly fear and quake:)

22 But ye are come unto mount Zion, and unto the city of the living God, the heavenly Jerusalem and to an innumerable company of angels,

23 To the general assembly and church of the firstborn, which are written in heaven, and to God the Judge of all, and to the spirits of just men made perfect,

[Underlines added for emphasis]

The heavenly Jerusalem, called mount Zion, is different than the large space vehicle that Moses and his people saw. It's a place where Jesus (the firstborn Son of God) and His Church reside. Those who have believed in Christ including all of God's covenant people, from the time of Adam on, who have been judged worthy will live alongside of an innumerable host of angels. Sounds like my kind of neighborhood!

The New Jerusalem

The prophet John was informed that the giant city where God dwells is called the "New Jerusalem" and that some of those who are accepted into its gates will go no more out.

REVELATION 3:12 *Him that overcometh will I make a pillar in the temple of my God, and he shall go no more out: and I will write upon him the name of my God, and the name of the city of my God, which is new Jerusalem, which cometh down out of heaven from my God: and I will write upon him my new name.* [Underlines added for emphasis]

An interesting point is the fact that God will "write" His name and the name of the city on those who dwell there. Sounds like the idea of angels wearing insignias or clothing with symbols on them is not totally unthinkable.

Another key instruction within this verse is that the New Jerusalem will "descend" out of heaven (meaning the sky above) and presumably rest near the Earth's surface (*Figures 33.6 & 33.7*).

The Bride of Christ

John further proclaimed that it will be a beautiful sight to behold when it descends upon the Earth in all its glory:

REVELATION 21:2 *And I John saw the holy city, new Jerusalem, coming down from God out of heaven, prepared as a bride adorned for her husband.*

When the "Bride of Christ" is mentioned in Scripture, it is referring to this magnificent city, along with all its inhabitants.

Big Enough For Everyone

The Bible goes even further with its description of heaven. We are given its actual size and shape. In Revelation, John reveals that the city is shaped like a cube, or foursquare:

> REVELATION 21:16 *And the city lieth foursquare, and the length is as large as the breadth; and he measured the city with the reed, twelve thousand furlongs. The length and the breadth and the height of it are equal.*
>
> 17 *And he measured the wall thereof, an hundred and forty and four cubits, according to the measure of a man, that is, of the angel.*

A furlong is one-eighth of a mile, so the city is 1,500 miles square. To give you an idea just how large that is, the tallest mountain in the world is Mount Everest. Its height is 29,028 feet or roughly 5 ½ miles above sea level. It actually rises just over 4 ½ miles above Katmandu, Nepal, the beginning point of most climbing expeditions. The sight is spectacular from Katmandu as Everest's jagged snow-capped peaks rise majestically into the clouds.

Can you imagine a mountain over three hundred times as high? If Zion were floated down to Earth into a position just a few miles overhead, the base of the gigantic superstructure would fill the entire sky from horizon to horizon! It's no wonder the Bible says the people of the Earth will fear at the sight of it (see *Figure 33.7*).

It's difficult to visualize something this large but I'll try to paint you a mental picture. If it were centered over the city of Jerusalem in Israel, it would cover all of Israel, Syria, Jordan, Egypt, Iraq and Turkey, most of Saudi Arabia and Greece and parts of Libya, Sudan, Iran and Russia. Its borders would extend on its northern side from the edge of Yugoslavia and Bulgaria, across the northern boundaries of Turkey to the southern edge of Russia. Its eastern border would go from the northern edge of Iran south to the southern borders of Saudi Arabia.

On its southern side it would cut across the northern border of Sudan and the edge of Chad. Up through Libya and north to the center of Greece; the massive structure would complete its Western front.

But, of course, that's just what its base would cover: 2,250,000 square miles. Remember it's as tall as it is wide: 1,500 miles. The Bible says it has twelve separate levels...and who knows how many sub-levels? If divided equally, each of the twelve levels would be 125 miles apart. If you lived in any of these levels there is the possibility that it would appear much like it does in Earth's atmosphere today. It's doubtful you would be aware that you were enclosed in a super structure because of its size and because of the light emanating from the layer above (explained next). Each level's atmosphere would extend upward 125 miles. By comparison: our own stratosphere, which contains all our clouds, extends only 12-15 miles up. Our highest manned jet flight (the X-15) only flew to a height of 67 miles. It would be a very spacious feeling to live in the New Jerusalem, and of course the sights God has planned must be spectacular! Jesus said the angels are busy building mansions in heaven for its future inhabitants.

If you could cut a swath around the diameter of the Earth a mile wide and a half-mile high, you would have to go around our planet five hundred and sixty-eight times to create as much space as the New Jerusalem contains. We're talken' BIG! Spacious and, no doubt, opulent surroundings for untold billions of people! And, of course, the universe will be the playground of its inhabitants.

Like A Huge Square Moon Rising

The glory of the presence of God will cause the whole structure to glow from within. There will be no night in the city or any need of the sun or moon to shine on it. As the nations of the Earth come to pay tribute to the LORD, the light from Zion will illuminate the entire countryside. Like a magnificent moon rising on the distant horizon, Zion will leave the world's travelers breathless (see *Figure 33.6*):

ISAIAH 60:1 *Arise, shine; for thy light is come, and the glory of the LORD is risen upon thee.*

2 *For, behold, the darkness shall cover the earth, and gross darkness the people: but the LORD shall arise upon thee, and his glory shall be seen upon thee.*

> 3 *And the Gentiles shall come to thy light, and kings to the brightness of thy rising.*
>
> 4 *Lift up thine eyes round about, and see: all they gather themselves together they come to thee: thy sons shall come from far, and thy daughters shall be nursed at thy side.*
>
> 5 *Then thou shalt see, and flow together, and thine heart shall fear, and be enlarged; because the abundance of the sea shall be converted unto thee, the forces* [resources] *of the Gentiles shall come unto thee.*

The nations of the Earth will bring great treasures: gold, silver and precious stones. And the riches of the sea will be given to the Lord of hosts to be used by the inhabitants of the New Jerusalem.

Christ Will be the Light of the City

John describes how New Zion will be lit from within by the mere presence of God.

> REVELATION 21:23 *And the city had no need of the sun, neither of the moon, to shine in it: for the glory of God did lighten it, and the Lamb* [Christ] *is the light thereof.*

Malachi refers to this city in the masculine, but is clearly speaking of the sight of the giant glowing city when he says "the Sun." This is not in reference to Jesus as the Son of God, but to this city whose appearance is bright like a sun, as denoted by the spelling of the carefully worded descriptive. It's inhabitants shall fly down to Earth on "wings" who bring healing with them. Always read Scripture in context. Malachi is speaking about the time called "the day of the Lord," when Christ returns with all His city's inhabitants who will discern between the righteous and the wicked (see *Malachi 3:17-18*).

MALACHI 4:2 *The Sun of righteousness shall arise with healing in his wings...*

A Beautiful Sight

John told us, in his visitation, that the city appeared to be transparent and the walls glowed like a green jasper stone:

REVELATION 21:11 *Having the glory of God: and her light was like unto a stone most precious, even like a jasper stone, clear as crystal;*

18 *And the building of the wall of it was of jasper: and the city was pure gold, like unto clear glass.*

Inside, the city glistened like pure gold that was as clear as glass. Twelve levels or foundations give off their own beautiful light, each different than the other:

REVELATION 21:19,20 *And the foundations of the wall of the city were garnished with all manner of precious stones. The first foundation was jasper; the second, sapphire; the third, a chalcedony; the fourth, an emerald; the fifth, sardonyx; the sixth, sardius; the seventh, chrysolyte; the eighth, beryl; the ninth, a topaz; the tenth, a chrysoprasus; the eleventh, a jacinth; the twelfth, an amethyst.*

21 *And the twelve gates were twelve pearls; every several gate was of one pearl: and the street of the city was pure gold, as it were transparent glass.*

The main street leading into the city shown with a gold transparent light.

All Will Pay Homage

The leaders of the nations from all the Earth will travel to pay tribute to Christ and bring Him gifts:

REVELATION 21: 24 *And the nations of them which are saved shall walk in the light of it; and the kings of the earth do bring their glory and honour into it.*

25 *And the gates of it shall not be shut at all by day: for there shall be not night there.*

26 *And they shall bring the glory and honour of the nations into it.*

Rewards For The Faithful

The Bible says that everyone will be given rewards in heaven according to their works on Earth and that those who win many to Christ will shine like stars:

MATTHEW 16:27 ...and he shall reward every man according to his works.

...

REVELATION 22:12 *And, behold, I come quickly; and my reward is with me, to give every man according as his work shall be.*

...

DANIEL 12:3 *And they that be wise shall shine as the brightness of the firmament; and they that turn many to righteousness as the stars for ever and ever.*

Perhaps the different levels of Zion have something to do with the Saint's faithfulness. Not everyone can live next to Moses or Ezekiel, but everyone will bathe in the glory of God. I personally would like to get as close to Christ as possible.

Angels On The Move

As people from far away nations approach the magnificent city they'll see its inhabitants moving about inside 24 hours a day. People of Earth will bring gifts into the gates of Old Jerusalem as an offering to the LORD who resides above the city in His holy mountain. They'll see the angels descending and ascending to the Holy city as they go about their appointed tasks:

ISAIAH 60:8 *Who are these that fly as a cloud, and as the doves to their windows?*

9 Surely the isles shall wait for me, and the ships of Tarshish first, to bring thy sons from far, their silver and their gold with them, unto the name of the LORD thy God, and to the Holy One of Israel, because he hath glorified thee.

10 And the sons of strangers shall build up thy walls
[Author's note: speaking of the Old Jerusalem that

the LORD will preserve and restore], *and their kings shall minister unto thee, for in my wrath I smote thee, but in my favour have I had mercy on thee.*

11 *Therefore thy gates shall be open continually: they shall not be shut day nor night; that men may bring unto thee the forces* [resources] *of the Gentiles, and that their kings may be brought.*

12 *For the nation and kingdom that will not serve thee shall perish; yea, those nations shall be utterly wasted.*

...

14 *The sons also of them that afflicted thee shall come bending unto thee; and all they that despised thee shall bow themselves down at the soles of thy feet; and they shall call thee, The city of the LORD, The Zion of the Holy One of Israel.*

Jesus also spoke of the free movement of angels in heaven:

ST. JOHN 1:51 *And he saith unto him, "Verily, verily, I say unto you, Hereafter ye shall see heaven open, and the angels of God ascending and descending upon the Son of man."*

Christ Will Reign from Mount Zion

When Mount Zion has descended out of heaven and positioned itself over Israel the Lord Jesus will be the "Prime Minister" of the world. Those who are on Earth and left to repopulate the world will teach their children the meaning of God's laws and tell of His greatness:

MICAH 4:1 *But in the last days it shall come to pass, that the mountain of the house of the LORD shall be established in the top of the mountains, and it shall be exalted above the hills; and people shall flow unto it.*

2 *And many nations shall come, and say, Come, and let us go up to the mountain of the LORD, and to the house of the God of Jacob; and he will teach us of his ways, and we will walk in his paths: for the law shall go forth of Zion, and the work of the LORD from Jerusalem.*

. . .

ZECHARIAH 2:12 *And the LORD shall inherit Judah his portion in the holy land, and shall choose Jerusalem again.*

13 *Be silent, O all flesh, before the LORD: for he is raised up out of his holy habitation.*

The law will come directly from God in His holy mountain which is "raised up" above Judah (Israel), but the works on Earth shall originate from His earthly Priests who dwell in Old Jerusalem below.

PSALM 22:28 *For the kingdom is the LORD's: and he is the governor among the nations.*

29 *All they that be fat upon earth shall eat and worship: all they that go down to the dust shall bow before him: and none can keep alive his own soul.*

30 *A seed shall serve him; it shall be accounted to the LORD for a generation.*

31 *They shall come, and shall declare his*
righteousness unto a people that shall be born, that
he hath done this.

As you recall, the Lord's earthly priests are those who were killed for not taking the mark of The Beast during the Tribulation Period and were resurrected to rule on Earth with Christ. These priests shall declare to those yet to be born that Jesus Christ is King. I truthfully believe that the rest of the Saints, those of us who are raptured and those Christians and Saints who died prior to the Rapture, will be busy in other parts of the universe, perhaps even ministering to other Earthlike creatures on far-away planets.

As Reverend Chuck Smith, founder of Calvary Chapel, has pointed out in his excellent book, *What the World is Coming to*: "It...doesn't seem likely that God would create anything without form and void. God has had such a beautiful design in all His creation. Isaiah said that God did not create the Earth a waste but He created it to be inhabited.

"By the same token, it doesn't seem logical that the Earth is the only area where God would place created, intelligent beings. The Bible doesn't tell us anything about people on other planets, but would God create this entire vast universe and only choose one little part to populate? No reason exists for us to believe that we're exclusive in the universe.

"Of course, God could have thrown the stars out into space just for your enjoyment. However, that doesn't seem likely to me. Having created the vast universe, He's probably populated other parts of it, too."[33-6]

Well Defensed

Just as the craft that led Moses and the tribe of Judah through the wilderness for forty years, the New Jerusalem will be covered in a mist during the day, but at night it will glow like fire:

ISAIAH 4:5 *And the LORD will create upon every*
dwelling place of mount Zion, and upon her

*assemblies, <u>a cloud and smoke</u> by day and the
shining of the flaming fire by night: for upon all the
glory shall be a defence.*

The word "defence" (King James' spelling) in the original Hebrew meant covering or encasement. Jeremiah also spoke of the protected city:

JEREMIAH 1:18 *For, behold, I have made thee this day a
defenced city, and an iron pillar, and brasen walls
against the whole land, against the kings of Judah,
against the princes thereof, against the priests
thereof, and against the people of the land.*

In this passage the term defensed city meant fortress or castle. Why would God need to protect Zion from anything? The truth is, men are born inherently wicked. Even during the Millennial Reign of Christ, the Earth will be inhabited by mortal, Adamic men. When they see the riches being poured into this city some will, no doubt, be tempted to pillage the wealthy fortress.

The Tree of Life

The tree of life is a mysterious object described in Scripture with leaves that contain great healing powers. Many of our modern medicines are derived from plants. So, too, will the Godly people of the Earth benefit from the leaves of the Tree of Life. Many will covet its powers and will be tempted to get a cutting or perhaps some seeds.

REVELATION 22:2 *In the midst of the street of it [the new
Jerusalem], and on either side of the river, was there
the tree of life, which bare twelve manner of fruits,
and yielded her fruit every month: and the leaves of
the tree were for the healing of the nations.*

...

REVELATION 22: 14 *Blessed are they that do his commandments, that they may have right to the tree of life, and may enter in through the gates into the city.*

15 *For without are dogs, and sorcerers, and whoremongers, and murderers, and idolaters, and whosoever loveth and maketh a lie.*

Where do these wicked people come from? Who is it that will inhabit the Earth after Armageddon?

God's Remnant

During the battle of Armageddon the wicked will be destroyed – which will probably include all of the people on the battlefront. However, in some parts of the planet a remnant will be left to re-populate the Earth. They and their offspring will journey to Zion after the great Day of the Lord:

ZECHARIAH 14:16 *And it shall come to pass, that every one that is left of all the nations which came against Jerusalem shall even go up from year to year to worship the King, the LORD of hosts, and to keep the feast of tabernacles.*

17 *And it shall be, that whoso will not come up of all the families of the earth unto Jerusalem to worship the King, the LORD of hosts, even upon them shall be no rain.*

ZECHARIAH 14: 18 *And if the family of <u>Egypt</u> go not up, and come not, that <u>have no rain; there shall be plague</u>, wherewith the LORD will smite the heathen that come not up to keep the feast of tabernacles.*

For those men left on Earth who choose to return to their old heritage of false Gods, the Lord will punish with plagues and drought.

Priests Among Us

Ezekiel was given a glimpse of the future by the angels of God and described a group of men who would be set apart during the battle of Armageddon:

EZEKIEL 9:4 *And the LORD said unto him* [an angel in white linen], *Go through the midst of the city, through the midst of Jerusalem, and <u>set a mark upon the foreheads</u> of the men that sigh and that cry for all the abominations that be done in the midst thereof.*

5 *And to the others he said in mine hearing, Go ye after him through the city, and smite: let not your eye spare, neither have ye pity.*
[Underlines added for emphasis]

When God's angels are sent to protect the temple at Jerusalem during Jesus' Second Coming, the people in the city that are righteous will be spared. This clearly indicates they are set apart. Perhaps they are among the people that will be chosen to inhabit the Earth during the Millennium. Likely, most of these inhabitants of Jerusalem will be Jews.

Isaiah speaks of these special Millennial Saints with the mark on their foreheads:

ISAIAH 66:19 *And I will set a sign among them, and I will send those that escape of them unto the nations, to Tarshish, Pul, and Lud, that draw the bow, to Tubal, and Javan, to the isles afar off, that have not heard my fame, neither have seen my glory among the gentiles.*

20 *And they shall bring all your brethren for an offering unto the LORD out of all nations upon horses, and in chariots, and in litters, and upon mules, and upon swift beasts, to my holy mountain Jerusalem, saith the LORD, as the children of Israel bring an offering in a clean vessel into the house of the LORD.*

They are the ones who shall go into all the nations and preach of Christ's glory and will return with peoples of the nations to offer gifts to the inhabitants of God's holy mountain:

JOEL 2:32 *And it shall come to pass, that whosoever shall call on the name of the LORD shall be delivered: for in mount Zion and in Jerusalem shall be deliverance, as the LORD hath said, and in the remnant whom the LORD shall call.*

[Underlines added for emphasis]

"Remnant" refers to those that are left or that survive the Lord's wrath. These special priests will rule along with the resurrected Saints who did not take the mark of the Beast. But the duty of the Remnant is to reach out to the nations and solicit offerings to the Lord. The untold billions of us living in the New Jerusalem will enjoy the riches of the Earth, I firmly believe, and will sample the best the Earth has to offer. That includes all the finest foods and garments and whatever else we might righteously desire. And why not? The whole universe belongs to the King and His faithful servants.

Those who die during the Tribulation Period for a witness of Christ will also become priests of the Earth and special resurrected holy men as mentioned previously:

REVELATION 20:4 *...and I saw the souls of them that were beheaded for the witness of Jesus, and for the word of God, and which had not worshipped the beast, neither his image, neither had received his mark upon their foreheads, or in their hands; and they lived and reigned with Christ a thousand years.*

God's Holy Highway

The New Jerusalem will have a golden road leading from Earth to its gates, but only the redeemed will be allowed to use it. I think the Saints who have become priests will journey far and wide to preach the gospel of Christ to a newly populated world and then return to have counsel with Jesus. Sort of like recharging their spiritual batteries in order to obtain "joy and gladness."

ISAIAH 35:8 *And an highway shall be there, and a way, and it shall be called The way of holiness; the unclean shall not pass over it; but it shall be for those: the wayfaring men, though fools, shall not err therein.*

9 No lion shall be there, nor any ravenous beast shall go up thereon, it shall not be found there; but the redeemed shall walk there:

10 And the ransomed of the LORD shall return, and come to Zion with songs and everlasting joy upon

*their heads: they shall obtain joy and gladness, and
sorrow and sighing shall flee away.*

No More War

The strong rulership of Christ will ensure peace on Earth:

> MICAH 4:3 *And he shall judge among many people,
> and rebuke strong nations afar off; and they shall
> beat their swords into plowshares, and their spears
> into pruning hooks: nation shall not lift up a sword
> against nation, neither shall they learn war any
> more.*

Eden In Jerusalem

The prophet Ezekiel tells us that at one time Lucifer himself dwelt in the garden of Eden:

> EZEKIEL 28:13 <u>*Thou hast been in Eden the garden
> of God;*</u> *every precious stone was thy covering, the
> sardius, topaz, and the diamond, the beryl, the onyx,
> and the jasper, the sapphire, the emerald, and the
> carbuncle, and gold: the workmanship of thy tabrets
> and of thy pipes was prepared in thee in the day that
> thou wast created.*

He further tells us that this place where the garden of Eden existed was covered with many of the same precious stones that are in the New Jerusalem as described by John in the book of Revelation.

The prophet then revealed an incredible insight in the following passage:

EZEKIEL 28:14 *Thou art the anointed cherub that covereth; and I have set thee so:* thou wast upon the holy mountain of God; *thou hast walked up and down in the midst of the stones of fire.*

15 *Thou wast perfect in thy ways from the day thou wast created, till iniquity was found in thee.*

16 *By the multitude of thy merchandise they have filled the midst of thee with violence, and thou hast sinned: therefore I will cast thee as profane out of the mountain of God: and I will destroy thee, o covering cherub, from the midst of the stones of fire.*

17 *Thine heart was lifted up because of thy beauty, thou hast corrupted thy wisdom by reason of thy brightness: I will cast thee to the ground, I will lay thee before kings, that they may behold thee.*
[Underlines added for emphasis]

Satan, called here "the anointed cherub," once lived in the presence of God in His holy mountain, presumably before the Earth was created and before the creation of man. And he dwelt in the "Garden of Eden" at the time of his ousting. Does this tell us he is a "gray"? Interesting.

Apparently the garden of Eden is located in God's holy mountain. The same holy mountain known as the New Jerusalem in Revelation. If that's true, the garden of Eden still exists today as it did during the time of Adam and Eve. It was never located on the Earth, as many Bible scholars have hypothesized, but is located in the glorious HFO that awaits all believers.

We will all, as true believers (more accurately...seekers of truth), enjoy this glorious city with its magnificent garden and pristine river running through its center who's banks are lined with mysterious trees which heal the nations' diseases (that would be the earthly nations living below who's mortal bodies will be susceptible to disease). From this home port, I believe, we will be dispatched to carry out the affairs of God in all parts of His vast universe, never to suffer or die again. What a fabulous, and extremely interesting existence!

Forever!!

*   *   *   *   *

(Illustration Courtesy Alexander Preuss)

Figure 33.1 – Futurists envision that, one day in the not-too-distant future, giant circular space stations, like the one pictured above, will orbit Earth as huge laboratories producing American industrial products and will hold cities of people. They will be preceded by commercial ventures, such as space hotels, like the one pictured in *Figure 33.2*, and the smaller Axiom and Bigelow Space Stations, currently under construction *Figures 33.3-4*. The areas closer to the centers of the giant rings will produce a zero-gravity environment. Imagine the floating recreation and games that could be invented for the structure's inhabitants.

Partial list of space tourism companies' websites:

https://gatewayspaceport.com/von-braun-station | https://www.axiomspace.com
https://bigelowaerospace.com   https://www.virgingalactic.com

The Future of Space Habitation

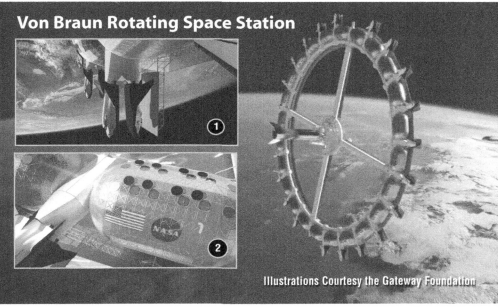

Figure 33.2 – Another project currently being pursued is the Von Braun Space Station with 24 seperate habitation modules and a center core for construction and maintenance. Each habitation module will have two SNC Space Planes attached (inset 1) for emergency escape to ensure a safe stay at the world's first orbiting hotel. Individual mods may also be assigned corporate sponsers (inset 2) or can be used for scientific and medical research. The center core may also be used for weightless fun and games. Notice that one side of the formation is shielded from the intense heat of the sun's side of orbit.

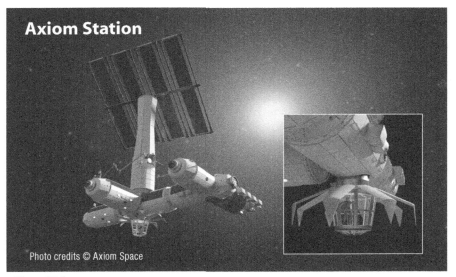

Figure 33.3 – Axiom Station, Nadir view (above) is an American-based space tourist project which has already attached a habitable pod to the International Space Station. They will eventually debark from the ISS and begin to build a space port of their own, complete with 360 degree space viewing cupola (inset). Axiom Station will complete construction and detach to operate into the future as a free-flying complex for living and working in space – marking humankind's next stage of LEO (low earth orbit) settlement. Habitation modules contain eight crew quarters and features a crew-capable airlock for venturing outside the commercial space station.

468

Figure 33.4 – Bigelow Aerospace is also building space tourism modules and has come up with a unique version for construction with expanding modules which are light weight, ergo cheaper to send into space. They also have installed a prototype module on the International Space Station and successfully expanded their habitation mod as the first step in building the Bigelow Space Station seen above.

Traditional church's limited vision of heaven:

"Arise, shine; for your light has come, and the glory of the LORD has risen upon you."

קוּמִי אוֹרִי כִּי בָא
אוֹרֵךְ וּכְבוֹד
יְהוָה עָלַיִךְ זָרָח:

Figure 33.5 – Here's an example of the traditional view of the New Jerusalem suspended "above the hills" of old Jerusalem. Micah 4:1. Remember, this city will hold untold millions, if not billions, of angels and saints, along with Christ and his special assembly of elders and priests. It is described as 1,500 miles cubed in Revelation 21, so the vision above is vastly underscale (see Figure 33.7). Another note, there are no hills above Jerusalem as illustrated above, I've been there. So what is Isaiah describing? The following illustration will explain.

Figure 33.6

ike a huge square moon rising on the distant horizon, sojourners from distant lands traveling in passenger jets and ocean liners will be left breathless as they approach the magnificent city named Zion: God's holy mountain. They will come from all the nations to pay tribute and offer gifts to the inhabitants of the earthly Jerusalem. Special priests will use the "Golden Highway" to bring those gifts – both precious objects like jewelry and art, and materials like gold, gems, spices, and even culinary delights – from around the globe to the privileged occupants of the holy city, New Jerusalem, suspended directly above them.

Revelation 21:23-26, 3:12   Psalms 22:25-31

Isaiah 60:1-5, 66:19-23   Micah 4:1-2

Zechariah 2:10-13, 8:3   Hebrews 12:22-24

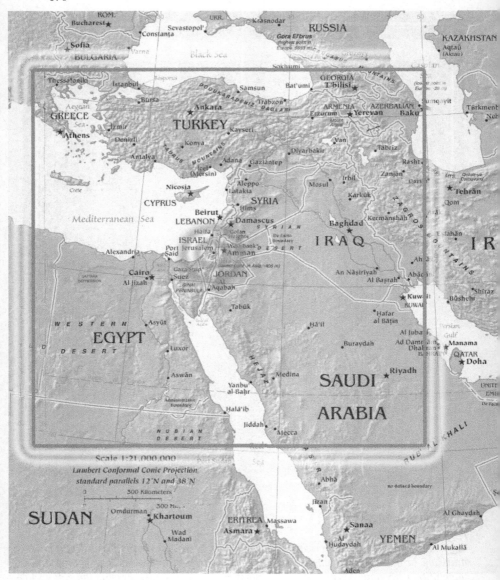

Figure 33.7 This is an aerial vew of the land mass the New Jerusalem will cover. It is 1,500 miles on each side, or 2,250,000 square miles. The continental United State is roughly 3 million square miles and would nearly fit into just one level of Zion. Therefore, the New Jerusalem, because it is a twelve-level cube, will contain nearly the same land mass as is contained on planet Earth. It is the magnificent, spacious home of countless angels and saints, along with Jesus and the Godhead. Its walls are 250 feet thick, too, so it's a very sound structure. The Great Wall of China is only 100 feet thick and we think of it as arguably the greatest structure man has ever built, but it is made mostly of mud and straw. God's building materials, of course, are not of this world, but are no doubt the best, most fortified and beautiful in the universe. Hope to see you there!

see **Revelation** 21:16-18

Your Ticket to Paradise

A Master's Plan

Most people view the Bible as a difficult and confusing manuscript written "perhaps" thousands of years ago by self-proclaimed prophets and changed many times to suit those who copied it. They have never taken the time to understand what is called "the plan of salvation," let alone, the vast array of insights and wisdom contained in its pages.

I, too, found it difficult to make myself read a book written in Elizabethan English. After spending some time with it, however, I discovered an incredible wealth of information...all of it intended for the benefit of mankind. Its "do's produce joy, and its "don'ts" avoid pain.

Before we get into this Master Plan let's review man's origin quickly, as it is related in the Bible.

Created in God's Image

As we already explained, man was created in the image of God. Obviously, man's powers are very limited by comparison, but his basic physical appearance is godlike.

The Same, But Different

Man was created in God's image, however, man was fashioned in three separate parts, according to Scripture. He has a physical body – we all are aware of this. He has an intellectual, emotional, willful part which the Bible calls his "soul." And he has a "spiritual" existence, the one the Bible refers to as the "hidden man." This is the part of man that is godlike: man's individual link to his Creator. This hidden part of man is the one that no psychologist or psychiatrist can explore and it is the part of a man that becomes "born-again" once he accepts God's new contract (as we shall explain further).

Man Once Lived in the Presence of God

In the beginning man lived in the presence of God. He dwelled in the Garden of Eden which, as we have explained, was in God's holy mountain. This holy city was positioned on Earth then just as it will be again one day. Adam and Eve, as exemplary figures of mankind, lived in this glorious city in the presence of God...then something quite dreadful happened.

Separation from God

God had rules of conduct for man in His city and told His creation not to eat of the "fruit of the tree of the knowledge of good and evil." But God allowed Satan to tempt Adam and Eve to test their true natures. Satan, who was created an eternal creature, went to Eve and told her a lie. He said "If you eat of this fruit, you'll be like God." When Eve, and then Adam, succumbed to Satan's temptation it ushered in the fall of mankind. This first act of sin sealed man's fate. The word "sin" simply means disobedience to God. Sin resulted in separation.

The Wage of Sin is Death

When Adam and Eve disobeyed God they were forced to suffer the consequences...separation from God with the curse of death. Eternal man became a human who must grow old and eventually suffer and die without ever living in the presence of God where there is no pain, suffering or death. But it was the spiritual side of Adam and Eve that actually died to the communion with God with that first act of disobedience. Their spiritual (or Godlike) part was isolated from their Creator along with their physical and intellectual selves. They suddenly became aware of their sin nature and hid their nakedness.

Even before the creation of man, God had trouble with some of His other creations: Lucifer (Satan) and his followers. They, too, rebelled against Him and forced Him to banish them to Earth.

This was very similar to the situation that man was forced into. God cast man down to Earth where he must dwell in the presence of the spirits of Satan and his demons. That's why Earth is such a rough place. Satan is allowed to roam around causing trouble in the realm of the spirit.

I PETER 5:8 *Be sober, be vigilant; because your adversary the devil, as a roaring lion, walketh about, seeking whom he may devour.*

This is the curse that all humans are born with... thanks to Adam and Eve. That's why humans are inherently evil. They suffer from the same affliction as Satan: separation from God because of vanity, lust and greed. But wait! This is not the final chapter in God's plan. God promises to reinstate us into our rightful position if we will make the "right" choice. The plan will be revealed in this chapter so please stay with me...it will be the best thing you ever did.

Jesus was Made a Man

God decided to show man the kind of life he should live in order to fully enjoy the privileges of his existence. He sent His Son into this world as an example that we might see that it is possible to follow His rules of conduct. "Hold on," you say, "He wasn't just a man like me...He was God... it was easy for Him."

In actuality, by becoming a man, Jesus was separated from God His Father just as we are. He endured the same pains and temptations that we all do as human beings, only more so. In the end, however, this innocent man suffered a terrible death for the sins of all mankind to fulfill God's promise:

HEBREWS 2:9 *But we see Jesus, who was made a little lower than the angels for the suffering of death, crowned with glory and honour; that he by the grace of God should taste death for every man.*

Sins for All

The promise that God made to man is that He would send His Son to die in our place – to consummate His terms of forgiveness. That's what it means when we say "Christ died for our sins." This will be explained in greater detail as we proceed (see *Hebrews 10:7-17*).

Less than Angels

Just as Jesus took on the traits of man and was made a little lower than the angels, so, too, are we given that distinction:

> **PSALM 8:4** *What is man, that thou art mindful of him? and the <u>son of man</u>, that thou visitest him?*
>
> *5 For thou hast made him a little lower than the angels and hast crowned him with glory and honour.*
>
> *6 Thou madest him to have dominion over the works of thy hands: thou hast put all things under his feet:*
>
> *7 All sheep and oxen, yea, and the beasts of the field;*
>
> *8 The fowl of the air, and the fish of the sea, and whatsoever passeth through the paths of the sea.*

AUTHOR'S NOTE: For the writers of the King James version of the Bible, the use of a lower case "s" in "son of man" indicates humankind. An upper case "S" would indicate the deity of Jesus Christ.

Angels Among Us

In the kingdom of God, those who hold places of distinction are those who are subservient to all...not those who try to be important because of their own abilities i.e. ego:

MATTHEW 20:27 *"And whosoever will be chief among you, let him be your servant:*

28 *"Even as the Son of man came not to be ministered unto, but to minister, and to give his life a ransom for many."*

...

MATTHEW 23:11 *"But he that is greatest among you shall be your servant."*

12 *"And whosoever shall exalt himself shall be abased; and he that shall humble himself shall be exalted."*

That explains why holy angels are assigned to watch over the body of Christ: Christians (see *Hebrews 1:13-14*). We call these protective spirits our "guardian angels," and, all too often, speak of them as if they were subservient to us.

It's quite true that they will assist us in our desperate times, having been dispatched by the Father, but in God's eyes, the angels are far superior creatures, even those of the lowliest rank:

MATTHEW 11:11 *"Verily I say unto you, Among them that are born of women there hath not risen a greater than John the Baptist: notwithstanding he that is least in the kingdom of heaven is greater than he."*

Guardian angels, then, are assigned to watch over Christ's followers. These angels must, on occasion, do battle with Satan's evil forces but will always win if the person who called them forth will remain faithful. Again, these spirits usually do their work in unseen arenas of battle. Just because we don't always see them at work certainly doesn't mean that they aren't there. We would all agree that we have ungodly thoughts from time to time, but because we don't see these thoughts, doesn't mean that they aren't real. As we've pointed out, Satan's angelic forces (demons) are free to tempt everyone and even to torment those who are ignorant or who's faith is not fully developed.

Be on alert for his temptations, but fear not, for God's power is much greater and we can overcome anything Satan places in our way through the authority we have in Christ Jesus.

We Are the Firstfruits

As Christians, and having been created slightly lower than the angels, we are the "firstfruits" of His spiritual creatures:

> **JAMES 1:18** *Of his own will begat he us with the word of truth, that we should be a kind of firstfruits of his creatures.*

I liken us to God's spiritual larva. Just as worker bees attend the hive to protect and care for their young, so too, our guardian angels care for us.

One day we will blossom out as butterflies and become eternal spirit beings in the kingdom of God! Then we will also become as angels and minister to others in God's kingdom (see *St. Luke 20:35-36*).

Why Man ... Why Not Angels Directly?

It's my opinion the reason God has insisted that man go through this "larva stage" is to weed out any potential creations that may go bad, even as Satan did.

Satan was God's masterpiece but he was a creation that didn't have to go through any preexistence test to reveal his true character.

He was allowed the privilege to live in God's presence among His precious creatures and was able to corrupt many. Satan in his glorious state persuaded one-third of the heavenly angels to forsake God's law. That must have been a terrible experience for the Creator of the universe to endure.

I personally don't think God wants any more of His creatures to betray Him in His presence, especially if they are to be sent on assignment in other parts of the universe. Corruptible spirits can do a lot of harm as we can attest to in the misery perpetrated here on Earth by Satan and his followers.

I believe that God created His angels to carry out His affairs throughout the universe. Since we become as angels, if we will accept the free gift of salvation, we will also, one day, travel throughout the universe on assignment from God. That totally excites me! What strange and wondrous adventures await the faithful!

Free Moral Agents

God made man a free moral agent. That means he has the right to obey or ignore any of His advice.

Why would He do such a thing? If you think about it, it makes perfect sense. Would you love your wife or husband if they were forced to love you? Would you have the same intimate feelings knowing that your mate was duty-bound to please you? I don't think so. It makes us feel special to be loved, doesn't it? Being in love requires a two-way commitment. God gives us His love freely, all we need do is return the gesture to create the most wonderful experience in the universe. One day we'll receive the full impact of His love and we'll be eternally grateful for our choice.

If God's angels were to reveal their reality to the world by landing at the White House and announcing their purpose, men would not be given the opportunity to exercise their faith...to freely make a choice. It would motivate most to believe their story...but it would do little to change their hearts. The Bible addresses this:

> ROMANS 8:24 *For we are saved by hope: but hope that is seen is not hope: for what a man seeth, why doth he yet hope for?*

> 25 *But if we hope for that we see not, then do we with patience wait for it.*

That explains the absence of any conspicuous contact by the HFOs that invade our skies from time to time. Their main purpose is to be a sign to the believer…a sign that the end is very near. Very soon they will reveal God's total plan to everyone when Christ returns at His Second Coming…unfortunately, by then it will be too late for the wicked of the Earth. God's deadline will have elapsed.

Man's Contractual Inheritance from God

There seems to be a lot of confusion and ignorance regarding the Bible's make-up. I hope the following will help clarify the significance of its organization. The Bible is divided into two main sections: The Old Testament and The New Testament.

Just why are they called "testaments?" The word testament refers to a promise of inheritance. Everyone has heard of the legal document called the "last will and testament." In its proper context, then, testament refers to an inheritance from God to man. A kind of legal will who's terms will be fulfilled at death.

Contained within the Books of the Bible are the various articles of this legal agreement. God's terms are called His "covenant" which is really just another word for "contract." His old covenant in the Old Testament has been superseded by His new one in the New Testament, as we shall see.

We've explained that God is truth and if He says He will do something, we can count on His faithfully carrying out His promise:

> DEUTERONOMY 7:9 *Know therefore that the LORD thy God, he is God, the faithful God, which keepeth covenant and mercy with them that love him and keep his commandments to a thousand generations;*

Those who do as He says will be greatly rewarded, but for those who break the terms of His contract there are stiff penalties:

> DEUTERONOMY 7:10 *And repayeth them that hate him to their face, to destroy them: he will not be slack to him that hateth him, he will repay him to his face.*

Why Do We Need Convenants?

That's a valid question. Why do we need any "terms" from God? Why doesn't He just let us do our own thing? As we have explained, men are so wicked by nature that they will abandon healthy lifestyles and instead seek to do what "feels good." Out of this comes only perversion, suffering and ultimate destruction. Here's a little analogy of the need for rules between God and men:

Let's suppose that Mitsubishi Corporation had sufficient technology to build a robot with phenomenal capability. To ensure its durability let's imagine they made it of a new polymer that simply cannot be destroyed... fire won't burn it and high impacts are easily repelled.

Next, imagine a great demand for these helpers throughout the world. To make them more pleasant, Mitsubishi decided to design them in the image of humans. Just as the Cabbage Patch Dolls developers used computer-aided technology to ensure that no two dolls were alike, so too, Mitsubishi's robots are individuals.

Well, everything is great and the demand is high...but something seems to be missing. The owners want to befriend their new companions. They want an intellectually intimate relationship with them.

Mitsubishi scientists soon realize the only way to achieve that is to allow their friends to make their own choices. If not, all they have accomplished is the creation of a "yes man." So they install a Self-Perpetuated Random Access Capability (SPRAC).

The well-meaning Mitsubishi Corporation created these helpers to be their friends. In fact, they've become very attached to them. Unfortunately, some of these valuable robots appear to have faulty SPRACs. Several of the models exhibit defects in their random access mechanism because they are making choices which Mitsubishi realizes may cause harm to their customers.

Remembering that these are indestructible machines, an executive decision is reached on how to deal with the problem.

An island is created and all of these creatures are sent there to be self-tested before Mitsubishi will allow them back into the homes of their customers. Mitsubishi is very disappointed because most of their robots are defective in one way or another. Their ability to use their Self-Perpetuated Random Access Capability wisely is questionable. These little guys have forgotten who they are and have become arrogant and destructive.

"Well," Mitsubishi scientists say to themselves, "Why don't we set some rules and guidelines for proper conduct on the island. The parameters will obviously be formulated to ensure the best possible existence for these creatures. If they are given rules of conduct they will surely obey them. Those who don't, we'll consider faulty. Since they are made of invincible material, we can't destroy them. We'll simply put them in a container at the bottom of the ocean where they can't do anyone any harm. We'll put them in permanent isolation along with the faulty deluxe prototype, Lucifer."

We could go on with this analogy but I think you get the picture. It is totally logical to think of God the Creator in very similar terms. He created us to be His companions and helpers – the Bible explains. When He realized that some of His creations got caught up in themselves and rebelled against His authority He had no choice but to isolate them from the rest of His creatures.

I can understand God's displeasure with mankind, can't you? To weed out the faulty creations, God established some rules of conduct for man to follow. Simple enough.

The Sacrifice Begins

From the beginning of time men have offered gifts to God as a way to honor Him. Cain and Abel both gave burnt offerings to the Lord. This ceremony was apparently introduced by God, Himself, to help men to remember their Maker.

To test the sincerity of men, God asked them to offer their finest possession as a symbol of their devotion. In early times a man's wealth was measured by the number of livestock that he attended. One's very life depended on these reliable animals. That's probably why God asked men to sacrifice their most prized possessions on stone altars…to show that God was more important to them than their possessions.

In the fourth chapter of Genesis we find that Cain made an offering of fruit to the Lord, while Abel offered a prize lamb. Cain's offering met with dishonor while God greatly respected Abel for his. Clearly, the Lord was displeased with Cain's gift. This was the incident that prompted Cain to kill his brother out of jealousy and perhaps anger at God.

Many generations later we find animal sacrifice still a part of the ceremony of worship. Abraham, considered the father of Israel, was a very honorable man in God's eyes. One day the Lord decided to test Abraham to see if he was totally committed to Him. To test him He asked that he sacrifice his only son, Isaac, in place of the livestock that had become the traditional offering. This sacrifice would seal Abraham's contract with God and prove his sincerity.

What more could anyone ask of a man? To seal an agreement today, the courts ask only that we simply sign a document as a symbol of our intention to keep the agreement. If we were asked to offer the life of our only child as a symbol of our sincerity, I would imagine the contract would have to be very important to us, indeed, in order to agree to the terms. It's hard to imagine anything any more important than the life of a beloved child.

Abraham was undeniably sincere in his devotion to God because he took his son to the altar he had built and was prepared to kill Isaac, as the Lord had requested. But God, in His mercy, spared the life of Isaac, having been assured of Abraham's devotion (see *Genesis, chapter 22*).

The bond between God and Abraham's lineage remains to this day a very unique one. It was through Abraham's descendants that God decided to conceive His only begotten child, Jesus. And it was as a symbol of His mercy and love for mankind that one day led to the sacrifice of His Son on a cross in Jerusalem. God has been very sincere about His contract with man.

The Old Contract

When the Earth was first inhabited with men, God was hopeful that they would turn to Him for guidance. However, seeing that they were inherently wicked and lusting after evil things only, the Lord decided that mankind should be totally destroyed *(Genesis 6:12,13)*. He wanted to start over, but He was able to find one man who remained faithful to Him. His name was Noah. Because of Noah's devotion He spared him and his family, but the rest of the world perished in the great flood (see *Genesis chapters 6-9*).

After thousands of years, Noah's descendants repopulated the Earth. One of Noah's descendants also found great favor with God. His name was Abraham. As we have indicated, Abraham was truly a beloved follower of God, so the Lord promised him that his seed would multiply throughout the Earth. From his lineage arose the Jewish race.

Through Divine circumstance a great Jewish prophet became the second in command over all of Egypt. Joseph, the great grandson of Abraham was warned by God that a terrible famine was coming on the

482

land. Joseph warned the Pharaoh of Egypt of the impending disaster and proved he was a prophet and a man of his word. To show his gratitude the Pharaoh gave Joseph a position of great authority and respect and put him in charge of storing up vast amounts of surplus grain throughout the land in preparation for the draught.

Just as Joseph had predicted, a seven year famine gripped the entire area and all the nations of the world came to Egypt to buy their surplus grain. Because of this the Pharaoh collected the wealth of the nations and Egypt became the greatest nation on Earth.

The Jewish tribe also moved to Egypt, at Joseph's insistence, to wait-out the famine. They were welcomed by a grateful Pharaoh and were given the very finest land in the country in which to settle.

But circumstances changed, as they always do. Joseph died of natural causes at an old age and a new Pharaoh took command of Egypt. The new Pharaoh never knew Joseph and he harbored ill feelings for the Jews who had by now become extremely wealthy and populous. He feared they would join his enemies one day in rebellion so he made a proclamation throughout Egypt. The Jews would now become the slaves of the native Egyptians. That would prevent them from becoming too powerful and taking over the entire kingdom.

Once again, there arose a leader of the Jews who found great favor with God because of his faithfulness. Moses was directed to lead the tribe of Judah out of Egypt and to a land called their "promised land." This was the land that God had given to Abraham and his descendants centuries before.

It was while God's "chosen" people were on their way to their promised land that He realized they needed some rules to abide by. The people had soon forsaken what Moses had taught them and returned to their pagan ways – worshipping the false idols of the Egyptians.

God came to Earth in a great holy mountain covered in clouds as described in detail in chapter 21 of this book. He gave Moses the ten commandments and told His people that if they would obey Him, they would be judged worthy to inherit eternal life and be restored to their rightful place in His presence. All they had to do was live perfectly by the "Law." That proved too difficult, as we all know, so the Lord made a covenant with His people that was easier to adhere to.

Moses and his people were instructed to sacrifice an unblemished lamb once a year during the Day of Atonement ceremony. The lamb symbolized the sins of the people and was offered to God by the High

Priest wearing special protective clothing supplied by God. The ceremony was rather intricate and exacting with each part having great symbolic significance to the Jewish people. Each served as a reminder of God's specific agreement with them. The lamb's blood was sprinkled on the Mercy Seat of the Ark of the covenant, an oblong golden chest and the permanent holding place for (1) the Laws of God: the Stone Tablets with the 10 Commandments on them, (2) a container of Manna: the food God sent to the Jews to feed them in the wilderness (symbolizing how God had taken care of His people), and (3) Aaron's Rod also known as "The Rod of God." (We're not really sure what significance the rod played but it apparently had great powers and perhaps symbolized God's protective power: read *Exodus 17:1-16*).

This was the ceremony that God introduced as a replacement for living a perfect life according to the L aw. Realizing that no man was able to live a perfect life, and in honor of the covenant He made with Abraham, the Lord forgave the people who came to the Lord's temple during the Day of Atonement ceremony.

This special promise was given to the tribe of Judah and any others who would submit to God's agreement, however, not many outside of the Jewish race even knew of its existence. That was the old contract...what about God's new contract?

The New Contract

The people who lived prior to the time of Jesus were living under the terms of the old covenants of God. But a new contract has been drawn up for man with the birth and subsequent sacrifice of God's Son, Jesus. The New Testament brings us the good news of God's new agreement with mankind.

HEBREWS 10:7 *Then said I, Lo, I come (in the volume of the book it is written of me,) to do thy will, O God.*

8 Above when he said, Sacrifice and offering and burnt offerings and offering sin thou wouldest not, neither hadst pleasure therein; which are offered by the law:

9 Then said he, Lo, I come to do thy will, O God. He taketh away the first, that he may establish the second.

10 *By the which will we are sanctified through the offering of the body of Jesus Christ once for all.*

As witness to God's new covenant with mankind He sent His Son, Jesus, to Earth. To show His devotion and love for mankind He allowed His "only begotten Son" to be killed as a symbol of His sincerity, just as Abraham had offered to do generations earlier with his son Isaac.

HEBREWS 12:24 *And to Jesus the mediator of the new covenant, and to the blood of sprinkling, that speaketh better things than that of Abel.*

Blood has always played a key part in sealing contractual agreements in various societies. The American Indians would cut two rival Chief's arms and bind their wounds together, intermixing (at least symbolically) their blood. This mixing of bloods made them blood brothers and nothing could void the contract between them. Religions throughout history, from sophisticated to very primitive cultures, have all used blood as a significant part of their religious rituals and beliefs.

It's not surprising to know that the "shed blood" of Jesus Christ is the symbol that seals God's New Contract with man.

LEVITICUS 17:1 *For the life of the flesh is in the blood, and I have given it to you on the altar to make atonement* [ask forgiveness for wrong doing] *for our souls; for it is the blood by reason of the life that makes atonement.*

NAS

Animal sacrifice by the early Jews was the symbol, or precursor, of a newer and better contract for forgiveness that was yet to come and which would be validated by Christ's sacrificial death on the Cross. Satanic and pagan rituals today mock God's provision through sacrificial offering in their sadistic and evil ceremonies, right down to the defiant drinking of blood – something strictly prohibited by God's edict (see *Leviticus, Chapter 17*). Satan always has a false counterpart to God's gifts and activities. Always.

God in His infinite love has decided to allow even pagans (non-Jews) the opportunity to get in on the inheritance of ever-lasting life. What a fantastic thing for the people of Earth. Imagine being able to live in the magnificent holy mountain, converse with the Saints of old and sit in the presence of the Creator of the universe! "What joy unspeakable," as the Psalmist has said. To comprehend the joy of such an experience is about as far from our understanding as is the technology of the UFO.

But the truth is so simple that many men miss it. All it requires is an open heart...a desire to know the truth, and the desire to do the will of God, but certainly not to be equal to God, as so many promote in the New Age movement.

The New Covenant Plan

Here is the New Covenant plan in brief:

1. God wants men to realize that there is only one true God:

   ISAIAH 43:11 *I, even I, am the LORD: and besides me there is no saviour.*

2. Believe that Jesus came to Earth and lived the perfect life, but was wrongly crucified as a propitiatory price for our sins... and arose again, in full authority, to prove His deity:

   ROMANS 10:9 *...if thou shalt confess with thy mouth the Lord Jesus, and shalt believe in thine heart that God hath raised him from the dead, thou shalt be saved.*

3. Confess your beliefs openly:

   ROMANS 10:11 *For the scripture saith, Whosoever believeth on him shall not be ashamed.*

   ...

   10 *For with the heart man believeth unto righteousness;   and with the mouth confession is made unto salvation.*

   ...

   ST. LUKE 12:8 *"Also I say unto you, Whosoever shall confess me before men, him shall the Son of man also confess before the angels of God:*

9 *"But he that denieth me before men shall be denied before the angels of God."*

4. Turn from your old sinful habits and walk in the light of God:

ST. JOHN 14:21 *"He that hath* (knoweth) *my commandments, and keepeth them, he it is that loveth me: and he that loveth me shall be loved of my Father, and I will love him, and will manifest myself to him."*

5. And if you mess up, as we all do, know that the LORD will forgive you if you will simply ask His forgiveness sincerely in your heart:

I JOHN 1:9 *If we confess our sins, he is faithful and just to forgive us our sins, and to cleanse us from all unrighteousness.*

If you'll sincerely do this, right now, wherever you are or whatever your sins, you'll be assured of your ticket to Paradise. Welcome aboard!

When Aliens Become In-laws

Once you've made this all-important decision to become a follower of Christ, you have joined the heavenly family according to God's law. We are all brothers and sisters in Christ, even joint heirs with angels (including the occupants of many of the UFOs we read about today):

EPHESIANS 2:19 *Now therefore ye are no more strangers and foreigners, but fellow citizens with saints, and of the household of God;*

Be On Guard Always

As a sign of the End Times, UFOs are invading the airways of the world. They are here to remind us all that Christ is returning soon.

ST. LUKE 21:11 *"...and fearful sights and great signs shall there be from heaven."*

Be on guard, for the redeemer will return and rescue those who have remained faithful from the terrible times coming upon the Earth, to transport them to a wonderful new existence with Him.

ST. LUKE 21:36 *"Watch ye therefore, and pray always, that ye may be accounted worthy to escape all these things that shall come to pass, and to stand before the Son of man."*

...

NEHEMIAH 1:9 *But if ye turn unto me, and keep my commandments, and do them; though there were of you cast out unto the uttermost part of the heaven, yet will I gather them from thence, and will bring them unto the place that I have chosen to set my name there.*

We'll be given a special place in heaven, according to our works here on Earth, and we'll live in the presence of God in The New Jerusalem in mansions that will make earthly mansions look like shacks. Not that possessions should be our focus. I'm sure that heaven is a place of communal living. But God will be faithful to reward us, as He has promised, with special crowns denoting our earthly accomplishments, and assigning us to duties accordingly. We'll be on eternal assignment with God our Creator doing His tasks, based on our abilities and faithfulness. What more could anyone ever hope for?

My Final Wish

I hope that this book has been a tool to help open your eyes to the mysterious side of the Bible. I've attempted to cover many subjects and reveal many of the hidden truths within its texts, but I want to encourage you to read it for yourself. "Faith cometh by hearing the Word of God," the Scriptures say. That process should include attending Bible-based churches and listening to good teachers, and can include watching sound (and I emphasize "sound", which is a rarity, unfortunately) Christian programming. But the most enriching route is the persistent individual study of the Holy Bible, along with a daily routine of prayer and thanksgiving. That will ensure that you'll recognize sound doctrine when you see, hear or read it. May you keep an open heart and continue to grow in the saving knowledge of Christ Jesus.

– END –

Bibliography

End Notes

Index

Gathering Clouds

1. John G. Fuller, *Incident at Exeter,*
   (New York: Bantam Books, 1975).
2. Josef F. Blumrich, *The Spaceships of Ezekiel,*
   (New York: Lyle Stuart, 1966).
3. Dr. Billy Graham, *Angels - God's Secret Agents,*
   (New York: Pocket Books, 1977).
4. Travis Walton, *The Walton Experience,*
   (New York: Berkley books, 1978).
5. Gray Barker, *They Knew too Much About Flying Saucers*
   (New York: University Books, 1956).
6. Dr. J. Allen Hynek, *The Hynek UFO Report,*
   (New York: Dell Publishing, 1972).
7. Brad Steiger, *Mysteries of Time and Space,*
   (New York: Dell Publishing and Confucian Press, Inc., 1974).
8. Hal Lindsey, *The Late Great Planet Earth,*
   (New York: Bantam Books, 1975).
9. Raymond Moody Jr., M.D., *Life After Life, The Investigation of a Phenomenon–Survival of Bodily Death,*
   (Bantam Books; New York, 1976)
10. Raymond E. Fowler, *The Andreasson Affair,*
    (New Jersey: Printice-Hall, Inc., 1979).
11. T.A. Heppenheimer, *Toward Distant Suns,*
    (New York: Fawcett Columbine Books, 1980) ©1979 T.A. Heppenheimer.
12. Maurice Rawlings, M.D., *Beyond Death's Door,*
    (Nashville, TN, Thomas Nelson, 1993)
13. Donald E. Keyhoe, *Aliens from Space,*
    (New York: New American Library 1974).
    (New York: Doubleday & Company, 1973).
14. Arthur Shuttlewood, *UFO Prophecy,*
    (New York: global Communications, 1968).
15. Budd Hopkins, *Missing Time,*
    (New York: Berkley Books, 1981).
16. John G. Fuller, *The Interrupted Journey,*
    (New York: Berkley Publishing Corp., 1974) © 1966 John G. Fuller.
17. Hal Lindsey, *There's a New World Coming,*
    (New York: Bantam Books, 1975).
18. Frank Edwards, *Flying Saucers - Serious Business,*
    (New York: Lyle Stuart, 1966).
19. Coral & Jim Lorenzen, *Flying Saucer Occupants,*
    (New York: Signet Books, 1967).
20. Aime Michel, *The Truth About Flying Saucers,*
    (New York: Criterion Books, 1956).
21. Edward J. Ruppelt, *The Report on Unidentified Flying Objects,*
    (Garden City, NewJersey: Doubleday & Co., 1956).
22. Aime Michel, *Flying Saucers and the Straight-Line Mystery,*
    (New York: S.G. Phillips, Inc., 1958).
23. Isaac Asimov, *Extraterrestrial Civilizations,*
    (New York: Fawcett Columbine, 1980), ©1979 Isaac Asimov.
24. Charles Berlitz & William L. Moore, *The Roswell Incident,*
    (New York: Grosset & Dunlap Publishers, 1980).

25. Lee J. Elders, Brit Nilsson-Elders and Thomas K. Welch,
    UFO...Contact from the Pleiades,
    (Phoenix, Arizona: Genesis III Productions, Ltd., 1979).

26. Donald E. Keyhoe, *Flying Saucers from Outer Space,*
    (New York: Henry Holt and Company, 1953).

27. John G. Fuller, *Aliens in the Skies,*
    (New York: G.P. Putnam's Sons, 1969).

28. Dr. J. Allen Hynek & Jacques Vallee, *The Edge of Reality,*
    (Chicago: Henry Regnery Company, 1975).

29. Frank Scully, *Behind the Flying Saucers,*
    (New York: Henry Holt and Company, 1950).

30. R. L. Dione, *God Drives a Flying Saucer,*
    (New York: Bantam Books, 1973).© 1969 by R.L. Dione.

31. Jeffrey Goodman, *We are the Earthquake Generation,*
    (New York: Berkley books, 1982) © 1979 by Jeffrey Goodman, Phd.

32. Morris K. Jessup, *UFO and the Bible,*
    (New York: The Citadel Press,1956).

33. Morris K. Jessup, *The Case for the UFO,*
    (New York: The Citadel Press,1955).

34. David Michael Jacobs, *The UFO Controversy in America,*
    (Bloomington & London: Indiana University Press, 1975).

35. Nigel Calder, *Einstein's Universe,*
    (New York: Greenwich House, 1982) © 1979 by Nigel Calder.

36. Paul Thomas, *Flying Saucers Through the Ages,*
    (London: Neville Spearman Ltd, 1962). © Paul Thomas, 1962, 1965.

37. Fritz Ridenhour, *Who Says God Created?,*
    (Glendale, California: G/L Regal Books, 1969) © 1967 by G/L Publications.

38. Blum & Blum, *Beyond Earth: Man's Contact with UFOs,*
    (New York: Bantam Books, 1974).

39. Kevin McClure, *The Evidence for the Visions of the Virgin Mary,*
    (Wellingborough, Northamponshire: The Aquarian Press,

40. Constance Cumby, *The Hidden Dangers of the Rainbow, The New Age
    Movement and our Coming Age of Barbarism* (Huntington House, Inc., 1983)

41. Dave Hunt, *Peace Prosperity and the Coming Holocaust,*
    (Eugene, Oregon: Harvest House Publishers, 1983).

42. Jacques Vallee, *Anatomy of a Phenomenon,*
    (Chicago: Henry Regnery Company, 1965).

43. Frank Edwards, *Stranger than Science,*
    (Secaucus, New Jersey: Citadel Press, 1959)

44. Ann Druffer & D. Scott Rogo, *The Tujunga Canyon Contacts,*
    (Englewood Cliffs, New Jersey: Prentice-Hall, Inc., 1980).

45. Walter Sullivan, *We Are Not Alone,*
    (New York: McGraw-Hill Book Company, 1964).

46. Hal Lindsey, *The Rapture: Truth or Consequences,*
    (New York: Bantam Books, 1983), © Copyright 1983 by The Aorist Corporation.

47. Coral & Jim Lorenzen, *Abducted! Confrontations With Beings From
    Outer Space,*
    (New York: Berkley Publishing Corp., 1977).

48. David Haisell, *The Missing Seven Hours,*
    (Markham, Ontario, Canada: PaperJacks Ltd., 1978).

49. Arthur Blessitt, *Arthur: A Pilgrim,*
    (California: Blessitt Publishing, 1985)

50. Holy Spirit, *The Holy Bible, King James Version/
    New American Standard Bible,*
    Copyright © The Lockman Foundation 1960, 1962, 1963, 1968, 1971, 1972, 1973, 1975, 1977.

51. Rev. Chuck Smith, *What The World is Coming To,*
    (Costa Mesa, California: Maranatha House Publishers, 1977).

52. Josh McDowell, *Research in Christian Ethics,*

53. Horst de la Croix, *Gardner's Art Through the Ages, (fifth edition),*
    Richard G. Tansey and Dale E. Bellis

54. Peter W. Stoner and Robert C. Newman, *Science Speaks,*
    (Chicago: Moody Press, © 1958, 1963, 1968).

55. J. A. Seiss, *The Epocolypse,*
    (Grand Rapids, MI: Zondervan Publishing House, 1981)

56. Hal Lindsey, *The Promise,*

57. The Hunger Project, *Ending Hunger:
    An Idea Who's Time Has Come*

58. Wayne Weible, *Medjugorje: The Message,*
    (Orleans, Massachusetts: Paraclete Press, 1989).

59. Flavius Josephus: *translated by G.A. Williamson, The Jewish War,*
    (London, England, Penguin Books, 1970, 1981)

60. J. Allen Hynek and Philip J. Imbrogno, *Night Seige*
    (New York: Ballantine books,1987).

61. Raymond E. Fowler, *The Andreasson Affair Phase II,*
    (Englewood Cliffs, New Jersey: Prentice-Hall, Inc., 1982).

62. Whitley Strieber, *Communion,*
    (New York: Avon Books, 1988).

63. Robert Jastrow, *God And The Astonomers,*
    (New York: Warner Books, 1984) Copyright ©1978 by reader's Library, Inc.
    Afterword Copyright © 1980 by John A. O'Keefe and Steven T. Katz.

64. Frank Edwards, *Flying Saucers Here And Now!*
    (New York: Lyle Stuart, Inc., 1967).

65. Major Donald E. Keyhoe, *Flying Saucers–Top Secret,*
    (New York: G.P. Putnam's Sons, 1960).

66. Frank Edwards, *Flying Saucers – Serious Business,*
    (New York, Bantam Books, 1966).

67. Robert Emenegger, *UFOs – Past, Present, & Future,*
    (New York: Ballantine Books, 1974).

68. Howard Blum , *The Gold of Exodus,*
    (Publisher: Simon & Schuster, February 9, 1998)
    Copyright 1997 Reed Business Information, Inc.

69. Bob Cornuke and Larry Williams,
    The Search for the Real Mt. Sinai
    Documentary film, 2002
    – and –

    Dean River Productions,
    Mountain of Fire: The Discovery of the Real Mt. Sinai
    Documentary film, 2002

Forward

F-1   Gallup Poll, Taken in 1987

F-2   Gallup Poll Projection (based on past reports) / Marist Institute for Public Opion Survey 1997, Marist College , Poughkeepsie, N.Y.

Chapter 1

1-1   Victor Trombettas , "Flight 587 Update - Witness Reliability" June 25, 2002, *U.S. Read, http://usread.com/flight587/Reliability/Reliability.html*

Chapter 2

2-1   Aime Michel, *The Truth About Flying Saucers,* (New York: Criterion Books, 1956), p. 31.

2-2   Gray Barker, *They Knew too Much About Flying Saucers* (New York: University Books, 1956), p. 31.

2-3   Aime Michel, *Flying Saucers and the Straight-Line Mystery,* (New York: S.G. Phillips, Inc., 1958), p. 31.

2-4   Ibid

2-5   Ibid, p. 43.

2-6   John G. Fuller, *The Interrupted Journey,* (New York: Berkley Medallion Books, 1966), © 1966 John G. Fuller, p. 158.

2-7   John G. Fuller, *Incident at Exeter,* (New York: Berkley Medallion Books, 1966), p. 32.

2-8   Ibid, p. 17.

2-9   Ibid, pp. 6, 17.

2-10   Ibid, p. 73.

2-11   Ibid, pp. 126-129.

2-12   Ibid, p. 181.

2-13   Ibid, pp. 109-111.

2-14   Edward J. Ruppelt, *The Report on Unidentified Flying Objects,* (Garden City, New Jersey: Doubleday & Co., 1956), pp. 133-134.

2-15   Aime Michel, *Flying Saucers and the Straight-Line Mystery,* (New York: S.G. Phillips, Inc., 1958), p. 93.

2-16   Donald E. Keyhoe, *Aliens from Space,* (New York: New American Library 1974). (New York: Doubleday & Company, 1973), p. 93.

2-17   John G. Fuller, *Incident at Exeter,* (New York: Berkley Medallion Books, 1966), p. 40.

2-18   Ibid, p. 164.

2-19   Edward J. Ruppelt, *The Report on Unidentified Flying Objects,* (Garden City, New Jersey: Doubleday & Co., 1956), pp. 187-189.

2-20   Donald E. Keyhoe, *Aliens from Space,* (New York: New American Library 1974). (New York: Doubleday & Company, 1973), p. 135.

2-21   John G. Fuller, *Incident at Exeter,* (New York: Berkley Medallion Books, 1966), p. 124.

2-22   Ibid,, p. 133.

Chapter 3

3-1   Edward J. Ruppelt, *The Report on Unidentified Flying Objects,* (Garden City, New Jersey: Doubleday & Co., 1956), p. 229.
Coral & Jim Lorenzen, *Flying Saucer Occupants,* (New York: Signet Books, 1967), p. 129.
Charles Berlitz & William L. Moore, *The Roswell Incident,* (New York: Grosset & Dunlap Publishers, 1980), p. 18.

3-2   George Gallup, *Gallup Poll Service,* 1947 National Survey.

3-3   George Gallup, *Gallup Poll Service,* 1973 & 1978 National Surveys.

3-4   Marist Institute for Public Opinion Survey - 1997, *The Denver Post,* December 16, 1997.
National Enquirer Poll - 1996, *National Enquirer,* July 23, 1996.

3-5   *ABC News,* UFOs: Seeing Is Believing, February 24, 2005. 2-hour special , hosted by Peter Jennings

3-6   George Gallup, *Gallup Poll Service,* 1987 National Survey, Report No. 258, March, 1987.

3-7   Frank Edwards, *Flying Saucers - Serious Business,* (New York: Lyle Stuart, 1966), pp. 45-46.

3-8   Ibid., p. 44.

3-9   Ibid., pp. 41-43.

3-10   Ibid., pp. 48-49.

3-11   Frank Edwards, *Flying Saucers - Serious Business,* (New York: Lyle Stuart, 1966), pp. 36-39.

3-12   Edward J. Ruppelt, *The Report on Unidentified Flying Objects,* (Garden City,
            New Jersey: Doubleday & Co., 1956), p. 5.

3-13   Ibid,, p. 77.

3-14   Edward J. Ruppelt, *The Report on Unidentified Flying Objects,* (Garden City,
            New Jersey: Doubleday & Co., 1956), p. 77.

3-15   Ibid, p. 80.

3-16   Frank Edwards, *Flying Saucers - Serious Business,* (New York: Lyle Stuart, 1966) pp. 67.

3-17   Ibid, pp. 68.

3-18   Donald E. Keyhoe, *Aliens from Space,* (New York: New American Library 1974). (New York:
            Doubleday & Company, 1973), p. 161.
            Frank Edwards, *Flying Saucers - Serious Business,* (New York: Lyle Stuart, 1966) pp. 69.

3-19   Donald E. Keyhoe, *Aliens from Space,* (New York: New American Library 1974). (New York:
            Doubleday & Company, 1973), p. 163.

3-20   Dr. J. Allen Hynek, *The Hynek UFO Report,* (New York: Dell Publishing, 1977), p. 139.

3-21   Ibid, pp. 137-139.

3-22   John G. Fuller, *Incident at Exeter,* (New York: Berkley Medallion Books, 1966), pp. 181-182.

3-23   Dr. J. Allen Hynek, *The Hynek UFO Report,* (New York: Dell Publishing, 1977), pp. 134-135.

3-24   Ibid, pp. 135-136

3-25   Ibid, pp. 127-129, 87-89.

3-26   Aime Michel, *The Truth About Flying Saucers,* (New York: Criterion Books, 1956), pp. 170-172.

3-27   Ibid, p. 123.

3-28   Dr. J. Allen Hynek, *The Hynek UFO Report,* (New York: Dell Publishing, 1977), pp. 129-134.

3-29   Aime Michel, *The Truth About Flying Saucers,* (New York: Criterion Books, 1956), p. 87.

3-30   Budd Hopkins, *Missing Time,* (New York: Berkley Books, 1981), p. 32.

3-31   Frank Edwards, *Flying Saucers - Serious Business,* (New York: Lyle Stuart, 1966), pp. 238.

3-32   Ibid, pp. 239-241.

3-33   Ibid, pp. 205.

3-34   Dr. J. Allen Hynek & Jacques Vallee, *The Edge of Reality,* (Chicago: Henry Regnery Company, 1975), p. 63.

3-35   Ibid, p. 63.

3-36   Ibid,, p. 63.

3-37   Ibid, p. 64.
            Frank Edwards, *Flying Saucers - Serious Business,* (New York: Lyle Stuart, 1966), pp. 226.

3-38   Dr. J. Allen Hynek & Jacques Vallee, *The Edge of Reality,* (Chicago: Henry Regnery Company, 1975), p. 64.
            Frank Edwards, *Flying Saucers - Serious Business,* (New York: Lyle Stuart, 1966), pp. 208.
            Charles Berlitz & William L. Moore, *The Roswell Incident,* (New York: Grosset & Dunlap Publishers,
            1980), p. 8.

3-39   Dr. J. Allen Hynek & Jacques Vallee, *The Edge of Reality,* (Chicago: Henry Regnery Company, 1975), p. 64.

3-40   Ibid, p. 64.

3-41   Frank Edwards, *Flying Saucers - Serious Business,* (New York: Lyle Stuart, 1966), pp. 206.

3-42   Donald E. Keyhoe, *Aliens from Space,* (New York: New American Library 1974). (New York:
            Doubleday & Company, 1973), pp. 91, 212.
            Charles Berlitz & William L. Moore, *The Roswell Incident,* (New York: Grosset & Dunlap
            Publishers, 1980), p. 8.

3-42   Dr. J. Allen Hynek & Jacques Vallee, *The Edge of Reality,* (Chicago: Henry Regnery Company, 1975), p. 64.

3-43   Ibid

3-44   Charles Berlitz & William L. Moore, *The Roswell Incident,* (New York: Grosset & Dunlap Publishers, 1980), p. 9.

    Dr. J. Allen Hynek & Jacques Vallee, *The Edge of Reality,* (Chicago: Henry Regnery Company, 1975), p. 64.

3-45   Charles Berlitz & William L. Moore, *The Roswell Incident,* (New York: Grosset & Dunlap Publishers, 1980), p. 9.

3-46   Donald E. Keyhoe, *Aliens from Space,* (New York: New American Library 1974). (New York: Doubleday & Company, 1973), p. 101.

    Charles Berlitz & William L. Moore, *The Roswell Incident,* (New York: Grosset & Dunlap Publishers, 1980), p. 8.

    Dr. J. Allen Hynek & Jacques Vallee, *The Edge of Reality,* (Chicago: Henry Regnery Company, 1975), p. 64.

3-47   Charles Berlitz & William L. Moore, *The Roswell Incident,* (New York: Grosset & Dunlap Publishers, 1980), p. 9.

    Dr. J. Allen Hynek & Jacques Vallee, *The Edge of Reality,* (Chicago: Henry Regnery Company, 1975), p. 64.

3-48   Ibid, p.64.

3-49   Ibid,

    Charles Berlitz & William L. Moore, *The Roswell Incident,* (New York: Grosset & Dunlap Publishers, 1980), p. 9.

3-50   Ibid,

3-51   Ibid, pp. 9-10.

    Dr. J. Allen Hynek & Jacques Vallee, *The Edge of Reality,* (Chicago: Henry Regnery Company, 1975), p. 64.

3-52   Charles Berlitz & William L. Moore, *The Roswell Incident,* (New York: Grosset & Dunlap Publishers, 1980), p. 9.

    Dr. J. Allen Hynek & Jacques Vallee, *The Edge of Reality,* (Chicago: Henry Regnery Company, 1975), p. 65.

3-53   http://www.nasa.gov/mission_pages/apollo/index.html

    Gallery – http://science.ksc.nasa.gov/mirrors/images/html/as16.htm

    Image – AS16-114-18423

    Text – Astronaut Charles Duke photographed collecting lunar samples at Station 1

3-54   Charles Berlitz & William L. Moore, *The Roswell Incident,* (New York: Grosset & Dunlap Publishers, 1980), p. 9.

3-55   Donald E. Keyhoe, *Aliens from Space,* (New York: New American Library 1974). (New York: Doubleday & Company, 1973), p. 97.

    John G. Fuller, *Incident at Exeter,* (New York: Berkley Medallion Books, 1966), p. 7.

    Dr. J. Allen Hynek & Jacques Vallee, *The Edge of Reality,* (Chicago: Henry Regnery Company, 1975), p. 201.

3-56   Charles Berlitz & William L. Moore, *The Roswell Incident,* (New York: Grosset & Dunlap Publishers, 1980), p. 130.

3-57   *The Arizona Republic,* July 1983, , pp. H1,2.

3-58   Edward J. Ruppelt, *The Report on Unidentified Flying Objects,* (Garden City, New Jersey: Doubleday & Co., 1956), p. 167.

3-59   Donald E. Keyhoe, *Aliens from Space,* (New York: New American Library 1974). (New York: Doubleday & Company, 1973), p. 91.

3-60   Frank Edwards, *Flying Saucers - Serious Business,* (New York: Lyle Stuart, 1966), p. 304.

3-61   Mel Gibson, writer, actor and director Passion Of The Christ (among others), Interview with *ABC Good Morning America, FOX Television,* ????2006.

3-62   "Prime minister's plane has close enounter with UFO in otherworldly incident", Jim Bronskill, *Canadian Press,* March 28, 2004.

3-63   David Sereda, Dan Aykroyd, C.M., D. Lit. (H.C.), *http://ufonasa.terra-ent.com/,* Web article from the documentary film: *Evidence: The Case for NASA UFOs.*

3-64   [1] Jim Brochu, *"Lucy in the Afternoon: An intimate Memoir of Lucille Ball"*
          (William Morrows and Company New York 1990), p. 125.

          [2] Alan Braham Smith and Ken Potter, *""Reagan Saw UFO While Flying – And Ordered His Pilot*
          to Follow It," National Enquirer, October 11, 1988.

          [3] UFO Researcher Stanton Friedman interview with Reagan's pilot Col. Bill Paynter
          (Subject: Re: Reagan And The Aliens – Friedman, Sept. 16, 2003 "UFO Updates" List.)

          [4] Many of Reagaon's speeches can be seen on http://www.youtube.com

3-65   Dr. John Jackson, physicist Sandia National Laboratory, lead investigator on the study of the
          Shroud of Turin.

Chapter 4

4-1   Edward J. Ruppelt, *The Report on Unidentified Flying Objects,* (Garden City,
         New Jersey: Doubleday & Co., 1956), pp. 214-215.

4-2   Frank Edwards, *Flying Saucers - Serious Business,* (New York: Lyle Stuart, 1966), pp. 291.

4-3   Dr. J. Allen Hynek & Jacques Vallee, *The Edge of Reality,* (Chicago: Henry Regnery Company, 1975), p. 7.

4-4   Edward J. Ruppelt, *The Report on Unidentified Flying Objects,* (Garden City,
         New Jersey: Doubleday & Co., 1956), p. 116.

4-5   Frank Edwards, *Flying Saucers - Serious Business,* (New York: Lyle Stuart, 1966), p. 145.

4-6   Charles Berlitz & William L. Moore, *The Roswell Incident,* (New York: Grosset & Dunlap
         Publishers, 1980), pp. 2-145.

4-7   Donald E. Keyhoe, *Aliens from Space,* (New York: New American Library 1974). (New York:
         Doubleday & Company, 1973), pp. 142-145.

4-8   Aime Michel, *Flying Saucers and the Straight-Line Mystery,* (New York: S.G. Phillips,
         Inc., 1958), p. 233.

4-9   Aime Michel, *The Truth About Flying Saucers,* (New York: Criterion Books, 1956), pp. 115-116.

4-10   Dr. J. Allen Hynek, *The Hynek UFO Report,* (New York: Dell Publishing, 1977), pp. 83-86.

4-11   John G. Fuller, *Incident at Exeter,* (New York: Berkley Medallion Books, 1966), p. 39.

4-12   Ibid, p. 43.

4-13   Ibid, p. 45.

4-14   Aime Michel, *Flying Saucers and the Straight-Line Mystery,* (New York: S.G. Phillips,
         Inc., 1958), p. 180.

4-15   Ibid, p. 217.

4-16   Edward J. Ruppelt, *The Report on Unidentified Flying Objects,* (Garden City,
         New Jersey: Doubleday & Co., 1956), pp. 152-169, 173.

4-17   Donald E. Keyhoe, *Aliens from Space,* (New York: New American Library 1974). (New York:
         Doubleday & Company, 1973, pp. 132-134.

4-18   Aime Michel, *Flying Saucers and the Straight-Line Mystery,*
         (New York: S.G. Phillips, Inc., 1958), p. 236.

4-19   Frank Edwards, *Flying Saucers - Serious Business,* (New York: Lyle Stuart, 1966), pp. 128.

Chapter 5

5-1   Edward J. Ruppelt, *The Report on Unidentified Flying Objects,* (Garden City,
         New Jersey: Doubleday & Co., 1956), pp. 147, 154, 211.

5-2   John G. Fuller, *Incident at Exeter,* (New York: Berkley Medallion Books, 1966), p. 160.

5-3   Donald E. Keyhoe, *Aliens from Space,* (New York: New American Library 1974). (New York:
         Doubleday & Company, 1973), p. 14.

5-4   Ibid

5-5   Ibid

5-6   Aime Michel, *The Truth About Flying Saucers,* (New York: Criterion Books, 1956), p. 76.

5-7   Edward J. Ruppelt, *The Report on Unidentified Flying Objects,* (Garden City, New Jersey:
         Doubleday & Co., 1956), p. 132.

5-8   Charles Berlitz & William L. Moore, *The Roswell Incident,* (New York: Grosset & Dunlap
        Publishers, 1980), pp. 113-114.
5-9   Edward J. Ruppelt, *The Report on Unidentified Flying Objects,* (Garden City,
        New Jersey: Doubleday & Co., 1956), p. 132.
5-10   Ibid, p. 132.
5-11   David Michael Jacobs, *The UFO Controversy in America,* (Bloomington & London: Indiana
        University Press, 1975), p. 105.
5-12   Edward J. Ruppelt, *The Report on Unidentified Flying Objects,* (Garden City,
        New Jersey: Doubleday & Co., 1956), p. 228.
5-13   Donald E. Keyhoe, *Aliens from Space,* (New York: New American Library 1974). (New York:
        Doubleday & Company, 1973), p. 86.
5-14   Ibid
5-15   Ibid, p. 164.
5-16   Frank Edwards, *Flying Saucers - Serious Business,* (New York: Lyle Stuart, 1966), pp. 253-254.
5-17   Ibid
5-18   John G. Fuller, *Incident at Exeter,* (New York: Berkley Medallion Books, 1966), p. 91.
5-19   Aime Michel, *Flying Saucers and the Straight-Line Mystery,*
        (New York: S.G. Phillips, Inc., 1958), pp. 252-255.
5-20   Edward J. Ruppelt, *The Report on Unidentified Flying Objects,* (Garden City,
        New Jersey: Doubleday & Co., 1956), p. 218.
5-21   Donald E. Keyhoe, *Aliens from Space,* (New York: New American Library 1974). (New York:
        Doubleday & Company, 1973), p. 17.
5-22   Charles Berlitz & William L. Moore, *The Roswell Incident,* (New York: Grosset & Dunlap
        Publishers, 1980), p. 131.
5-23   *The Arizona Republic* , March 9, 1982, p. A14.
5-24   Donald E. Keyhoe, *Aliens from Space,* (New York: New American Library 1974). (New York:
        Doubleday & Company, 1973), p. 104.
5-25   Budd Hopkins, *Missing Time,* (New York: Berkley Books, 1981), p. 217.
5-26   Ibid
5-27   Donald E. Keyhoe, *Aliens from Space,* (New York: New American Library 1974). (New York:
        Doubleday & Company, 1973), p. 85.

Chapter 6

6-1   David Michael Jacobs, *The UFO Controversy in America,* (Bloomington & London: Indiana
        University Press, 1975), pp. 94, 98.
        Edward J. Ruppelt, *The Report on Unidentified Flying Objects,* (Garden City,
        New Jersey: Doubleday & Co., 1956), p. 229.
6-2   Donald E. Keyhoe, *Aliens from Space,* (New York: New American Library 1974). (New York:
        Doubleday & Company, 1973), pp. 6-7.
        Edward J. Ruppelt, *The Report on Unidentified Flying Objects,* (Garden City,
        New Jersey: Doubleday & Co., 1956), pp. 15-16.
6-3   Donald E. Keyhoe, *Aliens from Space,* (New York: New American Library 1974). (New York:
        Doubleday & Company, 1973), p. 7.
6-4   Edward J. Ruppelt, *The Report on Unidentified Flying Objects,* (Garden City, New Jersey:
        Doubleday & Co., 1956), p. 87.
6-5   Donald E. Keyhoe, *Aliens from Space,* (New York: New American Library 1974). (New York:
        Doubleday & Company, 1973), p. 14.
6-6   Edward J. Ruppelt, *The Report on Unidentified Flying Objects,* (Garden City, New Jersey:
        Doubleday & Co., 1956), p. 59.
6-7   Ibid, pp. 65,66.

6-8   Ibid,, p. 114.
6-9   Ibid, p. 83.
6-10   Ibid, p. 131.
6-11   Ibid,pp. 135, 137, 139.
6-12   Ibid,pp. 165-169, 173.
6-13   Ibid,, p. 162.
6-14   Ibid,, p. 197.
6-15   Ibid, p. 85.
6-16   Dr. J. Allen Hynek, *The Hynek UFO Report,* (New York: Dell Publishing, 1977), p. 78.
6-17   Dr. J. Allen Hynek & Jacques Vallee, *The Edge of Reality,* (Chicago: Henry Regnery Company, 1975), p. 204.
6-18   Ibid, p. 193.
6-19   Donald E. Keyhoe, *Aliens from Space,* (New York: New American Library 1974). (New York: Doubleday & Company, 1973), p. 96.
6-20   Budd Hopkins, *Missing Time,* (New York: Berkley Books, 1981) pp. 132,133.
6-21   Donald E. Keyhoe, *Aliens from Space,* (New York: New American Library 1974). (New York: Doubleday & Company, 1973), p. 97.
6-22   Dr. J. Allen Hynek & Jacques Vallee, *The Edge of Reality,* (Chicago: Henry Regnery Company, 1975), pp. 191-195.
6-23   David Michael Jacobs, *The UFO Controversy in America,* (Bloomington & London: Indiana University Press, 1975), pp. .134-135.
6-24   Dr. J. Allen Hynek & Jacques Vallee, *The Edge of Reality,* (Chicago: Henry Regnery Company, 1975), p. 197.
6-25   David Michael Jacobs, *The UFO Controversy in America,* (Bloomington & London: Indiana University Press, 1975), p. 135.
6-26   Ibid,p. 143.
6-27   Ibid, p. 151.
6-28   Ibid,, p. 166.
6-29   Ibid, p. 212.
6-30   Ibid,, p. 253.

Chapter 7

7-1   David Michael Jacobs, *The UFO Controversy in America,* (Bloomington & London: Indiana University Press, 1975), pp. 90,91.
7-2   Ibid,pp. 90-95.
7-3   Ibid, p. 99.
7-4   Ibid, p. 105.
7-5   Ibid, pp. 73,86,87,90,105,138-140.
7-6   Ibid,, pp. 132-139.
7-7   Ibid, pp. 146,147.
7-8   Ibid, pp. 149-154.
7-9   Ibid, p. 187.
7-10   Ibid,p. 197.
7-11   Ibid, pp. 204-205.
7-12   Ibid, pp. 207-210.
7-13   Ibid,pp. 226,227.
7-14   Ibid, p. 227.
7-15   Ibid,, p. 229.
        Donald E. Keyhoe, *Aliens from Space,* (New York: New American Library 1974). (New York: Doubleday & Company, 1973), p. 222.
7-16   David Michael Jacobs, *The UFO Controversy in America,* (Bloomington & London: Indiana University Press, 1975), p. 230.

7-17   Morris K. Jessup, *The Case for the UFO,* (New York: The Citadel Press,1955),p. 224.
7-18   David Michael Jacobs, *The UFO Controversy in America,*(Bloomington & London: Indiana University Press,1975),p. 233.
7-19   Ibid,p. 238.
7-20   Ibid,pp. 242,243.
7-21   Donald E. Keyhoe, *Aliens from Space,*(New York: New American Library 1974).(New York: Doubleday & Company, 1973),p. 220.
7-22   Ibid,p. 224.
7-23   Ibid,,p. 228.
7-24   David Michael Jacobs, *The UFO Controversy in America,*(Bloomington & London: Indiana University Press,1975),p. 241.
7-25   Dr.J.Allen Hynek & Jacques Vallee, *The Edge of Reality,* (Chicago:Henry Regnery Company,1975),p. 195.
7-26   Edward J. Ruppelt, *The Report on Unidentified Flying Objects,* (Garden City, New Jersey: Doubleday & Co., 1956),p. 66.
7-27   Ibid,p. 10, 211.
7-28   Edward J. Ruppelt, *The Report on Unidentified Flying Objects,* (Garden City, New Jersey: Doubleday & Co., 1956),p. 174.
7-29   Dr.J.Allen Hynek & Jacques Vallee, *The Edge of Reality,* (Chicago:Henry Regnery Company,1975),p. 21.
7-30   Ibid,p.197.
7-31   David Michael Jacobs, *The UFO Controversy in America,*(Bloomington & London: Indiana University Press,1975) p. 253.
7-32   Ibid,pp. 264-265.
7-33   Donald E. Keyhoe, *Aliens from Space,*(New York: New American Library 1974).(New York: Doubleday & Company, 1973) Pages 63-71.

Chapter 8

8-1   Donald E. Keyhoe, *Aliens from Space,*(New York: New American Library 1974).(New York: Doubleday & Company, 1973) Page 209.
        Dr. J. Allen Hynek, *The Hynek UFO Report,* (New York: Dell Publishing, 1977) pp. 244.
8-2   Dr. J. Allen Hynek, *The Hynek UFO Report,* (New York: Dell Publishing, 1977) pp. 245.
8-3   John G. Fuller, *Incident at Exeter,* (New York: Berkley Medallion Books, 1966), p. 146.
8-4   Frank Edwards, *Flying Saucers - Serious Business,* (New York: Lyle Stuart, 1966) pp. 300-303.
8-5   Donald E. Keyhoe, *Aliens from Space,*(New York: New American Library 1974).(New York: Doubleday & Company, 1973) Pages 66-67.
8-6   Edward J. Ruppelt, *The Report on Unidentified Flying Objects,* (Garden City, New Jersey: Doubleday & Co., 1956)Pages 219-223.
8-7   David Michael Jacobs, *The UFO Controversy in America,*(Bloomington & London: Indiana University Press,1975) p.98.
8-8   Ibid,p. 236.
8-9   Dr. J. Allen Hynek, *The Hynek UFO Report,* (New York: Dell Publishing, 1977) pp. 251.
8-10   Edward J. Ruppelt, *The Report on Unidentified Flying Objects,* (Garden City, New Jersey: Doubleday & Co., 1956)Page 219.
8-11   Lee J. Elders, Brit Nilsson-Elders and Thomas K. Welch, *UFO...Contact from the Pleiades,* (Phoenix, Arizona: Genesis III Productions, Ltd., 1979) Entire Book.

Chapter 9

9-1   Aime Michel, *Flying Saucers and the Straight-Line Mystery,* (New York: S.G. Phillips, Inc., 1958). Page 25.
9-2   Ibid, Page 277.
9-3   Edward J. Ruppelt, *The Report on Unidentified Flying Objects,* (Garden City, New Jersey: Doubleday & Co., 1956) p. 249.

9-4   Ibid, pp. 11, 95-96.
9-5   1986 Brazilian film crew capture footage of small sphere. Shown on network television.
9-6   Dr. J. Allen Hynek, *The Hynek UFO Report,* (New York: Dell Publishing, 1977) pp. 168.
9-7   Budd Hopkins, *Missing Time,* (New York: Berkley Books, 1981) p. 106.
9-8   Coral & Jim Lorenzen, *Flying Saucer Occupants,* (New York: Signet Books, 1967) pp. 27-29.
9-9   Frank Edwards, *Flying Saucers - Serious Business,* (New York: Lyle Stuart, 1966) pp. 122-126.
9-10   Aime Michel, *The Truth About Flying Saucers,* (New York: Criterion Books, 1956) p. 173.
9-11   Ibid, pp. 131-133.
9-12   Coral & Jim Lorenzen, *Flying Saucer Occupants,* (New York: Signet Books, 1967) pp. 143-147.
9-13   Dr. J. Allen Hynek & Jacques Vallee, *The Edge of Reality,* (Chicago: Henry Regnery Company, 1975) p. 43.
9-14   John G. Fuller, *The Interrupted Journey,* (New York: Berkley Medallion Books, 1966),
        © 1966 John G. Fuller, p. 224.
9-15   *Arizona Republic Newspaper,* December 26, 1985.
9-16   Dr. J. Allen Hynek & Jacques Vallee, *The Edge of Reality,* (Chicago: Henry Regnery Company, 1975) p. 64.
9-17   Ibid, p. 64.
9-18   Budd Hopkins, *Missing Time,* (New York: Berkley Books, 1981) p. 246.
9-19   Freddy Silva, *Secrets In The Fields*
        http://www.cropcirclesecrets.org/
9-20   UFO fleets over Mexico: Rosario Oviedo / Arturo Robles /*UFOCasebook.com*: Santiago Yturria
9-21   UFO fleet over M25 Highway near London: Gene Harley: October 20, 2005
        http://www.ufos-aliens.co.uk/M25UFOs.htm -or- www.ufos-aliens.co.uk
9-22   CTV Sky News, Channel 4, North Battleford, Saskatchewan, Canada. *Strange Noises Heard in The Battlefords on Sunday the 23rd.* 6 pm News Report, January 25, 2012,

Chapter 10

10-1   John G. Fuller, *The Interrupted Journey,* (New York: Berkley Medallion Books, 1966),
        © 1966 John G. Fuller. Pages115,120,133,145,153.
10-2   Aime Michel, *Flying Saucers and the Straight-Line Mystery,*
        (New York: S.G. Phillips, Inc., 1958). Pages 40-42.

Chapter 11

11-1   Dr. J. Allen Hynek & Jacques Vallee, *The Edge of Reality,* (Chicago: Henry Regnery Company, 1975) p. 103.
        Dr. J. Allen Hynek, *The Hynek UFO Report,* (New York: Dell Publishing, 1977) pp. 213.
        Frank Edwards, *Flying Saucers - Serious Business,* (New York: Lyle Stuart, 1966) pp. 172.
11-2   Dr. J. Allen Hynek & Jacques Vallee, *The Edge of Reality,* (Chicago: Henry Regnery Company, 1975) p. 102.

Chapter 12

12-1   John G. Fuller, *The Interrupted Journey,* (New York: Berkley Medallion Books, 1966),
        © 1966 John G. Fuller.Pages 83-84.
12-2   Ibid, p. 98.
12-3   Budd Hopkins, *Missing Time,* (New York: Berkley Books, 1981), p. 232.
12-4   Ibid
12-5   Ibid, p. 233.
12-6   John G. Fuller, *The Interrupted Journey,* (New York: Berkley Medallion Books, 1966),
        © 1966 John G. Fuller.Pages 78-79.

Chapter 13

13-1   Raymond E. Fowler, *The Andreasson Affair,* (New Jersey: Printice-Hall, Inc., 1979) Entire Book.

Chapter 14

14-1   NOVA Television Documentary, PBS, 1984.
14-2   Isaac Asimov, *Extraterrestrial Civilizations,* (New York: Fawcett Columbine, 1980),
        ©1979 Isaac Asimov, p. 6.

14-3   Ibid, p. 203.
14-4   John G. Fuller, *Incident at Exeter,* (New York: Berkley Medallion Books, 1966), p. 28.
14-5   David Michael Jacobs, *The UFO Controversy in America,* (Bloomington & London: Indiana University Press, 1975) p. 216.
14-6   Ibid, p. 216.
14-7   Isaac Asimov, *Extraterrestrial Civilizations,* (New York: Fawcett Columbine, 1980), ©1979 Isaac Asimov, p. 219.
14-8   Edward J. Ruppelt, *The Report on Unidentified Flying Objects,* (Garden City, New Jersey: Doubleday & Co., 1956), p.59
14-9   David Michael Jacobs, *The UFO Controversy in America,* (Bloomington & London: Indiana University Press, 1975) p. 137.
14-10   Aime Michel, *Flying Saucers and the Straight-Line Mystery,* (New York: S.G. Phillips, Inc., 1958). pp. 5-6.

Chapter 15
15-1   Donald E. Keyhoe, *Aliens from Space,* (New York: New American Library 1974).(New York: Doubleday & Company, 1973), pp. 54,55.
15-2   Ibid, p. 62.
15-3   Ibid, p. 186.
15-4   Data in the first three columns are taken from *Habitable Planets for Man* by Stephen H. Dole, (New York, Blaisdell, 1964), pp. 102 and 104. The fourth column was computed from equations given by Michael Hart; see references to papers in the Bibliography. The last column again uses data by Dole, pp. 91 and 92.
15-5   T.A. Heppenheimer, *Toward Distant Suns,* (New York: Fawcett Columbine Books, 1980) ©1979 T.A. Heppenheimer. pp. 47-49.
15-6   Isaac Asimov, *Extraterrestrial Civilizations,* (New York: Fawcett Columbine, 1980), ©1979 Isaac Asimov, p. 204.
15-7   Ibid

Chapter 16
16-1   Budd Hopkins, *Missing Time,* (New York: Berkley Books, 1981) Entire Book.
16-2   Nigel Calder, *Einstein's Universe,* (New York: Greenwich House, 1982) © 1979 by Nigel Calder, p. 20.
16-3   Ibid, p.14-20.
16-4   Ibid, p.14-20.
16-5   Ibid, pp.all.

Chapter 18
18-1   Fritz Ridenour, *Who Says God Created?,* (Glendale, California: G/L Regal Books, 1969) © 1967 by G/L Publications, pp. 60-66.
18-2   Josh McDowell, *Research in Christian Ethics,* pp. 20-26.
18-3   Fritz Ridenour, *Who Says God Created?,* (Glendale, California: G/L Regal Books, 1969) © 1967 by G/L Publications, pp. 69-70.
18-5   Ibid, 79.
18-6   Ibid, pp. 87-88.

Chapter 20
20-1   Lee J. Elders, Brit Nilsson-Elders and Thomas K. Welch, *UFO...Contact from the Pleiades,* (Phoenix, Arizona: Genesis III Productions, Ltd., 1979), Entire Book.
20-2   Ibid,
20-3   John G. Fuller, *The Interrupted Journey,* (New York: Berkley Medallion Books, 1966), © 1966 John G. Fuller, pp. 172-173.
20-4   Ibid,, p. 175-180.

Chapter 21

21-1   Aime Michel, *Flying Saucers and the Straight-Line Mystery,*
        (New York: S.G. Phillips, Inc., 1958). p. 25.

21-2   Ibid, p. 26.

21-3   Ibid, p. 23-24.

21-4   Larry Williams, *The Mouintain of Moses: The Discovery of Mount Sinai,* (Wynwood, 1990).
        Bob Cornuke and Larry Williams, *The Search for the Real Mt. Sinai,* Documentary film, 2002.

Chapter 22

22-1   Kevin McClure, *The Evidence for the Visions of the Virgin Mary,* (Wellingborough,
        Northamponshire: The Aquarian Press), p. 75.

22-2   Ibid, p. 77 .

22-3   Aime Michel, *The Truth About Flying Saucers,* (New York: Criterion Books, 1956) pp. 146-147

22-4   Paul Thomas, *Flying Saucers Through the Ages,* (London: Neville Spearman Ltd, 1962)
        © Paul Thomas, 1962, 1965, pp. 77-78.

22-5   Kevin McClure, *The Evidence for the Visions of the Virgin Mary,* (Wellingborough,
        Northamponshire: The Aquarian Press), pp. 83-84.

22-6   Wayne Weible, *Medjugorje: The Message,* (Orleans, Massachusetts: Paraclete Press, 1989),
        Entire Book.

22-7   *Associated Press,* "It's Jesus, look! – Parishioners claim sightf of Christ, Mary" August 16,
        1988.

22-8   *Today's Catholic,* August 26, 1988, Archdiocese of San Antonio, pp. 9-11

Chapter 24

24-1   Budd Hopkins, *Missing Time,* (New York: Berkley Books, 1981) pp. 23-24.

24-2   Raymond E. Fowler, *The Andreasson Affair,* (New Jersey: Printice-Hall, Inc., 1979), Entire Book.

24-3   John G. Fuller, *The Interrupted Journey,* (New York: Berkley Medallion Books, 1966),
        © 1966 John G. Fuller. Page 167.

24-4   Ibid, p. 189.

24-5   Ibid, p. 264.

24-6   Frank Edwards, *Flying Saucers - Serious Business,* (New York: Lyle Stuart, 1966) pp. 172.

24-7   Dr. J. Allen Hynek, *The Hynek UFO Report,* (New York: Dell Publishing, 1977) pp. 214.

24-8   Ibid, pp. 213.

Chapter 25

25-1   Arthur Blessitt, *Arthur: A Pilgrim,* (California: Blessitt Publishing, 1985) Entire Book.

25-2   Dr. Billy Graham, *Angels - God's Secret Agents,* (New York: Pocket Books, 1977), pp. 21-23.

Chapter 28

28-1   Donald E. Keyhoe, *Aliens from Space,* (New York: New American Library 1974).(New York:
        Doubleday & Company, 1973) Page 8.

28-2   Aime Michel, *Flying Saucers and the Straight-Line Mystery,* (New York: S.G. Phillips, Inc.,
        1958) Entire Book.

28-3   Donald E. Keyhoe, *Aliens from Space,* (New York: New American Library 1974).(New York:
        Doubleday & Company, 1973) Page 117

28-4   Dr. J. Allen Hynek, *The Hynek UFO Report,* (New York: Dell Publishing, 1977) pp. 141.
        Frank Edwards, *Flying Saucers - Serious Business,* (New York: Lyle Stuart, 1966) pp. 205,238.
        Edward J. Ruppelt, *The Report on Unidentified Flying Objects,* (Garden City, New Jersey:
        Doubleday & Co., 1956) pp. 23, 151.
        Aime Michel, *Flying Saucers and the Straight-Line Mystery,* (New York: S.G. Phillips, Inc.
        1958) p. 238.

28-5   Edward J. Ruppelt, *The Report on Unidentified Flying Objects,* (Garden City,
        New Jersey: Doubleday & Co., 1956) p.116.

28-6   *OMNI Magazine,* February 1985, Pages 112-113.

ENDNOTES (cont'd)

505

28-7   John G. Fuller, *Incident at Exeter,* (New York: Berkley Medallion Books, 1966), p. 98.
28-8   Ibid, p. 126.
28-9   Ibid, p. 198-199.
28-10   Donald E. Keyhoe, *Aliens from Space,* (New York: New American Library 1974). (New York:
        Doubleday & Company, 1973) Page 174.
28-11   Frank Edwards, *Flying Saucers - Serious Business,* (New York: Lyle Stuart, 1966) pp. 257-258
        Donald E. Keyhoe, *Aliens from Space,* (New York: New American Library 1974). (New York:
        Doubleday & Company, 1973) p. 181.
28-12   Ibid, p. 181.
28-13   Donald E. Keyhoe, *Aliens from Space,* (New York: New American Library 1974). (New York:
        Doubleday & Company, 1973), p. 181.
28-14   Frank Scully, *Behind the Flying Saucers,* (New York: Henry Holt and Company, 1950), p. 173.
28-15   Frank Edwards, *Flying Saucers - Serious Business,* (New York: Lyle Stuart, 1966) pp. 262.
        John G. Fuller, *Incident at Exeter,* (New York: Berkley Medallion Books, 1966), p. 205.
28-16   Ibid, p. 205.
28-17   Donald E. Keyhoe, *Aliens from Space,* (New York: New American Library 1974). (New York:
        Doubleday & Company, 1973) p. 177.
28-18   Ibid, p. 178-179.
28-19   Raymond E. Fowler, *The Andreasson Affair,* (New Jersey: Printice-Hall, Inc., 1979) p. 140.
28-20   *The Arizona Republic,* March 1, 1984, p. 1.
28-21   Ibid, p. October 3, 1984,p. B2.
28-22   Ibid, p. October 1, 1984, p. B1.
28-23   Ibid, p. March 26, 1985.
28-24   Ibid, p. May 26, 1985.
28-25   *Arizona Gazette Newspaper,* October 9, 1985.
        Tucson Daily Star Newspaper, October 8, 1985.
28-26   Aime Michel, *The Truth About Flying Saucers,* (New York: Criterion Books, 1956) p. 63.
28-27   Donald E. Keyhoe, *Aliens from Space,* (New York: New American Library 1974). (New York:
        Doubleday & Company, 1973) Page 155.
28-28   David Michael Jacobs, *The UFO Controversy in America,* (Bloomington & London: Indiana
        University Press, 1975) p. 197.
28-29   Ibid, p.p. 265.

Chapter 29

29-1   The Hunger Project, *Ending Hunger: An Idea Who's Time Has Come,* pp. 6-30
29-2   'Millions more starving' by 2015, By Ania Lichtarowicz, *BBC News,* St Louis, Missouri, 17
        February 2006. Chart resources too numerous to list see: *http://en.wikipedia.org/
        wiki/List_of_famines#Main_article_lists*
29-3   Mrs. Thatcher's physician warns of AIDS epidemic, *San Francisco Chronicle,* May 23, 1986
29-4   U.S. Geological Survey, *http://earthquake.usgs.gov/earthquakes/world/historical.php.*
29-5   Frank Edwards, *Flying Saucers - Serious Business,* (New York: Lyle Stuart, 1966) pp. 273-275.

Chapter 30

30-1   Raymond E. Fowler, *The Andreasson Affair,* (New Jersey: Printice-Hall, Inc., 1979) p. 140.
30-2   Maurice Rawlings, M.D., *Beyond Death's Door,* (Thomas Nelson, 1978) entire book.
30-3   Ibid, p. p. 101.

Chapter 31

31-1   Yue Wang, *You Don't Need A Wallet In China, Just Your Smartphone*
        (Forbes Magazine-online dateline May 15, 2017)
        https://www.forbes.com/sites/ywang/2017/05/15/your-mobile-money-surviving-
        a-day-in-china-without-cash-or-cards/#39664d537626
31-2   • World Bank in Brussels, Belgium • Call to acquire new world-class supercomputers in
        Europe, Bulgaria, Slovenia, Czech Republic, and Portugal
        https://ec.europa.eu/newsroom/index.cfm?itemFinalType=825
        • *Financing the future of supercomputing : How to increase investments in high performance
        computing in Europe* (European Commission/European Investment Bank) p.12
31-3   • National Security Agency's Domestic Surveillance Directorate/Utah Data Center
        https://nsa.gov1.info/utah-data-center/
        • SLT.com
31-4   • Stephen Shankland, *IIBM now has 18 quantum computers in its fleet of weird machines*
        (cnet.com online, May 6, 2020)
        • Stephen Shankland, *Google's quantum supremacy is only a first taste of a computing revolution
        "Quantum supremacy" is nice, but more broadly useful quantum computers are probably still
        a decade away.* (October 25, 2019 cnet.com online)
31-5   • Stephen Shankland, *Honeywell says it's got the fastest quantum computer on the planet
        - For now...* (https://www.cnet.com/news/honeywell-says-its-got-the-fastest-quantum-
        computer-on-the-planet/ June 18, 2020 online)

- Stephen Shankland , *Our quantum computer will get 100,000x faster by 2025, Honeywell says It hopes to leapfrog rivals as it reenters the computing business.* (cnet.com online, March 3, 2020)

31-6   *Accenture, Microsoft Create Blockchain Solution to Support ID2020* (unlock-bc.com January 22,2018) https://www.unlock-bc.com/news/2018-01-22/accenture-microsoft-create-blockchain-solution-to-support-id2020
- *ID2020 Summit 2016* (United Nations Office for Partnerships, May 20,2016) https://www.un.org/partnerships/news/id2020-summit-2016
- *ID2020 Alliance Unveils Digital ID Program* (PYMENTS.com, September 19, 2019)
- *Mastercard joins ID2020 Alliance* https://www.finextra.com/pressarticle/82606/mastercard-joins-id2020-alliance
- *Mastercard Joins ID2020 Alliance Partnership accelerates access to and adoption of digital identity solutions* (May 21, 2020 | PURCHASE, NY) https://mastercardcontentexchange.com/newsroom/press-releases/2020/may/mastercard-joins-id2020-alliance/

31-7   - *Bill Gates' Quantum Tattoo, Coronavirus and ID2020 Connection* https://www.youtube.com/watch?v=Jw-ogFR0tR0
- Victor T. Angermann, *An Invisible Quantum Dot 'Tattoo' Could Be Used to ID Vaccinated Kids* (ScienceAlert.com December 21, 2019)

31-8   Dave Hunt, *Peace Prosperity and the Coming Holocaust,* (Eugene, Oregon: Harvest House Publishers, 1983), p. 62.

31-9   Constance Cumby, *The Hidden Dangers of the Rainbow: The New Age Movement and our Coming Age of Barbarism* (Huntington House, Inc., 1983), p. 83.

31-10   Ibid, pp. 149-150.

3111   Dave Hunt, *Peace Prosperity and the Coming Holocaust,* (Eugene, Oregon: Harvest House Publishers, 1983), p. 90.

31-12   Constance Cumby, *The Hidden Dangers of the Rainbow: The New Age Movement and our Coming Age of Barbarism* (Huntington House, Inc., 1983), p. 69.

31-13   Ibid, p. 120.

31-14   Ibid, p. 142-143.

31-15   Ibid, p. 111.

31-16   *UFO Review,* Issue No. 17-65661
UFO Review, Issue No. 16-6566

31-17   Ibid

31-18   Dave Hunt, *Peace Prosperity and the Coming Holocaust,* (Eugene, Oregon: Harvest House Publishers, 1983), p. 85.

31-19   Ibid, p. 113.

31-20   Ibid, p. 109.

31-21   Ibid, p. p. 117.

31-22   Ibid, p. pp. 59-60.

31-23   Constance Cumby, *The Hidden Dangers of the Rainbow: The New Age Movement and our Coming Age of Barbarism* (Huntington House, Inc., 1983), p. 58.

31-24   Ibid, p. 58.

31-25   Ibid, p. 55.

31-26   Ibid

Chapter 32

32-1   Lee J. Elders, Brit Nilsson-Elders and Thomas K. Welch, *UFO...Contact from the Pleiades,* (Phoenix, Arizona: Genesis III Productions, Ltd., 1979), Entire Book.

32-2   Flavius Josephus: translated by G.A. Williamson, *The Jewish War,* (London, England, Penguin Books, 1970, 1981), pp. 1-13, 360-361.

32-3   Ibid, pp. 1-13, 360-361.

32-4   Ibid, pp. 1-13, 360-361.

32-5   Ibid, pp. 1-13, 360-361.

32-6   Ibid, pp. 1-13, 360-361.

32-7   CTV Sky News, Channel 4, North Battleford, Saskatchewan, Canada. *Strange Noises Heard in The Battlefords on Sunday the 23rd.* 6 pm News Report, January 25, 2012,

32-8   Nationally televised MLB Game: *Tampa Bay Rays vs. Detroit Tigers* on August 23, 2011, Tropicana Field, Tampa Bay, Florida.

Chapter 33

33-1   *Arizona Republic,* March 16, 1985

33-2   T.A. Heppenheimer, *Toward Distant Suns,* (New York: Fawcett Columbine Books, 1980) ©1979, T.A. Heppenheimer. pp. 50-54

33-3   Newsweek, June 1, 1987

33-4   T.A. Heppenheimer, *Toward Distant Suns,* (New York: Fawcett Columbine Books, 1980) ©1979,T.A. Heppenheimer. pp. 188-196

33-5   Arcosanti, Cordes Junction, Arizona

33-6   Rev. Chuck Smith, *What The World is Coming To,* (Costa Mesa, California: Maranatha House Publishers, 1977), p. 205.

508 INDEX (cont'd)

GATHERING CLOUDS
J. Allen Jackson
March 21, 1998

Mordant winds blow over a reprobate remnant, the sky troubled in rebuke. Smoldering cylinders descend the foreboding curtain of dark, eager to dispense their work.

Blackcap, whinchat and rhebok hide among rocks; terror seizing both man and beast. Flames of fury reflect on tortured countenances: the scourge from on High has finally arrived.

Who are these who dart about the countryside like flickering fireflies on midsummer breezes; their blinding aim direct and purposeful?

They are the wrath of God; His judgement on malevolent blackguard souls great and small. Arrogant poltroon, violent righteous, false prophet and temptress.

They swirl down in wheels of fire, each saddened from prideful rebuff, mournful pleas left unheeded; the task too gruesome and final to relish.

Their infliction dealt in wisdom, guided by the great Knowing. A fiery sword in their right hands, red garments betoken their solemn duty.

Targeted with the lot of Sodom and Suleiman; struck down and crushed, the fouled streams and valleys run deep with the blood of the defiled.

The day has come scorned by haughty, loathsome flesh: first scoffed in closets the small and pious, their disdain made bold by new-found power and false perpetuity.

The roiling dark consumes both day and night, sun and stars swallowed in its path; His Earth swept clean for the New Day on the morrow.

Oh cursed dark, the moribund fool in regal refinery, his riches powerless to turn back swift retribution. No man can escape the King.

'Tis the smoldering furnace from Abram's encounter; Moses' pillar of fire revisited; the lamps of Aaron, their flashes inserting final authority.

This, the eve of reward; that long-awaited design from David's lineage. But first comes the day of darkness and weeping, followed closely by eternal Light.

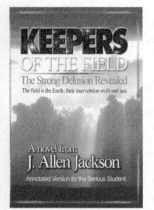

If you've enjoyed Aliens & In-laws perhaps you would also enjoy Keepers Of The Field, a novel from the same author.

Keepers of the Field is a fictional exposition of the material revealed in Aliens & In-laws, staying as true to actual prophetical events as I am able, and presented for mass consumption in an accepted, more traditional form. This may be the ideal way to present the provocative material found herein to the less daring friend or relative.

The main character is a veteran space shuttle pilot who is asked to command a secretive flight aboard America's newest SSTO shuttle to the International Space Station where the U.S. President and his military advisors intend to arm an experimental, and highly classified, defensive laser in response to troop mobilizations in Eastern Europe and the Middle East. Because the U.S. military is no longer able to respond on two fronts simultaneously, the true danger lies in the temptation to use the device as an offensive weapon against recent Russian aggressions, which risks almost certain escalation to all-out nuclear war, in the estimation of our main protagonist.

Integral to the plot is the life style and adventures of an Arab Pakistani youngster in Persia (Iran) who's uncle is an agent for the West in the midst of a massive mobilization by an Islamic league of nations. The Islamic Confederation is led by a charismatic Ayatollah who claims to be the Twelfth Imam, known as the Mahdi or "God-guided One," as prophesied in Moslem Shia texts for centuries. The coalescing Mahdi – Savior of Islam – is bent on a final assualt (or Grand Jihad) on the nation of Israel. He has allied and armed his ragtag military forces with the help of Russian hard-liners who have taken over in their nation, now known as the Union of Sovereign Social-democratic Republics, not coincidentally, once again the U.S.S.R. or Sovereign Union in short.

We live in a time of escalating danger brought on by the folly of world political leaders and misguided pronunciations from "progressive recidivists" around the planet. But fear not. Look up. For we are not alone in our plight. The Keepers are watching and awaiting their marching orders. **Look for Keepers in theatres soon.**

Available at www.Amazon *Books › Mystery, Thriller & Suspense* or *www.aopublishers.com*

Made in the USA
Middletown, DE
19 February 2022

61511610R00298